The Vietnam War in the Pacific World

The Vietnam War in the Pacific World

....

EDITED BY
BRIAN CUDDY
FREDRIK LOGEVALL

The University of North Carolina Press Chapel Hill

© 2022 The University of North Carolina Press
All rights reserved
Set in Charis by Westchester Publishing Services
Manufactured in the United States of America

Library of Congress Cataloging-in-Publication Data
Names: Cuddy, Brian, editor. | Logevall, Fredrik, 1963- editor.
Title: The Vietnam War in the Pacific world / edited by Brian Cuddy and Fredrik Logevall.
Description: Chapel Hill : The University of North Carolina Press, [2022] | Includes bibliographical references and index.
Identifiers: LCCN 2022015995 | ISBN 9781469671130 (cloth ; alk. paper) | ISBN 9781469671147 (pbk. ; alk. paper) | ISBN 9781469671154 (ebook)
Subjects: LCSH: Vietnam War, 1961-1975—History. | Pacific Area—History—20th century. | Southeast Asia—History—20th century.
Classification: LCC DS557.7 .V5673 2022 | DDC 959.704/332—dc23/eng/20220414
LC record available at https://lccn.loc.gov/2022015995

Cover illustration: President Nguyen Van Thieu during meeting with President Lyndon B. Johnson in Hawai'i (LBJ Library photo by Yoichi Okamato).

In memory of our mothers, Veronica and Gerd-Louise

Contents

List of Tables and Graphs, ix

1 Fire in the American Lake, 1
   Toward a Regional Turn in Vietnam War Studies
   BRIAN CUDDY AND FREDRIK LOGEVALL

2 British Neocolonialism in Malaya and Singapore, and U.S. Empire in the Pacific, 16
   WEN-QING NGOEI

3 Made in Britain, 31
   The Fantasy Driving Australia's Involvement in the Vietnam War
   GREG LOCKHART

4 The War of Southeast Asia, 54
   Falling Dominoes, the 1967 Clifford-Taylor Mission, and the Fight for the Stability of the Pacific World
   A. GABRIELLE WESTCOTT

5 A Far Greater Prize than Vietnam, 69
   The United States, Indonesia, and the Vietnam War
   MARK ATWOOD LAWRENCE

6 The View from the Hill, 87
   Hawai'i's Congressional Delegation and the Struggle for Peace in Vietnam and Equity at Home, 1964–1975
   MARC JASON GILBERT

7 GI Resistance and Transpacific Activism in Iwakuni during the Vietnam War, 107
   A Piece of Forgotten History
   NORIKO SHIRATORI

8 The U.S. Military's R&R Program in Taipei, 1965–1972, 125
   ZACH FREDMAN

9   Taiwanese Economic Assistance to South Vietnam, 1955–1975, 142
    JASON LIM

10 The "Vietnamese" Skirt and Other Wartime Myths in Lee Yun-gi's "Trigonometric Functions," 162
    ALICE S. KIM

11 The American-Led Military Coalition in Vietnam, 182
    Interests, Incentives, and Interpretations
    DAVID L. ANDERSON

12 LBJ's Hessians?, 197
    Korean Troops' Dispatch to Vietnam
    CHRISTOPHER LOVINS

13 Strengthening the Regime, 214
    Singapore, the United States, and the War in Indochina
    S. R. JOEY LONG

14 Buying Time?, 231
    The Vietnam War and Southeast Asia
    MATTIAS FIBIGER

15 From Resident to Refugee, 257
    The Exodus from Southern Vietnam in the Late 1970s
    LISA TRAN

16 Vietnamese Refugee Status, Habeas Corpus, and Hong Kong, 1988–1997, 271
    JANA K. LIPMAN

17 Moving beyond the Past, 288
    Vietnamese Serving in the Australian Defence Force
    NATHALIE HUYNH CHAU NGUYEN

18 Veterans' Reflections on Legacies of War in Việt Nam at Peace, 305
    MIA MARTIN HOBBS

19 Colonial Legacies of Dioxin Contamination in Vietnam and Australia, 321
    BOI HUYEN NGO

Acknowledgments, 337

Contributors, 339

Index, 343

Tables and Graphs

Tables

9.1 Trade between Taiwan (ROC) and South Vietnam (RVN), 1956–1972, 151

9.2 Sino-Vietnamese Economic Cooperation Conferences, 154

Graphs

14.1 U.S. military and economic aid to ASEAN states, 1960–1980, 238

14.2 International aid and Indonesian government revenue, 1967–1981, 241

14.3 ASEAN exports to the United States and South Vietnam, 1965–1975, 244

The Vietnam War in the Pacific World

1 Fire in the American Lake
Toward a Regional Turn in Vietnam War Studies

BRIAN CUDDY AND FREDRIK LOGEVALL

Most Americans and many non-Americans know it as the Vietnam War. The Vietnamese refer to it as the American War, the concluding phase in their thirty-year war of resistance. And some historians prefer to label it the Second Indochina War, both to distinguish it from the French struggle to reestablish empire after World War II and to acknowledge the central place of Laos and Cambodia in the conflict. But the war waged in those countries during the 1960s and early 1970s was also connected to the broader Asia Pacific region. We hold that this regional context is central to any understanding of why, how, and to what effect the United States and its partners intervened in a contest between communist nationalists in the Democratic Republic of Vietnam, also known as North Vietnam, and the southern insurgent National Liberation Front on the one side, and anti-communist nationalists in the Republic of Vietnam, or South Vietnam, on the other side.[1] This volume is dedicated to exploring the regional dynamics of the origins, conduct, and legacies of the Vietnam War.[2]

The Vietnam War was fought for, by, and through the Pacific. Dwight Eisenhower's image of falling dominoes in the region was the most prominent early rationale for waging the war, and the idea that the American effort in Vietnam provided time and space for the strengthening of anti-communist states in the Asia Pacific still has traction today. Our volume investigates these controversial rationales and also gives more attention to the agency of the states and peoples the United States claimed to be saving. Not passive dominoes waiting to be tipped over by the communist advance, nor mere puppets and mercenaries doing Washington's bidding in exchange for economic benefits, the anti-communist states of the region had their own interests, motivations, and strategies for engaging in (and disengaging from) the regional war effort. Moreover, these nations did not just fight the war alongside the United States and South Vietnam. As well as sending troops to Vietnam, the war coursed through these countries in such forms as bases, rest and recreation (R&R) locations, and refugee camps. And it changed them. Just as the region shaped the war, so too was the war crucial in shaping, in Simeon Man's words, "an emergent Pacific world in the middle decades of the twentieth century."[3]

The importance of the wider regional and international contexts to the motivation and prosecution of the conflict has been recognized in English-language scholarship on the Vietnam War.[4] But much of this scholarship, rather than taking the region as a unit of analysis itself, focuses instead on the experiences of particular states and groups within the region.[5] Where such studies have a diplomatic focus, they tend to rest on the axis connecting the country in question with Washington—much like the American "hub and spoke" system of bilateral alliances in the region—thereby obscuring the "point to point" transnational cross-currents in the Pacific. Works that do center the region (or regional groupings of states) often privilege the Cold War as an analytical framework for understanding regional developments.[6] We agree that the Cold War is vital to understanding the regional dynamics of the Vietnam War, but it alone cannot tell the full story of American power in, and its effect on, the region. In casting the war as an important part of the history of imperialism and neocolonialism in the Asia Pacific, our volume also highlights both the perpetuation and transformation of American power in a decolonizing Pacific.

・・・・・・

When asked the question "How does the world work?" the political scientist Peter Katzenstein gave a compelling answer: "Think of the world as regions organized by America's imperium."[7] Our volume begins from a similar premise. While shifting attention away from America's Vietnam War and its national narratives, we do not seek to downplay the role of the United States in the region's Vietnam War or in the regional transformations prompted by the war. Washington remains a leading character in the stories that follow, as it must.[8]

The Pacific is, as Alison Bashford notes, "a very large historiographical ocean," with successive historiographical traditions describing and reinforcing different geographic constructions of the Pacific world—the Polynesian triangle, the South Sea, Oceania, the Pacific Rim, and Asia Pacific.[9] These "plural cartographies of the Pacific" have been joined most recently by the idea of the "Indo-Pacific."[10] Although the historiographic and geographic meanings of the Pacific have changed across time, a constant factor in their construction has been external intervention. The actions of states from outside the region have long been central to both the material and conceptual formation of the Pacific as a region. "Euro-American intermediation produced the regional structure," suggests Arif Dirlik, and "Euro-American activity, in giving the region its form, also shaped consciousness of it and resulted in an ideological hegemony that paralleled the invention of the region in actuality."[11] The American influence in shaping the Pacific world, then, builds on the longer history of European imperialism in the region. The Pacific as an "American lake" since the late nineteenth century follows its depiction first as a "Spanish lake" in the sixteenth and early seventeenth centuries, then as an "English lake" in the eighteenth and nineteenth centuries.[12]

The height of American power in the Pacific coincided, of course, with a much-reduced footprint of formal imperialism. Washington was alive to the push for decolonization in the Pacific world after 1945. A July 1949 National Security Council paper recognized that "19th century imperialism is no longer a practicable system in SEA [Southeast Asia]" and that the United States must "satisfy the militant nationalism" of the region's anti-colonial movements. Washington therefore sought and fostered anti-communist nationalists as collaborators in making the "SEA region an integral part of that great crescent formed by the Indian Peninsula, Australia and Japan."[13] Through such a process, the United States maintained its imperial position through more informal means. As Man notes, "Decolonization was not antithetical to the spread of U.S. global power but intrinsic to it."[14] This is exemplified by the case of the Philippines, where the United States acquiesced to formal independence in 1946 but retained rights to station U.S. air and naval forces in Philippine territory and continued to influence the country's political and economic direction through trade agreements and support for friendly elites—a situation described by the journalist Stanley Karnow as "dependent independence."[15]

The formation of Washington's network of influence in the Pacific might have differed from earlier, more formal, iterations of imperialism, but it nonetheless built on them, particularly the long tail of British imperialism in the Asia Pacific, which was itself morphing into neocolonial modes of influence. As Man suggests, the post-1945 U.S. empire in the Pacific "essentially reanimated old colonial dynamics in the region."[16] Wen-Qing Ngoei (Chapter 2) and Greg Lockhart (Chapter 3) show in detail how this Anglo-American imperial dynamic worked in the lead-up to the Vietnam War. Not only did the British Empire—and in particular, British officials like Commissioner-General for Southeast Asia Malcolm MacDonald—shape the intellectual construct that informed the American and Australian strategic commitment to Southeast Asia (the domino theory). It also continued to exert, albeit in a different guise, its own imperial influence in Malaya and Singapore in parallel with Washington's support of South Vietnam under Ngo Dinh Diem. The politically driven British and Australian race-based assessment of Chinese forces moving downward through Southeast Asia may have been fantastic rhetoric, indicated as such both by contemporary intelligence assessments and by the region's decided tilt toward the United States *before* Washington Americanized the Vietnam conflict in 1965, but it nonetheless exerted considerable influence.

A. Gabrielle Westcott (Chapter 4) and Mark Atwood Lawrence (Chapter 5) extend Ngoei's and Lockhart's analyses of the divergence between rhetorical devices and strategic realities in the 1950s to the period of heavy U.S. military involvement in Vietnam in the 1960s. As they ramped up the American commitment to South Vietnam, U.S. officials often claimed Southeast Asia and the western Pacific—and in particular Indonesia—as the real prize. But the documentary record suggests that Washington lacked a suitable appreciation of how the war in Vietnam was linked to the politics of the wider region, including Indonesia. Framing the war in regional terms had less to do with geopolitics than with rallying American domestic support for the war—or, from 1968 and especially with the advent of the Nixon administration in 1969, making the case that the United States should or could pull back from its military commitment to South Vietnam. That the framing of the region's importance to U.S. decision making regarding Vietnam could so easily be turned on its head—first requiring the American military commitment, then removing the need for it—exposes Washington's muddled and sometimes emotional regional strategic thinking.

Katzenstein defines imperium as "the conjoining of power that has both territorial and non-territorial dimensions."[17] If American imperialism in the Pacific mostly took the form of British-influenced nonterritorial neocolonialism, old-fashioned territorial aspects of empire nonetheless persisted. "It would be wrong to suggest this new U.S. empire was any less territorial than the colonial empire of the past," writes Man, pointing to Washington's formal control over Pacific island territories including "Guam, the Northern Marianas, the Marshall Islands, and Okinawa, as part of its expanding empire of bases for military deployment and weapons testing."[18] Such "tiny specks," writes Daniel Immerwahr, "are the foundations of U.S. world power. They serve as staging grounds, launchpads, storage sites, beacons, and laboratories."[19] Hawai'i served as all these things and more during the Vietnam War.

Having gained statehood in 1959, Hawai'i was now part of the American federal union rather than its empire, but as Sarah Miller-Davenport argues, its nineteenth-century strategic role as America's "gateway to Asia" persisted and intensified. As an "ambiguously foreign place within the nation," Hawai'i's geographic location, mix of cultures, and Asian connections were "strategically deployed in the postwar era to suit the demands of American expansion in the decolonizing world."[20] In short, "Hawai'i is central to understanding American imperial relations in the Pacific."[21] This was no more so than during the Vietnam War for which Hawai'i served both as key military staging post and command center, and as a model for the "other war" of pacification and winning hearts and minds. As home of United States Pacific Command, which had formal control over American forces engaged in the Vietnam War, and host to important conferences that discussed policy and strategy during the war, Hawai'i had clear military significance to the American war effort.[22] The U.S. military even established a mock Vietnamese village in the jungle of O'ahu Island as a counterinsurgency training site, which in Man's words, "collapsed the distinction between Hawai'i and Vietnam and made them interchangeable sites of war."[23] Building on Hawai'i's reputation for a culture of mutual understanding, the U.S. Agency for International Development also established a training center there in 1966 for its staff posted to Vietnam, which in turn, in Miller-Davenport's words, "collapsed the boundaries between military and cultural strategies for advancing American expansion."[24] Complementing this work uncovering "Hawai'i's obscured centrality to the US war in Vietnam,"[25] Marc Jason Gilbert (Chapter 6) examines how Hawai'i's congressional delegation navigated between its often competing commitments to an independent South Vietnam, a negotiated peace, party loyalty, and Indigenous land rights. If Hawai'i was central to the American war in Vietnam, the war also provided impetus to movements for change within Hawai'i.

Together with its spaces of direct and incorporated rule, Washington's *extra*territorial empire was particularly important during the Vietnam War. Along with formal imperial and national territories, a string of status of forces agreements (SOFAs) with Asian allies formed the nodes in what Immerwahr calls America's "pointillist empire" in the Pacific.[26] A SOFA is a (generally bilateral) treaty arrangement that allows the military forces of one state to be stationed in another state's territory while retaining varying degrees of immunity from local law. SOFAs regarding U.S. military bases in the region often predated the Vietnam War but took on renewed importance during the war years.[27] These basing agreements were then joined during the Vietnam War by agreements that allowed servicemen to take "rest and recreation" (R&R) leave in Tokyo, Singapore, Manila, Bangkok, Hong Kong, Taipei, Sydney, Kuala Lumpur, and Penang.[28] Noriko Shiratori (Chapter 7) and Zach Fredman (Chapter 8) cast a spotlight on two such nodes during the Vietnam War—Marine Corps Air Station Iwakuni, in Japan, and the R&R program in Taipei, respectively—exploring how American power was advanced, negotiated, and resisted in each. These chapters not only highlight a U.S. military presence in the Pacific built on sex and capitalist economic development but also reveal the possibilities that existed for transnational alliances between American and local anti-war groups. America's extraterritorial, pointillist Pacific network may have obviated some of the challenges associated with direct imperial rule and military occupation, but the load-bearing points of that network still generated complex questions of jurisdiction, sovereignty, and solidarity.

· · · · · ·

To focus on the nature of American power in the Pacific—territorial, extraterritorial, and neocolonial—is not to suggest that Washington alone was responsible for the shape and texture of its empire. Reducing American allies and partners in the Pacific to client states and puppets does not help in understanding the regional drivers and effects of the Vietnam War. A "Vietnamese turn" and, within that, a "South Vietnamese turn" in recent historical scholarship on the war have enhanced our understanding of the agency of Vietnamese actors in the war years.[29] With greater attention to the variety and vibrancy of southern politics has come a finer appreciation for where, how, and why the Republic of Vietnam's goals and strategies diverged from those of the United States. As Heather Stur observes of South Vietnam's capital, Saigon "was a politically vibrant city with dozens of newspapers and magazines that promoted political positions ranging from support for the Saigon government to neutrality to peace at any cost."[30] This appreciation of South Vietnam's "chaotic yet proto-democratic national culture" extends to its relationship with the wider network of anti-communist governments in the Asia Pacific region that contributed to the war effort.[31]

Frustrated by both their material reliance on U.S. aid and the image of a client state that this produced, South Vietnamese officials sought to diversify their state's diplomatic and trade footprint. Sean Fear writes of "the surprisingly global scale of South Vietnam's diplomatic ambitions, belying the presumed insularity of a government often dismissed as little more than a puppet regime of the United States."[32] Simon Toner further notes that just like their revolutionary counterparts, "authoritarian, counter-revolutionary regimes sought to borrow ideas from elsewhere in the Global South," and in the view from Saigon, "the image of the East Asian developmental states—particularly Taiwan and South Korea—loomed large."[33] The three states had more in common than just developmental strategies. Each also represented the anti-communist part of a divided nation and were central to the establishment of the Asian People's Anti-Communist League (APACL). Founded by the governments of Taiwan and South Korea in 1954, APACL quickly made the fate of South Vietnam central to its agenda. APACL was intended as something of an alternative to both the Western-aligned Southeast Asian Treaty Organization, established in 1954 but made up mostly of countries not facing a direct threat of communist takeover, and the Afro-Asian nonaligned movement prompted by the 1955 Bandung Conference.[34]

For all the commonalities between Taiwan, South Korea, and South Vietnam, however, their joint wartime efforts did not necessarily lead to greater alignment. Jason Lim (Chapter 9) and Alice S. Kim (Chapter 10) explore, respectively, Taiwan's and South Korea's complex relationships with South Vietnam's efforts to survive as a state both economically and militarily. Attempts to build a sustainable economic relationship between Taiwan and South Vietnam could never overcome the significant trade imbalance between the two places, and South Korea's participation in the war led not only to greater understanding of the Vietnamese people but also to a debased imaginary of what it meant for something to be "Vietnamese." The Vietnam War witnessed both the repurposing of old cultural hierarchies and the creation of new ones in the region as Taiwan and South Korea assisted Saigon with its nation-building and war-making programs, respectively.

Taiwan and South Korea represent two ends of a spectrum of countries contributing troops to the war effort. Taiwan stationed around thirty officers at any one time in Saigon as the Republic of China Military Advisory Group, Vietnam but sent no regular combat troops for fear of prompting a backlash from Beijing.[35] South Korea, in contrast, sent over 320,000 troops to South Vietnam between 1965 and 1973. Between those two poles sat the rest of the so-called free world forces: Australia (61,000), Thailand (40,000), and New Zealand (3,800).[36] The Philippine contribution was restricted to medical and logistical support and peaked at about two thousand personnel. David L. Anderson (Chapter 11) and Christopher Lovins (Chapter 12) provide, in turn, a general overview of the variety of interests and incentives that drove South Korea, Australia, New Zealand, Thailand, and the Philippines to contribute troops and a deeper dive into the motivations of South Korea as the largest (by far) of those regional troop-contributing governments. The governments of these countries each had their own strategic appreciation of the threat posed to the region by communist gains in Indochina, which often deviated from and frustrated opinion in Washington. As early as 1966, President Lyndon Johnson complained that "the countries [in Southeast Asia] don't want the war to go on."[37] Johnson was oversimplifying regional attitudes. Many states in the region did see value in America continuing to fight in Vietnam. But this assessment was often driven less by international security considerations than by political considerations of legitimacy, credibility, and stability at home. The U.S. aid received for sending troops to the war needs to be considered in the broader domestic political context in each country.

Revising the image of South Korean, Thai, and Filipino troops as nothing more than mercenaries is one aspect of a larger project to better understand the complex reasons regional states had for supporting the American war in Vietnam. Singapore did not send troops to South Vietnam but nonetheless endorsed and encouraged continuing U.S. involvement in the war. Visiting the United States in October 1967, Singapore's prime minister, Lee Kuan Yew, voiced support for Lyndon Johnson and the continuing American war effort. S. R. Joey Long (Chapter 13) shows how Lee and other Singaporean leaders used this support for the war to encourage Singapore's economic development and military defense while also consolidating their own position of power within the city-state. In mid-1966, Lee praised the American action in Vietnam, stating that Washington was buying time for noncommunist states like Singapore to develop. This "buying time" thesis was used during the war and has persisted ever since as a key justification for the military effort: even though the United States lost the war and Saigon fell, so the logic goes, the very act of fighting the war delayed the communist advance long enough to ensure regional stability and continued alignment with Washington. Mattias Fibiger (Chapter 14) examines the "buying time" thesis in more depth, finding that although the war did contribute to more stable regimes, economic growth, and greater international cooperation in the region, it also set these developments on particular trajectories that promoted authoritarian governments, oligarchic economies, and regional organizations with rigid sovereigntist principles—outcomes that, in turn, led to the rise of new challenges for the region.[38]

. . . . . .

As a justification for waging the Vietnam War, the buying time thesis is strategically and morally dubious—simply a more sophisticated cousin of the domino theory, as Fibiger notes. But it is helpful for focusing attention on the effects of the war in the region. Much of the historiography of the Vietnam War is focused on the origins and conduct of the war—the latter often as a means to debate whether the war was winnable. As the war recedes further into the past, however, historians have begun to trace the legacies of the war, particularly for the United States, Vietnam, and to a lesser extent, Laos and Cambodia.[39] The war's ripple effect across the wider Pacific world has received less attention and deserves greater consideration as part of a broader regional turn.

The movement of people from Vietnam into (and beyond) the wider region is one major legacy of Hanoi's victory. In the two decades after the end of the war, over two million Vietnamese left the country. Lisa Tran (Chapter 15), Jana K. Lipman (Chapter 16), and Nathalie Huynh Chau Nguyen (Chapter 17) trace the pathways of Vietnamese refugees across three different junctures in the years after 1975: leaving Vietnam, with a particular focus on the motivations for doing so; transiting the temporary—and some not so temporary—camps where refugee status was determined and where resettlement or repatriation was arranged; and the long multigenerational process of settling in a new country. These chapters highlight the diversity of the refugee experience, with each juncture focusing on the complex interplay of local and international politics in a particular place. Reassessing migration from the perspective of Cholon, Hong Kong, and Australia shows how the human challenges associated with the refugee experience intersected with other political contests that together reshaped broader ideas of nationality, sovereignty, and identity in the region.

Nguyen's exploration of military career choices among second-generation Vietnamese in Australia highlights the contrasting ways the war—and the South Vietnamese experience more generally—is acknowledged and remembered in the region today. Australia's formal recognition of the service of South Vietnamese veterans not only acknowledges a former ally but also takes into account the history and experiences of a significant refugee community. Like Nguyen, Mia Martin Hobbs (Chapter 18) uses oral history to explore differences in war narratives between the United States and Australia. Veterans of the war from both countries have been returning to Vietnam since the early 1980s—a confronting act but also one that tends to confirm rather than challenge their understanding of the war's purpose, conduct, and outcome. The stories that these regional partners tell—and the differences between those national stories—ossify over time, serving to reaffirm the authority of Western narratives about the war. Boi Huyen Ngo

(Chapter 19) suggests that different forms of storytelling are necessary to dismantle the colonial legacies of the war in the region. Those legacies include the slow and often invisible accretion of damage to human bodies and to the environment as a result of exposure to chemical agents used in and after the Vietnam War. Colonial mindsets accompanied both the use of Agent Orange in Vietnam and on Indigenous land in Western Australia and the process of diagnosing—or of failing to diagnose—the effects of these chemicals.[40] To acknowledge and stop this slow violence, Ngo argues that Western diagnostic frameworks need to be supplemented with other diagnostic techniques such as personal, family, and community storytelling.

Telling stories in new ways, and telling new stories, helps not only to broaden our view of the past, but also to make better sense of the present. We hope that by explicitly placing the Vietnam War in its regional context, this volume furthers—and also complicates—our historical understanding of the Vietnam War and the pathways that led into it, through it, and out of it. As Stur writes, "By placing South Vietnam in regional and international contexts, we can see a picture of the Vietnam War that is less clear but more complete."[41]

But studying the regional dynamics of the Vietnam War is not of purely historical interest. After decades of emphasis on the Middle East, American foreign policy is turning its attention—even if haltingly and haphazardly—back to the Pacific. Barack Obama's "pivot," Donald Trump's trade war with China, and Joe Biden's pledge to restore vitality and credibility to America's alliance system in the region are all indicative of a renewed focus on what the Pentagon terms "inter-state strategic competition" in the Pacific.[42] Vice President Kamala Harris, when she visited Singapore and Vietnam in August 2021, put the matter plainly: "As we move forward and think about where we go in the 21st century, Southeast Asia and the Indo-Pacific will, in large part I believe, dictate the future of our world."[43] Understanding how the region reacted to the American war in Vietnam and how that war changed the region might help the United States and its Asia Pacific partners to better navigate the currents of competition in the future.

Notes

1. Although we utilize the familiar designations of "North Vietnam" and "South Vietnam" in this volume, we recognize that these terms gloss over contested questions of nationhood and statehood.

2. The title of this chapter is of course a play on the title of the Pulitzer Prize–winning book by Frances FitzGerald, *Fire in the Lake: The Vietnamese and the*

Americans in Vietnam (Boston: Little, Brown, 1972). We make no claim to comprehensive coverage of the conflict's regional dimensions in this volume. The Pacific world is vast, and there is still much to explore in its relationship to the Vietnam War.

3. Simeon Man, *Soldiering through Empire: Race and the Making of the Decolonizing Pacific* (Berkeley: University of California Press, 2018), 3.

4. There are several volumes that have sought to put the war in an international or global context. Andreas Daum, Lloyd Gardner, and Wilfried Mausbach, eds., *America, the Vietnam War, and the World: Comparative and International Perspectives* (New York: Cambridge University Press, 2003) is perhaps the most prominent, but despite a chapter each on Thailand and Australia, the volume's other chapters are largely on European perspectives, thus privileging Atlantic over Pacific history—a general theme of the literature on the international dimensions of the Vietnam War. Two chapters in Marilyn B. Young and Robert Buzzanco, eds., *A Companion to the Vietnam War* (Malden, MA: Blackwell, 2002) are devoted to the experiences of Vietnam's near neighbors (Cambodia and Laos), but their effect is muted by the volume's twenty-plus chapters on U.S. perspectives. A more recent work exploring the global repercussions of the Vietnam War is Lien-Hang T. Nguyen, "The Vietnam Decade: The Global Shock of the War," in *The Shock of the Global: The 1970s in Perspective*, ed. Niall Ferguson, Charles S. Maier, Erez Manela, and Daniel J. Sargent (Cambridge, MA: Belknap Press of Harvard University Press, 2010). Robert M. Blackburn, *Mercenaries and Lyndon Johnson's "More Flags": The Hiring of Korean, Filipino and Thai Soldiers in the Vietnam War* (Jefferson, NC: McFarland, 1994) is a key early work focused on the makeup of the so-called free world forces from the region that assisted the South Vietnamese and American war effort. More recent regional works include Ang Cheng Guan, *Southeast Asia and the Vietnam War* (Abingdon, UK: Routledge, 2010); Setsu Shigematsu and Keith L. Camacho, eds., *Militarized Currents: Toward a Decolonized Future in Asia and the Pacific* (Minneapolis: University of Minnesota Press, 2010); Wen-Qing Ngoei, *Arc of Containment: Britain, the United States, and Anticommunism in Southeast Asia* (Ithaca, NY: Cornell University Press, 2019); and Man, *Soldiering through Empire*.

5. Important works on individual countries in the region include (but are not limited to) Richard Ruth, *In Buddha's Company: Thai Soldiers in the Vietnam War* (Honolulu: University of Hawai'i Press, 2010); Nick Cullather, *Illusions of Influence: The Political Economy of United States–Philippines Relations, 1942–1960* (Stanford, CA: Stanford University Press, 1994); S. R. Joey Long, *Safe for Decolonization: The Eisenhower Administration, Britain, and Singapore* (Kent, OH: Kent State University Press, 2011); Daniel Chua, *U.S.-Singapore Relations, 1965–1975: Strategic Non-Alignment in the Cold War* (Singapore: National University of Singapore Press, 2017); Pamela Sodhy, *The U.S.-Malaysian Nexus: Themes in Superpower-Small State Relations* (Kuala Lumpur: Institute of Strategic and International Studies, 1991); Bradley R. Simpson, *Economists with Guns: Authoritarian Development and U.S.-Indonesian Relations, 1960–1968* (Stanford, CA: Stanford University Press, 2008); Kenton J. Clymer, *A Delicate Relationship: The United States and Burma/Myanmar since 1945* (Ithaca, NY: Cornell University Press, 2015); Peter E. Hamilton, "'A Haven

for Tortured Souls': Hong Kong in the Vietnam War," *International History Review* 37, no. 3 (2015): 565–581. On the other two states in Indochina apart from Vietnam, see especially Kenton J. Clymer, *Troubled Relations: The United States and Cambodia since 1870* (DeKalb: Northern Illinois University Press, 2007); and Seth Jacobs, *The Universe Unraveling: American Foreign Policy in Cold War Laos* (Ithaca, NY: Cornell University Press, 2012).

6. Ang Cheng Guan, *Southeast Asia's Cold War: An Interpretive History* (Honolulu: University of Hawaiʻi Press, 2018); Albert Lau, ed., *Southeast Asia and the Cold War* (Abingdon, UK: Routledge, 2014); Malcolm H. Murfett, ed., *Cold War Southeast Asia* (Singapore: Marshall Cavendish, 2012).

7. Peter J. Katzenstein, *A World of Regions: Asia and Europe in the American Imperium* (Ithaca, NY: Cornell University Press, 2005), ix. Like Katzenstein, we are also interested in more than "searching for a simple American hook on which to hang [our] regional stories." Katzenstein, *A World of Regions*, xii. On the American imperium, see also Andrew Preston, "America's Global Imperium," in *The Oxford World History of Empire*, ed. Peter Fibiger Bang, C. A. Bayley, and Walter Scheidel (Oxford: Oxford University Press, 2020), 1203–1234.

8. Daniel Bessner and Fredrik Logevall, "Recentering the United States in the Historiography of American Foreign Relations," *Texas National Security Review* 3, no. 2 (Spring 2020): 38–55.

9. Alison Bashford, "The Pacific Ocean," in *Oceanic Histories*, ed. David Armitage, Alison Bashford, and Sujit Sivasundaram (Cambridge: Cambridge University Press, 2017), 68–71; "large historiographical ocean" at 69.

10. Bashford, "The Pacific Ocean," 68. On the Indo-Pacific as the latest geographic construction of the region, see Rory Medcalf, *Indo-Pacific Empire: China, America and the Contest for the World's Pivotal Region* (Manchester, UK: Manchester University Press, 2020); Michael R. Auslin, *Asia's New Geopolitics: Essays on Reshaping the Indo-Pacific* (Stanford, CA: Hoover Institution Press, 2020); and Hansong Li, "The 'Indo-Pacific': Intellectual Origins and International Visions in Global Context," *Modern Intellectual History* (2021): 1–27, doi:10.1017/S1479244321000214.

11. Arif Dirlik, "The Asia-Pacific Idea: Reality and Representation in the Invention of a Regional Structure," *Journal of World History* 3, no. 1 (Spring 1992): 69. Dirlik continues that "Asian and Pacific intermediation now plays the most significant role within it."

12. Dirlik, "The Asia-Pacific Idea," 69.

13. NSC 51 of July 1, 1949, was originally issued by the State Department's Policy Planning Staff as PPS 51 on March 29, 1949. John G. Reid and John P. Glennon, eds., *Foreign Relations of the United States, 1949*, Volume VII, The Far East and Australasia, Part 2 (Washington, DC: Government Printing Office, 1976), Doc. 317. See also Ngoei, *Arc of Containment*, 47–48.

14. Man, *Soldiering through Empire*, 8.

15. Ngoei, *Arc of Containment*, 48.

16. Man, *Soldiering through Empire*, 6. See also Anne L. Foster, *Projections of Power: The United States and Europe in Colonial Southeast Asia, 1919–1941* (Durham, NC: Duke University Press, 2010).

17. Katzenstein, *A World of Regions*, 2.

18. Man, *Soldiering through Empire*, 6.

19. Daniel Immerwahr, *How to Hide an Empire: A Short History of the Greater United States* (London: Bodley Head, 2019), 18.

20. Sarah Miller-Davenport, *Gateway State: Hawai'i and the Cultural Transformation of American Empire* (Princeton, NJ: Princeton University Press, 2019), 10. On the idea of Hawai'i as "gateway to Asia" emerging within American military and geopolitical thought in the nineteenth century, initially as a coaling station for navy steamships, see Miller-Davenport, *Gateway State*, 8, 108–109.

21. Miller-Davenport, *Gateway State*, 11.

22. Day-to-day command over U.S. forces in South Vietnam was delegated to United States Military Assistance Command, Vietnam and over naval and air operations to other subordinate commands. The major wartime conference staged in Hawai'i was the 1966 Honolulu Conference. For a recent assessment, see Gregory A. Daddis, "Planning for a War in Paradise: The 1966 Honolulu Conference and the Shape of the Vietnam War," *Journal of Cold War Studies* 21, no. 3 (Summer 2019): 152–184.

23. Simeon Man, "Aloha, Vietnam: Race and Empire in Hawai'i's Vietnam War," *American Quarterly* 67, no. 4 (December 2015): 1085.

24. Miller-Davenport, *Gateway State*, 110–111.

25. Man, "Aloha, Vietnam," 1085.

26. Daniel Immerwahr, "The Greater United States: Territory and Empire in U.S. History," *Diplomatic History* 40, no. 3 (2016): 373–391. See especially 389–390, where Immerwahr includes extraterritorial military bases in his conception of today's formal American "pointillist" empire. Immerwahr's focus on points is informed by William Rankin, *After the Map: Cartography, Navigation, and the Transformation of Territory in the Twentieth Century* (Chicago: University of Chicago Press, 2016). On the territorial "nodes" of America's Pacific empire, see also Man, "Aloha, Vietnam," 1086. For a deeper history of extraterritoriality and foreign enclaves in American foreign relations, see Brooke Blower, "Nation of Outposts: Forts, Factories, Bases, and the Making of American Power," *Diplomatic History* 41, no. 3 (2017): 439–459.

27. The scholarly literature on American military bases is now substantial. For an explicit comparison between the older territorial system of establishing bases on the legal right of conquest and the newer extraterritorial system of negotiated SOFAs, see C. T. Sandars, *America's Overseas Garrisons: The Leasehold Empire* (New York: Oxford University Press, 2000).

28. Honolulu was also an R&R destination, albeit with significant differences. It was where men in relationships could connect with their American wives and girlfriends "and avoid the temptations of debased Asian women." With R&R, then, Hawai'i became not a gateway *to* Asia but rather an escape *from* it and a stepping-stone back to the comforts of home. "For American servicemen, it turned out, the door to the Gateway to the Pacific swung both ways." Miller-Davenport, *Gateway State*, 140. Sydney similarly operated as an R&R destination somewhat distinct from the other R&R destinations.

29. See, for example, Edward Miller, "The Postcolonial War: Hue-Tam Ho Tai and the 'Vietnamese Turn' in Vietnam War Studies," *Journal of Vietnamese Studies* 12, no. 3 (2017): 14–22; Andrew Preston, "*Rethinking the Vietnam War*: Orthodoxy and Revisionism," *International Politics Reviews* 1, no. 1 (2013): 37–39; Sean Fear, "The Rise and Fall of the Second Republic: Domestic Politics and Civil Society in U.S.–South Vietnamese Relations, 1967–1971" (PhD diss., Cornell University, 2016).

30. Heather M. Stur, *Saigon at War: South Vietnam and the Global Sixties* (New York: Cambridge University Press, 2020), 2.

31. Stur, *Saigon at War*, 7.

32. Sean Fear, "Saigon Goes Global: South Vietnam's Quest for International Legitimacy in the Age of Détente," *Diplomatic History* 42, no. 3 (2018): 429.

33. Simon Toner, "Imagining Taiwan: The Nixon Administration, the Developmental States, and South Vietnam's Search for Economic Viability, 1969–1975," *Diplomatic History* 41, no. 4 (2017): 774.

34. Stur, *Saigon at War*, 131–142.

35. Malaysia similarly did not send combat troops to the war but instead "offered to help train South Vietnamese police and military personnel in the methods of guerrilla warfare." Stur, *Saigon at War*, 133.

36. The most prominent work on regional troop contributions to the war is Blackburn, *Mercenaries and Lyndon Johnson's "More Flags."* See also Fredrik Logevall, "America Isolated: The Western Powers and the Escalation of the War," in *America, the Vietnam War, and the World: Comparative and International Perspectives*, ed. Andreas Daum, Lloyd C. Gardner, and Wilfried Mausbach (New York: Cambridge University Press, 2003). From outside the region, only Spain made a nominal contribution of personnel to the war.

37. Lyndon Johnson cited in Fredrik Logevall, *Choosing War: The Lost Chance for Peace and the Escalation of War in Vietnam* (Berkeley: University of California Press, 1999), 378.

38. Fibiger's mixed scorecard on the buying time thesis somewhat parallels Stur's argument regarding the Vietnam War's effect on an independent South Vietnam: it "would both buy time for Saigon to develop its political institutions and destroy popular will to resist a Hanoi-led reunification of Vietnam." Stur, *Saigon at War*, 24.

39. See, for example, Scott Laderman and Edwin A. Martini, eds., *Four Decades On: Vietnam, the United States, and the Legacies of the Second Indochina War* (Durham, NC: Duke University Press, 2013); Brenda M. Boyle and Jeehyun Lim, eds., *Looking Back on the Vietnam War: Twenty-First-Century Perspectives* (New Brunswick, NJ: Rutgers University Press, 2016); Christian G. Appy, *American Reckoning: The Vietnam War and Our National Identity* (New York: Viking, 2015); and Amanda C. Demmer, *After Saigon's Fall: Refugees and US-Vietnamese Relations, 1975–2000* (Cambridge: Cambridge University Press, 2021).

40. As Ngo notes in her chapter, the Western Australian Legislative Council did not accept the designation of "Agent Orange" for the herbicides used in the Kimberly region of the state in the 1970s and early 1980s. Agent Orange is a fifty-fifty

mixture of two chemicals, 2,4-D and 2,4,5-T, and the Western Australian government did not mix them, instead using them as herbicides separately.

41. Stur, *Saigon at War*, 15.

42. Jim Mattis, "Summary of the 2018 National Defense Strategy of the United States of America: Sharpening the American Military's Competitive Edge," https://dod.defense.gov/Portals/1/Documents/pubs/2018-National-Defense-Strategy-Summary.pdf.

43. Chris Barrett, "Harris Reaffirms Pivot to Indo-Pacific as US Exits Afghanistan," *Sydney Morning Herald*, August 23, 2021, https://www.smh.com.au/world/asia/harris-reaffirms-pivot-to-indo-pacific-as-us-exits-afghanistan-20210823-p58l34.html.

2 British Neocolonialism in Malaya and Singapore, and U.S. Empire in the Pacific

WEN-QING NGOEI

On March 23, 1976, Colonel J. C. A. Swynnerton and twenty-two noncommissioned officers of the British army vacated the HMS Terror Naval Barracks in Singapore and checked into the Hotel Equatorial. Swynnerton had served in various corners of Britain's shrinking empire, including stints in Nigeria and Kenya in the 1950s as these two countries clamored for colonial rule to end. In Singapore, he was to transfer the Terror Barracks to local control. With that accomplished, he boarded a commercial jet bound for England eight days later. The local newspapers dubbed him the "last British soldier [to] leave Singapore."[1]

This "Brexit" of the late 1970s passed without fanfare. After all, Singapore had gained its independence from Britain some ten years earlier. Yet, Swynnerton's actions were doubtlessly significant—they represent the definitive end of Britain's protracted withdrawal from its military installations in Singapore, from its once mighty empire east of Suez. Indeed, Britain's imperial influence had endured in Southeast Asia longer than the other European colonial powers thanks to London's neocolonial strategies in Singapore and Malaya after 1945 and the efforts of local conservative elites. The French, by contrast, had departed Indochina some twenty years before Swynnerton came to Singapore; the Dutch had quit virtually all their possessions in the Netherlands East Indies even earlier after failing to quell the Indonesian nationalists. Only Britain's tenacious empire would overlap for a considerable time with the ascent of U.S. power in Southeast Asia, profoundly shaping U.S. involvement in Vietnam and the wider Asian region between the 1950s and early 1970s.

This chapter places the Vietnam War on that larger canvas of Southeast and East Asian history by studying the long shadow that Britain's empire cast over U.S. entanglements across the region. Although historians have studied Anglo-American relations in Cold War Southeast Asia, scholarship on the subject remains piecemeal. There are valuable studies of U.S.-British interactions in the early 1960s with respect to the Vietnam conflict or the Indonesia-Malaysia rivalry known as the Confrontation.[2] And there are insightful considerations of U.S. reactions to Britain's pullout from Singapore from the end of the 1960s.[3] However, only one recent study has attempted to analyze Anglo-American relations in the Southeast Asian context from the end of the Pacific war through America's retreat from Vietnam.[4] This chapter adopts a similar wide-angle lens to consider two key moments when British and U.S. empires were imbricated in Southeast Asia: The first unfolded between the late 1940s and early 1950s, when British officials in Malaya and Singapore directly influenced the expansion of U.S. commitment to Southeast Asia by contributing to the domino theory's emergence and America's earliest moves to support the French war against the Vietminh. The second moment this chapter examines occurred over the 1950s and 1960s, when Britain and its allies in Malaysia[5] undermined Sukarno's left-leaning regime in Indonesia and China's influence in Southeast Asia. Consequently, much of Southeast Asia was on a decidedly pro-U.S. trajectory in the mid-1960s when President Lyndon Johnson Americanized the Vietnam conflict on the premise of rescuing the region from communism. Britain's neocolonial machinations in Malaya and Singapore were fundamental to the expansion of U.S. empire in this corner of the Pacific once dominated by the European powers.

· · · · · ·

As World War II ended, British officials began contemplating ways to slow the empire's descent from the apex of global power and retain its valuable colonial possessions. Britain's economy had been drained by the conflict with Nazi Germany, and Japan's initial victories over the colonial powers—including Britain's humiliating loss of Singapore in 1942—had galvanized colonized peoples everywhere against Western imperialism. Thereafter, Britain sought to cultivate a "special relationship" with the predominant superpower, the United States; to become intimately involved in the decision making that would create and preside over the post-1945 world order. Of course, London hoped that the new U.S.-led order would preserve Britain's empire in some shape or form.[6] In effect, London's policy was neocolonial.

British neocolonialism was not unique. All the Western powers that possessed colonies in Southeast Asia harbored similar aspirations after 1945. The United States seemed to concede to Philippine nationalism by granting independence to its colony but sustained its influence in Southeast Asia by holding on to vast tracts of Philippine land to host its massive air and naval bases. The Dutch mounted an abortive campaign to recolonize the Netherlands East Indies by force.[7] The French, while fighting against the communist-dominated Vietminh, tried vainly to redirect local nationalist fervor from Ho Chi Minh toward a former Annamese emperor—the so-called Bao Dai solution—who was pliant and friendly to France.[8]

London, for its part, wished to maintain substantial influence over Singapore (home to vital British military installations) and Malaya (which produced much of the world's rubber and tin supplies). However, in 1948, the Malayan Communist Party (MCP), guerrilla fighters in the Malay Peninsula and subversive agents that had infiltrated Singapore's trade unions and Chinese-medium middle schools, revolted against British authority. Britain's cause was not helped by the fact that many of Malaya's ethnic Chinese (who comprised almost 40 percent of the population) initially revered the mostly Chinese MCP. Indeed, the MCP was somewhat popular across the Malay Peninsula since it had been the backbone of a resistance force during the Japanese occupation.

British leaders, aware that the Vietminh provided inspiration to the MCP, surmised that inoculating Malaya and Singapore against communism was inseparable from ensuring America lent material and political support to France's counterrevolutionary campaign in Indochina. The urgency to lock in U.S. commitment to Southeast Asia only increased in October 1949 when the Chinese communists seized the mainland, fueling preexisting suspicions among Western leaders that Beijing would support Southeast Asia's communists and court the region's millions-strong Chinese diaspora.[9]

For the European powers, collaborating with America to uphold Western imperialism in Southeast Asia was not new. In the early twentieth century, because the USSR aided and guided local communists throughout Asia, European officials easily drew America on board their anti-communist projects in the colonies.[10] Thirty years on, the Chinese communists' victory similarly boosted British leaders' hopes of having their U.S. allies perceive Southeast Asia through their eyes and thereby throw America's weight behind the remnants of the colonial order despite U.S. analysts explicitly deploring such an "anti-historical act."[11] Indeed, America's so-called loss of China to communism had spurred President Harry Truman to dispatch several fact-finding missions to Asia, eager to learn how America could support its allies against a communist bloc that with the addition of China impinged directly on the wider region. London perceived in these U.S. missions a heaven-sent opportunity. From late 1949 through 1950, three such missions traveled through Southeast Asia, each visiting with British administrators in Malaya and Singapore to seek, above all, British assessments of regional affairs. As Colonel R. Allen Griffin, leader of the second mission, made plain, U.S. officials must "talk with the British if [they] were to understand" Southeast Asia.[12] Like Griffin, Ambassador Philip Jessup who led the first mission, and John Melby, who led the third, were impressed by the British commissioner-general for Southeast Asia, Malcolm MacDonald, whom they encountered in Malaya and Singapore. Jessup underscored that his report to the State Department on Asian security matched the "British view" he had solicited from MacDonald; Melby described MacDonald as the "most constructive man I have talked with" in Asia.[13]

U.S. officials' willingness to trust their British allies' strategic analyses enabled Britain to directly influence U.S. stakes in Cold War Southeast Asia. Men like Malcolm MacDonald would help implant the principle of Southeast Asia's interconnected insecurity—the logic of the domino theory—in the minds of his U.S. counterparts. As U.S. records of meetings between MacDonald and Jessup, Griffin, and Melby demonstrate, American officials allowed MacDonald much room to press his case that the fates of Malaya and Singapore were tied to that of Indochina, Burma, and Siam.

MacDonald's genius was in rhetorically intertwining the campaigns of the Vietminh and the MCP with U.S. fears of China expanding southward into the subregion. He did this by taking American concerns that the Chinese diaspora of the region would serve as Beijing's fifth column and melding them with American and British memories of Japan's conquest of Southeast Asia.[14] As such, Jessup returned to Washington claiming that the "overseas Chinese communities form one of the most important elements in the strength of the Communists in Asia," that these views were "in accord" with those of "McD" (MacDonald) and British officials in Malaya and Singapore. Jessup even contended that countries with large Chinese populations might as well share "common borders" with an expansionist China.[15]

Griffin, subtly encouraged by MacDonald to tap his underlying racial thinking, read developments in Southeast Asia largely through the perceived threat from China and the Chinese diaspora which he assumed had "primary loyalty" to Beijing. His reports on each Southeast Asian country to the State Department either anticipated China would invade (Burma, Thailand, and Indochina), or else the "mother country" would mobilize Chinese diasporic networks to subvert U.S.-friendly governments (British authorities in Malaya and Singapore, Indonesia, and again, Thailand).[16] For Griffin, France's war against the Vietminh was embedded within a broader U.S. vision of Southeast Asia, a region presumably interconnected by its overseas Chinese and susceptible to China's hegemonic designs. Importantly, U.S. records underscore that Griffin's reports prompted Truman's decision in April 1950 to back the French in Indochina. These earliest steps for the United States into the Vietnam quagmire entailed increases of U.S. military aid to France, aid that added to Indochina's guaranteed share of the $36.5 million in U.S. military assistance already set aside for distribution among several countries in the wider region (including Thailand, Japan, and Indonesia).[17]

In August 1950, with the Korean War raging, John Melby and his team visited Malaya and Singapore, keen to hear MacDonald's analysis of Asia. For this group of U.S. officials, MacDonald conjured the image of a Chinese "highway to the rest of South East Asia" that stretched from Korea and plunged through Burma, Indochina, and Siam toward Malaya. This "route," he stated, would be forged by the "local fifth column" of Southeast Asian communists and "all the [overseas] Chinese community" in the region. He painted a vivid picture of vulnerable Southeast Asian states lined up from north to south, a veritable row of teetering dominoes with Indochina as the "place of attack" (he used this phrase repeatedly) for the communists to undermine Western power in the region. In a brilliant rhetorical move, he invoked the visceral memory of the Japanese Empire storming through Southeast Asia, knocking the colonial powers over one by one, a foretaste of what the Chinese communists might do. Indeed, Macdonald shrewdly mentioned Thailand's willingness to accommodate to a northern aggressor, which the Melby team acknowledged was a highly "relevant" reference to the "precedent" of Thai behavior in World War II. He also described Malaya and Singapore as the "great prize" at the southern tip of mainland Southeast Asia, which for the military men in Melby's team was sufficient proof that the Chinese would reprise "the Japs'" "overland invasion of Malaya" in the "last war" to seize Britain's fortress in Singapore.[18]

By October 1950, almost four years before President Dwight Eisenhower would enunciate his "falling domino principle," U.S. intelligence officers had elaborated the insights of the fact-finding missions to Asia into a formative rendition of the domino theory. In the words of these American analysts—reminiscent of those uttered by Malcolm MacDonald—the "fall of Indochina would provide the Communists with a staging area in addition to China for military operations against the rest of Southeast Asia, and this threat might well inspire accommodation in both Thailand and Burma . . . [meaning that] the already considerable difficulty faced by the British in maintaining security in Malaya would be greatly aggravated."[19] Eisenhower's peculiar choice of imagery echoed this. More to the point, U.S. planners had willingly absorbed the specific formulation of Southeast Asia's interconnectedness offered by MacDonald and his colleagues, affirming its racist underpinnings and the vague memories it borrowed from imperial Japan's southward drive. In this way, vital components of Britain's neocolonial agenda—its early vision of the domino logic intertwined with its emphasis on supporting France against the Vietminh—became lodged within U.S. strategy toward the wider region.

Over the 1950s and 1960s, British neocolonialism in Malaya and Singapore continued to shape the larger context of America's evolving empire in Southeast Asia. Although U.S. interventions in Indochina proved ineffective in halting the advance of indigenous communist groups, a wide-angle view of Southeast Asia reveals that the states with the most resources and largest populations in the region were ensconced in the U.S. orbit by the late 1960s. Anti-communist elites in Thailand and the Philippines had already risen to political dominance with U.S. assistance in the 1950s.[20] In Malaya and Singapore, similar factions did so with British support and would play a critical role in undermining the left-leaning Sukarno regime of Indonesia, propelling the world's fifth-most populous country to the right of the Cold War divide by the end of 1965.

To be sure, Britain's neocolonial strategies paralleled France's Bao Dai solution and America's alliance with South Vietnamese leader Ngo Dinh Diem.[21] British officials had also courted the anti-communist nationalists in their former colonies, Malaya and Singapore, intending for these conservative elites to eventually helm their countries and, following independence, remain aligned with London. However, unlike the French and U.S. forces in Indochina, British and Commonwealth troops, with their Malayan allies, decimated the MCP guerrillas in the Malay Peninsula by the mid-1950s. There were never more than five thousand MCP fighters in the first place, which made Britain's task easier. In 1957, Malaya gained its independence, led by Prime Minister Tunku Abdul Rahman, a Malay prince who proved more effective at securing the popular vote than British leaders anticipated.[22] In 1959, Britain advanced Singapore to a stage in decolonization it named internal self-government, which entailed electing its first prime minister, Lee Kuan Yew, and local representatives to administer all aspects of government except for foreign policy and defense, which Britain still controlled. The anti-communist Lee proceeded to crush his left-wing rivals in early 1963 by claiming that their leading lights had endorsed a violent anti-British revolt in Brunei and planned to spread it to Singapore. With these allegations (the evidence was circumstantial at best), Lee justified his use of the repressive internal security tools bequeathed by Britain and detained his opponents for years without due process.[23]

Making friends of former colonies aside, Britain sought to retain control of its strategic resources in Southeast Asia, the most important being the military bases in Singapore that enabled London to still crow its world power status and support the Southeast Asian Treaty Organization (SEATO) and other U.S. goals in the region.[24] After all, U.S. officials had confided in their British counterparts that Washington prized the Singapore bases in the "over-all defense against Communist expansion [in] SEA."[25] Washington even considered British naval bases in Singapore more vital to U.S. objectives in the region than America's "less desirable peripheral" naval base in the Philippines.[26] Happily for London, the Tunku would formalize the Anglo-Malayan Defense Agreement soon after Malaya's independence, requiring that Britain maintain a sizable and enduring military presence in Southeast Asia.[27] This requirement meant that Britain could access several of its bases in Malaya and, importantly, must have complete control of its Singapore bases. Doubly fortunate for Britain, then, its close relationship with Lee would guarantee the Singapore bases remained in British hands. Lee had no qualms about this arrangement, for an estimated 150,000 Singaporeans' livelihoods were connected in some way to the British bases (nearly one-tenth of the population); in fact, the bases generated at least 20 percent of Singapore's national income into the late 1960s.[28]

For Sukarno, watching warily from Jakarta, Malaya's intimate politico-military ties to Britain, and Britain's continued control of the Singapore bases, proved a British neocolonial plot against Indonesia was under way. His suspicions were not baseless. From the mid-1950s, Washington and London had become concerned about Sukarno's embrace of the Indonesian Communist Party (PKI). Although not a communist himself, Sukarno wished to exploit the PKI's extensive grassroots networks and repel any challenge from the right-wing elites of the Indonesian military. To U.S. and British leaders, though, Sukarno had made Indonesia increasingly vulnerable to communism. In 1958, the Anglo-American allies launched covert operations to topple Sukarno with the notable support of the Tunku and tactical use of the Singapore bases. (This plot against Sukarno failed badly when troops loyal to the Indonesian leader downed an American pilot.)[29] Sukarno survived, embittered by Malaya's part in the plot, fearful of the threat presented by the Singapore bases, and tacked even further to the left. From the early

1960s, despite America's generous offers of aid to smooth over its turbulent past with Sukarno, he gravitated toward China. Indeed, even though the USSR, too, made overtures to Sukarno, he disliked the Kremlin's pragmatic "peaceful coexistence" with America, enamored instead of the Chinese communists' revolutionary zeal and aggressive anti-imperialism.[30] In this period, Sukarno would coin the term *nekolim* to describe Britain's cozy relationship with its former colonies, Malaya and Singapore, a prime example of the new face of colonialism and imperialism after World War II.

One more provocation from Britain, Malaya, and Singapore would ignite the Indonesia-Malaysia Confrontation (known also as *Konfrontasi*) that began in 1963 and ended a few years later with the Indonesian army's right-wing coup against Sukarno, the massacre of the PKI, and the new Suharto regime's severing of Indonesia's relationship with China. This provocation was the planned merger of Malaya, Singapore, and two British-controlled Borneo territories, Sabah and Sarawak, to form the Federation of Malaysia in September 1963. On the surface, the creation of Malaysia showed Britain's willingness to liquidate its empire in the region, allowing Singapore, Sabah, and Sarawak to formally gain their independence by federating with Malaya.[31] Then again, Lee and his government were determined that even after independence, Britain would be allowed "unrestricted use" of the Singapore bases to meet its military obligations to SEATO and Malaya.[32] For Sukarno and his like-minded colleagues, the formation of Malaysia was intolerable—it would project the malign presence of Britain and the Tunku to the Indonesia border in Borneo. American views of Malaysia stoked Sukarno's paranoia. In April 1963, the *New York Times* described Malaysia as a "great counterweight . . . to the vague threats of Indonesian expansion from the south."[33]

Thus, Indonesian officials took their case against Malaysia to the United Nations (UN) General Assembly and targeted their message at the newly independent nations of the nonaligned bloc. The Indonesians insisted that Malaysia was not "truly independent" so long as Britain controlled its Singapore bases, that the enlarged federation was a "British neocolonial plot" to encircle Indonesia.[34] In early 1963, Sukarno preempted the scheduled creation of Malaysia later that year by launching *Konfrontasi*, a campaign to "crush Malaysia" by all means available. China, eager to strengthen its ties to the PKI and Indonesia, sympathized with Sukarno, agreeing that Malaysia was indeed a "neocolonial scheme" concocted by Britain and America.[35] Premier Zhou Enlai even signaled that China would aid the communists of Laos, Indonesia, and Vietnam in the contest for Southeast Asia. Beijing would regularly embolden Sukarno by assuring him that China would defend Indonesia against aggression from the Anglo-American powers.[36]

At this time in the early 1960s, with South Vietnam spiraling into instability despite (or perhaps due to) American involvement, U.S. leaders became concerned that their treaty obligations to SEATO and ANZUS (Australia–New Zealand–U.S. Security Pact) might drag American forces into a major war with Indonesia and possibly even its Chinese patron. On paper, Indonesia looked formidable, with about half a million combat troops and military equipment it had received from China, the United States, and the USSR. As *Konfrontasi* unfolded in 1963 and 1964, Sukarno cut communications and trade with Malaysia, authorized guerrilla warfare and subversion in Sabah and Sarawak, and had Indonesian bombing aircraft repeatedly buzz and threaten the Royal Air Force in Singapore. Also, Indonesian forces attacked parts of the Malay Peninsula and Singapore's offshore petroleum bunkering station, while Indonesian saboteurs bombed various sites in Singapore. Responding, Britain called on its Australian and New Zealand allies and marshaled more than a quarter of the Royal Navy into action. Some 60,000 British military personnel were mobilized during the conflict, many drawn from Britain's commitments to the North Atlantic Treaty Organization in Germany.[37]

Behind the attention-grabbing military engagements, but no less important, was the Malaysian diplomatic offensive that destroyed Sukarno's reputation among the nonaligned nations he wanted to win over. Lee Kuan Yew started the ball rolling in April 1962 before Malaysia had come into existence, before Sukarno even declared *Konfrontasi*. In a whirlwind trip, Lee visited Burmese leader Ne Win, Indian prime minister Jawaharlal Nehru, Egyptian president Gamal Abdel Nasser, and Marshal Josef Tito of Yugoslavia to convince these major nonaligned leaders that *Konfrontasi* endangered the genuine aspirations of Malaysians to "throw off the last remnants of colonialism." Of course, neither Singapore nor Malaya were spurning British imperialism, and Sukarno's accusations should have carried weight given his stature as a preeminent Afro-Asian leader. Yet, Lee's diplomatic endeavors met with unexpected success. Indeed, Tito had at first refused to see Lee but eventually, after an hour with Lee, promised to break with Sukarno on the Malaysia issue. Nehru, already friendly with the Tunku, gave Malaysia his blessings through Lee. Ne Win and his advisers were likewise sympathetic to Malaysia's cause. Nasser received the Singaporean contingent in a ceremony with "twelve outriders, horns blazing" (according to a British journalist accompanying Lee) and signed a joint statement expressing Egypt's support for Malaysia.[38]

Two years later, Lee embarked on a similar mission to the African continent. From January through February 1964, he and officials from Sabah and Sarawak traveled to seventeen African states. Lee stated the mission's goal in a letter to the British High Commissioner to Singapore: "Once we get [the African leaders] over this antipathy for foreign troops and bases, we can effectively isolate the Indonesians."[39] The Indonesians never attempted a diplomatic campaign of comparable scale. In any case, goodwill for Sukarno in the region was in short supply. The Malaysians managed to persuade virtually all the leaders they visited to endorse Malaysia or at least mute their criticism of Britain's military presence in Singapore. Many African leaders would condemn Sukarno's belligerence—two even compared him to Hitler. Importantly, the African leaders Lee visited believed that Britain's military role in *Konfrontasi* was merely defensive. None were aware of Britain's clandestine raids into Indonesian Borneo and covert British-Malaysian support for secessionist factions in Indonesia that destabilized the country. Because these maneuvers occurred out of sight, Lee could claim convincingly that Malaysia was the victim. Months later, in October 1964, at a nonaligned conference in Egypt, Afro-Asian delegates emphatically denounced Sukarno and *Konfrontasi*.[40]

Crucially, the Malaysians scored their prime objective in touring Africa: agreements from President Camille Alliale of the Ivory Coast and Prime Minister Jomo Kenyatta of Kenya to support Malaysia's nonpermanent membership in the UN Security Council. This, the Malaysians and British believed, would eviscerate Indonesia's allegations of British neocolonialism and legitimize the new federation in the international community. And it did, when in January 1965, Malaysia officially entered the Security Council over Indonesia's objections. Sukarno, incensed, withdrew Indonesia from the UN in futile protest.[41]

The diplomatic isolation of the Sukarno regime unfolded alongside Indonesia's bruising military engagement with the fading British Empire, a low-grade war that nevertheless hollowed out the Indonesian economy. For the right-wing army elites of Indonesia, suspicious of the PKI and Beijing's abetting of Sukarno, *Konfrontasi* was disastrous for other reasons. Britain and its allies' ferocious response meant that Indonesia's army was paying the price for Sukarno's belligerence and the ambitions of China and the PKI. (That said, China never rendered military support to Sukarno despite

Britain's repeated attacks.) The Indonesian army right-wingers, determined to prevent *Konfrontasi* from escalating, tamp down the instability it brought, and stop the communists from inveigling themselves deeper into Indonesian politics, sought to end the Sukarno regime. In effect, British neocolonialism in Malaya and Singapore had shoved Indonesia to the precipice. Now America's part was vital. Following the Eisenhower administration's failed plot against Sukarno, Washington had changed its approach and in addition to wooing Sukarno with aid packages, funneled U.S. resources into equipping, training, and funding the conservative elements of Indonesia's army. This strategy persisted through the 1960s, entrenching the U.S.-friendly, anti-communist worldview of the army elites. These elites were primed for a power grab when a small segment of the PKI (including its chairman D. N. Aidit) rightly intuited that an army-led coup against Sukarno was imminent but clumsily played into the army's hands by assassinating six generals suspected to be the core group of its right wing.[42]

Aidit's gambit, the doomed Thirtieth of September Movement (which occurred on October 1, 1965), sealed the PKI's fate. Major General Suharto of the Indonesian army stepped to the fore amid the initial confusion (Aidit had also sequestered Sukarno to protect him) and cannily blamed the PKI and China for attempting to subvert Indonesia. He rallied the Indonesian armed forces and the broader public with a call to destroy the PKI, a call amplified by misleading, Central Intelligence Agency (CIA)–supplied propaganda materials and technical equipment which alleged that Beijing was in on the PKI's plot (in fact, Chinese leaders were stunned by Aidit's move). A massacre ensued between 1965 and 1966, as the army and civilians aroused by the disinformation campaign and their own prejudices and paranoia, slaughtered PKI members, suspected communists, and ethnic Chinese believed to be loyal to Beijing. Upward of half a million Indonesians were killed. U.S. officials, aware that Indonesia was moving swiftly into the American orbit, helped to conceal the rising body count. Thereafter, Suharto assumed power, sweeping aside Sukarno who was ineffectual without the PKI. In 1967, Suharto broke Indonesia's diplomatic relations with China, leaving the communist powers with only Indochina as their toehold in Southeast Asia.[43]

Indonesia's historic turn, prodded along expediently by U.S. interference, spurred by Britain's endeavors to preserve its power in Southeast Asia, and the machinations of anti-communists in Malaya and Singapore, was part of the larger regional context that enclosed the Vietnam War. Given that by late 1965, much of Southeast Asia—the Philippines, Thailand, Malaysia, Singapore, and Indonesia—were firmly anti-communist, there is great irony in President Johnson's escalation of the U.S. role in Vietnam. The bloodbaths that flowed from his fateful choice within Vietnam, Laos, and Cambodia are all the more tragic because America had by then already attained predominance in Southeast Asia.

· · · · · ·

In effect, British neocolonialism in Malaya and Singapore from the end of World War II through the late 1960s was mutually constitutive with the growth of U.S. power in the Pacific. Throughout the long overlap of the declining British Empire and the ascendant United States in Southeast Asia, Britain astutely deepened U.S. commitment to Indochina and the broader region with an incipient version of the domino theory and, with Malaysia and Singapore, played a critical role in Indonesia's transformation. Subsequently, U.S. informal empire in Southeast Asia would further enlarge because British leaders, their nation's economic capacity depleted by *Konfrontasi*, at last decided they must relinquish their Singapore bases and pull their military from Southeast Asia. As Britain's withdrawal process dragged into the 1970s, Malaysia and the newly independent Singapore (which had left the federation in 1965) chose the United States as their new patron, avidly supporting U.S. policy in Vietnam and fastening their economies and security to the U.S.-dominated order in the region.[44] In other words, before and while the United States sank into failure in Vietnam, much of Southeast Asia transitioned through a period of shared U.S.-British predominance into American hegemony. Through a wide-angle lens, then, the ill-starred American war in Vietnam seems something of an anomaly for the post-1945 history of U.S.–Southeast Asian relations, an exception that proves the rule.

Notes

This essay is adapted from material in the author's book, *Arc of Containment: Britain, the United States, and Anticommunism in Southeast Asia* (Ithaca, NY: Cornell University Press, 2019). All rights reserved.

    1. "Why Army Meals Are as Good as Those in Some Singapore Hotels," *Straits Times*, March 24, 1976; "The Last British Soldier Leaves Singapore Tomorrow," *Straits Times*, March 30, 1976.

    2. Matthew Jones, *Conflict and Confrontation in Southeast Asia, 1961–1965: Britain, the United States and the Creation of Malaysia* (Cambridge: Cambridge University Press, 2002); Peter Busch, *All the Way with JFK? Britain, the U.S. and the Vietnam War* (New York: Oxford University Press, 2003).

3. Saki Dockrill, *Britain's Retreat from East of Suez: The Choice between Europe and the World?* (London: Palgrave Macmillan, 2002); P. L. Pham, *Ending East of Suez: The British Decision to Withdraw from Malaysia and Singapore, 1964–1968* (Oxford: Oxford University Press, 2011).

4. Ngoei, *Arc of Containment*.

5. To clarify the change in names from Malaya to Malaysia: The Federation of Malaya, which gained independence from Britain in 1957, refers only to the states of the Malay Peninsula. In 1963, Malaya merged with Singapore as well as Britain's Borneo territories, Sabah and Sarawak, to form Malaysia. In 1965, Singapore was ejected from the federation, though Malaysia would retain its name.

6. For more on U.S.-British-Singaporean relations in the 1950s, see S. R. Joey Long, *Safe for Decolonization: The Eisenhower Administration, Britain and Singapore* (Kent, OH: Kent State University Press, 2011).

7. Robert J. McMahon, *Colonialism and the Cold War: The United States and the Struggle for Indonesian Independence, 1945–1949* (Ithaca, NY: Cornell University Press, 1981); Frances Gouda and Thijs Brocades Zaalberg, *American Visions of the Netherlands East Indies/ Indonesia: U.S. Foreign Policy and Indonesian Nationalism, 1920–1949* (Amsterdam: Amsterdam University Press, 2002).

8. Mark Atwood Lawrence, *Assuming the Burden: Europe and the American Commitment to War in Vietnam* (Berkeley: University of California Press, 2005).

9. Sir William Strang, "Tour in South-East Asia and the Far East," March 17, 1949, CAB (Cabinet Files), 129/33, 11; NSC-51: U.S. Policy toward Southeast Asia, July 1, 1949, U.S. Declassified Documents Online (USDCO) (Gale document no. CK2349354016), 1–4, 5–6.

10. Anne L. Foster, *Projections of Power: The United States and Europe in Colonial Southeast Asia, 1919–1941* (Durham, NC: Duke University Press, 2010).

11. Memo, Secretary of State for Foreign Affairs to the Cabinet, November 26, 1949, CAB 129/37, The National Archives of the United Kingdom (TNA); Ngoei, *Arc of Containment*, 47.

12. Oral history interview with Colonel R. Allen Griffin, conducted by James R. Fuchs, February 15, 1974, 59, Oral History Program, Harry S. Truman Presidential Library (HSTL), https://www.trumanlibrary.gov/library/oral-histories/griffinr.

13. Memcon, "Oral Report by Ambassador-at-Large Philip C. Jessup upon His Return from the East," April 3, 1950, *Foreign Relations of the United States (FRUS)*, 1950, vol. 6, *East Asia and the Pacific*, ed. Neal H. Petersen et al. (Washington, DC: Government Printing Office, 1976), 68–76; Letter from Melby to John Davies (Policy Planning Staff, Department of State), August 31, 1950, Melby Papers, box 12, Melby Chronological File 1950 (August 16–31), HSTL.

14. Wen-Qing Ngoei, "The Domino Logic of the Darkest Moment: The Fall of Singapore, the Atlantic Echo Chamber and 'Chinese Penetration' in U.S. Cold War Policy toward Southeast Asia," *Journal of American-East Asian Relations* 21, no. 3 (2014): 215–245.

15. Memcon, "Oral Report by Ambassador-at-Large Philip C. Jessup upon His Return from the East," 70–71.

16. Ngoei, *Arc of Containment*, 37–39.

17. Memo, Rusk to Webb, Budgetary Plans for Fiscal Year 1951 for Assistance for Countries Eligible under Section 303 of the Mutual Defense Assistance Act, April 25, 1950, *FRUS*, 1950, vol. 6, *East Asia and the Pacific*, 83–84.

18. State Department, Report of the Joint MDAP Survey Mission to Southeast Asia—Malaya, undated, 1, 9; U.S. Navy, Joint MDAP Survey Mission in Southeast Asia: Malaya, August 17, 1950, 16, Melby Papers, box 12, Melby Chronological File 1950 (August 1–15), HSTL.

19. CIA, "Consequences to the U.S. of Communist Domination of Mainland Southeast Asia," October 13, 1950, 1–2, CIA FOIA Reading Room, https://www.cia.gov.

20. For U.S.-Philippine relations in the early Cold War, see Nick Cullather, *Illusions of Influence: The Political Economy of United States–Philippine Relations, 1942–1960* (Stanford, CA: Stanford University Press, 1994). For U.S.-Thai relations, see Daniel Fineman, *A Special Relationship: The United States and Military Government in Thailand, 1947–1958* (Honolulu: University of Hawai'i Press, 1997).

21. For more on U.S. policy toward Diem, see Jessica Chapman, *Cauldron of Resistance: Ngo Dinh Diem, the United States, and 1950s Southern Vietnam* (Ithaca, NY: Cornell University Press, 2013); Edward Miller, *Misalliance: Ngo Dinh Diem, the United States, and the Fate of South Vietnam* (Cambridge, MA: Harvard University Press, 2013).

22. Ngoei, *Arc of Containment*, chap. 2.

23. Matthew Jones, "Creating Malaysia: Singapore Security, the Borneo Territories and the Contours of British Policy, 1961–3," *Journal of Imperial and Commonwealth History* 28, no. 2 (2000): 85–109.

24. Inward Telegram, Selkirk to Secretary of State for the Colonies, April 24, 1962, DO (Dominions Office) 169/96, TNA.

25. Incoming Telegram, Baldwin to Secretary of State, October 20, 1961, folder "Malaya and Singapore, 1/61–10/61," box 130, President's Office Files, National Security File—Countries, John F. Kennedy Library (JFKL).

26. CIA, "Consequences to the U.S. of Communist Domination of Mainland Southeast Asia," October 13, 1950, 5.

27. "Tunku" is a Malay word for "prince." In British records, Abdul Rahman was consistently referred to as "the Tunku," a practice that U.S. records adopted from the 1960s.

28. Lee Hsien Loong, "Let's Pledge to Continue Building This Exceptional Nation," *Today Online*, March 30, 2015, https://www.todayonline.com/rememberinglky/mr-lee-kuan-yews-state-funeral-service-pm-lee-hsien-loong-delivers-eulogy; CIA, "Singapore on the Eve of Lee Kuan Yew's Visit to the U.S.," October 6, 1967, 7, CIA FOIA Reading Room, https://www.cia.gov/library/readingroom/docs/CIA-RDP79-00927A006000070008-3.pdf.

29. Audrey R. Kahin and George McT. Kahin, *Subversion as Foreign Policy: The Secret Eisenhower and Dulles Debacle in Indonesia* (New York: New Press, 1995).

30. Ang Cheng Guan, *Southeast Asia's Cold War: An Interpretive History* (Honolulu: University of Hawai'i Press, 2018), 85, 87–88.

31. By agreement with Britain and Malaya, Singapore would move from "internal self-government" to full independence as a part of Malaysia. See Albert Lau, *A

Moment of Anguish: Singapore in Malaysia and the Politics of Disengagement (Singapore: Times Academic Press, 1998).

32. Inward Telegram, Selkirk to Secretary of State for the Colonies, April 24, 1962, DO 169/96.

33. Seth King, "Malaysian Union: A Potential Giant," *New York Times*, April 5, 1963.

34. *A Survey on the Controversial Problems of the Establishment of the Federation of Malaysia* (Washington, DC: Information Division of the Embassy of Indonesia, 1963); Soekarno, *Sukarno: An Autobiography as Told to Cindy Adams* (Indianapolis, IN: Bobbs-Merrill, 1965), 302–303.

35. Taomo Zhou, "Ambivalent Alliance: Chinese Policy toward Indonesia, 1960–1965," *China Quarterly* 221 (2015): 215.

36. Taomo Zhou, "China and the Thirtieth of September Movement," *Indonesia* 98 (2014): 33.

37. Brian Farrell, "End of Empire: From Union to Withdrawal," in *Between Two Oceans: A Military History of Singapore from First Settlement to Final British Withdrawal*, ed. Malcolm H. Murfett, John N. Miksic, Brian P. Farrell, and Chiang Ming Shun (New York: Oxford University Press, 1999), 388–390, 392–393.

38. Ngoei, *Arc of Containment,* 137–141. Here, the author draws from the private papers of British journalist Alex Josey who accompanied Lee on these trips. Josey's notes are in the private papers collections of the ISEAS-Yusof Ishak Institute, Singapore.

39. Letter, Lee to Philip Moore, February 12, 1964, FCO (Foreign and Commonwealth Office) 141/14078, TNA.

40. Ngoei, *Arc of Containment,* 141–144; Raffi Gregorian, "CLARET Operations and Confrontation, 1964–6," *Journal of Conflict Studies* 11, no. 1 (1991): 46–72; David Easter, "British and Malaysian Covert Support for Rebel Movements in Indonesia during the 'Confrontation,' 1963–66," *Intelligence and National Security* 14, no. 4 (1999): 195–208; Daniel Chua, *U.S.-Singapore Relations, 1965–1975: Strategic Non-alignment in the Cold War* (Singapore: National University of Singapore Press, 2017), 73–74.

41. Ngoei, *Arc of Containment,* 142–144.

42. John Roosa, *Pretext for Mass Murder: The September 30th Movement and Suharto's Coup d'Etat in Indonesia* (Madison: University of Wisconsin Press, 2006), chaps. 5 and 6.

43. Zhou, "China and the Thirtieth of September Movement"; Ngoei, *Arc of Containment,* 146–147; Vincent Bevins, "What the United States Did in Indonesia," *The Atlantic*, October 20, 2017.

44. Wen-Qing Ngoei, "A Wide Anti-communist Arc: Britain, ASEAN and Nixon's Triangular Diplomacy," *Diplomatic History* 41, no. 5 (2017): 903–932.

3 Made in Britain

The Fantasy Driving Australia's Involvement
in the Vietnam War

••

GREG LOCKHART

Introduction

On April 29, 1965, Australian prime minister R. G. Menzies justified Australia's commitment to the Vietnam War in a speech to Parliament: "The take-over of South Vietnam would be a direct military threat to Australia and all the countries of South and South East Asia. It must be seen as part of a thrust by Communist China between the Indian and Pacific Oceans."[1] This claim, which suggests Australian involvement in Vietnam to fight China, was a piece of the so-called domino theory. As such, it was soon seen to be an embarrassment, the press largely mocked it, the governments (Australian and U.S.) who used it quickly forgot they had endorsed it, and the literature has since largely dismissed it.[2] Even the *Official History* describes Menzies's claim as "a gravely misleading interpretation of the policy making that led to the decision."[3]

We will see, however, that Menzies, who never changed his position,[4] was in line with official policy when he announced the downward "thrust of Communist China" in Parliament. By 1950, Australian policy had been shaped by early British versions of the domino thinking. These seemed to necessitate the containment of communism in Southeast Asia and had, by then, also influenced U.S. official thinking.[5] As President Dwight Eisenhower enunciated the theory for everyone on April 7, 1954, one month before the French colonial garrison at Dien Bien Phu fell on May 7, "You have a row of dominoes set up, you knock over the first one, and what will happen to the last one is the certainty that it will go over fairly quickly"—after Indochina, Burma, Malaya, and Indonesia, threatening Australia and New Zealand and forcing Japan into the communist bloc.[6]

My argument is that once the Japanese destroyed the Western, particularly British, imperial order in Southeast Asia in 1941–1942, the political-cultural tendency in white Australia was to encourage and support the reestablishment of that order in a new form. This largely meant Australian government opposition to the post-1945 process of decolonization going on in the countries to the north, opposition that was set in a sense of the menacing nearness of Asian geography and that was race-based. The imposition of the Cold War on the process of decolonization further meant that the race-based strategy, which Australia evolved to establish a neoimperial order in Asia, tended to be overlaid and camouflaged by anti-communist rhetoric.

From 1948, when the British declared the Malayan emergency, the "red peril" began to override the old "yellow" one in political commentary. In October 1949, the rise of the communist People's Republic of China (PRC) intensified the "red peril" rhetoric in the conservative Australian political discourse, which accompanied the rise of the conservative Menzies-led Liberal/Country Party Coalition government in December. In 1950, concerns about the Chinese communists "coming down" through Vietnam, Thailand, and Malaya had already consolidated the domino thinking in Australian foreign and strategic policy.

The associated "red peril" rhetoric then enabled Menzies's worldview. It disguised its race-based sense of the threat from Asia at a time when it would have caused hostility in decolonizing Asian nations. Whether politicians like Menzies believed the domino thinking, the theory also gave them a language that reinforced their positions in both domestic and foreign affairs. Domestically, "red peril" rhetoric empowered Menzies's political attacks on the Australian Labor Party (ALP) and its links with the trade unions. In foreign affairs, such rhetoric linked their geopolitical concerns with British and, particularly, American interests in forging neoimperial defense alliances in the Asia-Pacific region.

Between 1945 and 1965, no major official Australian intelligence assessment found evidence to support the domino theory. Quite the reverse, those assessments concluded that communist China posed no threat to Australia. Shaped by the geographical illusion that "China," or at least "Chinese," were "coming down" in a dagger-like *thrust* through the Malay Peninsula, the domino theory was the fearful side of the race fantasy, the nightmare that vanished once it had fulfilled its political function. That was to constitute the dream of a British race strategy, which would protect white Australia in the Asia-Pacific region by engaging it in the Vietnam War.

British Imperial Backstory

On December 7, 1941, the Japanese attacked south and sent shock waves through Australia. By "attacking Great Britain and the United States like an assassin in the night," Labor prime minister John Curtin informed Parliament on December 16, "The Japanese Empire struck at civilization. In that generic, if not quite properly understood, term, we include the Commonwealth of Australia. Therefore, the attacks made against Singapore and Pearl Harbour, against Great Britain and the United States of America, are attacks which the Commonwealth of Australia accepts as constituting a direct attack upon itself."[7] In the Commonwealth, where "civilization" could only be construed "generically" and, indeed, "properly" as British or, necessarily in 1941, as Anglo-American, it really had suffered a direct hit without yet being attacked itself. We can also be in no doubt that an attack on British "civilization" was also generally assumed to be an attack on the British "race." In 1944, widely read Australian government publications referred to "a quiet pride of race" being the first item of the "Australian Charter."[8]

Such a biological identification with British "race" and "civilization" in Australia revealed its imperial frame. In the same debate, conservative opposition leader Arthur Fadden emphasized that "our frontier today is definitely in Malaya. Our destiny is linked with the fate of the Philippines, the Netherlands East Indies, Borneo, and the other stepping-stones on which Japan is seeking to establish bases in a drive towards Australia."[9]

By "Malaya," "Borneo," or "the Philippines," Fadden did not mean our frontier lay among their peoples. He meant it lay on the boundaries of white British and American colonial rule there. The dependent colonial, as distinct from sovereign national status of the Commonwealth, was strongly asserted. Given Britain's "great strategic arc of control from Suez to Sydney harbour,"[10] the Commonwealth's integration into and dependence on the scaffolding of Western imperialism in Asia was assumed by Parliament the instant the Japanese attacked. That integration was moreover fundamental to the so-called white Australia policy, which had its legal foundation in the Immigration Restriction Act (1901) and which had been the basis for the defense of the Commonwealth since its formation in 1901.[11]

For Menzies, England was *the* "imagined place" and Britishness the source of all worth, the essence of Australia and its achievements.[12] In August 1941, his first government fell amid widespread concern that his attempts to balance early wartime assistance to Britain against Germany with local defense against the prospect of a Japanese attack in the Pacific erred on the side of Britain.

Menzies's biographer Judith Brett argues persuasively that the imperviousness of his British identification to political change, even changes as drastic as those of 1941–1942, plus his public expression of that identification, made him unusual.[13] Referring to the series of radio broadcasts he began in early 1942 for middle Australia, she observes that "as an empire man nationalism was unavailable to him and he relied, instead, on the symbol of the home which, while its national location remained unspecified, drew its meanings from the original Home, as England was still called by the Australian middle class. The unreality of Menzies' England was also theirs as well as the longing for 'something a little higher than the everyday' in which all conflict and all striving could be contemplated."[14]

As the mellifluous tones of Menzies's voice reached into middle-class homes in 1942, he assuaged those who lived like him in their "darkest hour," with barbarism broken into the buffer zone of white tranquility all around. He was evoking in the staid living rooms of middle Australia the interior monologue of a people of overwhelmingly British derivation, who felt geographically isolated in a vast continent on the edge of Asia, a people who craved security, identity, and importance within a regrouped illusion of unchanging British order and civilization.

If his tenacious Britishness did not serve him well in 1941, it began to revive his political fortunes soon after. In return for floating his dream of empire at such a critical time, middle Australia soon blew Menzies up like a political balloon. After coming back to prominence as conservative opposition leader in 1944, he rose again to be prime minister in December 1949, for a record seventeen years at the height of the Cold War. The heightened British race and cultural patriotism of that legacy then focused the unreal menace of Asian independence movements, which determined Australia's involvement in the Vietnam War.

The Threat of Decolonization

In August 1945, Australian euphoria with victory over the Japanese went with an Asian awakening, a sharp sense that the country's future was somehow linked to the postcolonial tide of national independence movements sweeping the Asia-Pacific region. But how? No one really knew: the regional transformation also aroused disquiet about the scope of what was going on.

A good idea of the overall ambivalence was conveyed in the volume of eighteen essays edited by Robert J. Gilmore and Denis Warner, *Near North: Australia and a Thousand Million Neighbours* (1948). The foreword was by Dr. H. V. Evatt, then-minister for external affairs in Ben Chifley's Labor government (1945–1949). By eliminating the "offensive" language of the "White Australia Policy" and making "earnest" attempts to assist our neighbors in trade, technical, and cultural areas, his postwar aim was not Australia's integration into the region. It was the reverse: to "maintain" white Australia as a "defensive policy, not political but economic in character and substance."[15] Still anxious, as one writer noticed, about "the coloured millions" to the *near north*,[16] Evatt said the aim was to "strengthen" *in Australia's northeast and northwest* "both our close relationship with the United States, and our still closer ties of kinship with Great Britain."[17]

The aim was, indeed, nothing less than a race-based desire to usurp geography. By forming alliances inside the region with kindred powers from outside it, white Australians sought to neutralize their impression of there being a geographical as well as racial menace to their survival.

The essays, largely by journalists with experience of the region in the Pacific war, read like sunny versions of new Asian holiday destinations. At the same time, they swam in somewhat ominous open-endedness. Alan Dower's vivid portraits of the Indonesian Republican leaders Sukarno and Sjahrir hover over a worry that, following Japan's "race war," a "brown avalanche might one day fall on Australia."[18] Writing on Malaya, Gilmore assumes a bright future for the British but can't escape the "shadow of the *Kris*[19] and the pistol, symbols and implements of the contagious revolutionary anarchy accompanying political 'freedom' in nearby Indonesia, Burma, Indochina and India."[20] And indeed, journalist Nigel Palethorpe captured the revolution in Vietnam. Ho Chi Minh's declaration of the independence of the Democratic Republic of Vietnam (DRV) on September 2, 1945, was his starting point. He sketched the French *coup de force*, which British Empire troops, who had been sent into the country to disarm the Japanese, facilitated in Saigon on September 23. Thus, capturing the outbreak of what would become that republic's thirty years war for national liberation, Palethorpe quoted a local spokesperson, Pham Ngoc Thach, who said, the Vietnamese "people would fight for their freedom."[21]

Still, most Australians were not able to relate unambiguously to that: the emergence of independent Asian nations beyond white political powers and their military control was largely beyond their ken. It was not something Evatt contemplated. Even his department head Dr. John Burton, who supported decolonization with conviction, could be disquieted by the thought that the entire hemisphere from India to China might slip out of Western control.[22] In 1945–1947, informed conservatives had generally adapted to the new associative form of liberal imperialism imagined by the Western powers in Asia itself;[23] the natives might participate in local government, but an unconcealed race-based sense of threat still left them in no doubt about the need to preserve white, neoimperial military control of the region.

Menzies's sense of that threat was not only blatant. Since he was postwar leader of the parliamentary opposition, it also had a significant audience. On March 6, 1946, he alluded to the Chifley government's sympathy for the new Indonesian Republic when he exclaimed,

> Sukarno the man who visited Japan to pay tribute to the Japanese people in this war! Sukarno the man who led the feeling against the British and the Americans in this war! If the Australian waterside workers,[24] with the Australian government doing nothing, are to install him in a position of authority in the Netherlands East Indies, then I say Australia must look to its security! Instead of having, in a political sense, a barrier reef in the north-west, Australia will have a potential base of attack against itself.

Without such a "barrier reef," Menzies believed like many others that national self-determination in Indonesia would "justify the eviction of Australia from New Guinea and the British from India, Burma and the Malay Peninsula" and produce "an ever-growing threat to Australia in the future."[25]

What could have been the threat of the newly emerging nations? Without white presence, he assumed Asian incapacity. On the cultural front, he thought that the only Indonesian "claim to history is that they collaborated with the Japanese during the war"; on the racial front, he said Indonesians were not "fit for self-government."[26] Instability and chaos would spread. There would be greatly diminished, if any, ways of protecting Australia from the impending geographic isolation and racial invasion. Neither Menzies's biographers nor defense historians have spelled this out. But there it was: countries to the north that were not only liberated from the ravages of Japanese rule but, almost unthinkably, from the repressive autocracy of British and European colonial regimes would be potential bases of attack on Australia *because they were inhabited by the people who lived there.*

Menzies would eventually be forced to refine his crude rhetoric. In a secret report before the federal elections, which brought him to power on

December 19, 1949, the conservative political secretary to the Australian Commission in Singapore, Francis Stuart, advised him of the need for a change in the Liberals' language of empire. Stuart's racial sense of the Asian threat was, as David Fettling says, "palpable." Stuart also found Asian control of Asia almost unthinkable. So as not to draw unnecessarily the new Asia's attention to white Australia, however, he reported to Menzies that the old sentiments on empire "would not do."[27] This, from the other side of politics, was also Evatt's ambivalent advice in *Near North*.[28]

By 1950, outpost anxiety about decolonization would resolve itself under Menzies into a smoldering silence, as his side of politics revived its fortunes by trumpeting the threat of communism.

Malayan Cold War Pivot: From "Yellow" Peril to "Red" Peril and the Origins of the Domino Theory

In 1948, the Cold War began as the influence of the Soviet Union increased in Eastern Europe. In February, the communist coup in Prague reminded many of the dangers of Neville Chamberlain's appeasement to Adolf Hitler in 1938. In June, Western land access to Berlin was closed. In February to March, hot on the heels of Indian independence in 1947, both the World Youth Conference and the Second Congress of the Indian Communist Party in Calcutta aroused fear of the expanding influence of the Soviet Union in the region among new imperialists in British Malaya and Australia. Assuming orders from "Moscow," they claimed that the so-called "communist insurrections" of 1948 in India, Burma, Malaya, Indonesia, and the Philippines were orchestrated by "Calcutta." Yet, recent historical research makes it clear that no explicit instructions were issued by the Soviet Union to Southeast Asian communist parties via Calcutta directing them to violent insurrection post-1945 and beyond.[29]

In relation to Malaya, the alleged "communist insurrection" assumed a certain salience in Australian thinking about Asian and world communism. Britain was still the most important power in the region, and Australians desired that remain so. This was especially with Malcolm MacDonald, the governor-general of British Southeast Asia (1946–1948) and commissioner-general for it (1948–1955). Son of former British socialist prime minister Ramsay MacDonald[30] and an old friend of Menzies and other conservative leaders including R. G. Casey, MacDonald saw it as his task to recover Britain's major economic interests in the rubber and tin of Malaya, while formally ending the old empire. He was determined to build a Malay federation with local leaders responsive to London, which was to say a colonial nation within the British Commonwealth.

To facilitate this project, he attempted in mid-1947 to ban the Malayan Communist Party (MCP), which had fought against the Japanese during the war. He insisted that although the Soviet Union's only representation in the region was a small consulate in Bangkok, Soviet allies were at work in Malaya and Singapore among the "gullible" Asiatic masses and that they would constitute a potential "fifth column" in wartime. This did not convince the British Labour government,[31] and it took the outbreak of the Malayan emergency to outlaw the party.

Christopher Bayly and Tim Harper have demonstrated that the outbreak of the emergency was "contingent on the actions of the British themselves."[32] It was in the context of a myriad of ethnic, industrial, and economic rivalries, over which the MCP had little, if any, control[33] that on June 16, 1948, a group of Chinese murdered three British estate managers in Sungei Siput. The murders were police, not national security, matters. But the British High Commissioner in Malaya, Sir Edward Gent, panicked under the pressure of British business interests and MacDonald, who urged him to use British troops to guard the estates. Gent declared the emergency across the entire country, for what was expected to be weeks but lasted twelve years.

MacDonald now leveraged his colonial nation with violence in Malaya. His endless search for hard evidence of an international communist "plot"— his classic authoritarian use of the "agitator from outside" trope—then exerted wide influence,[34] not least in the Australian press.[35] As early as June 8, 1948, eight days *before* the emergency was declared, the Sydney *Daily Telegraph* published a remarkable article based on a Malayan radio broadcast MacDonald had given on June 6. Called "Communist Violence in Asia Is a Threat to Australia," the article provides us with a good example of the early domino thinking in Australia's strategic outlook.

The article began, "Mr Malcolm MacDonald said: 'The Communists have capitalised on the nationalist movements in India and Burma.'" Overlaying the usual "yellow" coloring of the undifferentiated Asiatic hordes with a "red" topcoat, the article sought to manipulate old Australian fears: "If the Communists succeeded in setting fire to Asiatic passion, Australia would have something very serious to worry about. For a thousand million underprivileged and under-provided people could become a mighty militant force under the leadership of communist fanatics, following the directions of the Kremlin's able leaders. . . . Australia would come in for a lot of painful kicking around. The Communists' official policy, remember, is opposed to White Australia."

The unhappy Asiatic masses were not yet differentiated into separate domino-like countries ready to fall down toward Australia. Yet, on the eve of the Malayan emergency, the flames of "red peril" flared over the still-burning "yellow" one, as the *Daily Telegraph* article resoundingly linked "our Wharf Labourers" to "the Kremlin." Those workers were said to have done nothing less than "started the Soviet ball rolling in Asia"; their success in "carrying Red slogans to the Indonesian masses . . . was the first step of a campaign which is coming to a violent conclusion in Malaya today!"[36] This was published in Sydney eight days *before* the British declaration of the emergency.

In this context, some MacDonald-Menzies parallels are worth recalling. One was in 1949, as the Communist Party of Australia (CPA) launched its bid for control of the unions. MacDonald-like, Menzies informed the electorate he would ban the party when he was returned to power, even though no one has ever discovered CPA plans to overthrow violently the Australian state—any more than they have found MCP plans to overthrow the Malayan government before the emergency.

As fear of domestic communist influence cut across Australian racism to elevate anxieties about threats from the north, Menzies's political language also paralleled MacDonald's. This was in relation to the radio speeches wherein MacDonald exhorted Malayans to banish the MCP from society. His speeches repeatedly depicted the MCP, whose members were very largely ethnic Chinese, as being the agents of alien enemies—the Soviet Union and China, even before the latter was "communist." Those agents were assumed to be entering Malaya, stirring up trouble and threatening real Malayan patriots in their "homes."[37] In Australia, there was no bloody war, but Menzies used the same binary opposition to promote his British Empire "home" ascendency in the face of an alien enemy "coming down." Press statements often linked the Australian "waterside workers" and "communists" with the end of the Dutch colonial regime in Indonesia, the British one in Malaya, and Australian rule in Papua New Guinea.

In 1948, the inflation of MacDonald's Australian press image was, moreover, intimating the return of Menzies to power in a *dream* of British civilization in Asia—in opposition to the nightmare of a "Chinese Communist Republic," one might specify. Between 1946 and 1955, there were at least 2,300 Australian press articles on him; in 1948–1950, there were at least 1,300.[38] Among these, Denis Warner published a memorable one in the Melbourne *Herald* on September 10, 1949.[39] It captured MacDonald, the "romanticist" and "practical politician" at Bukit Serene, his palatial residence set in undulating lawns and gardens that swept down to the Straits of Johore where, not one to stand on ceremony, he could pull up a chair on the lawn and invite you to take off your coat, without thinking to remove his own:

> For a moment you are caught in the spell of his idealism. You too look beyond the slopes of Bukit Serene, beyond the murder and terror of Malaya, the smothering surge of communism to distant and brighter fields. And the emergence of a new and free dominion of South-East Asia, independent, but within the framework of the British Commonwealth does not seem so remote a possibility. It is the only hope for Britain in South-East Asia: equally certain it is the only hope for South-East Asia itself. And if it is a dream, it is well dreamt.

A presence rather than a power in a waning empire, Warner remarked that MacDonald had "no big stick."[40] Here, rather, was a British viceroy whose character was calibrated to manage a delicate imperial mission. Here was a British proconsul whose idealism drew Australian imagination into his sphere by assuaging anxiety about what might be going on in the near north. With Casey and Menzies coming to stay and others passing through, Bukit Serene was, for Australians in the old colonial twilight, British government house in the sky.

It was in such a fantasy that the political wheel was set to turn. On October 1, 1949, Mao Zedong inaugurated the PRC, and buoyed especially by that devil in the December 3 federal elections, the victory of the conservative Liberal/Country Party Coalition was borne on it. In domestic politics, Chifley's fiscal policy of nationalizing the banks had made his campaign vulnerable to anti-socialist propaganda. Outlawing the CPA was also a major issue.[41]

As for the external threat, Country Party leader Arthur Fadden came in on cue. With "Moscow centre" controlling the Asiatic as well as the Western dominions of world communism, Fadden imagined Chinese communist forces "thrusting their red spear points towards Australia." "With the advance guard of communist forces . . . extremely active in the pattern of guerrilla war through Burma, Siam, Malaya and Indonesia," he continued, no one could doubt that "a similar fifth column is operating in Australia, as part of a conspiracy of world conquest, sabotage of our Industries and defence activities."[42] And, it somehow seemed, as part of a conspiracy of Asian geography against Australia.

Specific countries had now been identified in the face of the "red spear points" showering down on them and Australia. Yet, this "red peril" had not overshadowed the "yellow" one as a more accurate measure of strategic risk. At any time between 1946 and 1965, it would have been impossible to define a plausible Chinese military threat to Australia. Counterfeit constructions of communist violence linking Asia and Australia simply worked to Menzies's political advantage, as he nurtured his dream of an empire-home in the colonial Commonwealth.

In 1950, the full-fledged form of the domino theory would do the same, as Mao's rise to power finally filled out MacDonald's "agitator from outside" fixation on Chinese communists descending on Malaya.

Indochina Pivot: Australia Adopts the Domino Thinking

In 1950, MacDonald had added a new and, indeed, pivotal element to his perception of the threat, as he drew official Australian and, as we will see, American attention toward French Indochina, particularly Vietnam. This Indochina element allowed him to conjure up not just agents of guerrilla war and terrorism—of "the murder and terror of Malaya"—but whole Chinese armies thrusting south.

In January 1950, the British Commonwealth Conference at Colombo, which convened to discuss the Commonwealth's response to the new communist China, provided him an opportunity to expand his work. As a British delegate to the conference, MacDonald met Menzies's first external affairs minister, Percy Spender. From that point, Australia's Vietnam policy began to take shape around MacDonald's expanded idea of the defense of Malaya. This meant preventing communist China "coming down" through Vietnam and "outflanking" Malaya by embracing MacDonald's questionable support for the "Bao Dai solution."

Note that Vietnam was not China. But without reference to Vietnam's thousand-year history of resistance to its northern neighbor, MacDonald submerged Vietnamese identity in it. He saw Ho Chi Minh's guerrilla resistance to French neocolonial rule in Vietnam as a part or, at least, an extension of communist China. At the Colombo conference, he compounded that crude calculation by dismissing Ho Chi Minh's leadership credentials. He strongly supported French attempts, which had been initiated in early 1949, to place Bao Dai, the former Vietnamese emperor, at the head of a government within the "French Union." At Colombo, MacDonald ignored the skepticism of the other delegates by asserting that Bao Dai, who had abdicated with Ho Chi Minh's rise to power in 1945, was "a sincere nationalist and not a tool of the French"[43]—even as French colonialists themselves were describing Bao Dai's ministers as "puppets."[44]

MacDonald's biographer Clyde Sanger suggests MacDonald's position was "naïve."[45] As a neocolonial strategist with his imagination, however, MacDonald was bound to support Bao Dai and did until the French were defeated in 1954. In 1951, for instance, MacDonald flew in a light plane with newly appointed commander of French colonial forces Marshal de Lattre de Tassigny over his defense lines around the Red River delta. Looking down on the fortifications, he knew de Lattre had been appointed to reverse the steadily worsening military situation, against which Bao Dai's government was helpless. However, as the plane swooped down with its engines roaring, thrilling the troops who could see their new commander waving to them at almost eye level,[46] any thought MacDonald had of a final French colonial defeat receded in such powerful company—and in the gallant dream of Bukit Serene.

Even before, Percy Spender had fallen like a domino for all that. Already, on February 8, 1950, one day after Britain and a wary United States recognized Bao Dai's government, Australia followed suit.[47] This was despite voices in Spender's own Department of External Affairs, that of diplomat Ralf Harry, for one, who stressed Ho Chi Minh's "unusual ability and unrivalled popularity" and his credentials as a "sincere nationalist."[48] Others warned of the dangers of investing Australia's longer-term interests in Bao Dai's government.

Still, on March 9, 1950, Spender domesticated the domino theory in Commonwealth policy. This was in a landmark speech he made in Parliament that not only embodied MacDonald's strategic outlook in Australia's Southeast Asia policy but did so for the next twenty years.

Now, in Spender's words, "Vietnam was the greatest present danger point in the South-East Asian area." He continued, "Should Vietnam come under the heel of Communist China, Malaya is in danger of being outflanked and it, together with Thailand, Burma and Indonesia, will become the next direct object of further Communist activities."[49] Such, at the heart of state policy in 1950, was the perceived threat to the revival of British rule in Southeast Asia. Adding to the naming of the countries that would fall—like dominos—we have the idea that these would fall successively as a result of communist "activities." This was the dark fantasy of the not-yet-named domino theory, which now revolved around Vietnam.

Although still unnamed, the theory had assumed its full-fledged form. Spender's phrases "coming under the heel" and "being outflanked" strongly implied the danger of "activities" for which there was no evidence: sweeping Chinese military maneuvers into the south. In fact, an April conference of British and Australian military intelligence authorities in Singapore assumed such movements were not possible. According to a report by Denis Warner, who was well informed in these matters, the conference believed that "Communist China, lacking ships and aircraft, could not undertake a major operation so far from home."[50]

A recurring theme in the adoption of Australia's version of the domino theory comes into view: determined political indifference to the informed military as well as political intelligence available to the government. Determining that indifference was, then, the white settler society's desire for the revival of the British Empire in the region after its fall in 1941–1942.

Lifting the Threat out of Historical Context

Consider now a historical analogy from World War II, which MacDonald used to reinforce his geopolitical musings on Indochina: the Japanese advance into the Pacific. This analogy had potent political implications in Australia, wherein the dagger of the *downward thrust* of Japan sunk deeply into popular awareness, as the relevant volume in the World War II Official Histories showed. When Lionel Wigmore's volume came out in 1957, it was called *The Japanese Thrust*.

Meanwhile, it will be helpful to appreciate the use MacDonald made of the analogy with some interested American officials in 1950. For the first time since 1945, the rise of the PRC in October 1949 had revived U.S. interests in Southeast Asia, within wider concerns about containing global communism. MacDonald then realized that Britain's power was waning and wanted eventually to hand over British interests in the region to U.S. hegemony for safekeeping in the Anglosphere.

On August 8, 1950, two months before the fact of China's involvement in Korea, MacDonald advised a U.S. fact-finding mission led by John F. Melby that if China's Korean expansion succeeded, "Indo-China is next."[51] Why? Let me cull my answer from the account of that meeting presented in Wen-Qing Ngoei's masterful 2019 book, *Arc of Containment: Britain, the United*

States and Anticommunism in Southeast Asia, while retaining its exact quotes from original documents.

Basically, MacDonald informed Melby Indochina had been the country from where, in 1941, the Japanese had launched their attack on Malaya to acquire its tin and rubber. Pursuing again what he liked to call the "great prize" of Malaya's resources and the communications hub at Singapore, MacDonald explained that the Chinese would again spring south from Indochina. It would be "the place of attack . . . the highway to the rest of Southeast Asia." Melby wanted to know if there were proven links between Peking and the MCP. Commander-in-Chief British Far East Land Forces General Sir John Harding, who was also at the meeting, could say that the MCP received "guidance from Peking." MacDonald buffed up the point: far from being delivered remotely by radio, he said, the "guidance" was given by Chinese communist messengers in person at meetings in "Bangkok, Hong Kong, much through the USSR embassy in Bangkok."[52] The succession of falling dominos was reimagined: Siam, Burma, Malaya, Singapore, Indonesia, and beyond. By August 1950, the U.S. State Department was officially saying the "Japanese had demonstrated the way" the Chinese would "invade" the region.[53]

This anticipation of the threat was obviously anachronistic. Presumably, in the United States, the chronological confusion was lost in a cosmic sense of confrontation with global communism. In Australia, the confusion rather drifted off in the white dream of British Southeast Asia. Whatever way, diverting attention from the absence of evidence for what British, U.S., or Australian officials were strongly predisposed to think, MacDonald's historical Japanese analogy was empowered in Australia, too. Following Spender's remarks in March, we are reminded how the September 1950 strategic appreciation of the Australian Chiefs of Staff spoke from all points of the Anglosphere when it said, "The front line in the cold war in south east Asia lies in Northern Indochina. If that front gives away . . . an invasion route to Malaya lies open to the Communist forces . . . because of its effect on the defence and internal security of Malaya, Indochina occupies an important part of our strategy."[54] This, we should add, was even though the available intelligence, which looked forward to "the next ten years," caused the same strategic appreciation to inform the government that "neither the Soviet nor the Chinese communists are likely to be able to mount a seaborne invasion of Australia." "The problem of Indonesia," it added, "is internal, there being no immediate threat of external aggression."[55]

Domino Fantasy and Fiction

Before 1953, Menzies had such little time for the domino theory that he did not seem to think it represented strategic reality. When, in May 1950, MacDonald arrived in Canberra to discuss Australian military assistance for Malaya, Menzies was preoccupied with bolstering the imperial center. At that point, he was planning for an Australian imperial force to return to the Middle East to support Britain in the event of World War III. All he could do to assist MacDonald in Malaya was to send five or six jungle warfare advisers, create the Australian Secret Intelligence Service to assist in the application of the dark arts, and make available six Lincoln bombers and eight Dakota transport aircraft.[56]

In June and July 1950, Menzies's response to the American request for assistance in Korea was again conditioned by his primary loyalty to the British imperial center. When the British made a Royal Navy ship available to the Americans, Menzies made two Australian frigates available. Spender further offered No. 77 Mustang Squadron, Royal Australian Air Force. Initially, however, Menzies made no offer of ground troops because Britain had not made one. An infantry battalion would eventually be forthcoming in late July once Britain decided to commit. The great flying of No. 77 Squadron in the desperate defense of Pusan then became a significant talking point around which the Australia, New Zealand, and United States (ANZUS) Pact was signed in 1951 to secure what Australians saw as the "bolt on the back door" to Asia.[57]

Still, French colonial setbacks in Indochina began to stretch Menzies's primary allegiance to Britain. In October 1953, by which time the Viet Minh were placing great pressure on French forces, Menzies hesitated when the British proposed a Far Eastern Strategic Reserve in Malaya to underwrite the Australia, New Zealand, and Malaya (ANZAM) area alliance.[58] The security situation in French Indochina caused him to seek U.S. support before he committed.[59] The threat of Chinese communism seemed so great to Menzies that only American power could guarantee ANZAM.

The fall of Dien Bien Phu—in Vietnam, not China—greatly exacerbated the distortions in that view. On May 7, 1954, five regular divisions of the Vietnamese People's Army, which Menzies would not have clearly differentiated from the Chinese one, had defeated an elite French force in an epic battle. The French compared the event with the fall of Constantinople in 1453. Not only the French colonial position in Indochina and the British one in Malaya but, since the British had left India in 1947, the entire Western position, which was to say the white man's position east of Suez, seemed to be at stake.[60]

On April 7, Eisenhower had said the potential effects of Dien Bien Phu were "just incalculable" and, as stated at the outset, enunciated the "domino theory." In September, the United States also set up at Manila the Southeast Asia Treaty Organization (SEATO) to prevent communism from advancing into the region along the theory's lines. Besides the United States, it was significant that an old imperial rear guard of white states, Britain and France along with Australia and New Zealand, still held the organization together with no more than three Asian signatories: Pakistan, the Philippines, and Thailand. South Vietnam, Laos, and Cambodia were offered protection. India, Indonesia, and Malaya declined to take part.[61]

On February 2, 1955, still in the aftermath of Dien Bien Phu, Menzies attended the Commonwealth Prime Ministers Meeting in London. There, the now Chief of the Imperial General Staff General Sir John Harding, with whom Menzies had chatted at Bukit Serene, reminded him in the defense discussions that Britain was interested in a contribution of Australian forces for its Far Eastern Strategic Reserve in Malaya. After noting the impressive fighting capacities of the Chinese in the Korean War, Harding said,

> In an attack on south-east Asia the Chinese forces would be limited for logistic reasons to five armies totalling about 250,000 men and a small force of about 200 aircraft mostly of the ground attack type. The main axis of their advance, in which they would have the support of the whole Viet Minh Army, would be through Hanoi to the Siamese border at Thaket and thence to Bangkok. A secondary line of advance would be through central Vietnam to Saigon. By these routes the enemy might reach Saigon about three months after passing the Chinese border. . . . The enemy might direct some forces against Burma. . . . But the real prize at stake would be the rubber and tin of Malaya and [the] focus of sea and air communications at Singapore. . . . From the strategic point of view Malaysia and Singapore were of critical importance for the defence of South-East Asia.[62]

Menzies replied, it was "certainly vital that the Treaty Powers build up a strategic reserve on the spot and have plans ready to dispatch supplementary forces if the need arose."[63]

He had agreed vacuously with a fantasy and a fiction. Harding had presented in the conditional tense, with no citation of Chinese plans or force analysis, a remarkably overdetermined forecast of Chinese aggression in *all* of Southeast Asia. His scenario had again contradicted concrete appraisals of strategic reality. A November 1954 ANZAM military intelligence assessment of the period to 1956 had concluded that "it was most unlikely that communist China would initiate aggression in the period under review."[64]

Still, the historical analogy of the Japanese attack south from Indochina in 1941–1942, which Harding's fiction centered, had caused Menzies to live through his "darkest hour." That was something the fiction could only have reminded him he would not want to relive. The MacDonald-Harding-Menzies-Chinese-downward-thrust line, which translated into Eisenhower's "falling dominos" now shaped Australian strategic planning all the way to Vietnam.

Race Strategy

By 1955, the defense of Australia was invested in its "collective security arrangements," which were all or for the most part *white*: ANZUS, ANZAM, and SEATO. Erected in the decade after 1945 but ostensibly to contain the Japan-like *downward thrust* of communist China post-1949, this race-based framework represented the new imperial imposition on Asia and the Pacific, which the British construction of Malaysia in 1963 was developed to reinforce.[65]

In April 1955, when ANZAM plans were to defend Malaya from China in Thailand, Menzies announced the centrality of Malaya in Australian defense thinking. "Malaya," he declared, "was vital to our defence, more vital, properly understood, than some point on the Australian coast."[66] What he meant was what Fadden did when the Japanese attacked in 1941: not the defense of Malaya but the British position in Malaya, which can be shown to have resulted in strategic planning to defend Malaya in Thailand.[67]

If one thought "China" and "Chinese"—communists—were "coming down," one obviously built barrier defenses forward. Much as the defense of Malaya was to be in Thailand and, with the United States bankrolling the Ngo Dinh Diem regime in Saigon since 1954, in Indochina, the Australian government had, by 1955, already adopted the strategic posture, which the Chiefs of Staff described in 1964 as "forward defense." As the chiefs saw it, Australian forces were "contributing to the security of the more immediately threatened areas in South East Asia, *and in turn attracting the support of powerful allies, particularly the United States.*"[68] Long since a cutting edge and yet on the margin of Australian strategic thinking, Vietnam was *a place* that would become increasingly central to perceived U.S. and, for that reason, Australian interests, as they intersected in the domino theory.

The immediate determinants of Australia's Vietnam involvement are clear. One was the 1962 opening in Saigon of the U.S. Military Assistance Command Vietnam (MACV), whose badge featured a stylized Great Wall of China pierced by a sword. As in Malaya, the Australian government attached to MACV a small number of Australian advisers—thirty-two in this case—experienced in jungle warfare. Other determinants were the strong fear in early 1965 of a communist takeover in Sukarno's Indonesia, coupled with indications that the United States was about to send ground troops to escalate and play the central role in the war they had been supporting in Vietnam since at least 1951. To encourage and support this escalation, the Menzies government deployed an Australian infantry battalion and, in 1966, a larger task force. That is how Australia would pay minimally for its "barrier reef" of U.S. forces against the incommensurable, geographically determined, and race-based threat of decolonization in the near north.

For the first time, Australia (and New Zealand) would be in a war that did not involve Britain. Still, the conservative Australian desire for imperial revival in the region, which determined the Australian version of the domino theory, was one of the fading British Empire.

For Menzies, the strength of the theory was paradoxically the great body blow Japan had historically dealt to the British Empire in Asia. For a man of his uncompromising Britishness, the perceived threat of communism coming down through Vietnam and Indonesia at the time of the Cold War could only leave him to build on a strategic illusion. Hence the cut-back version of Harding's 1955 fiction, which he delivered in his 1965 parliamentary statement about why Australian forces would be sent to Vietnam—to encourage and support the escalation of U.S. power in the region.

In 1965, Menzies's version of the threat contradicted the Defence Committee's last military intelligence assessment of the strategic basis for Australian defense policy. The assessment of October 1964, which only slightly revised the one of September 1950, was that Indonesia was the only country that might pose "a direct military threat to Australia," although its capacity to do so was still negligible.[69] China was not expected to act aggressively. It is clear once again that Menzies was always going to claim that the communists in southern Vietnam were the strategic spearhead of "a thrust by Communist China between the Indian and Pacific Oceans."

Postscript

On May 4, 1965, five days after Menzies made that claim, the leader of the Labor opposition, Arthur Caldwell, countered it in a famous parliamentary speech. Among other prescient points, he emphasized that in Menzies's domino reckoning, "the very map of Asia itself becomes a kind of conspiracy of geography against Australia."[70] Confirming this point, Menzies's claim was discarded once we got into Vietnam and found we were not at war with China. By substituting "North Vietnam" for "China," however, the now muted domino understanding reorganized itself in official thinking around the remarkable idea of "the north invading the south."

That is not the only major point the *Official History* elides. There is also its uncritical recording of the "buying-time" refrain; the mantra that the Vietnam involvement created a shield behind which the countries of Southeast Asia had a decade to consolidate their nation-states before their exposure to communism.[71] As with that work's denial of the importance of the domino theory for Australia's entry into the Vietnam War, the reverse was true. The U.S. strategic ambition of containing communism in Asia had been very largely achieved *before* the escalation of U.S. forces in Vietnam in 1965—and was confirmed by the formation of Association of Southeast Asian Nations (ASEAN) in 1967.

By 1965, the Vietnam War was to use Ngoei's word, strategically "anomalous."[72] Thailand was a U.S. client state, Malaysia a colonial nation, Singapore a prospering U.S.-aligned republic, the Philippines a right-wing U.S.-backed dictatorship. Indonesia was where the United States supported the right-wing coup of October 1965 and where, also with some British and Australian oversight, the massacre of half a million "communists" followed. All those Southeast Asian countries had anti-communist nation-states by the time the United States, urged and backed cleverly with small forces by the Australian government, seriously escalated the Vietnam War and the massacring of millions in Vietnam, Laos, and Cambodia seriously began. If there had ever been a need to contain communism, there was no "thrust by communist China between the Indian and Pacific Oceans," and the killing that went on in the aftermath of that illusion had no strategic justification.

Notes

1. *Commonwealth Parliamentary Debates (CPD)*, vol. House of Representatives 45, April 29, 1965, 1060–61.

2. One serious press rebuttal was "Domino Theory Attacked by Former Diplomat," *Canberra Times*, January 30, 1967, 6. The diplomat was Gregory Clark, whose book *In Fear of China* (Sydney: Lansdowne, 1967) almost alone realized the unwarranted centrality of China in Australian official thinking. Max Hastings, *Vietnam: An Epic Tragedy, 1945–1975* (New York: HarperCollins, 2018), 461, still recycles Menzies.

3. *The Official History of Australia in Southeast Asian Conflicts, 1948–1975*, 6 vols. (Sydney: Allen & Unwin in Association with the Australian War Memorial, 1992–2012); Peter Edwards with Gregory Pemberton, *Crises and Commitments: The Politics and Diplomacy of Australia's Involvement in Southeast Asian Conflicts 1948–1965* (Sydney: Allen & Unwin in Association with the Australian War Memorial, 1992), 372–373. Peter Edwards, *A Nation at War: Australian Politics, Society and Diplomacy during the Vietnam War 1965–1975*, (Sydney: Allen & Unwin in Association with the Australian War Memorial, 1997), 28, argues that departing from the draft statement his advisers had prepared for him, Menzies wrongly indicated that Australia was intervening in Vietnam to counter a direct Chinese military threat, when the advisers had in mind Chinese political influence. Yet, this argument misses much, including the influence of the domino thinking on Australian strategic policy from at least 1950.

4. In his memoirs, Robert Menzies, *The Measure of the Years* (London: Cassell, 1970), 217, the former prime minister still wrote that "I subscribe to the Domino Theory."

5. Wen-Qing Ngoei, *Arc of Containment: Britain, the United States and Anticommunism in Southeast Asia* (Ithaca, NY: Cornell University Press, 2019).

6. Eisenhower's Press Conference, April 7, 1954, *Foreign Relations of the United States*, 1952–54, vol. 13, pt. 1, 1280–1281.

7. *CPD*, House of Representatives, *Debates*, December 16, 1941.

8. *Stand Easy: After the Defeat of Japan 1945* (Canberra: Australian War Memorial, 1945), 10.

9. *CPD*, House of Representatives, *Debates*, December 16, 1941.

10. Christopher Bayly and Tim Harper, *Forgotten Wars: The End of Britain's Asian Empire* (London: Penguin, 2008), 159.

11. Peter Spartalis, *The Diplomatic Battles of Billy Hughes* (Sydney: Hale & Iremonger, 1983), 62.

12. Judith Brett, *Robert Menzies' Forgotten People* (Sydney: Pan Macmillan, 1992), 129–150, 145.

13. Brett, *Robert Menzies' Forgotten People*, 144.

14. Brett, *Robert Menzies' Forgotten People*, 143.

15. H. V. Evatt, foreword to *Near North: Australia and a Thousand Million Neighbours*, ed. Robert J. Gilmore and Denis Warner (Sydney: Angus & Robertson, 1948), vi.

16. R. B. Leonard, "Foreign Policy," in Gilmore and Warner, *Near North*, 69.

17. Evatt, "Foreword," v–viii.

18. Gilmore and Warner, *Near North*, 139–140, 143.
19. An asymmetrical Malay dagger with distinctive blade patterning.
20. Gilmore and Warner, *Near North*, 152.
21. Gilmore and Warner, *Near North*, 208–220, 218.
22. David Fettling, *Encounters with Asian Decolonisation* (Melbourne: Australian Scholarly Publishing, 2017), 188, 211, 223.
23. Bayly and Harper, *Forgotten Wars*, 121–129, 276–277, 281, 341.
24. Sukarno did visit Japan during the war. The Australian Waterside Worker's Union, which was influenced by the CPA, had placed a ban on working with ships carrying arms to support the Dutch against the Indonesian Republic. Rupert Lockwood, *Dark Armada: Australia and the Struggle for Indonesian Independence, 1942-1949* (Sydney: Australian Book Society, 1975).
25. *CPD*, House of Representatives, vol. 186, 6/3/46, 7–9.
26. Quoted in Fettling, *Encounters*, 43.
27. Fettling, *Encounters*, 81.
28. Evatt, "Foreword," vi.
29. Karl Hack and Geoff Wade, "The Origins of the Asian Cold War: Malaya, 1948," *Journal of Southeast Asian Studies* 40, no. 3 (October 2009): 443. This essay provides a good overview of the relevant historiography, while arguing for more indirect Soviet influence in the region than most scholars do.
30. He had written *Labour and the Empire* (1907), which deplored imperialism and militarism, after visiting Australia. See "Labor Rally," *Ballarat Star*, November 27, 1906.
31. Bayly and Harper, *Forgotten Wars*, 341.
32. Bayly and Harper, *Forgotten Wars*, 427.
33. Anthony Short, *The Communist Insurrection in Malaya, 1948-1960* (New York: Crane, Russak, 1975), 43–49, 26, argued that the "government was never properly re-established [in Malaya] after the war."
34. Bayly and Harper, *Forgotten Wars*, 346.
35. Trove, National Library of Australia. Between 1945 and 1955, there were over 100,000 Australian press articles on "Malaya." Over 32,600 were published in 1948–1950.
36. *Daily Telegraph*, June 8, 1948.
37. Ngoei, *Arc of Containment*, 55.
38. Trove, Newspapers, National Library of Australia. Most of the articles, however, were short.
39. *Herald*, September 10, 1949, 13.
40. *Herald*, September 10, 1949, 13.
41. Later, in April 1950, Menzies introduced the Communist Party Dissolution Bill into Parliament. In October, the bill passed. On appeal, the High Court ruled in March 1951 the act was unconstitutional.
42. *Sydney Morning Herald*, December 6, 1949.
43. Clyde Sanger, *Malcolm MacDonald: Bringing an End to Empire* (Montreal: McGill-Queens University Press, 1995), 347.
44. Général Yvres Gras, *Histoire de la guerre d'Indochine* (Paris: Plon, 1979), 251.

45. Sanger, *Malcolm MacDonald*, 347–348.

46. Sanger, *Malcolm MacDonald*, 348–350.

47. Meanwhile, Britain had recognized Mao's PRC on January 6, 1950 out of self-interest related to Hong Kong. Australia did not recognize the PRC until 1972 and the United States until 1979.

48. Edwards, *Crises and Commitments*, 85, quoting Memorandum, Harry to Shaw, June 19, 1950, DEA File 464/1/1 Part 1, CRS A1838, AA.

49. *CPD*, House of Representatives, March 9, 1950, 622–641.

50. Denis Warner, "Our War Plan Ignores East Asia," *The Herald* (Melbourne), April 11, 1950.

51. Ngoei, *Arc of Containment*, 39, 26–44, describes three missions between December 1949 and August 1950.

52. Ngoei, *Arc of Containment*, 41–42.

53. Quoted in Ngoei, *Arc of Containment*, 25.

54. "Appreciation of the Australian Chiefs of Staff (September 1950)," 6–9, in Minute by Chiefs of Staff Committee, December 14, 1950, Agendum No. 17/50 "Australian Strategy in Relation to Communist Expansion in the Pacific, South-East Asia and the Far East during the Cold War Period," Series A816/52, Item 14/301/447, 14, AA.

55. "Appreciation of the Australian Chiefs of Staff (September 1950)," 6–7, 9.

56. Greg Lockhart, "Into Battle," in *Vietnam Remembered*, ed. Gregory Pemberton (Sydney: Lansdowne, 1990), 40–43.

57. Quoted in Peter Cochrane, *Australians at War* (Sydney: ABC Books, 2001), 192. Andrew Kelly, *Anzus and the Early Cold War: Strategy and Diplomacy between Australia, New Zealand and the United States, 1945-1956* (Cambridge: Open Book Publishers, 2018), 2, says, "Australia, undeniably the most enthusiastic [Anzus signatory]" wanted to rebalance its defense ties from Britain to the United States, as "the treaty limited the likelihood of future existential threats such as those posed by Japan in late 1941."

58. Kelly, *Anzus and the Early Cold War*, chap. 2. W. David McIntyre, *Background to the Anzus Pact: Policy-Making, Strategy and Diplomacy, 1945-55* (London: Palgrave Macmillan, 1994), 210–222, 373–384.

59. Matt Radcliff, *Kampong Australia* (Sydney: NewSouth Books, 2017), 18–20.

60. Greg Lockhart, *Nation in Arms: The Origins of the People's Army of Vietnam* (Sydney: Asian Studies Association of Australia in Association with Allen & Unwin, 1989), xi–xii.

61. McIntyre, *Background to the Anzus Pact*, 385–393; Peter Busch, *All the Way with JFK? Britain, the US and the Vietnam War* (Oxford: Oxford University Press, 2009), chap. 1, especially 15–16.

62. *Commonwealth Prime Minister's Conference London 1955 Minutes of Meetings* (file with one attachment tied on), Defence Conference Papers, A1209/23, 1957/5981, AA, 1–4.

63. *Commonwealth Prime Minister's Conference London 1955 Minutes of Meetings.*

64. "ANZAM Intelligence Report on Probable Scale of Attack against Malaya up to the End of 1956," ANZAM Intelligence Meeting, Melbourne, November 1954, para 9, A1209/23, 1957/5980, AA.

65. Busch, *All the Way with JFK?* chap. 1.

66. *Current Notes on International Affairs* 26 (April 1955): 278–279.

67. Greg Lockhart, *The Minefield: An Australian Tragedy in Vietnam* (Sydney: Allen & Unwin, 2007), 14.

68. Gregory Pemberton, *All the Way: Australia's Road to Vietnam* (Sydney: Allen & Unwin, 1987), 205, quoting Chiefs of Staff Committee Minute No. 56/1964, April 6, 1964. Italics added.

69. Cabinet Submission 493, "Strategic Bases of Australia's Defence Policy," Paltridge, October 22, 1964, CS file C3640, CRS A4949/1, AA.

70. *CPD*, vol. House of Representatives 45, May 4, 1965, 1101.

71. Edwards, *Nation at War*, 107, 342. Ngoei, *Arc of Containment*, 167.

72. Ngoei, *Arc of Containment*, 9–10, 166–182, especially 182.

4 The War of Southeast Asia
Falling Dominoes, the 1967 Clifford-Taylor Mission,
and the Fight for the Stability of the Pacific World

A. GABRIELLE WESTCOTT

In July 1967, President Lyndon B. Johnson sent Clark Clifford and General Maxwell Taylor to meet with troop-contributing allies in South Korea, Thailand, New Zealand, and Australia.[1] After stopping in Saigon to review the situation in South Vietnam, Clifford and Taylor briefed allied leaders on the war and carefully broached the subject of increased allied troop commitments. In the summer of 1967, the Johnson administration faced a dilemma. Despite reports from U.S. officials in Saigon that the war in Vietnam was going well, a growing domestic anti-war movement threatened congressional support for additional U.S. troops and a tax increase. To convince the American public of the importance of the commitment to Vietnam, the Johnson administration deployed the well-worn domino theory. If the Johnson administration could show that regional allies believed the war was vital enough to send more of their men to fight, it could argue more persuasively that the war was essential for the stability of the region and the security of the United States.[2] The Clifford-Taylor mission exemplifies the ways that the Johnson administration strategically framed the Vietnam War as a regional conflict to defend the legitimacy of American involvement and rally domestic support.

The Clifford-Taylor mission also illustrates the emotional dimensions of Clifford's turn against the war as secretary of defense in 1968. Over the last decade, the study of emotions has gained increasing attention in U.S. foreign relations history. Scholars have demonstrated how the inner feelings of policymakers and nonstate actors have influenced how these players imagined the ostensibly more tangible military, political, economic, and cultural elements of international relations.[3] The emotionality of policymakers with reputations for being realists or pragmatists has often been overlooked when assessing their policy positions.[4] Clifford, who worked as a Washington, D.C. lawyer while serving as a personal adviser to President

Johnson, gained a reputation for his pragmatism. Journalist Patrick Anderson described him as "cold and shrewd" and as someone who was not "swayed by moralistic arguments."[5] His biographers described him as "above all else, . . . a pragmatic man."[6] Clifford did much to cultivate this image of himself. Before each meeting with the president, he meticulously prepared his arguments to deliver them with calm precision. He sought to present himself as an objective and rational observer. In one instance, while rehearsing an argument with his staff, he told them, "It has to be a *logical* presentation," in which he would emphasize that he had "*no previous posture, no previous position, no public record to defend.*" His conclusions would be based solely on the "facts."[7] The narrative that Clifford promoted to explain his shift in 1968 from being a staunch supporter of Johnson's policy to becoming an unrelenting advocate for de-escalation similarly suggested that he had engaged in a gradual and reasoned reassessment of evidence.[8] In retrospect, Clifford would identify the Clifford-Taylor mission as planting the seeds of doubt that led to this shift. For Clifford, the mission would come to represent two things: the illegitimacy of the domino theory, which held that if South Vietnam fell to communism, the rest of the region would quickly follow; and the futility of continued U.S. involvement in Vietnam. That the war was no longer a war for Southeast Asia became Clifford's primary rationale for disengagement.

In 1969, Clifford published an article in *Foreign Affairs* explaining the evolution of his thinking on Vietnam and calling for disengagement. He argued that the transformation in his thinking had been brought about by the conviction that U.S. military action in Vietnam was no longer necessary to secure the stability of Southeast Asia.[9] However, an examination of the evolution of Clifford's views on the relationship between the United States and its allies in Southeast Asia and the Pacific reveals a pattern of emotional thinking that challenges this narrative. Clifford's assessment that the war was not, in fact, a war for the stability of Southeast Asia came *after* he determined that a military victory was impossible. As the new secretary of defense grew increasingly certain of the impossibility of military victory, he also began to question the necessity of maintaining the U.S. commitment to Vietnam. This reassessment served a psychological purpose: it provided a justification for the withdrawal of American forces. If the war *could not* be won, perhaps it did not actually *need* to be won. Perhaps the stakes were not as high as he had believed previously. The emotional nature of his thinking is revealed in the emotionally charged language he used to describe the South Vietnamese and regional allies. As Clifford fought against a hardening of U.S. policy in the summer and fall of 1968, his perceptions of troop-contributing allies in Southeast Asia and the Pacific began to mirror his growing frustrations with South Vietnamese leaders. By the end of 1968, Clifford believed that the nations the United States was ostensibly fighting to save were hindering U.S. efforts to bring a rapid end to the war. That Clifford had been working relentlessly to push the president toward de-escalation (his secretary would later tell him, "That was a year that lasted five years. I thought it was going to kill you") made the allies' attempts to prolong U.S. involvement all the more personal.[10]

When Secretary of Defense Robert McNamara returned from a trip to South Vietnam in mid-July 1967, he came bearing good news. The embassy was under excellent leadership, military operations were proceeding well, and the pacification program was making progress that "exceeded [McNamara's] expectations." McNamara went so far as to say that "for the first time," he "felt that if we follow the same program we will win the war and end the fighting." To continue to make rapid progress, General William Westmoreland was requesting 100,000 additional troops. The greatest barrier to victory appeared to be American public opinion. Clifford, who was attending the meeting as an informal adviser to the president, pointed out that Americans sometimes referred to Vietnam as "the war that can't be won." The war weariness of the public would make it difficult to send the additional 100,000 troops necessary to maintain pressure on North Vietnam and ensure victory. McNamara believed that number could be shaved down by tightening up U.S. forces, pushing the South Vietnamese to extend tours of service, and asking allies in the region to contribute additional combat troops. In particular, he noted, "The Australians, Thais, Koreans, New Zealanders and Filipinos should be asked to carry more of their share of the burden."[11] On the basis of this meeting, Johnson proposed sending Clifford and Taylor on a presidential mission to meet with the leaders of troop-contributing allies in Southeast Asia and the Pacific. Senior foreign policy advisers also hoped that increased participation on the part of regional allies would help convince the American people to support expanded U.S. involvement. As Clifford would explain to Korean leaders, "The American people will want to know what our allies are sending since many of the people feel that the nations of Southeast Asia and the Far Pacific Area are closer to the danger than we are."[12] The American people needed to be convinced that the war in Vietnam was, in fact, a war for all of Southeast Asia. The commitment of regional allies would serve as a litmus test for the legitimacy of U.S. involvement.

From the outset, administration officials were aware that troop increases would create domestic political problems for allied leaders. Johnson wanted the mission to "be kept extremely quiet" and warned Clifford and Taylor to "get into the troop question slowly." Although there was hope that the Australians and the South Vietnamese would be willing to provide additional troops, Johnson's advisers were less optimistic about the mission's prospects in other troop-contributing countries. National Security Adviser Walt W. Rostow indicated that "the toughest area would be the Philippines," while Clifford cautioned against expecting the mission to return with any firm commitments.[13] These concerns were well founded, as President Ferdinand Marcos of the Philippines declined a visit from Clifford and Taylor after the press depicted the mission as "an arm-twisting delegation off to squeeze more troops from laggard allies reluctant to do their fair share."[14] Senior members of the administration, including Clifford, were clearly conscious of the challenges they faced in trying to secure additional forces from allied leaders in Southeast Asia and the Pacific.

Clifford and Taylor's official report on the mission contained both cautiously optimistic appraisals that the allies would contribute more troops and thinly veiled frustration at their reticence to do so. Summarizing the discussions surrounding troops with the allied leaders, they noted, "The response was always friendly but usually cautious and defensive. Our hosts liked to talk more about what they had done in the past, rather than what they would be willing to do in the future. . . . Nevertheless, their final position was never negative and, indeed, their statements lead us to believe that something will be forthcoming from all countries visited." In the case of Thailand and Korea, allied leaders cautiously indicated that they might be able to contribute additional forces, though with the implicit expectation that they would receive aid in return. Clifford and Taylor were less impressed by their meetings with allied leaders in Australia and New Zealand. When the Australians expressed a desire for the United States to maintain its commitment to the region but proved unwilling to make any contribution that would upset "the 'normal' course of Australian life," Clifford and Taylor concluded, "Either the Australians do not believe that their vital interests are at stake to a point requiring immediate sacrifice, or they believe that we are so deeply involved that we must carry through to a conclusion satisfactory to them as well as to us." They described Prime Minister Harold Holt's reading of a list of contributions as "designed to demonstrate that little Australia was 'doing its part' in the world." The reference to "little Australia" and the quotation marks around "doing its part" belittled both the contributions of the nation and the argument of its leader. They were similarly unimpressed with New Zealand's reluctance to provide more troops, noting that "while New Zealand sent 120,000 men overseas in World War II, they strain under the thought of even doubling up on the present 381-man deployment in South Viet-Nam."[15]

Two years later, Clifford would argue that it was his meetings with allied leaders in Australia and New Zealand that first planted doubts in his mind about the validity of the domino theory and the importance of Vietnam to regional stability. In a 1969 interview, he would recall, "I wondered as I flew back from New Zealand whether or not the attitude of the countries represented their evaluation of the comparative danger to which they were subjected in the second World War as compared to the danger that confronted them in the South Vietnamese War. . . . I could not find any sense of urgency, no feeling of emergency that they ought to get men over there and stop this conflict before it reached their shore."[16] In an article published in *Foreign Affairs* in 1969, Clifford recounted the impact of the trip on his thinking:

> I returned home puzzled, troubled, concerned. Was it possible that our assessment of the danger to the stability of Southeast Asia and the Western Pacific was exaggerated? Was it possible that those nations which were neighbors of Viet Nam had a clearer perception of the tides of world events in 1967 than we? Was it possible that we were continuing to be guided by judgments that might once have had validity but were now obsolete? In short, although I still counted myself a staunch supporter of our policies, there were nagging, not-to-be-suppressed doubts in my mind.[17]

Yet, any doubts that Clifford harbored regarding the allied leaders' assessments of the importance of South Vietnam were not expressed in his meeting with the president on August 5 to discuss the official report of the trip. To the contrary, he reported "an enormous feeling of friendship and goodwill" among the allied leaders.[18] At a press conference later that day, Clifford noted, "In each instance, also, there was a clear recognition on [the allies'] part that their welfare and their future, and the freedom of their nation, is involved in this conflict. I think that, curiously enough, as a matter of interest, we found again and again the statement made that this war was incorrectly described as the South Vietnamese War. It should be called the War of Southeast Asia. That is what our allies think is at stake in the conflict that is taking place."[19] If Clifford harbored private doubts, his public statements nonetheless reaffirmed the importance of the war to maintaining the stability of the entire region. Clifford's 1969 recollection of the trip would be called into question by Maxwell Taylor in a memorandum to Henry Kissinger. The memorandum, prompted by Clifford's *Foreign Affairs* article, argued that Clifford misrepresented the mood of allied leaders. Taylor noted, "While none of these governments were wildly enthusiastic over the thought of increasing their troop contributions, I certainly got no impression of indifference to the outcome of the war in Viet-Nam—quite the contrary." Furthermore, he quoted a televised interview that took place one week after the trip in which Clifford said, "General Taylor and I came back with a feeling of enthusiasm, with a feeling of renewed dedication, with a feeling of encouragement, and then we ran into this miasma of gloom here in Washington. You don't get it out there." For his part, Taylor interpreted allied leaders' reluctance to contribute more troops as stemming from the belief that the military requirements in South Vietnam were so great that any allied troop contributions would have an insignificant effect on the military outcome, and thus were not worth the domestic political problems that a troop increase would create.[20]

The Clifford-Taylor mission does not appear to have raised serious questions about the legitimacy of U.S. involvement in Vietnam among other senior foreign policy advisers. In the months following the trip, the Johnson administration continued to publicly frame Vietnam as a war for Southeast Asia and the Pacific in order to justify continued U.S. involvement to the American people. In September, in a speech to the National Legislative Conference in San Antonio, Texas, Johnson quoted President Dwight D. Eisenhower's 1959 warning that "the loss of South Viet-Nam would set in motion a crumbling process that could, as it progressed, have grave consequences for us and for freedom." He also pointed to the consensus among leaders in Southeast Asia and the Pacific that a communist victory would threaten the entire region.[21] The administration publicized allied support for the U.S. commitment in other forums as well. A publication by the Department of State, *Viet-Nam Information Notes*, devoted an entire issue to "Opinions of Asian and Pacific Leaders" in February 1968, when the administration was considering yet another troop increase in the face of growing public opposition. It quoted Asian and Pacific leaders on the threat that communist efforts in Vietnam posed to the entire region.[22]

However, such warnings were largely tailored for public consumption. Within the administration, national intelligence estimates cast a much less dire picture. A 1964 Special National Intelligence Estimate (SNIE) titled "Short-Term Prospects in Southeast Asia" indicated that the concern of the administration was not so much that a loss in Vietnam would lead the nations of Southeast Asia to fall to communism like dominoes but rather that it would "have a serious effect on the future willingness of governments in Southeast Asia to adopt anti-Communist, rather than neutralist, stances."[23] Neutralism, rather than communist takeover, posed the greatest threat to U.S. interests in the region. Policymakers believed that U.S. credibility was on the line in Vietnam.[24] A demonstration of the firmness of the United States' commitment was necessary to ensure that the countries directly threatened by communist aggression retained their anti-communist orientation. That same 1964 SNIE noted, "The struggle for South Vietnam will be a test, crucial for much of Southeast Asia, of US ability and will to preserve and protect anti-Communist regimes in the area—and, hence, of the feasibility of going along with the US response to Communist pressures rather than opting for some other course such as an attempt to negotiate livable settlements with the Communists."[25] According to this logic, the determination of allies to resist communism depended on a demonstration of U.S. commitment. This helped policymakers rationalize intervention on behalf of a people that seemed to lack the will to fight for themselves, both in the case of the South Vietnamese and regional allies. For most of Johnson's senior foreign policy advisers, reluctance on the part of regional allies to increase their commitment to the war was expected and thus did not call into question the legitimacy of the communist threat to the region.[26]

Clifford's personal assessment of the trip upon his return likely fell somewhere in between the unbridled optimism expressed in his public statements in 1967 and the certainty reflected in his 1969 accounts that troop-contributing countries in Southeast Asia and the Pacific did not share the United States' concern about the Vietnam War. He would explain in his 1969 interview that regarding his doubts, "I did not make much of a point on that. The record will show and I came back and submitted a report to the President—this was more of a nagging, uneasy, vague feeling within me. I just kind of wondered a little bit about it."[27] These doubts began to crystallize in 1968, as Clifford came to believe that the United States could not achieve a military victory in Vietnam and began to question the legitimacy of U.S. involvement in Southeast Asia. Justifying the United States' withdrawal from a war that could seemingly not be won required dismantling the logic that had made U.S. intervention seem like a necessity in the first place. In hindsight, the reluctance of Southeast Asian and Pacific allies to commit additional troops during the Clifford-Taylor mission provided a starting point for dismantling this logic.

In the first months of 1968, a number of events conspired to shake Clifford's faith in the ability of the United States to win the war in Vietnam. The Tet offensive at the end of January and General Westmoreland's subsequent request for 205,197 additional troops prompted a reevaluation of Vietnam policy. At the beginning of March, Clifford, who was now the secretary of defense, led a task force to examine this troop request. Through his participation in the Clifford Task Force, the new secretary of defense came to believe that a military victory in Vietnam was not possible. His recommendations contributed to a shift in U.S. policy. On March 31, 1968, Lyndon Johnson announced that he would be capping escalation in Vietnam, restricting the bombing of North Vietnam to the area directly above the demilitarized zone, and would pursue negotiations. However, disagreement over the meaning and intent of the speech and over the possibility of achieving a military victory in Vietnam meant that Clifford would have to fight to keep the president on the path toward de-escalation for the remaining ten months of his term.

Clifford would later refer to 1968 as "the most difficult year of my life"— one in which he was "engaged in a tense struggle for the soul and mind of Lyndon Johnson."[28] Over the course of the year, Clifford transformed from a Cold War hawk who staunchly supported the president's policy, into the most vocal proponent of de-escalation and disengagement among Johnson's senior foreign policy advisers. The evolution in Clifford's thinking is visible in the notes of his meetings with a small group of Department of Defense staff that would come to be known as the 8:30 Group. In these meetings, Clifford recalled, "I felt free to speak my mind, and to solicit the views of men I trusted and respected: they were the sounding board for ideas."[29] In this setting, Clifford was less reserved in offering his views and expressing doubts about the war than he was in other forums. In meetings with his 8:30 Group, Clifford's outlook on the war and questions about the legitimacy of U.S. involvement grew more emotional as the year progressed. He shifted from questioning continued U.S. involvement in 1968 to questioning the legitimacy of U.S. intervention in 1965.[30] This transition coincided with a trip to meet with South Vietnamese leaders in Saigon in July 1968. Clifford returned from Saigon convinced that South Vietnamese leaders were not interested in ending the war and that the United States needed to get out of Vietnam. Clifford would project his growing frustration with the Vietnamese onto allied leaders in Southeast Asia and the

Pacific. In doing so, he would reevaluate his experiences during the Clifford-Taylor mission to help dismantle the logic of credibility on which U.S. involvement was justified and to challenge the domino theory that had been used to sell the war to the American people.

By June 1968, Clifford was disillusioned by what he saw as a hardening of the president's Vietnam policy and an unwillingness on the part of Johnson and his other advisers to take steps that could lead to a breakthrough in negotiations. In a June 11 meeting with the 8:30 Group, Clifford was "moody" and expressed "a deeper concern as to whether we belong in V.Nam." For perhaps the first time, Clifford voiced his doubts about the validity of U.S. involvement in Southeast Asia because of what he perceived to be a lack of concern on the part of U.S. allies in the Pacific. His special assistant, George Elsey, recorded in his notes of the meeting, "[Clifford] is shaken because, he says, he doesn't think there is validity to [the] U.S. being out there—[neither the] Philippines, nor Australia, nor N[ew] Zeal[and] [are] concerned!!!"[31] Although the allies' reluctance to contribute to the war effort led Clifford to question the reasons for U.S. engagement in Vietnam, there was no indication that the secretary of defense felt animosity toward the Southeast Asian and Pacific allies.

Two and a half months later, Clifford's tone had changed. What he had originally presented as doubts about the legitimacy of U.S. involvement in Vietnam had turned into certainty that Vietnam posed no threat to U.S. national security. Clifford expressed indignation at the lack of effort on the part of Southeast Asian and Pacific allies. He told his staff on August 22, "Our Nat[ional] interest [is] *not* at stake; N.VNam [is] *no* threat; if it were a threat surely Australia, N[ew] Zealand, [the] Phil[lipines], Korea, etc would be active & none of them do more than barest lip service."[32] In a meeting a few days later, when Paul Warnke expressed concern over Australia's "isolationist mood and an expectation we'll do *all* the fighting," Elsey noted, "[Clifford]'s *mad* at them."[33] Clifford's reaction to the allies' lack of commitment was significantly more emotional than it had been in 1967 and more tinged with anger than it had been in early June.

Clifford's experiences in Saigon and Honolulu in July 1968 can help explain his increased animosity toward allied leaders at the end of the summer. In late July, Clifford traveled to Saigon to meet with South Vietnamese leaders, before continuing on to Hawai'i to attend the Honolulu Conference, where President Johnson was meeting with South Vietnamese President Nguyen Van Thieu. Clifford returned from Saigon infuriated by his perception that the South Vietnamese had no interest in ending the war. His meetings with South Vietnamese leaders solidified his belief that the United States needed to disengage from Vietnam. Clifford remarked to his staff upon his return, "If I needed any added proof we sh[ou]ld get out, this trip did it. I wonder how in [the] name of God we ever got in!" Clifford was not simply questioning the legitimacy of continued U.S. involvement; he was challenging the decision to intervene in the first place. Part of his frustration stemmed from the fact that he thought the South Vietnamese were taking advantage of the U.S. commitment to the war, noting, "The [Government of the Republic of Vietnam] does not want the war to stop now! I'm absolutely *certain* of it now. [T]hey're protected by 540,000 U.S. [troops] & [a] golden flow of money." He was particularly disturbed by the "shocking & outrageous list of equipment" the South Vietnamese government was requesting from the United States.[34] However, it was Vice President Nguyen Cao Ky's suggestion that the United States pay for salary increases for the Army of the Republic of Vietnam that he seemed to find most troublesome. In a more widely attended Department of Defense meeting, Clifford spoke in more measured tones, noting that the exchange provided "a little glimpse of the curious attitude that this is really an American war."[35] Clifford attempted to warn Johnson of his misgivings when he arrived in Honolulu, yet the joint communiqué signed by Johnson and Thieu that emerged from the conference was a firm restatement of the U.S. commitment to Vietnam.[36]

Compounding Clifford's anxieties about continued U.S. involvement in Vietnam was the fact that the Honolulu trip coincided with a substantial hardening of the president's position. At the beginning of August, he reported to the 8:30 Group that he was "astounded & then deeply disturbed by the substantial hardening w[hi]ch was reflected in [the] Honolulu communique."[37] He seemed to believe that Johnson's meeting with Thieu had stiffened the president's commitment to his South Vietnamese allies, when his sights should have been set on disengagement. In September, Clifford worried that another summit with Southeast Asian and Pacific leaders might lead to a further hardening of the president's position that could threaten peace talks in Paris. He expressed concerns that if the summit produced "another Honolulu[-]type communique," it "w[ou]ld wreck Paris." Elsey recorded in his notes that the "Greatest Fear of us all is the hard line." Clifford also projected his view that the South Vietnamese were taking advantage of the U.S. commitment onto all of the Asian allies in the region, referring to the proposed summit as "another way for Asians to suck us in."[38] Clifford's distrust of regional allies began to mirror his distrust of the South Vietnamese.

The language that Clifford used to describe Southeast Asian and Pacific allies in his 1969 *Foreign Affairs* article closely mirrored the language he used to describe the South Vietnamese after the Honolulu Conference. Given his increased animosity toward allied leaders in this moment, it seems likely that Clifford's views of troop-contributing allies, as expressed in 1969, solidified in the fall of 1968 in connection with his growing irritation with the South Vietnamese. Clifford projected his frustration that the South Vietnamese seemingly wanted the United States to pay for their war onto the allied leaders of troop-contributing countries. In 1969, he noted Asian leaders' willingness to contribute to the war only when they received financial and material assistance in return. In reference to Thailand, Clifford noted that they did eventually send an additional division, "but we had to arm them, equip them, train them and also deliver a substantial amount of other equipment to the Thais in order to persuade them that it was in their own best interest to send some more men to South Viet Nam." No such indignation had been present in his reports in 1967. Clifford also claimed that the Clifford-Taylor mission revealed that allied leaders viewed the war in Vietnam as primarily an American war. He recalled, "What proved to be such a shock to me was that it was our war! . . . I had started off with what was probably the rather ingenuous and unsophisticated thought that we were helping them."[39] However, Clifford had publicly stated in 1967 that the Clifford-Taylor mission left him with the sense that the allies felt the war was "the War of Southeast Asia," not an American war, or even a South Vietnamese war.[40] In his *Foreign Affairs* article, Clifford was actually restating the conclusion that he had reached after meeting with South Vietnamese leaders in 1968. The views that Clifford expressed about allied leaders in Southeast Asia and the Pacific in 1969 were likely influenced by his frustration with the South Vietnamese the summer before.

By December 1968, Clifford was questioning not only whether U.S. interests were at stake in the region but also the rationale behind intervention in 1965. On December 14, Clifford "meditate[d] aloud—& at length" on why the United States sent troops to Vietnam. Responding to reports of high numbers of desertions of South Vietnamese troops, he posed the question to his 8:30 Group, "What does it mean?" Deputy Secretary of Defense Paul Nitze interjected, "This was the 1965 issue—The people we were backing were known to be 'mushy[.]' It was clear then—The Society was lousy—the Gov't was lousy—No leaders we trusted[.] It was clear[.]" Clifford retorted, "*If* it was clear, why, why, *why* did we go in?"[41] If U.S. allies in Southeast Asia and the Pacific, and even South Vietnam, were unwilling to fight and die in a war that was ostensibly for their benefit, why should U.S. soldiers bear that burden? In asking this question, Clifford challenged the assumption that allied determination to resist communism was dependent on the United States maintaining credibility. He tied the legitimacy of U.S. involvement to the strength of the allies' commitment, which he found lacking.

Clifford crafted his message in his *Foreign Affairs* article to challenge the rationale behind continued U.S. engagement in Vietnam. He did so in terms that were, by this point, very familiar to the American people. Because the Johnson administration had argued that the war in Vietnam was necessary on the basis that a loss in Vietnam could lead the entire region to fall to communism, Clifford argued that the domino theory was obsolete to make a case for disengagement. However, he tempered his argument to avoid publicly criticizing Johnson's policies—policies that Clifford had helped shape. Although he defended the administration's decision to send ground troops in 1965, he argued that in years since, "the situation has altered dramatically. The armed forces of South Viet Nam have increased in size and proficiency. The political situation there has become more stable, and the governmental institutions more representative. Elsewhere in Asia, conditions of greater security exist." He argued that the stability of the region rendered continued American involvement unnecessary. The war for Southeast Asia and the Pacific had been won; all that remained was to begin withdrawing U.S. troops from Vietnam and transfer responsibility over to the South Vietnamese.[42]

Clifford used the Clifford-Taylor mission to provide a rational framework for the evolution in his thinking in 1968, suggesting that the reluctance of allies to contribute more troops revealed the logical fallacies behind continued U.S. involvement. If this transformation in Clifford's thinking was brought about by a reasoned reassessment of the available evidence, why did the trip not raise similar questions among Johnson's other advisers or for Johnson himself? In part, this is because senior members of the administration did not believe in the validity of the domino theory as it was presented to the public. They did not look to the strength of the allied commitment as a way to measure the severity of the communist threat to the region. Rather, they believed the determination of regional allies to resist communism depended on the strength of U.S. credibility. Furthermore, it is unlikely that the trip was transformative for Clifford in the way that he has suggested. This is not to say that Clifford returned from the Clifford-Taylor mission without any doubts as to the legitimacy of the domino theory or the importance of U.S. engagement in Southeast Asia. However, it is clear that Clifford's views on the troop-contributing allies in Southeast Asia and the Pacific continued to evolve throughout 1968. This transformation was driven by his conviction that the war in Vietnam could not be won. Johnson, Rostow, Taylor, and Rusk never became convinced, to the degree that Clifford did, that a military victory was not possible. Throughout the year, they all pushed, at one time or another, for an expansion of the bombing that had been restricted by the March 31 speech. As Clifford's certainty that the United States needed to disengage from Vietnam grew, so too did his emotionality. His growing disillusionment with the war and his animosity toward the South Vietnamese influenced how he interpreted his meetings with allied leaders. The Johnson administration strategically framed the Vietnam War as a war for all of Southeast Asia to gain public support for increased U.S. involvement. By turning this argument on its head, Clifford made the case that the stability of the region provided an opportunity for disengagement. That the war was no longer a war for Southeast Asia became a central part of the public narrative of his personal transformation from Cold War hawk to ardent dove.

Notes

1. Research for this chapter was made possible, in part, by a Moody Research Grant from the LBJ Foundation.

2. For a detailed history of the Johnson administration's attempts to solicit allied aid for South Vietnam between 1964 and 1969, see Robert M. Blackburn, *Mercenaries and Lyndon Johnson's "More Flags": The Hiring of Korean, Filipino and Thai Soldiers in the Vietnam War* (Jefferson, NC: McFarland, 1994).

3. Some recent works include Frank Costigliola, "Reading for Emotion," in *Explaining the History of American Foreign Relations*, 3rd ed., ed. Frank Costigliola and Michael J. Hogan (Cambridge: Cambridge University Press, 2016), 356–373; Barbara Keys, "The Diplomat's Two Minds: Deconstructing Foreign Policy Myth," *Diplomatic History* 44, no. 1 (2020): 1–21; Illaria Scaglia, *The Emotions of Internationalism: Feeling International Cooperation in the Alps in the Interwar Period* (New York: Oxford University Press, 2020).

4. Barbara Keys, in particular, has worked to correct this tendency. See Barbara Keys, "Henry Kissinger: The Emotional Statesman," *Diplomatic History* 35, no. 4 (September 2011): 587–609.

5. Quoted in John Acacia, *Clark Clifford: The Wise Man of Washington* (Lexington: University of Kentucky Press, 2009), 4.

6. Douglas Frantz and David McKean, *Friends in High Places: The Rise and Fall of Clark Clifford* (Boston: Little, Brown, 1995), 221.

7. Notes of Meeting, May 18, 1968, VanDeMark Transcripts, Papers of George Elsey, box 1, Lyndon B. Johnson Presidential Library (hereafter LBJL). Emphasis in original.

8. Clark Clifford with Richard Holbrooke, *Counsel to the President: A Memoir* (New York: Doubleday, 1991); Clark M. Clifford, "A Viet Nam Reappraisal: The Personal History of One Man's View and How It Evolved," *Foreign Affairs* 47, no. 4 (July 1969): 601–622.

9. Clifford, "A Viet Nam Reappraisal," 602–603.

10. Clifford, *Counsel to the President*, 461.

11. Notes of Meeting, July 12, 1967, U.S. Department of State, *Foreign Relations of the United States, 1964–1968*, 5: Document 238 (hereafter cited as *FRUS*).

12. Cable from the American Embassy in Seoul to the Secretary of State, "Clifford/Taylor Visit," August 3, 1967, NSF Country File, Vietnam, box 211, LBJL.

13. Notes of Meeting, July 14, 1967, *FRUS, 1964–1968*, 5: Document 244.

14. Maxwell D. Taylor, *Swords and Plowshares* (New York: Norton, 1972), 376.

15. Clifford-Taylor Report to the President, August 5, 1967, NSF Country File, Vietnam, box 91 [1 of 2], LBJL.

16. Transcript, Clark M. Clifford Oral History Interview III, July 14, 1969, by Paige Mulhollan, Internet Copy, 6, LBJL.

17. Clifford, "A Viet Nam Reappraisal," 607.

18. Notes of Meeting, August 5, 1967, *FRUS, 1964–1968*, 5: Document 270.

19. "Press Conference of General Maxwell D. Taylor and Clark Clifford upon Returning from Southeast Asia," August 5, 1967, NSF Country File, Vietnam, box 211, LBJL.

20. Maxwell Taylor to Henry Kissinger, "Clifford-Taylor Visit to Troop Contributing Countries, August 1967," June 26, 1969, Papers of Maxwell D. Taylor, box 58, National Defense University Archives.

21. *The Pentagon Papers: The Defense Department History of United States Decisionmaking on Vietnam*, Senator Gravel edition (Boston: Beacon Press, 1971), 4:678–679.

22. Department of State, "Opinions of Asian and Pacific Leaders," *Viet-Nam Information Notes*, no. 11 (February 1968, revised March 1968): 1–8, NSF Country File, Vietnam, box 91 [1 of 2], LBJL.

23. SNIE 50–64: Short-Term Prospects in Southeast Asia, February 12, 1964, NSF National Intelligence Estimates, box 1, LBJL. A 1968 National Intelligence Estimate would draw similar conclusions. See NIE 1–68: World Trends and Contingencies Affecting US Interests, NSF National Intelligence Estimates, box 1, LBJL.

24. For an explanation of the strategic use of the domino theory by senior foreign policy advisers, see Gareth Porter, *Perils of Dominance: Imbalance of Power and the Road to War in Vietnam* (Berkeley: University of California Press, 2005), 238–258. However, Porter understates advisers' concerns about neutralism in the region. For a better explanation of what policymakers believed was at stake in Vietnam and for more information on the administration's attempt to generate and publicize allied support for the war, see Fredrik Logevall, *Choosing War: The Lost Chance for Peace and the Escalation of War in Vietnam* (Berkeley: University of California Press, 1999).

25. SNIE 50–64: Short-Term Prospects in Southeast Asia, February 12, 1964, NSF National Intelligence Estimates, box 1, LBJL.

26. Frank Ninkovich, *Modernity and Power: A History of the Domino Theory in the Twentieth Century* (Chicago: University of Chicago Press, 1994), 298–299. Ninkovich argues, "But even the obvious absence of such a will would not have been decisive, since cold-war logic assumed that it was lacking in the first place. The American military presence was intended to nurture in the Vietnamese mind the logic, in Ambassador Lodge's words, 'If the Americans can commit themselves, then I can commit myself.'"

27. Transcript, Clark M. Clifford Oral History Interview II, July 2, 1969, by Paige Mulhollan, Internet Copy, 15, LBJL.

28. Clifford, *Counsel to the President*, 461, 507.

29. Clifford, *Counsel to the President*, 491.

30. Clifford opposed sending ground troops in 1965. However, once the decision had been made, he fell into line behind the president's policy and became a staunch supporter of the war. See Clifford, *Counsel to the President*, 425; Acacia, *Clark Clifford*, 240–243.

31. Notes of Meeting, June 11, 1968, VanDeMark Transcripts, Papers of George Elsey, box 1, LBJL.

32. Notes of Meeting, August 22, 1968, VanDeMark Transcripts, Papers of George Elsey, box 1, LBJL. Emphasis in original.

33. Warnke was the Assistant Secretary of Defense for International Security Affairs. Notes of Meeting, August 26, 1968, VanDeMark Transcripts, Papers of George Elsey, box 1, LBJL. Emphasis in original.

34. Notes of Meeting, July 22, 1968, VanDeMark Transcripts, Papers of George Elsey, box 1, LBJL. Emphasis in original.

35. Secretary of Defense Staff Meeting Notes, July 22, 1968, Papers of Clark Clifford, box 18, LBJL.

36. Notes of Meeting, July 19, 1968, *FRUS, 1964–1968*, 6: Document 304. See also Clifford, *Counsel to the President*, 552–553.

37. Notes of Meeting, August 9, 1968, VanDeMark Transcripts, Papers of George Elsey, box 1, LBJL.

38. Notes of Meeting, September 24, 1968, VanDeMark Transcripts, Papers of George Elsey, box 1, LBJL. Emphasis in original.

39. Transcript, Clark M. Clifford Oral History Interview III, July 14, 1969, by Paige Mulhollan, Internet Copy, 4–5, LBJL.

40. "Press Conference of General Maxwell D. Taylor and Clark Clifford upon Returning from Southeast Asia," August 5, 1967, NSF Country File, Vietnam, box 211, LBJL.

41. Notes of Meeting, December 14, 1968, VanDeMark Transcripts, Papers of George Elsey, box 1, LBJL. Emphasis in original.

42. Clifford, "A Viet Nam Reappraisal," 617–618.

5   A Far Greater Prize than Vietnam
The United States, Indonesia, and the Vietnam War

MARK ATWOOD LAWRENCE

A paradox runs through U.S. policymaking toward East Asia during the Vietnam War era. On the one hand, the documentary record reveals numerous U.S. officials, on numerous occasions, pointing to Indonesia as the most crucial nation in Southeast Asia, a territory whose vast population, abundant resources, political influence, and strategic location demanded strenuous efforts to fight communism there and in neighboring countries. As early as 1950, Secretary of State Dean Acheson contended that Indonesia's Cold War orientation would have a "profound effect" on the "rest of Asia."[1] Four years later, President Dwight D. Eisenhower invoked Indonesia's importance as a key reason for American alarm about communist advances in Vietnam, listing the archipelago as the ultimate Southeast Asian "domino" that might fall if Ho Chi Minh's armies defeated the French.[2] American officials offered similar assessments in the early 1960s as Indonesia seemed to wobble dangerously toward communism. "The stakes are very high," Secretary of State Dean Rusk told the National Security Council (NSC) in January 1964. "More is involved in Indonesia, with its 100 million people, than is at stake in Viet Nam," added Rusk, who saw the fight in Indochina as the front line of a struggle for the whole region.[3] Deputy National Security Adviser Robert Komer agreed a few months later, telling Lyndon B. Johnson (LBJ) that Indonesia's "strategic location and 100 million people make it a far greater prize than Vietnam."[4]

On the other hand, scholars of U.S. decision making toward Vietnam have had precious little to say about the place of Indonesia in American calculations about escalation, even in the all-important year of 1965 when Washington confronted acute crises in both countries. Lloyd C. Gardner's *Pay Any Price* contains just a single reference to Indonesia, for example, while David Kaiser's *American Tragedy* has just eight and Fredrik Logevall's

Choosing War—otherwise brilliant in its global scope—none at all.[5] A recent anthology exploring "international perspectives" on the war contains chapters on Thailand, Japan, Australia, and West Germany but nothing on Indonesia.[6]

The point here is not to criticize historians of the Vietnam War but to suggest a significant impediment to serious inquiry into the place of Indonesia in decision making about Vietnam. Although American officials consistently invoked the archipelago's population, resources, location, and political volatility as major reasons for resisting communist expansion in Indochina, they seldom developed the point in any detail or drew specific connections between events unfolding in the two places. The connection was more a rhetorical assertion and hypothetical supposition than a matter of detailed analysis. It is possible, of course, that Indonesia's importance and the connections between the anti-communist struggles in the two countries was so obvious and deeply ingrained in American minds that it did not require explicit discussion in the decision-making record. Yet the sheer volume and sophistication of that documentary record, in which few analytical stones were left unturned or generally accepted points left unexpressed, makes this possibility seem less likely than another alternative: policymakers themselves were uncertain about the precise links between Indonesia and the war in Vietnam.

This chapter contends that despite all the platitudes about the urgency of resisting communist expansion in Indochina in order to protect the more important territories farther to the south, U.S. officials lacked any clear or consistent sense of the link between the anti-communist struggles in Vietnam and Indonesia until at least 1969. At that time, the Nixon administration came to view General Suharto's regime in Jakarta as a key bulwark of stability that would ensure defense of Western interests in the region following the U.S. military withdrawal from Indochina. Ambivalence about American decision making in earlier years took two distinct forms: uncertainty about the effect of the American intervention in Vietnam on the political situation in Indonesia and, conversely, about the meaning of Indonesia's political development for Washington's conduct of the war in Vietnam. The following pages examine the Indonesia-Vietnam connection from each of these angles, arguing in sum that Washington, in the peak years of escalation in Vietnam, lacked a clear vision of the war's relationship to Indonesia and the rest of Southeast Asia.

Effects of Escalation on Indonesia

U.S. officials consistently justified escalation in Vietnam as a way to block communist advances to the south, including above all in resource-rich Indonesia. In this vision of an interconnected region, Vietnam furnished the principal battleground for the defense of crucial territories lying at one or two removes from Indochina's borders. American leaders were particularly prone to this way of thinking in the 1950s, but the idea remained powerful in the key period of escalation. LBJ encapsulated the outlook in his April 1965 speech at Johns Hopkins University, perhaps his fullest explanation of his administration's decisions for a U.S. combat role. "The contest in Vietnam," asserted the president, "is part of a wider pattern of aggressive purposes." To abandon Vietnam would only expose other territories to Chinese domination. "The battle would be renewed in one country and then another," LBJ insisted.[7]

Although LBJ did not specifically mention Indonesia, other officials did, contending above all that an American failure to prevent communist takeover of South Vietnam would embolden Sukarno's radical regime in Jakarta to deepen its reliance on the vast Indonesian Communist Party (PKI) and to move closer to China. More specifically, noted a Central Intelligence Agency (CIA) study in June 1964, Indonesia would likely be "emboldened" to escalate its military effort to "crush" Malaysia, the nation established by Britain in 1963 as a successor to its colonial rule in Malaya, Singapore, and other Southeast Asia territories. Sukarno strenuously opposed creation of the new nation as a thinly veiled effort to perpetuate Western control in the region and an affront to Indonesian nationalism. Most worrying of all to American officials was the possibility that intensification of Sukarno's "confrontation" (*Konfrontasi*) policy would lead Britain, Australia, and Malaysia itself to demand U.S. military assistance. This prospect stirred anxiety in Washington, where no one wanted any part of a new military embroilment in Southeast Asia.[8] If there were no settlement between Indonesia and Malaysia, Secretary of State Dean Rusk told British prime minister Harold Wilson, Washington would be "up to the neck" in the region.[9]

The question for policymakers at the time as well as for historians ever since is whether the rapidly mounting U.S. commitment in Vietnam actually had the effect of helping to avoid the nightmarish outcomes that Americans contemplated in Indonesia if South Vietnam collapsed. Johnson administration officials, eager for evidence to support the theory that the commitment in Vietnam was paying regional if not global dividends, were quick to assert that the answer was yes. Even as U.S. relations with Sukarno deteriorated in early 1965, the ambassador in Jakarta, Howard Palfrey Jones, insisted that U.S. military escalation in South Vietnam, along with signs of determination to keep other areas of Southeast Asia in the Western fold, would have a "salutary effect" on Indonesian behavior.[10] However, claims about the regional benefits of the American war effort in Vietnam intensified sharply after the complicated series of events on September 30 and October 1, 1965, that marginalized Sukarno, gave the Indonesian military a key role in national government, and sparked a brutal military campaign against the PKI. Within hours of an apparent communist coup attempt and a successful countercoup led by General Suharto, U.S. leaders speculated that a nation leaning dangerously toward China had lurched toward the West. In a memo on October 2, Assistant Secretary of State William Bundy and Walt Rostow, the director of the State Department's Policy Planning Staff, concluded that Indonesia offered "one of the most favorable situations on the world scene in recent years."[11]

Further steps by the Indonesian army to marginalize Sukarno in March 1966 produced a flurry of self-congratulatory comment within the Johnson administration as the war in Vietnam ground on with no end in sight. The U.S. ambassador in Saigon, Henry Cabot Lodge, was one of the first to strike the theme, telling an NSC meeting in May 1966 that the destruction of the PKI was "a direct result of our having taken a firm stand in Vietnam."[12] A lengthy State Department assessment of Southeast Asia repeated the claim a month later. While denying that the United States had played a "direct part" in provoking the Indonesian army to act in Indonesia, the report asserted that U.S. escalation in Vietnam had "unquestionably" bolstered "the courage of the anti-Communist leaders." The study even asserted a retrospective correlation between the relative ineffectiveness of U.S. policy in Vietnam in earlier years and the "marked pro-Communist trend" that had played out in Indonesia in the months preceding the coup. Without Washington's "evident determination" to resist communism throughout the region, the paper claimed, Suharto and the other generals would have been "very much less likely to have acted" against Sukarno and the PKI.[13] The new U.S. ambassador to Jakarta, Marshall Green, wrote in February 1967 that the American military campaign in Vietnam had a "definite and favorable impact" on events in Indonesia, where Suharto and other anticommunist generals could not have behaved as they had if a "serious threat from the North had existed."[14] Defense Secretary Robert McNamara joined the chorus a few days later, asserting that Washington's "firm policy" in Vietnam had "played a part" in emboldening the Indonesian army to act.[15]

Were these assertions accurate? In the final analysis, it is impossible to say. Inaccessibility of Indonesian sources makes it difficult to judge the extent to which the generals drew confidence from the American war effort in Vietnam, and even if extensive documentation was available, it might be hard to draw conclusions about intangible matters of perception. However, U.S. sources, imperfect though they are for gauging Indonesian decisions, raise doubts about whether Americans had any good reason for their claims about the beneficial effects of escalation. Before October 1, 1965, in fact, U.S. observers reported far more extensively on the ways in which the expanding war in Vietnam made U.S. objectives more difficult by fueling anti-Americanism in Indonesia. Just after the start of U.S. bombing against North Vietnam in February 1965, for example, Secretary of State Dean Rusk noted that U.S. policy in Vietnam had become the focal point for "the latest series of outrages" against American property in Indonesia, including attacks on the U.S. Information Service libraries in Jakarta and Medan, and predicted more violence to come.[16] Historian Matthew Jones has shown, moreover, that LBJ's decisions to escalate in Vietnam disempowered U.S. officials with a relatively sophisticated understanding of the delicate political situation in Indonesia and aligned Washington more closely with the British government, which strongly backed Malaysia and had no interest in cultivating the Indonesian military as a partner in the region.[17] The ability of the United States to protect its interests in Indonesia, that is, may have diminished rather than increased as a consequence of the war to the north.

American sources show, too, that the Indonesian generals, for all their anti-communism, expressed scant enthusiasm for the U.S. war in Vietnam following the countercoup that brought them to power and presumably freed them to speak their minds in their interactions with U.S. officials. A State Department assessment in November 1965 noted that Indonesian officers had a "friendly, professional" attitude toward the United States, resulting in part from the fact that many had received training at Fort Leavenworth, Fort Benning, or Fort Sam Houston. Yet, this "association founded on trust, respect, and a network of deep personal friendships," as the State Department report put it, did not mean that the Indonesians would readily line up behind American geopolitical aims. Not only were the generals prepared to defy Western hopes by carrying on the *Konfrontasi* with Malaysia, but they also opposed U.S. policy in Vietnam and clung to nonalignment even as they rejected Sukarno's pro-Chinese orientation. The army, noted the State Department, "considers our military presence as western intervention encouraging rather than deterring Chinese intervention in Southeast Asia."[18] As Suharto's regime gained power and confidence over the next two years, Indonesian officials occasionally expressed greater tolerance for U.S. policy in Vietnam, and on one occasion in 1966, the newly appointed Indonesian foreign minister, Adam Malik, told Vice President Hubert Humphrey that the generals had been "directly influenced" by the American commitment in Vietnam.[19] A year later, the senior economic adviser to the new government, Widjojo Nitisastro, similarly told members of the U.S. House of Representatives that the American presence in Vietnam had had "an effect" on his country's rightward turn. It is revealing, however, that Malik and Widjojo made their comments in the process of buttering up U.S. interlocutors to support American economic aid and did not specify how Indonesian behavior had been affected by the war in Vietnam.[20] In any case, Suharto revealed no change in his attitude toward the war when he publicly addressed the subject a few weeks later. In a speech, the Indonesian leader offered no hint of supporting the American military effort, insisting that the United States could not prevail in Vietnam and calling for negotiations to end the war.[21]

The most striking evidence that the American commitment in Indochina played little or no role in Indonesia, however, lies in candid assessments by U.S. experts pointing to this conclusion. In the spring of 1966, LBJ, apparently eager to validate the idea of a direct connection, asked the CIA to study the issue. The resulting report, dated May 13, led off with a blunt assertion that presumably disappointed the president. "We have searched in vain," CIA analysis asserted, "for evidence that the US display of determination in Vietnam directly influenced the outcome of the Indonesian crisis in any significant way." Rather, the Indonesian army's efforts to marginalize Sukarno and eradicate the PKI appeared "to have evolved purely from a complex and long-standing domestic political situation." To be sure, the study acknowledged that "it is possible—though there is no evidence for this—that US determination in Vietnam did indirectly have some influence in shaping events." Without the introduction of American combat forces, most of Vietnam would have been in communist hands by the fall of 1965. That result would have left no "barrier of US force" between China and Indonesia, said the CIA, making it conceivable that army leaders would have lacked confidence to act against Sukarno and the PKI. "However," the report hastened to add, "no Indonesian leader among those now in ascendancy has ever given us any indication that he viewed the situation in this way." Events of September 30–October 1, 1965 were driven by political rivalries peculiar to Indonesia, contended the report, while pervasive anti-Chinese sentiment in Indonesia made it easy to see the army's hostility to Beijing as driven by internal rather than geopolitical calculations.[22]

The report did not end speculation among American leaders, and LBJ was drawn to the idea that Indonesia was a "dividend" of the war in Vietnam, as Ambassador Green phrased it in 1967.[23] By the time LBJ published his memoir, *The Vantage Point*, in 1971, he had fully embraced the idea. The "brave men" who carried out the countercoup in 1965 and destroyed communism in Indonesia, wrote LBJ, would probably never have acted if the United States had not "taken a stand in Vietnam."[24] There remained virtually no hard evidence to support this claim, but LBJ, like many advisers who surrounded him, had an obvious interest in finding silver linings on the Vietnam cloud and was in no mood to investigate too carefully.

Effects of Indonesian Events on the War in Vietnam

The persistence with which American leaders asserted that the U.S. stand in Vietnam encouraged the political turnabout in Indonesia attests to Washington's conviction that the war served important purposes in the region. It is thus relatively easy to conclude that events in Indonesia, regardless of whether the U.S. role in Vietnam actually had anything to do with encouraging them, had the effect of stiffening U.S. determination in Vietnam. That belief was never clearer than at the end of 1967, when the Johnson administration engaged in a broad public relations campaign to bolster public and congressional support for the war. In a speech on December 4, 1967, LBJ deployed several of the arguments he had used two and a half years earlier to justify American escalation in Vietnam, but he came down hardest on a new theme: the U.S. military effort in Vietnam provided a "shield" behind which a virtuous cycle of political and economic development was occurring throughout Southeast Asia. Nothing less than a "domino theory in reverse"—a toppling of nations in the direction of the West—was playing out across the region. The main lesson for LBJ was that the United States must not buckle under the weight of the difficulties and controversies that the war had caused. Likening opponents of the war to appeasers who had failed to see the dangers posed by Adolf Hitler and Benito Mussolini, Johnson urged redoubled commitment in Vietnam. It was clear to Asian leaders, if not always to Americans, said the president, "that our presence in Vietnam is vital, is necessary, is a must to Asia's tomorrow."[25]

Few Americans disputed the president's analysis. Most policymakers surely agreed with him, while anti-war critics had little to say about the regional dimensions of the war effort. (If they had, they might well have focused on the deeply authoritarian character of the pro-American governments that increasingly dominated the region rather than challenging LBJ's core contention.) But a few voices—at the time and again in later years—disputed LBJ's logic, even contending that Indonesia's lurch to the right, far from justifying the war in Vietnam, made that campaign unnecessary by successfully resolving Washington's major problem in the region. From abroad, for example, the shah of Iran, a keen observer of geopolitical trends in Asia, told U.S. diplomats in November 1966 that he had dropped his earlier "hawk-like" support for American escalation due to the "favorable developments" in Indonesia and now favored a negotiated solution.[26] In Washington, a similar view came from the iconoclastic American diplomat George F. Kennan, who asserted during testimony before a Senate Committee in February 1966 that events in Indonesia made the risk of communism spreading through the region "considerably less" than it had been a year earlier.[27]

Perhaps the closest the U.S. decision-making bureaucracy came to this view during the war came in the form of a September 1967 CIA assessment of the likely geopolitical consequences of a communist takeover of South Vietnam. The thirty-three-page study, a top secret exercise that made no discernable impact on LBJ's thinking, concluded that the United States would suffer no permanent or devastating setbacks anywhere in the world, including even in the areas closest to the Indochinese states, as long as Washington made clear its determination to remain active internationally after a setback in Vietnam. With respect to the leaders who had come to power in Indonesia in 1965, CIA analysts saw no reason to believe that a communist success in Vietnam would cause them to "falter in their determination to cope with their own internal communist problem." Rather, said the report, they would likely remain determined to "move ahead with orderly development" of their own society, particularly if Thailand remained in pro-Western hands and thereby created a buffer between communist Indochina and the Indonesian archipelago.[28]

Long after the war ended, in the 1990s and early twenty-first century, a significant body of commentary drew out the implications of the CIA's report to suggest that the Johnson administration had learned the wrong lesson about the connection between the Vietnam War and political change elsewhere in Southeast Asia. Far from clarifying the necessity of the war, this view suggested, the consolidation of pro-American governments should have demonstrated to Washington that it had achieved its principal goals in the region and could have withdrawn in confidence that, at worst, only Vietnam, Cambodia, and Laos would fall to the communists. Robert McNamara, the former secretary of defense who presided over American escalation in Vietnam, gave this view its classic formulation in his 1995 memoir *In Retrospect: The Tragedy and Lessons of Vietnam*. American leaders including himself, asserts McNamara, missed the fact that the military takeover in Indonesia amounted to a massive setback for China, depriving Beijing of its best prospect for expanding communist influence in Southeast Asia and contributing to the inward turn that produced the Cultural Revolution. Quoting Kennan's contention that the army's move against Sukarno "greatly reduced America's stakes in Vietnam," McNamara raised a tantalizing counterfactual scenario: if only U.S. leaders had appreciated which way communist fortunes were trending in the region, they would have attached less significance to Vietnam and questioned the escalatory path down which they were headed.[29] Thirteen years later, historian Bradley R. Simpson, author of the most authoritative study of U.S.-Indonesian relations in the 1960s, made the point even more explicitly. The destruction of the largest communist party outside the Eastern bloc, wrote Simpson, eliminated "at a stroke the chief threat to the Westward orientation of the most strategically and economically important country in Southeast Asia" and "vividly undermined the rationale for the escalating U.S. war in Vietnam."[30] Journalist Vincent Bevins came to a similar conclusion in a 2020 study, asserting simply "McNamara was right": Indonesia's reorientation essentially secured core American objectives in the region.[31]

The problem with this line of reasoning is that it assumes American policymakers could—and should—have recognized the bold moves by the Indonesian army in the fall of 1965 as a profound break with heavy implications for the overall Cold War balance in Asia. In fact, difficult U.S. relationships with India, Pakistan, and Iran, as well as persistent concern about Chinese expansionism around the same time, made it unlikely that Americans would view the changed status of a single territory—even one as important as Indonesia—as valid reason to scale back in Vietnam. By 1965, after all, U.S. leaders had repeatedly insisted that the fighting was connected to anticommunist efforts not only in Southeast Asia but throughout the world. But the bigger problem with the idea of a missed opportunity in 1965 is abundant evidence that it took years for U.S. policymakers to become satisfied that a permanent shift had occurred in Indonesia. In retrospect, it may seem that the generals' countercoup eliminated the communist danger "at a stroke," but the Johnson administration did not see the events of the fall of 1965 in that way. For this reason, American officials had a hard time seeing clear or direct implications of Indonesian events for their decisions regarding Vietnam. U.S. officials gained some confidence by 1967 that Indonesia was firmly in the Western camp—hence LBJ's speech about the "reverse domino effect"—but uncertainty persisted until at least 1969, when the Suharto regime's behavior became a significant factor as the Nixon administration made policy toward Indochina. The bottom line is that LBJ and his supporters, just like critics such as Kennan and Simpson, erred in viewing the events of the fall of 1965 as a clear-cut rupture with direct implications for the U.S. role in Vietnam, whether that implication buttressed or undercut the rationale for the American war.

American leaders unquestionably exulted about the army's bold move in the fall of 1965 and threw their support behind the anti-communist repression that followed, implicating the United States deeply in the moral abominations that ensued. Still, they had difficulty assessing the meaning of the countercoup for U.S. policy toward Indonesia narrowly or the region more generally. For one thing, it seemed possible that the shift in Indonesian politics would be limited and incremental rather than decisive. Just two weeks after the countercoup, Ambassador Green offered a pessimistic assessment. Although the communists had been badly weakened, he foresaw "prolonged maneuvering" between Sukarno and the army and cautioned that the resolution might do "little more than paper over" lines of fracture among Indonesian elites since neither contender for power wanted a total break. Green predicted "changes of emphasis" in political sloganeering but warned that "the basic framework of Indonesia's domestic ideology will be retained," including Sukarno's long-standing emphasis on unity among nationalist, communist, and religious elements of Indonesian society.[32] The British Foreign Office reinforced this gloomy assessment, noting on November 6 that the army had made no effort to "mend fences" with the West, an assessment shared in Washington.[33] To Washington's distress, the generals showed no inclination to soften Sukarno's hostility to the U.S. war in Vietnam and seemed determined to press on with the *Konfrontasi* against Malaysia, raising the frightening spectacle of British military action to weaken the Indonesian military while it was distracted with internal concerns.[34] The CIA noted, meanwhile, that the army remained heavily dependent on Soviet assistance and contained many officers and enlisted personnel sympathetic to communist ideology, if not the PKI per se.[35]

Meanwhile, U.S. observers fretted that Sukarno might yet find ways to bolster both his own power and that of the PKI at the expense of the army and its allies. Although Sukarno's power had been undercut, U.S. assessments following the countercoup noted that he seemed in good health and, as the CIA put it in a briefing for the president, appeared eager to use his "political magic" to restore the status quo ante.[36] The nightmare scenario was a political comeback by the PKI, which Green believed could occur in one of two ways. Sukarno might be able to establish a "new-style PKI" more closely aligned with Moscow than Beijing. Alternatively, the party might adopt a "violent anti-government guerrilla warfare strategy," a development that would likely lead to even tighter bonds between Indonesian communists and Beijing than ever before.[37] Such concerns made U.S. leaders wary of surrendering their leverage over Jakarta by aiding the army too quickly. If Washington showed too much enthusiasm, warned Secretary of State Dean Rusk, "[the] Indonesian army and other elements friendly to us could be led to believe they can count on us whatever their posture on Viet-Nam, Malaysia and other issues important to us."[38]

Only in March 1966 did a new flurry of dramatic events in Indonesia significantly boost Washington's optimism about the nature of the new regime in Jakarta. Anxious that Sukarno seemed to be making precisely the sort of comeback that Americans feared, the army mobilized a large student movement that it had nurtured in earlier months and took deliberate steps to damage the nation's economy. Amid mounting chaos that he had instigated, Suharto succeeded on March 11 in manipulating Sukarno into signing a landmark document known as the *Supersemar*, which gave the generals authority to restore order. Although Sukarno remained the nation's figurehead president, the document effectively concentrated all executive power in Suharto's hands. Within days, Suharto had banned the PKI—mostly a formality since little of it remained following months of organized killing—and arrested several Sukarno-appointed cabinet members who had refused to resign. At last, the CIA advised LBJ, the generals had cut their ties to Sukarno and were going "their own way."[39]

This was the context within which Henry Cabot Lodge and other U.S. officials began voicing their view that American escalation in Vietnam had helped bring positive results in Indonesia. As noted above, there was no clear evidence for such a claim, though Americans were surely correct in believing that Suharto would feel freer to side openly with the West. For the first time, Suharto referred to China as "the enemy," explicitly vowed to protect American investment in Indonesia, and indicated his desire to wind down the Confrontation with Malaysia.[40] The new Indonesian foreign minister, Adam Malik (later exposed as a CIA asset), even expressed a degree of sympathy for the U.S. commitment to Vietnam and made his comment to Vice President Humphrey about the effect of the American war on inspiring the generals to act.[41] Newly confident of the Suharto regime, which LBJ suggested in 1967 might even provide a "showcase" for the rest of the world, Washington began seriously considering large packages of development and food assistance.[42]

Still, there were problems. Malik's strongly pro-U.S. opinions were not widely shared among Indonesia's new leaders, and it was clear that the regime remained wedded to nonalignment in the Cold War. Given the broad hostility to Washington's Vietnam policy among nonaligned nations, it was surely difficult to imagine Suharto veering significantly toward Washington's outlook. To be sure, Suharto's version of nonalignment was a far cry from Sukarno's strongly pro-Chinese orientation. Yet, the new regime clearly appreciated the popularity of nonalignment across Indonesian society and repeatedly declared its determination to rid Southeast Asia of foreign forces. A State Department study cautioned in 1966 that Indonesia under Suharto would "undoubtedly resume its position as one of the more militant [members] of the Asian-African bloc" and would surely oppose Washington on "many key questions." As for Vietnam, the government would likely remain "publicly critical" of U.S. policy even if Malik attempted from time to time to soften the impact through private reassurances.[43] A British assessment in June 1967 reached a similar conclusion, finding "no evidence" that the war would affect U.S.-Indonesian relations adversely but attributing Jakarta's moderation more to Indonesian dependence on U.S. economic aid and fear of a sudden U.S. defeat in Vietnam than any real enthusiasm for American policy.[44]

Concerns about the government's orientation following the *Supersemar* paled, however, in comparison to the danger that Indonesia's dysfunctional economy and sclerotic administrative apparatus would undermine the new regime's ability to play even the moderately helpful role that Americans hoped for. At the start of 1968, analysts in the U.S. embassy in Jakarta worried that a combination of persistent food shortages and inflation, among other woes, still imperiled Indonesia's stability. "The average Indonesian," read one embassy study, "had no more rice in the pot at the end of 1967 than at the beginning, and what he did have cost him considerably more."[45] So immense were the problems that even a modest improvement in Indonesia's economic conditions would be a "sizeable achievement," the U.S. Agency for International Development concluded later in the year.⁴⁶

Only after Richard Nixon took office in 1969 did Washington become fully confident of Indonesia's economic progress and status as a pro-Western bastion whose reliability could be factored into U.S. policymaking in Vietnam. The connection between events in Indonesia and Vietnam, so often invoked in earlier years, finally morphed from the realm of the hypothetical and aspirational into a pillar of U.S. policymaking. Nixon and his top foreign policy lieutenant, National Security Adviser Henry Kissinger, increasingly accepted Indonesia as a regional power that could serve Western economic and geopolitical objectives following the withdrawal of American forces from Vietnam. In this sense, Indonesia fit neatly within the so-called Nixon Doctrine, the new administration's policy of reducing the need for direct U.S. military intervention around the world by building up regional partners that Washington could rely on to uphold its interests. Suharto, increasingly confident in his power within Indonesia and eager to play a role in international affairs, saw his nation's role in a similar way.

This harmony of U.S. and Indonesian visions for Southeast Asia gave rise to what the American diplomat Paul F. Gardner dubbed the "apex of the bilateral relationship" between Washington and Jakarta.⁴⁷ U.S. officials lauded Suharto for Indonesian leadership within the Association of Southeast Asian Nations, the grouping of anti-communist nations established in 1967 to promote economic development, and welcomed Jakarta's increasingly supportive attitude toward American decision making in Vietnam. Indonesian leaders clung to their nation's nonalignment and broadly urged the withdrawal of all outside military forces, including the remaining American contingent, from the region. However, wary of any extension of Chinese influence, they also spoke favorably of American bombing, warned against an overly hasty U.S. withdrawal, and toyed with the idea of inserting Indonesian peacekeeping forces to uphold a peace settlement preserving an independent South Vietnam.⁴⁸ This willingness to project Indonesian power made Indonesia "the key to at least South and Southeast Asia" following the U.S. withdrawal from Vietnam, Kissinger wrote.⁴⁹ Washington, that is, could pull its forces out of Indochina in the knowledge that Indonesia was playing a leadership role in what historian Wen-Qing Ngoei has called the "arc of containment" stretching from Malaysia to the Philippines.⁵⁰

American expectations escalated as Jakarta showed signs of filling the regional role that Washington hoped for as the United States pulled back.

In 1969, the Indonesian regime gratified U.S. officials by peacefully incorporating West Irian, a formerly Dutch territory claimed by Indonesia, into the nation, resolving a potentially dangerous regional flash point. Suharto impressed Americans even more the following year by throwing Indonesian political and even military support behind Lon Nol, the military officer who came to power in Cambodia through a U.S.-backed coup d'état in March 1970. Indonesian hostility to the previous Cambodian ruler, Prince Norodom Sihanouk, for allowing Vietnamese communist forces to operate with impunity in Cambodian territory aligned closely with Washington's outlook, and Suharto's backing for Lon Nol remained steadfast even after Nixon ordered a controversial U.S. military incursion into Cambodia at the end of April. Suharto sent Indonesian military assistance to the new regime in Phnom Penh and, in May, risked his nonaligned credentials by convening an emergency meeting of Southeast Asian governments aimed at bolstering Cambodia's anti-communists. Kissinger welcomed signs of Jakarta's growing capacity for "organization and leadership" in a region that would need both of those qualities as Washington removed its forces. "What Suharto has done and is doing," Kissinger wrote to the president, "accords perfectly with your concept of Asian responsibilities under the Nixon Doctrine."[51]

Conclusion

To argue that Americans drew contradictory and imprecise connections between Indonesia and Vietnam does not mean that U.S. leaders, including LBJ, were insincere in their assertions on the subject or pursued policies they did not earnestly embrace. However, the intermittent and inconsistent ways in which they invoked the connections and the ambiguity that surrounded the issue suggests that the regional implications of the anti-communist fight in Vietnam were less important to their decisions than the bold rhetoric that they sometimes used on the subject would suggest. Indeed, this chapter has argued that U.S. officials, when they studied the matter, saw only loose connections between the war in Vietnam and developments in Indonesia. Although they could not resist the temptation to ascribe the Indonesian generals' willingness to act against Sukarno in 1965 to American determination in Vietnam, careful study of the issue indicated that Indonesia's rightward lurch sprang from domestic causes. Meanwhile, LBJ's certainty that Indonesia's turn indicated the need to carry on the war in Vietnam coexisted with a contrary line of thinking that suggested events in Indonesia made it possible to draw down in Vietnam. In fact, most American officials had a hard time drawing implications of Indonesian events because the new regime there evolved slowly, and Americans gained full confidence in Suharto's New Order as a factor in regional geopolitics only around the time Nixon took office. Perhaps Americans *should* have felt more immediate confidence about the dramatic events that played out in Indonesia in the fall of 1965 and the brutal destruction of the PKI that quickly ensued. Yet the sheer complexity of events, combined with American intolerance for ambiguity, made it unlikely that the Johnson administration would abruptly shift course.

Historians and memoirists have long highlighted the tragic nature of the American commitment in Vietnam by demonstrating the ways in which preconceived and often simplistic notions about the need to contain communist expansion, to bolster American credibility with adversaries and allies alike, to secure political advantage by demonstrating determination to stand up to the Soviet bloc, and to protect personal reputations for toughness drove deeply flawed decisions to escalate the war in Vietnam. The murkiness of the connection between the greatest "prize" in Southeast Asia and the war in Vietnam provides yet another example of the ways in which American policymakers invoked flawed certainties as they made decisions that resulted in catastrophe. Breezy assumptions about falling dominoes and the interconnections among Southeast Asia societies proved iffy at best when put to the test at the time, just as they appear problematic when viewed with the benefit of a half century of hindsight and access to the bulk of the American decision-making record.

Notes

1. Acheson to Harry S. Truman, January 9, 1950, *Foreign Relations of the United States, 1950* (Washington, DC: U.S. Government Printing Office, 1976), vol. 6, doc. 608.

2. Editorial Note, *FRUS, 1952–1954*, vol. 13, pt. 1, doc. 716.

3. Record of the 521st National Security Council meeting, January 7, 1964, *FRUS 1964–1968*, vol. 26, doc. 8.

4. Komer to Johnson, August 19, 1964, *FRUS, 1964–1968*, vol. 26, doc. 61.

5. Lloyd C. Gardner, *Pay Any Price: Lyndon Johnson and the Wars for Vietnam* (Chicago: Ivan R. Dee, 1995); David Kaiser, *American Tragedy: Kennedy, Johnson, and the Origins of the Vietnam War* (Cambridge, MA: Belknap, 2000); Fredrik Logevall, *Choosing War: The Lost Chance for Peace and the Escalation of War in Vietnam* (Berkeley: University of California Press, 1999).

6. Andreas W. Daum, Lloyd C. Gardner, and Wilfried Mausbach, eds., *America, the Vietnam War, and the World* (New York: Cambridge University Press, 2003).

7. Johnson speech, "Peace without Victory," April 7, 1965, American Presidency Project, https://www.presidency.ucsb.edu/documents/address-johns-hopkins-university-peace-without-conquest.

8. Board of National Estimates to John McCone, June 9, 1964, *FRUS 1964–1968*, vol. 1, doc. 209.

9. Memorandum of conversation, January 29, 1965, PREM 13/1914, National Archives of the United Kingdom, Kew (NAUK).

10. Jones to State Department, March 4, 1965, *FRUS, 1964–1968*, vol. 26, doc. 113.

11. Rostow and William Bundy to Ball, October 2, 1965, Record Group 59, Policy Planning Council, Subject and Country Files, 1965–1969, box 304, National Archives and Records Administration, College Park, MD.

12. Record of the 557th National Security Council meeting, May 10, 1966, *FRUS, 1964–1968*, vol. 4, doc. 135.

13. State Department paper for the president, June 8, 1966, National Security File (NSF), Country File (CF), box 248, Lyndon B. Johnson Presidential Library, Austin, TX (LBJL).

14. Rostow to Johnson, February 21, 1967, NSF, CF, box 248, LBJL.

15. McNamara to Johnson, March 1, 1967, *FRUS, 1964–1968*, vol. 26, doc. 232.

16. Rusk to Jakarta embassy, February 20, 1965, NSF, CF, box 246, LBJL; Rusk to Jakarta, February 22, 1965, NSF, CF, box 246, LBJL.

17. Matthew Jones, "U.S. Relations with Indonesia, the Kennedy-Johnson Transition, and the Vietnam Connection, 1963–1965," *Diplomatic History* 26, no. 2 (Spring 2002): 249–281.

18. David Cuthell to William Bundy, "Indonesian Army Attitude toward the United States Government," November 3, 1965, *FRUS, 1964–1968*, vol. 26, doc. 167.

19. Humphrey to Johnson, September 25, 1966, *FRUS, 1964–1968*, vol. 26, doc. 222.

20. Memorandum of conversation, "U.S. Economic Assistance to Indonesia," June 28, 1967, NSF, CF, box 248, LBJL.

21. Green (Jakarta) to State Department, July 19, 1967, NSF, CF, box 249, LBJL.

22. CIA report, "The Indonesian Crisis and US Determination in Vietnam," May 13, 1966, NSF, CF, box 248, LBJL.

23. Memorandum of conversation, Green with Vice President Hubert Humphrey, March 13, 1967, NSF, CF, box 248, LBJL.

24. Lyndon Baines Johnson, *The Vantage Point: Perspectives on the Presidency, 1963–1969* (New York: Holt, Rinehart, and Winston, 1971), 357.

25. Johnson speech to the Foreign Policy Conference for Business Executives, December 4, 1967, American Presidency Project, www.presidency.ucsb.edu/node/238100.

26. Rome embassy to State Department, November 3, 1966, *FRUS, 1964–1968*, vol. 22, doc. 181.

27. "Excerpts from Kennan's Statement to Senators on Vietnam," *New York Times*, February 11, 1966, 2.

28. CIA report, "Implications of an Unfavorable Outcome in Vietnam," September 12, 1967, CIA Electronic Reading Room, https://www.cia.gov/library/reading room/document/0001166443.

29. Robert S. McNamara, *In Retrospect: The Tragedy and Lessons of Vietnam* (New York: Times Book, 1995), 215–219.

30. Bradley R. Simpson, *Economists with Guns: Authoritarian Development and U.S.-Indonesian Relations, 1960–1968* (Stanford, CA: Stanford University Press, 2008), 2. See also Errol Morris, "The Murders of Gonzago," *Slate*, July 10, 2013, http://www.slate.com/articles/arts/history/2013/07/the_act_of_killing_essay_how _indonesia_s_mass_killings_could_have_slowed.html.

31. Vincent Bevins, *The Jakarta Method: Washington's Anticommunist Crusade & the Mass Murder Program That Shaped Our World* (New York: Public Affairs, 2020), 160.

32. Green to State Department, October 17, 1965, *FRUS, 1964–1968*, vol. 26, doc. 156.

33. Foreign Office to Washington embassy, November 6, 1965, PREM 13/2718, NAUK.

34. Cuthell to William Bundy, November 3, 1965, *FRUS, 1964–1968*, vol. 26, doc. 167.

35. CIA report, "Indonesian Army Attitudes toward Communism," November 22, 1965, CIA Electronic Reading Room, https://www.cia.gov/library/readingroom /document/cia-rdp79t00472a000600040009-3.

36. President's Daily Brief, October 5, 1965, CIA Electronic Reading Room, https://www.cia.gov/library/readingroom/docs/DOC_0005967926.PDF.

37. Green to State Department, October 19, 1965, NSF, CF, box 247, LBJL.

38. Rusk to Jakarta, December 8, 1965, NSF, CF, box 248, LBJL.

39. President's Daily Brief, March 16, 1966, CIA Electronic Reading Room, http://www/cia.gov/library/readingroom/document/0005968207.

40. Green to State Department, May 27, 1966, *FRUS, 1964–1968*, vol. 26, doc. 209.

41. Humphrey to Johnson, September 25, 1966, *FRUS, 1964–1968*, vol. 26, doc. 222; Tim Weiner, *Legacy of Ashes: The History of the CIA* (New York: Doubleday, 2006), 299.

42. Notes of National Security Council meeting, August 9, 1967, Tom Johnson's Notes of Meetings, box 1, LBJL.

43. State Department report, "Indonesia," August 1, 1966, *FRUS, 1964–1968*, vol. 26, doc. 215.

44. Joint Intelligence Committee report, "The Outlook for Indonesia Up to the End of 1970," June 12, 1967, PREM 13/2718, NAUK.

45. Embassy report, "Trends during 1967 and Problem Areas for 1968," January 12, 1968, RG59, Policy Planning Council, Subject and Country Files, 1965–1969, box 304, NARA.

46. AID study, "Indonesia's Current Development Position," October 7, 1968, NSF, CF, box 248, LBJL.

47. Paul F. Gardner, *Shared Hopes, Separate Fears: Fifty Years of U.S.-Indonesian Relations* (Boulder, CO: Westview, 1997), 265.

48. For example, Kissinger to Nixon, March 26, 1969, *FRUS, 1969–1976*, vol. 20, doc. 266; and memorandum for the record, July 27, 1969, *FRUS, 1969–1976*, vol. 20, doc. 271.

49. Kissinger to Nixon, July 18, 1969, https://nsarchive2.gwu.edu/NSAEBB/NSAEBB242/.

50. Wen-Qing Ngoei, *Arc of Containment: Britain, the United States, and Anticommunism in Southeast Asia* (Ithaca, NY: Cornell University Press, 2019), 159–160.

51. Kissinger to Nixon, May 26, 1970, NSC Files, VIP Visits, box 919, Richard Nixon Presidential Library, Yorba Linda, CA.

6   The View from the Hill
Hawai'i's Congressional Delegation and the Struggle for Peace in Vietnam and Equity at Home, 1964–1975

MARC JASON GILBERT

Although the American War in Vietnam had a considerable role in shaping the foreign relations and domestic affairs of Asia-Pacific nations, scholars of the war have evaluated Hawai'i's role largely in terms of the state's strategic and logistical contributions to the war effort.[1] However, in many ways, the impact of the war in Hawai'i was similar to that experienced by the rising nation-states of the region. Many of Hawai'i's people had idealistically fought for statehood to liberate themselves from an avowedly racist colonial U.S. territorial administration, much as the citizens of then-new nations of Asia sought or were then still seeking liberation from their own oppressive colonial past. Like many of the peoples of the noncommunist nations of Southeast Asia, Hawaiians had hopes of a bright postcolonial future, but it had fallen short of expectations. Like them, Hawaiians found themselves increasingly governed by a moneyed political elite that was desirous to a fault to partner with international investors whose projects brought jobs and prosperity to some, while shunting aside the poor and ignoring the interests of their own Indigenous people. As a result, many Hawaiians entered the Vietnam era resentful of what they perceived as a dependent economy, rising inequality, and the usurpation of their land to serve the Cold War needs of the U.S. military.[2]

These postcolonial ills led many Hawaiians to ask uncomfortable questions regarding their place in the U.S. and the Asia-Pacific world. They acknowledged that serving as the point of America's spear in the region helped sustain the Hawaiian economy but feared it came at the cost of militarization of their society and despoliation of their land.[3] Its majority Asian population (a majority of whom were of Japanese ancestry) was unique in terms of American polity. They had established cultural bonds between themselves and the small surviving Indigenous (native Hawaiian) population, thus helping to preserve the island's Polynesian traditions, only to find that the native Hawaiian community was harboring thoughts of recovering their lost sovereignty.[4] Like many Hawaiians, they looked with approval at the post-statehood economic boom driven by the American tenet that "growth is progress and progress is good" and embraced the accompanying boom in tourism. Others joined with those who challenged the state's political leadership to address the accompanying loss of traditional lifestyle and unprecedented increases in poverty and air and water pollution, arguing that Hawai'i "must not become Los Angeles."[5] Given these developments, it should come as no surprise that ambiguity characterized the Hawaiian response to the Vietnam War.

That ambiguity was reflected in the desire of most Hawaiians to hold to the traditional belief in the value of *aloha* (the sharing of life with others in peace), while at the same time, they were deeply concerned with the rising communist threat to the security of all Asia-Pacific peoples, to whom most of the population was connected by heritage due to decades of Asian immigration and intermarriage and who expected their leaders in Washington to respond with force if necessary to a communist attempt to subvert the Republic of Vietnam, a free and fledgling democratic regime. However, as early as 1965, the special circumstances of that conflict (decolonization, insurgency, rivaling states in the aftermath of Geneva, and no U.S. declaration of war) indicated to them that a lasting peace in Vietnam could only be achieved via negotiations, not by a "total" military victory, leaving Hawaiians divided between those favoring "more bombing" to achieve a settlement and those who preferred "peace with aloha" over "our bombing our way to peace," which carried the risk of "a worldwide global thermonuclear holocaust."[6] For the next ten years, as their home-grown faith in what would come to be called "limited war" in Southeast Asia ebbed and flowed, so did their support for and opposition to the war. On the surface, this ambiguity mirrored the "push-pull" of pro- and anti-war opinion in the United States and in some Asia-Pacific nations, but its roots were unique and its impact far reaching for the Hawaiian people, for national policy, and for the Asia-Pacific world.

The Hawai'i Congressional Delegation

The burden of translating Hawai'i's limited-war mandate into policy at the national level fell to members of the Hawai'i congressional delegation. Serving together from 1964 to 1975, they sought to balance America's national defense and foreign policy interests with the Hawaiian guiding value of peace to which they were committed by long experience shaped by the islands' recent history and cultural environment. Their individual and collective performance in office played an important role in shaping the course of the Vietnam War and waging peace in its aftermath. Their parallel quest to achieve the return of Hawaiian lands held by the U.S. military provides insight into how this fundamental issue in modern Hawaiian history became entangled with American militarism so as to contribute to the development of the native Hawaiian (*Kanaka Maoli*) renaissance and the Hawaiian sovereignty movement.[7]

Hawai'i's wartime delegation consisted of three Democrats and one Republican. The Democrats were Daniel K. Inouye (senator, 1963–2012), Spark Masayuki Matsunaga (representative, 1963–1977; senator, 1977–1990), and Patsy Takemoto Mink (representative, 1965–1977).[8] All three were nisei, second-generation Japanese Americans, who came from humble immigrant backgrounds where they experienced racial discrimination and even challenges to their right to citizenship, especially after the Japanese attack on Pearl Harbor in 1941. Inouye and Matsunaga were battle-scarred veterans of the now famous units composed of Japanese Americans, determined to demonstrate on the battlefield their loyalty as American citizens.[9] Mink also emerged from the war as a soldier, if out of uniform, in the parallel fight against racism and for democracy and also against virulent paternalism (she had been denied entrance into medical school on the basis of her sex). All emerged from the war embittered that this global conflict had in no way dimmed the discrimination applied to Asians by the Republican and Caucasian plantation-owning minority that dominated the U.S. territorial government.

All three were soon swept up into the epic postwar Democratic Party–led campaign for statehood convinced that this was the only practical way to end discriminatory territorial rule. The delegation's three Democrats went to law school so as to aid in that fight from which they emerged leaders of the fiftieth state in 1959. In Congress, they were respected for their personal qualities, including party loyalty, that earned them placement on important committees of their choice. Inouye had an engaging personality and strength of character, which President Lyndon Baines Johnson admired as Inouye overcame racism within Johnson's own former Texas congressional delegation.[10] Matsunaga's colleagues in the House and later in the Senate saw him as "modest in his manner and bearing" but "ambitious in the interest of justice and humanity."[11] Patsy Takemoto Mink's dynamic personality helped her overcome paternalism as well as racism to achieve victory in twelve campaigns for the House. Yet, her colleagues never looked at her "simply because she was a woman or an Asian-American. . . . Patsy was a moral filter for the Congress, a questioning and unflappable inquisitor of whether an initiative moved justice forward in America and the world or did not. And woe to the proposal . . . that failed to meet that test."[12]

Republican Hiram L. Fong (senator, 1959–1977) rose from poverty as the son of Chinese immigrants. After his war service, he mixed business with local politics until 1959, when he was elected senator on a social reform platform (civil rights and immigration reform) similar to that of his liberal Democratic colleagues and favored by President Johnson. His electoral success in a majority Democratic state owed much to his skill at coalition building: he provided legal services to a financial pillar of the Hawai'i Democratic Party, the leftist International Longshoreman and Warehousemen's Union (ILWU). When asked to explain how a millionaire businessman and enemy of international communism like himself could be allied with the avowed Marxist leaders of the ILWU, Fong said of them, "From my viewpoint, knowing these people, I think what they were doing was that they were just protesting the rule [of] the people in control."[13]

All the members of the Hawai'i delegation were part of the politically and economically dominant Asian community of Hawai'i, which largely avoided the inequality produced by Hawai'i's post-statehood economic boom driven by foreign investment and a surging tourism industry. However, all four members of Hawai'i's congressional delegation began life on plantations or in working-class neighborhoods. They came of age in Hawai'i's unique, if imperfect, multiracial and multicultural society, and had a deep respect for local traditions with Polynesian roots. None but the entrepreneurial Fong had profited from the post-statehood boom other than from fees as lawyers, while Fong, who prided himself on his independence, often put Hawai'i's public land interests above his own.

The delegation's like-mindedness extended into the area of foreign affairs to the degree that at no time did any member of the Hawai'i delegation, even at the height of American divisiveness over the Cambodian incursion in 1970, publicly depart from their own and the majority of their constituents' belief that peace in Vietnam could only come through a negotiated settlement achieved within the parameters of limited war. To a large extent, that unity was based on their preference for "soft power."

Seeking Peace through Soft Power in Southeast Asia

At the time of the passage of the Gulf of Tonkin Resolution in August 1964, the members of the Hawai'i delegation already had a well-established interest in the building of peace between the United States and the countries of Asia. A self-described "Pacific man," Fong had toured thirteen countries in 1959. There he found no "ugly Americans" among Americans working in Asia; he believed that they were "winning the battle for the minds of people in neutral and free countries of Asia" through the exercise "of economic and cultural influence to improve relations in Asia." His preference for "soft power"[14] in Asia was fully shared by Matsunaga. He, too, was a Pacific man, who built close connections with Asian governments from Japan to India, and sought congressional support for rural development, health, and educational infrastructure he believed was necessary for peace in and the growth of postcolonial nations. Matsunaga believed he was "born and raised in the spirit of *aloha*," as was reflected in a student paper he wrote declaring that "we are living in a society based too largely on a militaristic foundation. . . . We must replace attitudes favorable to war with attitudes opposed to war," which became his life's work, "directly due to his experiences in war."[15] That work began in earnest in 1962, when Matsunaga ran for office as a peace candidate.

Proof that the delegation's preference for soft power was consistent with contemporary local and national policy was then literally rising in their own backyard. In 1959, Hawai'i's Democratic governor, John A. Burns, a mentor to the delegation's Democratic members, convinced his friend, Senator Lyndon Baines Johnson, to introduce legislation, soon integrated into the Mutual Security Act of 1960, supporting the creation in Honolulu of an East-West Center as a bridge between the United States and Asia that would stimulate dialogue aimed at peace building between the United States and the peoples of Asia.[16] Fong and Inouye were avid supporters of the center; for Matsunaga, its only flaw was that it was not practical enough. He preferred to build an academy to train American diplomats working in Asia to develop sensitivity to Asian political and social life.[17] All four members of the Hawai'i delegation were realists in terms of understanding that obstacles to peace making were manifold and military action in pursuit of national interests often necessary. They were steadfast in their support of troops in the field. To make that clear, Fong and Matsunaga rejoined the military as colonels in the army reserve. They did not fear sending Americans to their deaths in battle when the cause was just, nor, it proved, did they fear calling them back when they felt the national interest required. As will be seen, their personal integrity in the face of both options was so complete that even Fong, who was in a very delicate electoral position late in the war, never let political polls influence their views. That integrity would extend to the controversial subject of the federal control of Hawaiian lands which, in terms of intensity as well as cultural and political significance, began to impact Hawai'i from the very outset of the war.

The Vietnam War Comes to Hawai'i

The Hawai'i land issue had both local political and federal military dimensions. Most of the state's population had hoped that statehood in 1959 would lead to the creation of a "New Hawai'i" that would be multiracial, multicultural, and politically and economically egalitarian. As briefly mentioned above, the "New Hawai'i" resulted in private profit for investors, while holding out the promise of increased opportunities for public officials to boost the state's economy. Together, these interests were able to influence public institutions and private trusts to sweep away low-income urban housing in favor of hotels and evict poor Hawaiians from their rural settlements to make way for suburban housing and resorts. The Cold War, and the Vietnam War in particular, led to the expansion of American military bases in Hawai'i that put more pressure on the availability of land and affordable housing: less than half of Hawaiian homes were owned by its residents and almost half of new housing built during the 1960s was beyond the reach of the average resident.[18]

These developments served to stimulate long-standing grievances over the federal government's failure to return "ceded lands" promised in the Organic Act that spelled out the terms of America's assumption of sovereign power over the islands in 1900. Hawai'i's congressional delegation was especially desirous to secure the return to Hawaiians of those lands rendered surplus for military purposes. The handover of such lands was required by law but was never acknowledged by U.S. military authorities, though it amounted to one-third of the islands' land mass. When Hawaiian appeals for redress failed in the courts, Inouye and Fong sought to secure remedial bipartisan legislation in the form of Senate Bill S. 227, introduced on October 25, 1963. This bill was submitted along with a letter to the then-president of the Senate, Lyndon Baines Johnson, asking him to consider claims that had been recognized by the United States for many years and also address further losses of land via executive orders. However, when the president did turn to the subject of Hawaiian lands, within days after the passage of the Gulf of Tonkin Resolution, he issued three executive orders reserving additional public land and private property for military use. These properties, Fort Shafter Military Reservation, the Makua Military Reservation, and at the Pohakuloa Training Area, were expected to and delivered vital assistance to military operations in Indochina but were to become important targets of both the anti-war movement and the Hawaiian movement.[19] In the short term, the land issue was overshadowed by the delegation's more immediate concern: how to preserve the noncommunist Republic of Vietnam (the south) from an insurrection that was managed and supplied by the communist Democratic Republic of Vietnam (the north).

Testing the Limits of Limited War

The Gulf of Tonkin Resolution marked the beginning of the delegation's war-long effort to reconcile their commitments to peace with the determination of successive presidential administrations to employ escalating force to thwart the communist threat to the existence of South Vietnam. The delegation's labors passed through three distinct phases.

In the first phase, lasting from 1964 to 1965, the delegation accepted the burden of defending South Vietnam on the condition, laid down explicitly by President Johnson, that the United States was committed to waging a limited war with limited objectives that were to be achieved through negotiation and not the destruction or conquest of North Vietnam. They had voted for the Gulf of Tonkin Resolution because, due to their long interest in Asia, the delegation was well aware of the developing crisis that led the president to request more freedom to confront acts of war by the north against U.S. forces assisting in the defense of the south. Along with virtually every member of Congress, they also deferred to the long-standing tradition of presidential leadership of the country's foreign affairs. However, their support of the president's actions chiefly arose from their trust in his concern for world peace, as did the people of Hawai'i through their local leaders: on August 24, 1964, the state of Hawai'i's House and Senate endorsed the delegation's position on the Gulf of Tonkin legislation in a concurrent resolution to that effect.[20]

Unfortunately, the situation in Vietnam during the winter of 1964 deteriorated to the point that by the spring of 1965, Johnson believed he had no choice but to send American troops to Vietnam in increasing numbers and approve bombing inside the borders of North Vietnam. The Hawai'i delegation did not fault Johnson for taking these steps in the defense of the south, as once American forces were engaged in warfare, they believed they should do everything necessary to support them. However, there were doubts, especially for Matsunaga, until a meeting with the president on March 9, 1965, after which Matsunaga spoke for all in confiding to their constituents:

> Because of the strong position I had taken towards continuing the advancement of world peace, initially I, too, was seriously disturbed by the Administration's action in Vietnam. I was therefore especially glad to have had the opportunity recently to engage in a frank discussion with the President himself. He assured me . . . that he is against escalating the war as much as anyone else, but sees no other alternative. He has, as you know, made repeated overtures to negotiate to no avail.[21]

Matsunaga's confidence in the correctness of the administration's approach was bolstered by a visit to Vietnam made in connection with a trade mission to countries in Asia in November and December 1965. His briefing in Vietnam on November 30, conducted by U.S. ambassador Henry Cabot Lodge, confirmed his belief that the "fastest way to peace is to convince Hanoi we in the U.S. are fully united in our effort against any form of military aggression as a means of settling disputes between political entities" and that the current level of American military operations would soon lead the north to enter negotiations as had been and remained their intent. He told his constituents that "after viewing the situation at first hand, I am convinced what we are doing is right," which he defined as "a limited war, for limited objectives."[22] On his return from his own trip to Asia, Daniel Inouye expressed similar views.[23]

Staying the Course (1966–1970)

During the second phase, the Hawai'i delegation was forced to grapple with further American escalation—troop increases and intensified bombing—in the face of Hanoi's refusal to negotiate on terms acceptable to the White House. The Hawai'i delegation approved each of these steps. However, with each step, their concern grew that the war in Vietnam was exceeding the president's limited war remit. In the fall of 1966, the delegation supported efforts to invite third parties to jump-start negotiations, such as those involving U Thant, the secretary-general of the United Nations (UN) and the American ambassador to the UN, Arthur Goldberg. Senator Ernest Gruening attributed the failure of these overtures to the president's unwillingness to give these initiatives a chance.[24] That fall, Mink and Matsunaga lost patience with American failed peace initiatives in the face of both the north's and the south's intransigence: they were among forty-five House Democrats and two Republicans protesting calls by the Republic of Vietnam vice president Nguyễn Cao Kỳ for an invasion of the north. This action led Matsunaga to be called out for taking his "first flight as a Dove."[25] The following month, Mink opposed the president's request for an income tax increase. She believed the funds it generated would be used to "feed the ever-expanding cost of the war machine," which was like "administering aspirin to a seriously ill patient who needs major surgery."[26]

Later, Mink alone seemed to take issue with the intensification of the air war over North Vietnam, which came to include the bombing of the largest petroleum depot in that country and of its international port at Haiphong. Sensing a story could be made of a fight between Fong-Matsunaga versus Mink, the editor of the *Honolulu Star-Bulletin* created a forum for the delegation to air its views on the war. Despite the forum's sensational headline, "Two Hawks, One Dove," this discussion, which Inouye joined, established that the delegation had more in common than not. Fong agreed with Matsunaga that oil depots were legitimate targets, but both shared Mink's recognition of the danger that more bombing of the north would increase the chance of war with communist China. They acknowledged the failure of previous air operations and past bombing halts to produce movement toward negotiations, leading them to be dubious that any more could do so. They all rejected the "possible invasion of North Vietnam" as an option, with Fong reminding the newspaper's readers that "our mission there is stop the North Vietnamese invasion and aggression [against] South Vietnam." They all remained opposed to unilateral withdrawal and any political settlement that would impose a government on the people of South Vietnam against their will. Based on his knowledge of the fate of China in 1949, Fong was convinced an American withdrawal would lead to the "abandonment of 15 million Vietnam to the hands of their enemy, and end in a bloodbath." Inouye declared that an unconditional and immediate withdrawal was unacceptable.

This being so, Mink addressed a question that would come back to haunt them: would the throwing of more rocks at the problem solve anything? She drew attention to Secretary of Defense Robert McNamara's grudging admission that the air war ("Rolling Thunder") failed to generate progress toward a settlement, interdict a significant amount of aid from the north, or have any discernable impact on the Democratic Republic of Vietnam's capacity to continue to wage war. There was thus no reason to continue the bombing. Like Matsunaga and Fong, Mink refused to blame the president for this situation as it did take two to negotiate. What was to be done? Her best hope lay in President Nguyễn Văn Thiệu's remark that he might be calling for a bombing halt as a prelude to a meeting between himself and Hồ Chí Minh, which never materialized.[27]

Mink appears to have tried to establish a baseline for the delegation's consideration of the futility of proceeding along the current lines, but her colleagues chose to stay the course. Inouye, a member of the Armed Services Committee, did his best to grill administration officials on strategy and tactics, but his friendship with and trust in the president kept him in check. Ironically, Inouye was describing himself when he later faulted his fellow senators for not speaking up to a president who had surrounded himself with advisers who would not disagree with him. Yet, though Inouye believed the president welcomed dissenting views, he chose not to offer any until after Johnson decided not to seek reelection.[28] Another reason none of the delegation questioned the authority of the president to seek his own way out of the war was that they all believed he was doing his best to do so under challenging circumstances, as did the Hawaiian public: polls showed strong support for the president's continued leadership of the war effort (initially 10 percent opposed it, 59 percent agreed with it, and 20 percent wished him to be more aggressive).[29] Yet, like their delegates in Congress, they became frustrated by the lack of movement toward peace. In early 1967, the Hawai'i State Senate resolved to press the president to "continue all efforts to prevent the expansion of the war in Vietnam and end the war through negotiation."[30]

The Tet offensive, beginning in January 1968, did not change the delegation's overall assessment of the war. Their mandate had always been an end to the war via negotiations rather than an outright military victory. That now seemed inevitable, as CBS newsman Walter Cronkite famously concluded his television commentary that February. They took heart in Johnson's March 31 decision to cap U.S. forces in Vietnam and halt the bombing north of the demilitarized zone and were encouraged by the president's announcement that he would send U.S. representatives to meet with the enemy's representatives in Paris. A drawback for the Democrats in the delegation was that the president had declined to run for reelection, though this freed Inouye from whatever bonds of loyalty he still felt toward the administration's escalatory policies. This was apparent in Inouye's closing remarks at the Democratic National Convention in Chicago that summer, which combined a heartfelt call for peace with a condemnation of the growing "immorality of the war."[31] When Republican Richard M. Nixon succeeded Johnson as president in the ensuing elections, Fong welcomed Nixon's plan for an honorable peace in Vietnam, which Nixon announced along with notice of his candidacy for the presidency on January 30, 1968, and hoped Nixon's new initiative might just lead to negotiations with Hanoi.[32]

End Game

The last phase of the Hawai'i delegation's engagement with the war began with President Nixon's announcement on April 30, 1970, of what became known as the Cambodian incursion. That event marked the parting of ways between Fong and his Democratic colleagues over the further prosecution of limited war. It also came to spur a connection between anti-war sentiment in Hawai'i and the Hawai'i land movement. That division and its results will be addressed from each side of the now divided delegation.

Fong believed that the president's speech to the nation announcing the latest escalation of the war fell within the parameters of limited war he and his colleagues had followed since 1964: coercive measures as a stimulus for negotiations leading to an honorable peace. The Cambodian incursion, followed by the resumption of bombing of the north (expanded to include the mining of the approaches to Haiphong) and the soon-to-be not-so-secret bombing campaigns in Cambodia and Laos, was just an increase in coercive levels to achieve that end. Fong agreed with the president that expanding the war geographically and aggressively would interdict enemy troops and supplies and, when combined with Vietnamization, would quell growing American dissatisfaction with the level of American casualties, compel Hanoi to resume long-stalled peace talks in Paris, and speed the release of American prisoners of war held in the north with peace, as Nixon suggested, achieved by the end of 1971. Unfortunately, much of the country was not prepared for what to them was a peace plan based on expanding the war to other countries and mining another nation's ports without a declaration of war. Others drew attention to confrontations between students protesting the Cambodian incursion that led to clashes with Ohio National Guardsmen at Kent State University that left four dead and a police encounter with students that left two dead in Jackson, Mississippi, as among the rising human cost of the war. Fong was little moved by such criticism. The incursion deeply satisfied those members of his constituency, particularly from the veteran community, who sought more vigorous prosecution of the war. They considered the Cambodian incursion as an opportunity for Americans to "act like men" and thus dispel the "weakness" they believed was spreading across American society, as exemplified by student protestors, who "should be killed," while others hoped Nixon's actions were but a prelude to invasion of North Vietnam.[33] Henrietta G. Rauch wrote, "Why not invade North Vietnam and destroy this cancer at its root, if necessary with nuclear weapons, and when that was accomplished, turn those weapons against China and Russia," moving Fong, often called a "hawk," to note, "Now *that* is a Hawk!"[34]

Yet, Fong replied to each of those letters of support in the same measured voice the entire delegation had used for years in answering both pro and con letters on Vietnam: that he was glad to have their opinion and remained strong in his long-term commitment to peace through negotiations. In one such letter recalling Mink's warning that they should not try to "solve the problem by throwing more rocks at it," Fong noted that the delegation "had all agreed that the war must end in negotiations, which were intended to produce a political settlement that would not impose a government on the people of South Vietnam against their will." Still believing that any alternative outcome would lead to a bloodbath, Fong placed his faith in Nixon's stated commitment to those same objectives.[35]

However, Fong failed to take adequate notice of several developments. Many Hawaiians who, like Fong, believed that foreign policy was the domain of the president, were now asking him how Fong could support a president's "blitzkrieg" as a representative of the Hawaiian people who were so urgent about peace. They told Fong that "saving our face is not worth more than the two million Vietnamese which [have] already been lost in Vietnam" and took him to task for opposing the values of the East-West Center he helped found. Republican members of the "establishment" and "not hippies" announced that they were no longer members of the "silent majority" which they believed Nixon had relied on for support for military action. A veteran back from service with the 82nd Airborne begged Fong to "stop this insane war," while one still-serving soldier simply wrote, "In Nam, act for peace."[36]

Moreover, the anti-war students at the University of Hawai'i at Mānoa had emerged as a political threat. Fong's conservative base once thought them to be a nonfactor in Hawai'i politics, as both "Orientals [Asian Americans] and *Haoles* [here meaning students not born and reared in Hawai'i] were believed to be apathetic and too shy to speak out," and even when some had engaged in anti-war activities, their lack of unity and pursuit of the same tactics as mainland anti-war students alienated as many as it attracted to their cause.[37] However, anti-war students grew in strength with their embrace of the Hawaiian land issue, claiming that America's war in Indochina was motivated by the same imperial impulse that led to Hawai'i's loss of independence and the U.S. military's illegal retention of Hawaiian lands. On May 7, 1970, Fong received a letter from a constituent informing him that he had just come from a protest at the university's amphitheater in which "a co-ed, a local girl, gave an impassioned speech calling on the people of Hawai'i to rise up and unite to oppose this war and diminish the military's stranglehold on valuable Hawaiian land. She received a standing ovation. The times they are a-changing."[38] They were changing for students (by May 16, 85 percent of students were opposed to the war)[39] and changing for Fong in terms of his overall political support. He was reelected to the Senate in late 1970 by only 8,000 votes, the smallest margin of his career.

Nevertheless, Fong was committed to support Nixon's Vietnam policy. Between 1970 and 1975, Fong helped fight off, with some early success, congressional efforts to cut off funding for the war, effect the immediate withdrawal of American troops, and curtail the ability of the president to commit the country to acts of war without any consultation with Congress and "hoping and praying" that the Paris Accords would work. He believed that Nixon had strengthened President Thiệu by securing his role as a principal in the future negotiations and expected that the U.S. government "would not tolerate violations of the Paris Accord's provisions."[40] However, he soon was moved to "vote with the majority" to cut funding for the war and, on April 30, 1975, echoed President Gerald Ford's sentiments, telling his constituents, "Our long and controversial involvement is over."[41] The pro-war segment among his constituents blamed Congress for the defeat in Indochina, including Mink and, most particularly, "Benedict Arnold Inouye," who had called the war a "mistake" at the height of the Cambodian protests.[42] They kept Fong informed of their efforts to deny South Vietnamese and Cambodian former leaders any *aloha* by affording them housing in Hawai'i; they derided the courage of the Republic of Vietnam's lost soldiers and fought to stop any Vietnamese refugees from arriving in the state.[43] However, Fong grew detached from these subjects except the POW/MIA movement. Claiming exhaustion, he declined to run for reelection.

The Democratic Members' Response

Fong had supported Nixon's plan to end the war as just a more muscular extension of the Johnson administration's war policy. The Democratic members of the Hawai'i delegation condemned it for the same reason, as the perceived continuation of the failed policies of the past that were driven by the assumption that the right amount of coercion short of all-out war would bring the enemy to enter into genuine negotiations. It was now clear to them that Hanoi would not sign a peace agreement acceptable to the United States (which would insist on the preservation of a free, sovereign regime in the south). Saving the south might likely require a level of destruction of the north at the cost of thousands more American lives and certainly thousands more Vietnamese lives and raised to a higher level their long-standing concern that American action on the Sino-Vietnamese border might produce a catastrophe. The bitter truth was that a limited war could not deliver the negotiated settlement that they had pledged to support in 1964. Freed from the bounds of loyalty to President Johnson and as shocked as most of their constituents at Nixon's abuse of his constitutional power as they perceived it, Matsunaga and Mink in the House and Inouye in the Senate supported, wrote, or cosponsored many of the earliest pieces of legislation aimed at achieving reductions in military spending on the war in Vietnam and Cambodia, developing a definite date for the withdrawal of American military forces, and restricting the president's war powers. From 1970 to the end of the war, Matsunaga worked closely with Senator Mark Hatfield (D-OR), effectively keeping anti-war legislation in the House in play by arguing how changes in the war situation warranted a reconsideration of the American policy in Southeast Asia, especially in the wake of the rapid reductions in U.S. forces that, he argued, jeopardized the safety of the decreasing number still in the south: the passage of the War Powers Act in 1973 owed much to Matsunaga's almost three years of persistent work and eloquent speech in its support.[44]

Mink took the war to the American people in two ways. She mounted a campaign for the Democratic nomination for the presidency on an anti-war platform in 1972 and, on April 21 of that same year, visited the then-stalled peace negotiation in Paris. There, she met with U.S. delegates, North Vietnamese officials, and Mme. Nguyễn Thi Binh, foreign minister of the Provisional Revolutionary Government of South Vietnam. Neither action had the impact that she hoped, while the latter earned her the epithet Pink Patsy. She was then asked how she expected to fare among her constituents in a state "with a heavy military presence." She replied, "It was a case of living up to my own views and my own conscience. If I was defeated for it, that's the way it had to be."[45] Just how attuned Mink was in matters of conscience with her electorate is suggested by her winning reelection in all her subsequent runs for a seat in the House.

By then, Inouye had already grasped the importance of the anti-war movement's growing connection not only with the illegal retention by the military of Hawaiian lands but also with the economic and cultural plight of native and poor Hawaiians. These concerns were thrown into high relief by events occurring in Oʻahu's Kalama Valley, where families pushed by developers and land speculators out of the cities and prime rural land had taken up residence. Many were native Hawaiians, but there were others who shared their poverty and also shared a love of the Hawaiian traditions and lifestyles that were falling away after statehood. Beginning in 1969, the trust that owned the land, influenced by pro-development interests, began to evict them from the valley. Even as their numbers dwindled, they began to organize to resist their eviction, which was noticed by anti-war students at the University of Hawaiʻi at Mānoa. Between 1970 and 1971, student protest took on a local character by aligning itself, carefully and with great respect, to those *kamaʻāina* (those at one with the spirit of the land) fighting homelessness and the growing material despoliation of the land. This battle was a key contributor to the evolution of the "Hawaiian movement," an element of which would evolve into the Hawaiian sovereignty movement.[46] Inouye took notice of the symbolic tent city for the homeless erected at the University of Hawaiʻi at Mānoa campus and inserted the Hawaiian land issue into the 1970 gubernatorial campaign. That he then did not do more, he later attributed to the struggle to end the war, but would soon return to it.[47]

Building the Peace

Within five years after the end of the Vietnam War, the Democratic wartime members of the Hawaiʻi delegation were working on ways to heal the divisions and address the setback to peace they believed to have been occasioned by the conflict in Southeast Asia. They paid particular attention to advancing legislation restoring and expanding civil liberties, addressing the health and educational needs of veterans, and providing manifold public services to native Hawaiians and the Indigenous peoples, minorities, and marginalized populations of the Asia Pacific. Mink pursued those goals as the assistant under secretary of state for oceans and international environmental and scientific affairs in the Carter administration from 1977 to 1979. During her time in the House of Representatives, her sponsorship of pioneering gender equality legislation culminated in the passing of Title IX in 1972, now known as the Patsy T. Mink Equal Opportunity in Education Act.

After the Paris Accords, Matsunaga returned to his concern that although there were military academies to train and teach doctrines of warfare, his country had yet to build an academy to teach peace making. He led a successful drive to create the Senate-funded Commission on Proposals for the National Academy of Peace and Conflict Resolution that culminated in the creation of United States Institute of Peace (USIP) in 1985. Richard Solomon, as president of USIP, attributed its very existence to Matsunaga, remarking that "Senator Matsunaga was ahead of his time. He wanted a peacemaking institution in the middle of the Cold War. He recognized the need to defend our country in war, but also demonstrated his commitment to peace."[48]

In 1977, Senator Matsunaga (elected to Fong's seat) joined with Inouye and Daniel K. Akaka[49] in engaging the Hawai'i land issue. All three addressed the current focal point of Hawaiian interest—the return to the Hawaiian people of the island of Kaho'olawe. This island was often called Target Island in derision, as it was long used as a bombing range by the U.S. Navy. In the 1970s, supporters of the Hawai'i movement organized as Protect Kaho'olawe 'Ohana (PKO). They then began a series of occupations of the island in an effort to halt bombing. As a result of the PKO's unrelenting pressure, in 1990 President George H. W. Bush ended the bombing of Kaho'olawe. Inouye was chiefly responsible for Title X of the 1994 Department of Defense Appropriations Act, which authorized the conveyance of Kaho'olawe and its surrounding waters back to the state of Hawai'i. The Hawai'i land issue and related sovereignty claims remain controversial, but the war marked an important watershed in the political and social history of Hawai'i.[50]

Conclusion

This chapter examined Hawai'i's engagement with the Vietnam War through the lens of its wartime congressional delegation with a view toward providing a richer, more complex understanding of the period in its own history and in its nation's foreign affairs. This analysis reminds us that unlike any other American state or territory, its majority Asian American population had ties with Asian nations struggling against communist aggression. In the effort to assist them, the delegation drew on their own experience of combat and/or public service in the cause of self-determination and democracy. They were also guided by their exposure to the Hawaiian values they shared with the majority of their constituents, who endorsed the delegation's effort to pursue peace through negotiations encouraged by limited military action. When the level of violence employed to achieve the ends of limited war in Indochina reached beyond acceptable levels, they chose peace over any other consideration. Although the delegation's efforts to secure a negotiated peace "through aloha" failed, their preference for soft power still has resonance in conflict resolution circles, and they succeeded in building lasting local and national institutions for the promotion of peace across the Asia Pacific.

Notes

Citations to the Congressional Collection, Archives and Manuscripts Department, Hamilton Library, University of Hawai'i at Mānoa (CC) refer to the papers of Daniel Inouye (DI), "Spark" Masayuki Matsunaga (SMM), and Hiram Fong (HF), by box number (BN) and folder name. For example, Hiram Fong, box 80, Legislative/Foreign Relations/Vietnam/Cambodia reads, CC/HF/BN80/LFRVN/CAM/Correspondence Supporting the War.

1. There is only one study that has as yet offered an in-depth analysis of the impact of the Vietnam War on an American state, and through it, the nation, as opposed to how it serviced the war effort and addressed its local human and material cost. See Marcia Eymann and Charles Wollenberg, eds., *Next Stop Vietnam: California and the Nation Transformed* (Berkeley: University of California Press, 2004), which addresses subjects such as how Silicon Valley was a product of wartime federal funding for California's aerospace industries and research universities.

2. See George Cooper and Gavan Daws, *Land and Power in Hawai'i: The Democratic Years* (Honolulu: Benchmark Books, 1988); Tom Coffman, *The Island Edge of America: A Political History of Hawai'i* (Honolulu: University of Hawai'i Press, 2003); and Susan Y. Najita, *Decolonizing Cultures in the Pacific: Reading History and Trauma in Contemporary Fiction* (New York: Routledge, 2006).

3. Noel E. Kent and Dan Boyland, *Hawai'i: Islands under the Influence* (Honolulu: University of Hawai'i Press, 2016); Kyle Kajihiro, "Nation under the Gun: Militarism

and Resistance in Hawaiʻi," *Cultural Survival Quarterly* (March 2002), https://www.culturalsurvival.org/publications/cultural-survival-quarterly/nation-under-gun-militarism-and-resistance-hawaii.

4. Haunani-Kay Trask, "The Struggle for Hawaiʻian Sovereignty—Introduction," *Cultural Survival Quarterly* (March 2002), https://www.culturalsurvival.org/publications/cultural-survival-quarterly/ struggle-hawaiian-sovereignty-introduction.

5. Tom Coffman, *Catch a Wave*, 2nd ed. (Honolulu: University of Hawaiʻi Press, 1973), 9, 54.

6. Masatochi Fujimoto, October 29, 1965, and William H. Ewing, "The Time Has Come," *Honolulu Star Bulletin*, June 9, 1965 (clipping), CC/HF/BN80/LFRVN/January–November/1965; Paul Lovinger to Matsunaga, May 28 and July 1, 1965, CC/SMM/BN250-C-316/FRVN/Folder/1.

7. Milani B. Trask, "The Hawaiʻian Sovereignty Movement," *Cultural Survival Quarterly* (March 2002), https://www.culturalsurvival.org/publications/cultural-survival-quarterly/Hawaiʻian-sovereignty.

8. Thomas P. Gill served one term in the House of Representatives (1962–1964), declined to run for reelection, voted in favor of the Gulf of Tonkin Resolution in August 1964, and thereafter focused solely on the race for governor of Hawaiʻi.

9. See James M. Caffrey, *Going for Broke* (Norman: University of Oklahoma Press, 2017).

10. "Recording of Telephone Conversation between Lyndon B. Johnson and Hubert Humphrey, 10:41AM, Citation #30, Recordings and Transcripts of Conversations and Meetings, the Lyndon Johnson Presidential Library and Museum, Austin, TX.

11. Richard Halloran, "Sparky, a New Book Explores the Life of Sen. Spark M. Matsunaga, a Kauai Boy Who Helped a Reluctant Nation Accept Its Asian-American Brothers," *Honolulu Star Bulletin*, July 11, 2002, http://www.archives.starbulletin.com/2002/07/07/editorial/indexspecial.html.

12. George Miller, "Memorial Addresses and other Tributes held in the House of Representatives and the Senate of the United States together with Memorial Services in Honor of Patsy T. Mink Late a Representative from Hawaii, One Hundred Seventh Congress Second Session," 150, https://www.govinfo.gov/content/pkg/CPRT-107JPRT82489/pdf/CPRT-107JPRT82489.pdf.

13. Michaelyn Pi-Hsia Chou, "The Education of a Senator: Hiram L. Fong from 1906 to 1954" (PhD diss., University of Hawaiʻi, 1980), 733.

14. "Hawaiian Senator Here; Praises Aid for Asians," *Los Angeles Times*, January 5, 1960, https://history.house.gov/People/Detail/15032451315.

15. Diana Leone, "Peace Institutes Realize Vision," *Honolulu Advertiser*, August 20, 2009, http://the.honoluluadvertiser.com/article/2009/Aug/20/In/Hawaii908/20034.

16. Howard E. Howland, "The East-West Center," *International Education & Cultural Exchange* (Fall 1965): 33–34.

17. Vincent Esposito to Matsunaga, July 3, 1963, SMM/BN267-C-333/East-West Center, Part 2 of 2.

18. "Talks on the Land Problem," *Honolulu Hochi*, April 13, 1968, among many related clippings in SMM/BN591-C-117/Hawaiʻi Lands/1963 [1963–1969].

19. "Conveyance of Certain Lands to the State of Hawai'i," *Congressional Record* (Bound), 109, Part 15, October 31, 1963, 20786, and Executive Orders 11165, 11166, and 11167, accessed June 11, 2021, https://www.archives.gov/federal-register/executive-orders/1964.html. The resistance to these bases is traced in Kyle Kajihiro, "A Brief Overview of Militarization and Resistance in Hawai'i," A DMZ-Hawai'i / Aloha 'Aina Paper (2007), accessed December 2020, http://www.dmzHawai'i.org/dmz-legacy-site/overview_military_in_Hawai'i.pdf.

20. State of Hawai'i, "Concurrent Joint Resolution No. 2, Southeast Asia," SRJ 189 and HJR 115, August 24, 1964.

21. Matsunaga to Margaret Grey, March 12, 1965, CC/SMM/BN250-C-316/FR/Foreign Aid/Vietnam. See like-minded sentiments expressed by Fong to Harold Shin, October 25, 1965, CC/HF/BN80/LFRVN/January–November/1965.

22. Matsunaga to Major Kenneth K. Ikeda, March 9, 1966, SMM/BN250-C-316/Foreign Aid/Vietnam/1966–1967.

23. "Oral History Transcript, Daniel K. Inouye," interview 2 (II), 5/2/1969, by Dorothy Pierce (McSweeney), LBJ Library Oral Histories, LBJ Presidential Library, 27–30, accessed June 10, 2021, https://www.discoverlbj.org/item/oh-inouyed-19690502-2-75-27-b.

24. "Widening the Credibility Gap," *Congressional Record* (Bound), 112, Part 20, October 17, 1966, 27247 (Statement by Senator Gruening).

25. Robert K. Walsh, "47 in House Blast Ky for Urging a Wider War," *Evening Star*, July 30, 1966; and "Matsunaga Takes First Flight with the Doves," *Honolulu Advertiser*, July 31, 1966, attached to Robert E. Gibson to Matsunaga, August 2, 1966, CC/SMM/BN251-C-316/FR/Foreign Aid/Vietnam/Part 2.

26. Matthew Andrew Wasniewski, ed., *Women in Congress* (Washington, DC: U.S. Government Printing Office, 2006), 426.

27. Frank Hewlett, "Three Hawks and One Dove, Isle Delegation Bares Views on War, U.S. Goals," *Honolulu Star-Bulletin*, October 14, 1967, 1, 4, clipping in SMM/BN250-C-316/LFRVN/1966–1967.

28. McSweeney, "Oral History Transcript, Daniel K. Inouye," 24–27.

29. "Vietnam at the Polls," *Honolulu Advertiser*, November 20, 1965, clipping at CC/SSM/BN250-C-116/FRVN/1965/Part 1; Fong, "Special Note on Poll," CC/HF/BN80/LFRVN/1967.

30. State of Hawai'i, Fourth Legislature, "Senate Concurrent Resolution (Yoshinaga)," No. 216, April 20, 1967.

31. "Transcript of the Keynote Address by Senator Inouye Decrying Violent Protests," *New York Times*, August 27, 1968, https://www.nytimes.com/1968/08/27/archives/transcript-of-the-keynote-address-by-senator-inouye-decrying.html.

32. Fong to Roy L. Farrow, November 24, 1969, CC/HF/BN83/LFRVN/CAM/1969–1970.

33. L. Hancock, May 15, 1970; Terry Lawrence, May 15, 1970; Ralph Seeley, May 20, 1970; J. Walter Silver, May 20, 1970; to Fong, CC/HF/BN81/LFRVN/CAM/1970–1976/Correspondence/Supporting War/1970.

34. Note by Fong on Letter from Henriette G. Rutch to Fong, June 9, 1970, CC/HF/BN81/LFRVN/CAM/1970–1976/Correspondence/Supporting War/1970.

35. Fong to R. A. Stewart, May 27, 1970, CC/HF/BN81/LFRVN/CAM/1970–1976/Correspondence/Supporting War/ 1970.

36. Larry LeDoux, May 8,1970; Stuart Bolden, May 7, 1970; Doris Aragaki, May 13, 1970; Louis Box, May 7, 1970; Mary and Arthur Smith, May 21, 1970; John C. Swindell, May 6, 1970; and Philip Hunnicutt, May 7, 1970, to Fong, CC/HF/BN80/LFRVN/CAM/1970–1976/Correspondence/Opposing War.

37. Joycelyn Yamamoto, May 6, 1970; and Rose Louie, May 9, 1970, to Fong, CC/HF/BN80/LFRVN/CAM/1970–1976/Correspondence/Opposing War.

38. D. Kamins Quenes to Fong, May 7, 1970, CC/HF/BN80/LFRVN/CAM/1970–1976/Correspondence/Opposing War.

39. Gaius Thede to Fong, May 16, 1970, CC/HF/BN80/LFRVN/CAM/1970–1976/Correspondence/Opposing War.

40. Fong Note, January 24, 1973, composed after a briefing by Henry Kissinger, CC/HF/BN81/Peace Settlement/1973–1975/Part 2.

41. Fong to Leon A. Thevin, April 30, 1975, HF/BN81/LFR/VN/CAM/Opposition to Vietnamese Refugees.

42. George P. Gordon to Fong, May 22, 1970, CC/HF/BN81/LFRVN/CAM/Correspondence Supporting War.

43. See large collection of such letters in CC/HF/BN81/Opposition to Immigration of Vietnamese Refugees.

44. "End of Indochina Conflict," *Congressional Record* (Bound), House, 116, Part 2, February 1, 1971, 2181 (Statement by Mr. Matsunaga); *The War Powers Resolution: Relevant Documents* (Washington, DC: U.S. Government Printing Office, 1975), 18–19.

45. "Mink, Patsy," *Current Biography, 1968* (New York: H. W. Wilson, 1968), 255.

46. Haunani-Kay Trask, "The Birth of the Modern Hawai'ian Movement: Kalama Valley, O'ahu," accessed February 24, 2021, https://www.marxists.org/history/erol/ncm-1a/hawaii.pdf.

47. Interview with Daniel K. Inouye by Gavan Daws, University of Hawai'i at Mānoa, Hamilton Library, Rare Book, Asia Collection, DU627.5.A2.J46.no. 27 np.

48. Richard H. Solomon, "Spark Matsunaga's Legacy: The United States Institute of Peace," accessed June 18, 2021, https://www.usip.org/spark-matsunagas-legacy-united-states-institute-peace.

49. Daniel K. Akaka (1924–2018) was the first Hawaiian of native ancestry to serve in Congress. As senator, he sponsored the Akaka Bill, a failed attempt to advance Hawaiian sovereign rights.

50. Rob Perez, "The U.S. Owes Hawaiians Millions of Dollars' Worth of Land," *Honolulu Star Advertiser*, May 7, 2021, https://www.staradvertiser.com/2021/05/07/breaking-news/promised-land-the-u-s-owes-hawaiians-millions-of-dollars-worth-of-land-congress-helped-make-sure-the-debt-wasnt-paid/.

7 GI Resistance and Transpacific Activism in Iwakuni during the Vietnam War
A Piece of Forgotten History

NORIKO SHIRATORI

During America's infamous war in Vietnam, global waves of anti-war protests erupted. People in the Asia-Pacific region protested, too, especially in countries with prominent U.S. military bases. Among those countries was Japan—the launching pad for the U.S. armed forces into the wider region. When the United States started a bombing campaign in North Vietnam in February 1965, Beheiren (**Be**tonamu ni **Hei**wa wo! Shimin **Rengō** [Citizens' Committee for Peace in Vietnam]) was launched in Tokyo with the sole purpose of bringing peace to Vietnam. Beheiren quickly became the driving force of an anti–Vietnam War movement that spread across Japan with 393 (known) local chapters. Engaged in various activities, the Beheiren movement was active from 1965 to 1974. This chapter focuses on Beheiren's collaboration with GI resistance in Iwakuni, where Americans have been stationed at the U.S. Marine Corps Air Station (MCAS) since 1945.

Iwakuni is a conservative small town, located in southwest Japan in Yamaguchi prefecture, a one-hour train ride from Hiroshima. Yamaguchi has produced eight prime ministers, including most recently, Abe Shinzo. Abe's grandfather Kishi Nobusuke, a former class A war criminal, was prime minister from 1957 to 1960 but was forced to resign after the 1960 protests against the Japan-U.S. Security Treaty. His grand-uncle and Kishi's brother, Sato Eisaku, was the prime minister during the critical years of the Vietnam War, from 1964 to 1972. Ironically, in the early 1970s, transpacific activism by transnational anti-war actors flourished in Iwakuni, the electoral base of Japan's right-wing political family.

This chapter is based on archives including newsletters published by Beheiren such as *Beheiren Nyūsu*, *Dassōhei Tsūshin*, and *JATEC Tsūshin*, from 1965 to 1974, other publications by former Beheiren activists, and interviews with some of them. After introducing the origins of Beheiren and its development, the chapter shows how transpacific activism emerged and developed in Iwakuni by examining several major examples of transpacific collaboration.

Origins of the Beheiren Movement and Its Transnational Development

Beheiren was founded by postwar Japanese intellectuals who possessed experience abroad and already had broad transnational networks, both of which were uncommon in 1965 Japan. Their networks included academics, artists, and American civil rights activists. Inspired by theories used in the civil rights movement, Beheiren's activity was based on the principle of nonviolent direct action. The core actors of Beheiren were born in the 1930s and were elementary school children when they learned of Japan's defeat through Emperor Hirohito's radio broadcast on August 15, 1945.[1] Some children felt that they were deceived by the adults because their teachers immediately reversed the narratives from "imperialism" to "democracy" and that was not what those children had been taught throughout elementary school. Takahashi Taketomo and Motono Yoshio, who played a critical role in assisting American deserters in the late 1960s, were among those children who witnessed the adults suddenly change their positions. Takahashi, a former professor of French literature, said, "The adults could reverse their minds overnight, but we children could not, so there was a great sense of betrayal."[2] He decided never to become an adult who deceived children. Motono, a former TV producer, also stressed, "Our generation is skeptical toward power. I don't trust those who support power. That has become my lifestyle."[3] Twenty years later, the war in Vietnam triggered their sense of distrust of authority.

Beheiren was managed loosely by a fraction of this wartime generation of writers, philosophers, mathematicians, scientists, professors, artists, musicians, filmmakers, TV producers, and students. War-weary ordinary citizens who were sick of anything concerning "war" also actively joined them. In its first phase, Beheiren focused on publicity that included posting anti-war ads in the *New York Times* in 1965. Tsurumi Yoshiyuki, an anthropologist, pointed out that anti-war ads in the *New York Times* were emblematic of Beheiren's style of "turning daily mannerisms upside down" because it reversed postwar Japan-U.S. relations by giving money to the American press to express "our" idea, instead of "we" receiving money and the "right" idea from America as had been the case for the previous twenty years.[4] Beheiren also held various lectures and conferences by inviting internationally known figures such as Jean-Paul Sartre, Simone de Beauvoir, Howard Zinn, Thích Nhất Hạnh, and Joan Baez to Japan. They also handed out flyers directly to GIs around the U.S. bases, urging them to desert.

Starting in 1967, when American deserters actually emerged on the streets of Tokyo and found the organization, Beheiren underwent a transformation as it became involved in underground activities. Countless ordinary people took turns sheltering American deserters in their homes and helped them move out of Japan to Sweden in cooperation with the Soviet Union at the height of the Cold War. By the late 1960s, however, as the number of deserters increased, there were several incidents involving American intelligence officials masquerading as GIs, whom the Japanese media called spies. After some arrests of deserters by American military police (MP) in cooperation with Japanese police made national and international headlines, Beheiren realized that assisting deserters had become unsustainable.

By 1970, while the civil rights movement was already declining in the United States, its successor, the Black Power movement, was thriving beyond U.S. borders along with the anti–Vietnam War movement. Black GIs who were empowered by the Black Power movement were active players in the GI movement wherever there were U.S. military bases. David Cortright, who had served in Vietnam himself, observed that fragging, mutiny, soaring desertions, and rising dissent threatened to destroy the American military apparatus.[5] Underground GI newspapers distributed by GIs played a critical role in sustaining the resistance. The year 1970 was also the designated time for renewing the Japan-U.S. Security Treaty—the same treaty that had mobilized Japanese to an unprecedented scale of anti-security treaty protests, so called ANPO Tōsō in 1960, in which future founders of Beheiren had fought fiercely. A decade later, Japan was again in a tumultuous period of political protest, which was also directly connected to the Japan-U.S. Security Treaty, which allowed for the widespread and permanent presence of U.S. bases in Japan.[6] At the time, young American anti-war activists and young Beheiren activists connected through their passion of stopping America's war in Vietnam.

As anti-war GI networks expanded overseas, American anti-war civilian activists flooded to Japan and U.S.-occupied Okinawa and worked closely with Beheiren. Although Japan itself had been fully independent after the Allied occupation ended in 1952, the United States retained control of what had been its southern-most prefecture of Okinawa for another twenty years. While anti-war activity was peaking in Japan, the Japanese and U.S. governments were negotiating the reversion of Okinawa to Japanese control, under the terms of the joint security treaty. Consequently, American activists could freely travel to U.S.-occupied Okinawa, but Japanese could not go there without a passport, and not many Japanese citizens had a passport. Japanese activists therefore learned information about conditions in Okinawa from American activists. Those American activists, already having information on Iwakuni and Beheiren, targeted Iwakuni as the front line for stopping the war in Vietnam.

The first important collaboration that American activists brought to Beheiren was the Pacific Counseling Services (PCS) that provided GIs pragmatic advice and helped them file for legal discharge such as through conscientious objector (CO) status. PCS was originally founded by Sidney Peterman, a Unitarian minister, in 1969 near Fort Ord in Monterey, California. PCS soon expanded across the U.S. bases in the Asia-Pacific region, including Iwakuni.[7] Hearing about the rise of GI resistance in Japan, Peterman, wearing his ankle-length black clerical robes and a high collar, visited the Beheiren office in Tokyo in early 1970.[8] Soon, a PCS office was added to the Beheiren office in June 1970.[9] This delighted Fujieda Mioko, a feminist scholar who had been recruited by Beheiren for her English proficiency. She had been frustrated by the gap between the slang-filled English that American GIs used and the English she knew, which she felt was too polite and middle class for the situation of screening young American GIs who had escaped from the base. "Our understanding had been simplistic. An American soldier who escaped from the base was a deserter. We had no idea about terms like AWOL (Absence Without Leave) or Conscientious Objection. So, when Sid (Peterman) appeared, I was delighted. It was like a ray of sunshine in the dark. Sid immediately started assisting GIs with applying for legal discharge."[10]

The PCS staff had the knowledge and skills to tackle the problems of antiwar GIs. Eric Seitz, a civil rights attorney who would later come to Japan, was the first student member of the National Executive Board of the National Lawyers Guild (NLG). Seitz explained, "The PCS was part of the group urging us because they knew we did most of the anti-war military representation. They urged us to go to Asia. I started military cases in the Bay Area in 1967 while still a law student at Berkeley. The NLG was the only organization that provided lawyers to people in the military. Nobody else was doing that."[11]

Through the American activists, Beheiren learned that helping GIs obtain legal discharge was more effective than assisting deserters to get out of Japan because that was what GIs wanted the most and what the American military authorities hated the most.[12] In the summer of 1970, Beheiren expanded GI counseling services around all the U.S. bases in Japan. One major event called the Vietnam Summer in Japan involved a collaboration between the PCS, Black Panthers, Student Nonviolent Coordinating Committee (SNCC), Asian American Committee, and Concerned Asian Scholars Committee.[13] Sidney Tarrow suggests that transnational brokers provide domestic activists with access to resources, information, and legitimacy.[14] Serving as transnational brokers, American activists certainly brought Beheiren new technical and legal knowledge with a pragmatic approach.

Transpacific Activism Developed in Early 1970s Iwakuni

Marine Corps Air Station Iwakuni is one of the largest U.S. Marine bases in the Asia-Pacific region. As it became the center of GI resistance, the Pentagon repeatedly sent more officials to Japan to repress the escalating GI resistance in Iwakuni around 1970.[15] Seitz recalled the global situation in this small base town. "Of all the places in Asia, Iwakuni was by far the hottest. There were great things happening in the Philippines because it was such a volatile place, but as far as the numbers of military people who got involved with 'things,' there was nothing like Iwakuni. Iwakuni was actually one of the most insurgent bases in the world. It was the place. There were very tightly organized Black GIs in Iwakuni. All of us were constantly watched and harassed by Japanese Security Police. But I fully enjoyed working with Beheiren."[16]

Cortright also pointed out that MCAS Iwakuni possessed one of the most consistently successful GI organizations in Asia.[17] One factor that contributed to the volatility in Iwakuni was racism, which was rampant in the U.S. military. From the late 1960s, Beheiren's newsletters continuously reported racism and race-related incidents in the U.S. bases, particularly that of Iwakuni, given its large number of Black GIs who were empowered by the Black Power movement. Because of this known volatility, Americans and Beheiren student activists from other parts of Japan headed to Iwakuni where they immediately collaborated to protest, marching past the base and flying massive kites by the MCAS runway to stop fighter planes such as the Phantom from leaving for Vietnam.

Among the events in Iwakuni that eventually hit both the Pentagon and the Japanese government, this chapter examines in chronological order five critical collaborations created by these rapidly emerging transpacific actors: (1) the underground GI newspaper *Semper Fi*, (2) the first U.S. court-martial in which an American GI was defended by a Japanese lawyer, (3) national news on nuclear weapons in Iwakuni, (4) the *Free the Army* (FTA) tour, and (5) the GI coffeehouse, called the Hobbit. As there was no internet or cell phones in those days, information about these things was mostly spread by word of mouth, globally from one U.S. base to another by GIs, and throughout Japan by Beheiren's newsletters.

Underground GI Newspaper: *Semper Fi*

GI newspapers, which peaked in 1971, provided rank-and-file GIs with the opportunity to see what was going on. Among at least 259 (known) such papers published by 1971, fifteen GI newspapers were published in Japan and seven in U.S.-occupied Okinawa.[18] One Black GI shared his experience with Beheiren:

> I'm black. All I did in high school was sports. I was not prepared for college, so I applied to the service. I didn't want to die, and in the military, we don't get the information we need. I started thinking about what was going on. I have seen people put in jail with no particular reason. In Germany, I gradually understood the truth about the military. I made a decision to disobey orders and to fight against the pigs. They didn't tell me anything about underground papers like *Black Panther*, but I found and read them. Eventually, a revolution that I never knew about occurred. A black revolution.[19]

Semper Fi, motto of the Marine Corps meaning "Always Faithful," was launched in January 1970 by members of the American Servicemen's Union in the Iwakuni marine base as a collaborative project. GIs wrote stories; Iwakuni Beheiren received the drafts and sent them to Chris Cowley at the World Friendship Center in Hiroshima, who typed up the draft. Hiroshima Beheiren then printed them and delivered the papers to Iwakuni, after which Iwakuni Beheiren activists handed the papers out to GIs around the bar area near the base.[20] Later, printing *Semper Fi* was all processed in Iwakuni. *Semper Fi* gained many readers, but its staff endured repeated harassment and arrests that often resulted in immediate repatriation to the United States. Such information was immediately reported by *Semper Fi*.

On Thursday, 23 April, Bob Dorton left Iwakuni for Camp Pendleton, California. Brother Bob was kicked out of MCAS by the brass for his part in the 12 April Peace Gathering at Kintai; he had been given less than 36 hours to check out and send home all his gear. Anyone growing weary of his role in the American military occupation of Japan and wishing to return home might take a hint from this episode and join the struggle. Just pack your bags first.[21]

Kintai, a bridge made of five wooden arches in Iwakuni built in 1673, is one of the three most famous bridges in Japan. Beheiren and American activists and GIs often gathered on the Kintai riverbank for rallies. Eventually, news on GI resistance in Iwakuni started appearing in the mainstream media. One TV program even broadcast a documentary in which an American Servicemen's Union member who had applied for conscientious objector status spoke about their movement in Iwakuni, and the public was sympathetic to American GIs.[22] Under these circumstances, a "riot" occurred in Iwakuni base.

The First U.S. Court-Martial in Which an American GI Was Defended by a Japanese Lawyer

On July 4, 1970, a disturbance broke out in the crowded military prison, or brig, on the marine base in Iwakuni. Having pent-up anger with their inhumane treatment, unjust confinement, and utter racism, the inmates destroyed the dining room, broke into a hangar, armed themselves, and occupied the brig for sixteen hours.[23] They did not harm anyone, but military authorities labeled it a "riot" and arrested thirteen GIs. Activists called them the Iwakuni 13. A flyer, *Iwakuni 13's Struggle*, indicated the impact of the transpacific collaboration:

> To this day supporters of the Iwakuni 13, Japanese and Americans alike, feel these 13 men were put in the brig for political, not legal reasons and were courageous to take action that was necessary to awaken the people to the brutal and lawless actions and conditions of the Iwakuni Brig. . . . The "riot" of the Iwakuni 13 and their trials became international news because of the involvement of American and Japanese civilians, including lawyers and newspapermen. There was news about the 13 across Japan and even in the *New York Times*.[24]

Usually, those GIs were immediately repatriated to other bases in the United States, but fearing that Beheiren would hold press conferences as they had always done, the U.S. military authorities instead made the Iwakuni 13 face court-martial right on the Iwakuni marine base. Beheiren formed a defense counsel that consisted of an American civilian lawyer, a Japanese lawyer, and Japanese witnesses who had once sheltered one of the Iwakuni 13, a nineteen-year-old GI named Noam Ewing.[25]

Ewing was in the brig on July 4 when the "riot" occurred because he had been arrested while staying at a local friend's apartment near the base. The first court-martial trial on a U.S. military base in Japan in which a Japanese lawyer defended an American GI was held on November 12, 1970, in the presence of Japanese reporters. The defense team argued that the court-martial was illegal because Ewing's arrest, made outside of the base, was a violation of the Japan-U.S. Security Treaty.[26] According to *Iwakuni 13's Struggle*, transpacific supporters of Ewing jammed the courtroom and formed the largest audience ever for an MCAS court-martial. There was testimony from a Japanese housewife who had sheltered Ewing for three weeks and Tsurumi Shunsuke, a philosopher and one of the Beheiren founders. Tsurumi reminded the audience that the Japanese constitution renounced war and it was the natural duty of Japanese people who lived under this constitution to help Ewing.[27] "Poll shows 80% of Japanese opposed the Vietnam War. So, ordinary Japanese are willing to help soldiers who left the military because of opposition to the war. As long as America has military bases in Japan, you should know that there are many Japanese who think this way. Today, I came here to tell you this."[28]

All the Iwakuni 13 GIs received bad conduct discharges or dishonorable discharges, with only a few months of sentence, which was much lighter than the maximum of forty years. Ono Nobuyuki, the Japanese lawyer who defended Ewing, pointed out that Ewing's behavior was totally legal and justifiable in Japan and that his only mistake was to become an enlistee, thinking there must be some justice in the Vietnam War.[29] Witnessing those events, Beheiren's student activists determined that Iwakuni needed a GI coffeehouse. Students from Kyoto, Hiroshima, and Fukuoka moved to Iwakuni in the fall of 1971 to build a coffeehouse. Right after they settled in Iwakuni, one of the most controversial issues in Japan occurred before their eyes.

National News on Nuclear Weapons in Iwakuni

"Nuclear Weapons in Iwakuni Base?" The headlines in national morning newspapers on November 17, 1971, marked the beginning of more turmoil. This bombshell report was initiated by Narazaki Yanosuke, a member of the House of Representative from the Japan Socialist Party at a meeting of the 67th Diet Okinawa Reversion Agreement Special Committee. Narazaki had obtained evidence of the U.S. military storing nuclear weapons on the Iwakuni base.[30]

Keeping nuclear weapons in Japan was an outright violation of Japan's three-part non-nuclear policy—not to make, possess, or allow entry of nuclear weapons into Japan. Moreover, Iwakuni is less than a one-hour train ride from Hiroshima on which the United States had dropped the first atomic bomb in 1945. This news enraged nuclear-sensitive postwar Japanese citizens and pressured the governments of both Japan and the United States. GIs living on the marine base at Iwakuni had already indicated to Beheiren activists where exactly the nuclear weapons were on the base map.[31] Interestingly, when students checked the actual site on the base after the news, the color was changed from its previous red to yellow within a day of the breaking news, which fueled further speculation.[32]

This was a nightmare for U.S. military authorities. Four GIs involved with *Semper Fi* suddenly disappeared. In his appeal published in Beheiren's newsletter, Seitz, who was to defend the four GIs, articulated why the arrest of the four GIs was unjust, how the Iwakuni base was the worst base in the world, and how he and Ono immediately took action to prepare for the court-martial to defend them.[33] This court-martial never happened because fearing more unwelcome media coverage, the military authorities sent the four GIs back to the United States very early in the morning before Beheiren's scheduled press conference was held.[34] Seitz, who traveled around U.S. bases in Japan, revealed that he might have been involved unknowingly in this matter:

> I went to see guys in the brig when I was in Iwakuni in May 1971. One of the guys gave me a diagram written on a napkin. I didn't know what it was. He didn't tell me what it was. He said, "Give this to the [Beheiren] boys, and they'll know what to do with this." I didn't ask questions. When I came back to Iwakuni in November, it was all over in the newspapers on the front page. I was like, "Oh, oh . . . I remember this. . . ." I was worried, but nobody tied it to me.

> It went through three, four people before it went to the people who published that ... so I don't know who they were, I don't want to know, and I didn't want to know at the time. The U.S. denied it, everyone denied it, flat denial.[35]

Seitz concludes that he does not know if it was true or not, but he does not see any reason it was not true. This news deeply depressed Japan, but Iwakuni came to life again with the news that the FTA show was coming to town the following month as part of its Asia-Pacific tour.

Free the Army Tour in Iwakuni

Beginning in the spring of 1970 in the United States, *Free the Army* (FTA) was a satirical play about the Vietnam War. Its name was a play on the GI expression "F—the army." It was performed only at a few military bases in the United States before it quickly disappeared. According to Seitz, who accompanied the tour, the FTA group initially wanted to go to Vietnam, but they could not, so they contacted PCS. As a result, they decided to come to the Philippines, Japan, and Okinawa. The FTA crew arrived in Tokyo on December 8, 1971, when the diet was still in chaos and the public was still angry about the nuclear weapons on Iwakuni base. The crew including Jane Fonda was initially refused entry to Japan. Beheiren staged a protest at the hotel where the crew was confined and gathered petitions which led to their release.[36] The released crew performed the show near U.S. bases in Yokota, Yokosuka, Iwakuni, and Misawa in Japan, Koza (now Okinawa City) in occupied Okinawa, and also for general audiences in Kyoto and Tokyo.

Beheiren activists coordinated the logistics of the show in Iwakuni, from finding the venue to preparing thousands of chairs.[37] This further strengthened the transpacific network. Seitz positioned the show in Japan as a highly political event implemented by political activists in a very political time. A Japanese student activist from Kyoto pointed out that the FTA tour in Asia was an extension of the struggles that American activists had been experiencing in fighting against their own imperial state in U.S.-occupied Okinawa and Japan.[38]

Decades later, Jane Fonda casually unveiled what she had heard directly from GIs in Iwakuni back then. "One very important thing happened while the tour was in Japan. We filmed an interview with several men at Iwakuni Marine Base who told us that despite the agreement between Japan and the United States following World War II that stipulated nuclear weapons were never again to be brought onto the island, they themselves were moving nuclear weapons around the bases, 'all in secret, all illegal.' They asked us to demand that a search be conducted to uncover the truth. We got nowhere."[39] Ken Cloke, a pioneer in the field of conflict resolution who had been to Japan for a Beheiren conference in 1968 and returned later, updated Fonda about his post-FTA episode in Japan. "Ken Cloke told me that when he'd gone to the Philippines and Japan to visit coffeehouses right after FTA had been there, bootlegged audiotapes of the show were 'selling like hotcakes' among soldiers and were even circulated in Vietnam."[40] A DVD, *FTA: The Show the Pentagon Couldn't Stop*, became available in 2008. A blurb on the back states, "Available for the first time since it mysteriously disappeared in 1972 'after only one week' in theaters, this raucous film is a riveting slice of the Vietnam antiwar movement."[41] While they kept working on building a GI coffeehouse in Iwakuni, Beheiren students also made sure that the FTA show in Iwakuni was successful. The coffeehouse that GIs were looking forward to was about to open.

GI Coffeehouse: The Hobbit

The first GI coffeehouse, UFO, was launched near Fort Jackson in Columbia, South Carolina, in January 1968 by Fred Gardner, a former editor of the *Harvard Crimson*. After his own active-duty tour, Gardner was convinced that anti-war groups needed to connect with GI movements.[42]

Beheiren's student activists who decided to build a GI coffeehouse in Iwakuni were middle school students when Beheiren was founded in 1965. They had been watching Beheiren thriving nationwide and were excited by it. They got involved when opportunities appeared. Older activists of Beheiren wholeheartedly supported whatever the younger activists did. Hearing that a GI coffeehouse would open in Iwakuni, *Semper Fi* informed its readers. "In the near future GIs stationed here at Iwakuni will have available to them a GI Coffeehouse. It will be maintained and staffed by Semper Fi supporters. Donations cards are being distributed to help cover expenses. Buy one and help get the Coffeehouse started. Power to the people!!!"[43] The *Semper Fi* members also helped with the carpentry work and GIs generously donated to the newspaper.[44] Its announcement of the naming of the coffeehouse, the Hobbit, indicates their excitement:

> This coffeehouse is for us, the G.I.s, so that we have a place to unwind and relax, to escape the stress of military hassles for a few

hours. It also provides a chance to meet and understand the Japanese people and their culture. . . . This coffeehouse is for us and our needs. . . . There will be free literature and a lending library. A lawyer from the National Lawyers Guild and a trained civilian counsellor are available if you have any legal questions or hassles. . . . Both are very knowledgeable in military matters and donate their services to G.I.s. . . . The coffeehouse will be what you make it.[45]

The Hobbit was opened in February 1972. *Semper Fi* made an announcement:

On the 25th of February the Hobbit had its grand opening. The atmosphere is beautiful, Japanese and GIs rapping over cups of coffee and cocoa, listening to the music of famous American and Japanese artists. Every room was filled; people browsing through the library, as well as a rap room filled with guys talking with the two lawyers, who are here. . . . If you haven't been there, you better check it out, because you'll be missing something that was created for and by you.[46]

Just as the UFO in Fort Jackson quickly became popular among local high school students and dissident college students, the Hobbit became the center of counterculture in Iwakuni. Rock music was an integral part of GI coffeehouses, and most of them had a small library with books that were not available on the base, such as Black liberation books. Seitz, who lived on the second floor of the Hobbit while serving as a lawyer for PCS, described what it was like inside the coffeeshop:

It was a very nice place. Very popular with a lot of younger Japanese in the community. They were out on the street every day, distributing literature and talking to GIs. Inside the Hobbit, we had a nice little library. There were a lot of books from the Black liberation movement. Eldridge Cleaver, Malcolm X, W. E. B. du Bois . . . There were a whole lot of things pretty much just for Black people because Black soldiers couldn't get anything. We of course had GI newspapers and periodicals from the anti-war movement. We had music from the '60s that was popular with young military people. We would sit and talk with people about what they were reading and what was going on. They were angry . . . very wonderful relationships.[47]

These descriptions show that the Hobbit contained the must-have characteristics of the GI coffeehouse that Gardner envisioned: music, library, legal counseling services, and people they could freely talk with. The Hobbit apparently achieved its purpose. "A small little coffeehouse, free to the public. It is operated by people who believe in freedom of the peoples. One small place of freedom in an oppressed city. The GIs of Iwakuni are oppressed to the fullest. The coffeehouse gives you a chance at life. It is very inspirational with its rap room, library, and the coffeehouse itself. There is music for everyone."[48]

Music always played an important role for the young Beheiren activists when communicating with American GIs. Yoshioka Shinobu, a nonfiction writer and the director of the Japan PEN Club who helped many deserters as a student, stressed that when he spent time with American deserters, "Music was the only thing we could talk about!"[49] Tomita Hiroaki, one of the creators of the Hobbit, said that a good mix of rock, jazz, and Japanese rock music was played at the Hobbit.

> Bob Dylan was the solid No. 1. For the Beatles, Abbey Road, White Album, Sergeant Pepper, were often played. For the Rolling Stones, there were many that we played, like Let It Bleed. John Lennon's Imagine was also a regular. Santana, Pink Floyd, Cream, Led Zeppelin, Jimi Hendrix, the Doors were also frequently played. Others also played often were the Who, Janis Joplin, Neil Young, CSNY, Carol King, King Crimson, Stevie Wonder, Jefferson Airplane, Deep Purple, Traffic, Simon and Garfunkel, Paul Butterfield, and James Taylor. . . . GIs brought Joni Mitchell, Moody Blues, Jethro Tull, Yes, and Woodstock! Also, CCR and Leon Russell too. Some of us liked jazz, so John Coltrane, Miles Davis, Billie Holiday, Weather Report, Bill Evans, Thelonious Monk, were frequently played as well. As for Japanese musicians, Asakawa Maki, Happy End, Okabayashi Nobuyasu, Endo Kenji were frequently played.[50]

These are exquisite selections of music that have lived well beyond the 1970s. In a small rural base town of Iwakuni, spending time off-base at a GI coffeehouse listening to this music, which was their common language, must have been a transformative and globalizing process for not only GIs but for everyone involved beyond its original purpose of ending the war.

The Hobbit was not just a GI coffeehouse. According to Washino Masakazu, another Beheiren student activist, who co-operated the Hobbit, a few Beheiren students from the Hobbit walked to the base every day watching the sky at the end of the base runaway all day long to count planes such as Phantom and A-6 Intruder jets leaving Iwakuni so they could tell the scale of the bombing in Vietnam.[51] This was happening in yet another violation of the Japan-U.S. agreement that prohibited fighter planes leaving for Vietnam from U.S. bases in Japan. Because of the accuracy of their information, media reporters came to the Hobbit to hear from them.[52]

On June 4, 1972, just about three months after its opening, the Hobbit was raided by twenty-three Japanese policemen for an alleged violation of the Firearm and Sword Control Law.[53] It was a made-up search. The real purpose was to search for materials related to the U.S. military base, GI movement, and personal diaries and letters.[54] The U.S. Marine Corps colonel H. L. Van Campen declared the Hobbit off-limits because "the Hobbit is harmful to the well-being of GIs, and the safety of the base and the United States."[55] Coming from the U.S. military, this statement looks like a joke, but the narrative resembled what happened to other GI coffeehouses in the United States.

Beheiren Nyūsu rightly pointed out that the U.S. military authorities felt threatened by the Hobbit, which represented transpacific anti-war activism. A representative of the Hobbit, along with nine GIs, filed a lawsuit against Col. Van Campen in the federal court of the United States in Washington, D.C.[56] *Semper Fi* dedicated its cover page to Colonel Heil L. Van Campen "for all of the good work he's done lately" by tipping their hats. A picnic, "Brig Riot" in honor of the 1970 Fourth of July "riot," was called for. "Hey kids!! When's the last time you went to a real down-home picnic?? Well, opportunity is knocking. . . . The same group of degenerates that brings you your Semper Fi, plus our Japanese friends, are putting on a picnic to celebrate the brig riot of 2 years ago on July 4th. Look for a red and blue flag at Kintai. . . . See you there."[57]

Transpacific activism was resilient, and Col. Van Campen was sent back to California soon after this picnic.[58] A GI coffeehouse, the Hobbit, born in Iwakuni during the Vietnam War, is legendary among certain people in Japan even though it is now a vacant lot.

In the 1970 Symington Report, a 2,500-page document from the hearings of a special Senate Foreign Relations Subcommittee on U.S. Security Agreements and Commitments Abroad chaired by Senator Stuart Symington in 1969–1970, hundreds of pages were devoted to Japan-Okinawa and U.S.-Japan relations, including issues in Iwakuni and Beheiren. Beheiren published a series from the Symington Report in *JATEC Tsūshin* for months.[59]

Conclusion

This chapter has shown how transpacific activism in Iwakuni developed and thrived by examining an array of related anti-war activities. The creation of *Semper Fi* and the Hobbit involved transpacific collaboration that made Iwakuni a hotbed of GI resistance and also involved higher level intervention by both the U.S. military and Japanese officials. In a base town with a population of 150,000 in 1970 in Yamaguchi prefecture, the constituency of Prime Minister Sato at the time, citizens of Iwakuni witnessed politically volatile events one after another in a short period. It is ironic that while transpacific actors worked collaboratively to stop the war, Japanese and U.S. authorities also collaborated to stop those activists. Who could have imagined then or now that Iwakuni, a rustic base town surrounded by lotus-root fields that relied on the base with its big government subsidy, would become the epicenter of GI resistance in the Asia-Pacific region and a threat to the U.S. military authorities?

Although this chapter shows an early example of transpacific activism, it also indicates that there must be more hidden history similar to Iwakuni in other parts of the globe that hosted U.S. bases during the Vietnam War. Meanwhile, nothing seems to have fundamentally changed in Iwakuni. Whether it was under Prime Minister Sato during the Vietnam War or more recently under his nephew, Prime Minister Abe. "Iwakuni is a sad town," said Iwase Jōko, a lifetime Iwakuni native, and former Hobbit customer who is a writer of children's literature.[60] The Vietnam War is now history, but Iwakuni's struggle with the Marine Corps Air Station continues to this day.

Notes

1. Noriko Shiratori, "Peace in Vietnam! Beheiren: Transnational Activism and GI Movement in Postwar Japan 1965–1974" (PhD diss., University of Hawai'i at Mānoa, 2018).

2. Takahashi Taketomo, interview, Tokyo, October 6, 2016.

3. Motono Yoshio, interview, Tokyo, October 6, 2016.

4. Tsurumi Yoshiyuki, "70 Nendai he muketeno Beheiren," in *Beheiren*, ed. Makoto Oda (Tokyo: San-ichi shobō, 1969), 85.

5. David Cortright, *Soldiers in Revolt: The American Military Today* (Garden City, NY: Anchor, 1975), 50.

6. Patricia Steinhoff, "Memories of New Left Protest," *Contemporary Japan* 25, no. 2 (October 2016): 127–165.

7. Cortright, *Soldiers in Revolt*, 61.

8. Motono Yoshio, "Hōshin tenkan to beigun kaitai undo," in *Tonari ni dassōhei ga ita jidai. Jattekku, aru shimin undō no kiroku*, ed. Shigeru Sekiya and Yoshie Sakamoto (Tokyo: Shisō no Kagakusha, 1998), 147.

9. Cortright, *Soldiers in Revolt*, 78; Motono, "Hōshin tenkan to beigun kaitai undo," 147–152; "PCS iyoiyo kaigyō!" *Dassōhei Tsūshin* 11 (June 15, 1970): 12.

10. Fujieda Mioko, "Kaisō Rasupūchin eno omaju," in *Tonari ni dassōhei ga ita jidai. Jattekku, aru shimin undō no kiroku*, ed. Shigeru Sekiya and Yoshie Sakamoto (Tokyo: Shisō no Kagakusha, 1998), 165–166.

11. Eric Seitz, interview, Honolulu, HI, January 18, 2016.

12. "Katsudō no sōkatsu to tenbō," *Dassōhei Tsūshin* 11 (June 15, 1970): 2–5.

13. "Betonamu samā Japan 1970," *Dassōhei Tsūshin* 11 (June 15, 1970): 5.

14. Sidney Tarrow, *The New Transnational Activism* (New York: Cambridge University Press, 2005), 199.

15. "Zainichi beigun kichi ha yureteiru," *Beheiren Nyūsu* 55 (April 1, 1970): 3.

16. Seitz, interview.

17. Cortright, *Soldiers in Revolt*, 104–105.

18. Cortright, *Soldiers in Revolt*, 283.

19. "Kuroi rutsubo," *Dassōhei Tsūshin* 4 (October 15, 1969): 5.

20. Kihara Shigeya, "Iwakuni hansen beihei shinbun Semper Fi ni tsuite no shiron. Fukugōgata taikō-teki kōkyō-ken no senzairyoku wo megutte," *Kure kōgyō kōtō senmon gakkō kenkyū hōkoku* 78 (2011): 17–22; Nakagawa Roppei, *Hobitto. Sensō wo tometa kissaten. Beheiren 1970–1975 in Iwakuni* (Tokyo: Kōdansha, 2009), 14.

21. "Human Relations: 'A Black GI Raps,'" *Semper Fi* 6 (May 1, 1970): 1, Yoshikawa Yūichi Collection, Research Center for Cooperative Civil Societies, Rikkyō University, Tokyo.

22. "Iwakuni kichi GI hansen undō no takamari," *Dassōhei Tsūshin* 12 (August 15, 1970): 7.

23. Nakagawa, *Hobitto. Sensō wo tometa kissaten*, 32; "Oretachi ha buta janai," *Dassōhei Tsūshin* 14 (October 15, 1970): 6–7.

24. "Iwakuni 13's Struggle, 1970," flyer, courtesy of Tomita Hiroaki.

25. "Atarimae no ningen ni natu tameni," *Beheiren Nyūsu* 63 (December 1, 1970): 4; Nakagawa, *Hobitto. Sensō wo tometa kissaten*, 41; "Nihonjin shimin mo shōgen dai he," *Dassōhei Tsūshin* 15 (November 15, 1970): 2–3.

26. "Iwakuni gunsai hajimaru," *Dassōhei Tsūshin* 15 (November 15, 1970): 2–3; Nakagawa, *Hobitto. Sensō wo tometa kissaten*, 41–42; Takashi Oka, "A U.S. Marine in Japan Becomes an Antiwar Symbol," *New York Times*, November 15, 1970, https://www.nytimes.com/1970/11/15/archives/a-us-marine-in-japan-becomes-an-antiwar-symbol-perplexing-problems.html; Ono Nobuyuki, "Hansen dassōhei bengo no imi," in *Tonari ni dassōhei ga ita jidai. Jattekku, aru shimin undō no kiroku*, ed. Shigeru Sekiya and Yoshie Sakamoto (Tokyo: Shisō no Kagakusha, 1998), 180–182.

27. "Iwakuni gunsai hajimaru," 2–3; Nakagawa, *Hobitto. Sensō wo tometa kissaten*, 49–51.

28. Tsurumi Shunsuke, as quoted in Nakagawa, *Hobitto. Sensō wo tometa kissaten*, 53.

29. Ono, "Hansen dassōhei bengo no imi," 179–180.

30. Kokkai Hakusho [White paper], Dai 067 kai kokkai, *Okinawa henkan kyōtei tokubetsu iinkai*, dai 7 gō, November 17, 1971, http://kokkai.ndl.go.jp/SENTAKU/syugiin/067/0707/06711170707007a.html; Nakagawa, *Hobitto. Sensō wo tometa kissaten*, 84–86; "Wareware ga chokumen suru genjitsu," *JATEC Tsūshin* 5 (December 20, 1971): 2–3.

31. Kakegawa Kyōko, "Iwakuni no ninen," in *Tonari ni dassōhei ga ita jidai. Jattekku, aru shimin undō no kiroku*, ed. Shigeru Sekiya and Yoshie Sakamoto (Tokyo: Shisō no Kagakusha, 1998), 168–177; "Zainichi beigun kichi no tetteiteki kenkyū 2. Iwakuni," *JATEC Tsūshin* 2 (May 5, 1971): 8–9.

32. Nakagawa, *Hobitto. Sensō wo tometa kissaten*, 85.

33. Eric Seitz, "Apīru," *Beheiren Nyūsu* 74 (December 1, 1971): 8.

34. "Konran shita beigun tōkyoku," *JATEC Tsūshin* 5 (December 20, 1971): 3.

35. Seitz, interview.

36. Nakagawa, *Hobitto. Sensō wo tometa kissaten*, 95.

37. Nakagawa, *Hobitto. Sensō wo tometa kissaten*, 83.

38. "Ajia wo kakemegutta FTA," *Beheiren Nyūsu* 77 (March 1, 1972): 4.

39. Jane Fonda, *My Life So Far* (New York: Random House, 2005), 275.

40. Fonda, *My Life So Far*, 275.

41. *FTA: The Show the Pentagon Couldn't Stop!* Docudramatists', 2008.

42. Cortright, *Soldiers in Revolt*, 53; David Parsons, *Dangerous Grounds: Antiwar Coffeehouses and Military Dissent in the Vietnam Era* (Chapel Hill: University of North Carolina Press, 2017), 16–17.

43. "Support Coffeehouse," *Semper Fi* 2, no. 14 (October 5, 1971): 17, Yoshikawa Yūichi Collection, Research Center for Cooperative Civil Societies, Rikkyō University, Tokyo.

44. Nakagawa, *Hobitto. Sensō wo tometa kissaten*, 105–110.

45. "Coffeehouse," *Semper Fi* 3, no. 3 (February 15, 1972): 16, Yoshikawa Yūichi Collection, Research Center for Cooperative Civil Societies, Rikkyō University, Tokyo.

46. "Coffeehouse Open," *Semper Fi* 3, no. 5 (March 16, 1972): 4, Yoshikawa Yūichi Collection, Research Center for Cooperative Civil Societies, Rikkyō University, Tokyo.

47. Seitz, interview.

48. "Coffeehouse Open," 4.

49. Yoshioka Shinobu, interview, Tokyo, October 6, 2016.

50. Tomita Hiroaki, email communication, September 28, 2017.

51. Washino Masakazu, interview, Iwakuni, October 1, 2016.

52. Tomita Hiroaki, interview, Iwakuni, October 1, 2016.

53. Nakagawa, *Hobitto. Sensō wo tometa kissaten*, 166.

54. "Keisatsu, masukomi. 'Tsukuri banashi' no decchiage," *Beheiren Nyūsu* 81 (July 1, 1972): 2; Tomita Hiroaki, email communication, March 29, 2018.

55. "Iwakuni Hobitto. Beigun GI wo tachi-iri kinshi," *Beheiren Nyūsu* 81 (July 1, 1972): 2; Nakagawa, *Hobitto. Sensō wo tometa kissaten*, 177.

56. "Hobitto no hangeki," *Beheiren Nyūsu* 81 (July 1, 1972): 2; Nakagawa, *Hobitto. Sensō wo tometa kissaten*, 181.

57. "It Can Happen Again," *Semper Fi* 3, no. 12 (June 30, 1972): 16, Endō Yōichi Collection, Research Center for Cooperative Civil Societies, Rikkyō University, Tokyo.

58. "Iwakuni Hobitto," *Beheiren News, Special Issue* (October 1, 1972): 10.

59. "Saiminton hōkoku. Bei gaikō shōi no chōmon-kai sokkiroku," *JATEC Tsūshin* 1–5 (April 15–December 1, 1971).

60. Iwase Jōko, interview, Iwakuni, October 1, 2016.

8 The U.S. Military's R&R Program in Taipei, 1965–1972

ZACH FREDMAN

On September 16, 2013, federal agents arrested Malaysian defense contractor Leonard Glenn Francis in the opening strike of a transpacific sweep that soon uncovered the worst corruption scandal in U.S. Navy history. Francis admitted to running a decade-long conspiracy to bribe officers from the U.S. 7th Fleet to look the other way while his company, Glenn Defense Marine Asia, defrauded the navy out of at least $35 million by overcharging for services at port facilities Francis controlled across the western Pacific.[1] The scandal ensnared hundreds of active-duty personnel, wreaking havoc on the navy's ability to fill senior leadership roles.[2] Francis, a six-foot-three, 350-pound smooth talker known in navy circles as "Fat Leonard," sometimes doled out cash or hotel stays, but his preferred enticement was sex. Court documents alleged that he "frequently sponsored wild sex parties" for officers from the 7th Fleet, including a Dom Perignon–fueled orgy in the Manila Hotel's MacArthur Suite where participants used "historical memorabilia" related to General Douglas MacArthur "in sexual acts."[3] The secretary of the navy attributed the scandal to the moral failings of individual officers whose behaviors were out of step with long-standing military values.[4] However, the inducements Francis offered—access to prostitutes and good times—have been cornerstones of the U.S. military presence in Asia for more than a half century.

Francis was just a kid growing up in Penang, Malaysia when nearly two million American servicemen participated in the U.S. military's rest and recreation (R&R) program during the Vietnam War. A central component of the "comfort-for-morale formula" that underpinned the U.S. war effort in Indochina, the R&R program guaranteed each American soldier serving a one-year tour in South Vietnam a five-night overseas excursion to one of the following destinations: Tokyo, Singapore, Manila, Bangkok, Hong Kong, Taipei (Taibei), Sydney, Honolulu, Kuala Lumpur, or Penang—where Francis's wealthy family ran a maritime logistics firm.[5] The program officially aimed to "provide a respite from the rigors of a combat tour in Vietnam." It also offered relief from the monotony of rear echelon duty, where most troops actually served. The historian Meredith Lair describes R&R as "the ultimate Vietnam consumer experience," but a closer look at Taiwan reveals that the program focused on the same enticements Francis offered.[6] R&R destination Taipei was a joint Sino-U.S. undertaking aimed at providing American personnel with hygienic, morale-boosting access to local women's bodies while promoting capitalist economic development and assuaging historically charged sensitivities about national sovereignty. Fat Leonards of all stripes—from heads of state to health inspectors to hostess bar pimps—were indispensable to the American way of war in Vietnam.

・・・・・・

Sexual relations between American military personnel and local women contributed to three crises for Republic of China (ROC) president Chiang Kai-shek's Nationalist government between 1945 and 1957, so Chiang gambled by supporting R&R. During the last year of World War II, resentment against sexual relations between poorly disciplined American servicemen and Chinese women led to widespread panic over rape, resulting in anti-American riots in the wartime capital of Chongqing.[7] Less than two years later, the rape of a nineteen-year-old Peking University student named Shen Chong by two intoxicated U.S. marines sparked a nationwide protest movement.[8] The Chinese Communist Party (CCP), which had helped to spearhead the initial protests in Beijing, harnessed the movement and used it to make a persuasive case that the Americans were imperialists and Chiang's Nationalists their lackeys.[9] After the Nationalists fled to Taiwan, the U.S. Military Assistance Advisory Group's (MAAG's) neocolonial footprint, including military prostitution catering to American personnel in Taipei, fomented ill-will throughout the 1950s. Tensions boiled over on May 24, 1957, when rioters stormed the American embassy and injured several diplomats after a U.S. military court acquitted MAAG sergeant Robert Reynolds on voluntary manslaughter charges for killing a Chinese man while off-duty.[10]

However, when debating whether to host R&R in Taipei in October 1965, ROC officials explored questions related to jurisdiction, not sex. American servicemen's exemption from Chinese law had played a central role in each previous crisis. Although Washington rescinded America's extraterritorial rights in China in 1943, the U.S. military retained exclusive jurisdiction over American servicemen deployed there during World War II, which facilitated sexual misconduct against women, ranging from aggressive heckling to rape. Newspaper articles and rumors about GIs committing rape in 1945 resonated widely by portraying women's bodies as territory to be recovered and inextricable from national sovereignty.[11] In 1947, demonstrators wanted Shen Chong's attackers tried in a joint Sino-U.S. court, but U.S. authorities rejected their demand, thus making Shen into a symbol of America's larger assault on Chinese nationhood.[12] In Taiwan, press coverage of the Reynolds case focused on the diplomatic immunity all MAAG personnel enjoyed, whereas in Japan, reporters noted, American soldiers who committed crimes against locals while off-duty could be tried in Japanese courts.[13] The August 1965 ROC-U.S. Status of Forces Agreement (SOFA) finally granted Taipei similar rights, most importantly, the right to jurisdiction in cases involving the death or rape of an ROC citizen at the hands of an American servicemen. However, the treaty did not enter force until April 1966.[14] The U.S. military wanted to begin R&R in Taipei in November, so ROC Foreign Ministry officials began investigating how jurisdiction would look in the interim.[15]

Officials in Taipei took it for granted that most R&R personnel would head straight to the hostess bars: the key issue was preventing drunken, carousing American troops from becoming involved in any incident that could damage the government's legitimacy or its ties with the Johnson administration. ROC officials, like U.S. military commanders, believed that sex bolstered morale. They credited the military brothel system established at garrisons around the island in the early 1950s with helping to keep ROC forces in fighting shape while protecting national morality. After Taipei sanctioned the opening of hostess bars in 1956, police strove to make establishments catering to MAAG personnel safe, hygienic, and comfortable in order to maximize foreign exchange earnings.[16] If managed carefully, ROC officials believed, R&R could bolster the economy and strengthen the crucial relationship with the United States.

ROC Foreign Ministry officials believed that Thailand offered a model for excluding visiting American personnel from coverage under the new U.S.-ROC SOFA. Although Bangkok was the first city to host American R&R personnel, Thailand had not concluded a SOFA with the United States. Jurisdiction over these troops relied on an informal arrangement whereby any soldier who committed a violent crime would be shipped off quietly to the United States for trial, while Thai authorities cooperated with a team of seventeen U.S. military policemen and liaison officers to keep visiting troops out of trouble.[17] Authorities in Taipei recommended a similar arrangement. Taiwan Garrison Command, the state security body responsible for enforcing martial law, sought to prevent conflict between R&R personnel and locals through a system of joint patrols by U.S. military and ROC foreign affairs police.[18] The Foreign Ministry wanted to classify the American visitors as tourists rather than foreign soldiers. Tsai Wei-ping, head of the Foreign Ministry's North American Department, asserted that "there was a difference between those U.S. forces coming to Taiwan for holiday . . . and those serving there in its defense, so their [legal status] is not the same."[19]

U.S. State Department officials disagreed. They insisted that R&R personnel came under the SOFA "by virtue of the term 'members of the U.S. armed forces'" contained in the agreement's first article. American diplomats recognized that officials and civilians in Taiwan had long resented how the U.S. government granted Japan greater rights over the American troops stationed on its soil compared to what Washington offered Taipei. So U.S. embassy staff in Taipei emphasized that the language in the U.S.-ROC SOFA regarding military personnel on leave was identical to that used in the agreement the United States had concluded with Japan, "where R&R personnel are given SOFA status." These diplomats did not refer to Thailand, but they noted that even though the North Atlantic Treaty Organization (NATO) SOFA specifically excluded military personnel on R&R, America's NATO allies had in fact allowed the U.S. military to maintain jurisdiction over these troops.[20]

The first batch of eighty R&R personnel arrived in Taipei on November 26, 1965, before the two governments had reached an agreement about their legal status. Earlier in the month, an advance team comprising liaison personnel and representatives from different military branches had worked alongside local foreign affairs police to set up an R&R Service Center on Taipei's North Zhongshan Road, just north of the hostess bar district.[21] The first few R&R visits ended without incident, but State Department officials threatened to pull the plug unless the two sides could reach a mutually satisfactory agreement.[22]

Each country had a substantial stake in continuing the R&R scheme. U.S. military commanders had already made the sexualized "R&R" holiday a centerpiece of their efforts to maintain morale in Vietnam.[23] U.S.-ROC cooperation on military tourism, meanwhile, dated back to 1956, with the creation of Taiwan's Tourism Council (*Guanguang shiye weiyuanhui*), an institution that worked with advisers from the U.S. Department of Commerce and other government agencies to promote Taiwan as a holiday destination for U.S. troops stationed in the region.[24] During his March 1963 visit to Saigon, ROC premier Chen Cheng had actually pushed U.S. officials to send American servicemen in Vietnam to Taiwan on R&R leave.[25] R&R also provided a means to make up for the ROC's loss of nonmilitary U.S. foreign aid, which ended in 1965 after years of gradual reductions.[26] The Tourism Council expected a daily average of four hundred R&R visitors, each spending around $200 per five-day trip.[27] R&R thus offered a timely economic windfall. Ending the program also carried political costs, especially after President Ferdinand Marcos and Prime Minister Lee Kuan Yew agreed to open Manila and Singapore as R&R destinations while U.S. and ROC officials were still arguing over jurisdiction.[28]

The ROC accepted the U.S. government's position on April 15, 1966, placing all R&R personnel under the authority of the U.S. Taiwan Defense Command but with crucial exceptions.[29] In accordance with the SOFA, the ROC waived its primary jurisdiction rights in cases involving American servicemen. However, according to Assistant Secretary of State for Far Eastern Affairs William Bundy, Taipei reserved the right to recall this waiver "in specific cases where major interests of Chinese administration of justice make the exercise of Chinese jurisdiction imperative," including security offenses against the government or offenses "causing the death of a human being, robbery or rape."[30] Police in Taiwan also had the power to arrest American personnel, a privilege the ROC lacked before the two governments concluded the SOFA. These key components of the jurisdiction agreement assured Chiang that R&R personnel could be detained and tried in Chinese courts if they committed any of the crimes that had sparked crises for his government in the 1940s and 1950s.[31]

Taiwan's state-controlled press promoted R&R by building up American servicemen as "warriors" defending the "free world" from communism while also infantilizing them as lovable but unsophisticated "children." As such, they deserved both fairness and forbearance. In a series of articles published in leading newspapers during the weeks leading up to the scheme's November 26 launch, authors warned against price gouging and emphasized R&R's importance to U.S.-ROC relations.[32] The author of an unattributed November 22 op-ed in the popular *Zhengxin xinwen bao* (Credit newspaper) admitted that the program would bring challenges. "The great majority of visitors will be enlisted men," the author wrote, "ordinary Americans and definitely not high-level intellectuals." Most Chinese they would interact with, the piece continued, "won't exactly be high-level intellectuals either." But just as ROC citizens would not want Americans judging Taiwan by the "swindlers" they would inevitably encounter in Taipei's red light districts, Chinese should not allow the conduct of these "innocent overgrown kids," to color their perceptions of American youth.[33] R&R would be disreputable, but it would be out of sight and out of mind for most, its burden falling on the lower-class young Chinese women who would provide morale-boosting sexual services to lower-class young American men.

Taipei quickly became a popular R&R destination. In 1966, 19,684 American servicemen spent their holiday in Taiwan, and nearly 50,000 came in 1967.[34] Specialist John Haydock sung Taipei's praises in *Thunder*, the official publication of the Army's 25th Infantry Division. "The girls of Taipei are very friendly, Americanized almost totally in dress and taste, and like all Oriental women, are set on satisfying the male's every need," he wrote.[35] Soldiers from South Korea, Australia, and New Zealand also participated in the scheme, as did Central Intelligence Agency agents and American commandos fighting the secret war in Laos, who were eligible for R&R after only four weeks in the field.[36] U.S. government-sponsored R&R visits to Taiwan continued for more than six years, ending on April 5, 1972, a considerable time after R&R centers had closed in Hong Kong, Sydney, Singapore, Tokyo, Manila, Kuala Lumpur, and Penang.[37] According to ROC sources, more than 211,000 American troops spent an estimated U.S.$52.8 million while on R&R in Taiwan.[38]

R&R visits to Taiwan began with a stay at Camp Alpha, the U.S. military's $7.5 million R&R out-processing center near Tan Son Nhut Air Base outside Saigon. Any soldier with ninety days of service in country could apply for R&R leave, with a certain number of slots allocated to each destination. Those signing up for R&R ranked their top three destinations. To prevent soldiers from departing with insufficient funds, staff at Camp Alpha made sure each man had a minimum of $250 in cash.[39] Uncle Sam paid for the flights, but American troops had to cover their own expenses while away. Medical personnel gave out vaccinations and tested the men for venereal disease (VD). The men were also isolated from the civilian population at Camp Alpha for twenty-four hours before departure. This procedure helped to meet VD control requirements in the various host countries.[40]

Once cleared, R&R personnel boarded a Pan American Airways commercial airliner for the two-hour-and-forty-minute flight to Taipei's Songshan Airport. Pan Am won an exclusive contract for the R&R program in 1965 and devoted thirteen DC-6 and two Boeing 707 aircraft to R&R flights, a fleet as large as any transcontinental service operating in the mid-1960s.[41] For American personnel, the trip to Taiwan required only travel orders, an ID, and a vaccine record.[42] After deplaning at Songshan Airport, the visitors passed through an abbreviated immigration inspection by ROC authorities (after one last chance to throw away any contraband) and then boarded buses for the R&R service center on North Zhongshan Road.[43]

While on the bus, the men heard a lecture from an American service representative that confirmed what they already knew: their stay in Taiwan would revolve around intoxication and intercourse. A crew from San Francisco's KGO-TV News captured the scene when accompanying a group of R&R personnel in 1967. After warning the men not to discuss Vietnam or try to handle any disputes on their own, a Marine Corps gunnery sergeant from the R&R center spent the rest of the bus ride discussing Taipei's hostess bar system. Women in bars wearing triangular pins worked as hostesses, available to sit and talk for four drinks per hour at $1 a round. Those wearing circular pins, "she's what we call a thoroughbred," said the sergeant, "and she's got plenty of practice." The soldiers aboard the bus giggled knowingly as the sergeant explained how these women could be hired out of the bar for sexual intercourse after the men signed a contract, "just like buying a car."[44]

The gunnery sergeant was not exaggerating. Each bar catering to R&R personnel commodified female sex workers by requiring American customers to fill out a legally binding contract titled "Registration Form for Outgoing of Waitress" before leaving the premises with a licensed prostitute. In 1967, the form was filled out in duplicate, with one copy for the customer and the bar holding on to the second. The waitress herself was regarded as a piece of merchandise rather than a party to the agreement, though later versions of the contract distributed in 1969 were filled out in triplicate, with one copy going to the woman. The form included spaces for the soldier and the waitress's names, the number of hours, and price, marked down as "money paid for business losses." Official charges for "business losses" were NT$200 for the first two hours (U.S.$5), NT$50 for every additional half hour, and the maximum charge limited to NT$600, or $15 for a whole day. Later versions of the form also dispensed with the "no prostitution" pretense contained in the 1967 contract. All bars adhered to the same price standard, and soldiers were eligible for a refund if the "waitress" left him before the allotted time had expired. The form listed six categories as reasons for the waitress's outgoing: dancing, movie, restaurant, party, club, and number six—left blank. "Number six, the blank one," wrote Darrell Houston of the *Seattle Post-Intelligencer*, "is far and away the most popular selection. In fact it's the only one that's ever checked off."[45]

In official correspondence and press releases, U.S. and ROC authorities described R&R as a means of showcasing Chinese culture and strengthening

Sino-American friendship, but journalists like Houston told readers back home what their tax dollars were really supporting. "Don't tell Mom and Dad," he wrote after an April 1969 visit to Taiwan, "but Uncle Sam is the biggest panderer in the world." Houston mocked the "great lengths" U.S. and ROC authorities went "to conceal what is really little more than bilateral concubinage." The ROC's Hotel Business Association, which ran R&R on the Taiwan side, deployed euphemisms like "hostesses" to refer to licensed prostitutes, or "business losses" when describing income from prostitution. U.S. commanders also played the game. A framed certificate of appreciation for "contributing to the morale and welfare of U.S. and other Free World troops" signed by General Creighton Abrams, commander of U.S. forces in Vietnam, hung on the briefing officer's wall at the R&R center. Some Americans were more forthcoming with Houston, with one "old Taiwan hand" telling him, "After decades of pretending that our troops are made of flesh-colored plastic, the military is finally wising up. They are recognizing that the primary need of healthy, normal young Americans fresh from a war zone is S-E-X."[46]

After being processed at the R&R center, American personnel were free to enjoy their holiday. Hotel representatives waited outside and competed for their business. Thirty-two hotels catered the Americans, with rooms going for an average of around $4 per night in April 1967. A survey carried out by ROC authorities that same month reported that 96 percent of R&R personnel visited one of twenty-six Taipei Police Bureau–approved hostess bars. Almost all these drinking establishments were located within stumbling distance along North Zhongshan Road, beginning a block south of the R&R Service Center and continuing down three-quarters of a mile to Changchun Road. Representatives from the bar owner's association distributed a business card–sized booklet to servicemen arriving in Taipei, which included a map, emergency phone numbers, exchange rate conversion table, and standard menu for drinks, with Taiwan Beer at seventy-five cents a glass and "drinks for girls" priced between $1 and $1.50. Soldiers were supposed to sleep only with the circular pin–clad licensed prostitutes working at the bars, but the April survey showed that many men spent the night with unlicensed sex workers introduced to them by hotel staff.[47]

U.S. and ROC officials worked together behind the scenes to guarantee R&R personnel access to VD-free sex workers. Drawing on a history of gendered, imperialist discourse, U.S. commanders viewed local prostitutes, rather than American visitors, as the main source of infection.[48] R&R personnel were tested for VD before leaving Saigon, but that did not stop them from causing a syphilis outbreak in Taipei just months into the program.[49] Sex workers in Taipei, however, faced a more intrusive testing and treatment regime. The ROC had outlawed compulsory genital inspections for sex workers in 1962, and when the R&R program began, licensed prostitutes were required to take a blood test four times per year to continue working legally. However, complaints from the R&R center about hostesses spreading VD resulted in the imposition of fortnightly vaginal inspections and blood tests every other month starting in April 1967, carried out by the Taipei City Government's Health Bureau. Women who tested positive were subjected to compulsory quarantine and treatment.[50] In 1969, American epidemiologists helped set up the Taipei Municipal Venereal Disease Control Institute, which carried out inspections and treatment of sex workers. American epidemiologists in Saigon, meanwhile, interviewed soldiers who tested positive for VD after returning from Taiwan, and they reported their findings to the institute in Taipei, which carried out contact tracing.[51] As for American personnel in Taiwan on R&R, Houston wrote that the service representative told them on the bus from Songshan Airport, "Don't worry too much about VD. . . . Uncle Sam can cure anything you can catch."[52]

The construction of race and gender at Asian R&R destinations like Taipei differed from Sydney, where the white Australia policy had created a population that remained of overwhelmingly European descent in the 1960s. Unlike in Taiwan, sex tourism was not the central focus of R&R in Australia. U.S. authorities encouraged visiting personnel to see Australians, including women, as people similar to themselves. "There is a well-rounded reason why" Sydney was the most popular R&R destination in 1970, according to *First Team*, the 1st Cavalry Division's official publication: "round-eyed girls" who "live, work and play like state-side dandies."[53] GIs might have flocked to Kings Cross to visit Sydney's red light district, but they were also invited into thousands of homes for sit-down meals with local families.[54] The Australian-American Association organized numerous social functions for them, and nearly all visitors joined some kind of sightseeing or organized sporting tour, such as deep-sea fishing, surfing, or a harbor cruise.[55] In Taiwan, on the other hand, R&R center staff instructed visiting personnel not to bother with anything other than drinking and fornicating. "You're not supposed to marry these girls, so don't go falling in love," said the army official giving the bus ride briefing during Houston's trip to Taipei. "All you're doing is renting a body."[56] Contemporary reporting and military publications on R&R in Taipei consistently emphasized the exoticism, servility, and affordability of the city's female sex workers.[57]

Not everyone in Taiwan was comfortable with the focus on sex. Women's groups and conservative intellectuals criticized R&R as an adoption of Western immorality.[58] Tatung Institute of Technology president T. S. Lin wrote to Executive Yuan's Tourism Policy Committee in December 1968 to request that the Taipei City Government move the R&R Center to a new location. His institution, which ran cooperative programs with Harvard and MIT, was located just eighty meters from the R&R center. "All day long," he wrote, the school was surrounded by "an endless stream of bar girls." Making matters even worse, this was all taking place two years into the ROC's Chinese cultural renaissance movement, the appeal to traditionalism Chiang launched in 1966 in response to the People's Republic of China's Cultural Revolution. The presence of so many sex workers and foreign guests, according to Lin, "was having a huge influence on the physical and spiritual health of the institution's young students."[59] The government relocated the center to a new location on Taiyuan Road in 1969 as a result of Lin's complaints.[60] However, none of the hostess bars along the strip catering to American personnel just south of the Tatung Institute were closed.

ROC officials also voiced concerns, though rarely in public. In October 1966, the GMD Central Committee's 5th Group submitted a report to Minister of Foreign Affairs Wei Daoming, describing problems that had emerged since Taiwan had joined the R&R program. In addition to causing a syphilis outbreak, American troops had beaten up hostess bar owners. The *Taiwan Daily*, the report noted, had also published a series of articles describing how Malaysians had encouraged visiting R&R personnel to travel to Taiwan instead because "women there were easy," unlike local prostitutes, many of whom refused to sleep with American men. "If foreigners only come to Taiwan to look for women, this is a great attack on our national honor," the report concluded. The authors also warned Wei of the likelihood of soldiers leaving behind mixed-race children like the Japanese had, which "could become a serious social problem."[61] Despite these concerns, ROC authorities allowed the R&R program to grow much larger in 1967. However, when speaking to reporters about R&R in March 1968, Taiwan Tourism Bureau director Jiang Lianru still recommended that "licensed prostitution should be abolished for the sake of dignity."[62] Jiang's statement came not long after ROC officials had been embarrassed by a *Time* magazine feature on R&R that included a photo of two topless Chinese women bathing an American soldier at Beitou hot springs north of Taipei.[63]

From Taipei's perspective, however, sex tourism was not the scheme's leading threat to national dignity. Foreign Ministry files and meeting records from the government committees responsible for managing R&R on the ROC side devote much more space to other American actions and policies that officials viewed as threats to Chinese sovereignty. ROC authorities were especially incensed about U.S. military police inspecting bars and hotels in Taipei without being accompanied by local foreign affairs police. The Ministry of State Security, meanwhile, lodged complaints with the Foreign Ministry about U.S. military officials, rather than local customs officers, carrying out baggage inspections, while bar and hotel owners fretted over what they described as the arbitrary standards R&R center staff employed when placing establishments off-limits for visiting personnel. These American staff members, the committee alleged, were also soliciting bribes from hotel owners in exchange for steering visitors toward their establishments. These problems, the R&R committee chair concluded in an April 1967 meeting, "besmirch the reputations of the majority of honest business owners in the tourism industry and insult the dignity of our country to an unbearable degree."[64]

R&R's disreputable side became a problem for ROC authorities when it moved outside established boundaries. The Taiwan Garrison Command demanded that foreign affairs police crack down on hotels that allowed unlicensed prostitutes to accompany American visitors to their rooms. Although ostensibly for disease-control purposes, this measure ensured that the state received its proper cut of sex industry revenue.[65] In 1968, intense competition among hostess bars and hotels spilled over at Songshan Airport, where bar girls, pimps, and touts started gathering in order to vie for the business of arriving American personnel before they boarded buses for the R&R center. "Because of this group of people, Taiwan is becoming a cheap red-light district suitable only for servicing vulgar interests in the eyes of foreigners," argued one writer in a July 15 *Zhengxin xinwen* op-ed.[66] A Taipei police spokesman announced that same day that bar girls would henceforth be kept away from U.S. servicemen near the airport.[67]

U.S. military commanders in Taiwan, for their part, tried to keep the good times rolling. At their request, public health authorities in Taipei implemented a more intrusive disease-control regime for local sex worker while the Taiwan Garrison Command oversaw crackdowns to halt price gouging at bars or hotels that deviated from government-approved rates. R&R center staff had the power to place any establishment off-limits to American personnel, so police urged bar and hotel owners to keep their premises clean and treat R&R personnel with respect.[68] So long as R&R personnel enjoyed Taipei and returned to Hanoi VD-free, the scheme achieved its purpose from the U.S. military's perspective. "Your adventures in Taipei will be remembered until you check into a home for the aged," wrote one sergeant with the army's 23rd Infantry Division in 1969.[69]

The R&R program ran for more than six years in Taipei, as U.S. and ROC authorities succeeded in jointly intervening to control women's bodies for the sexual pleasure of visiting military personnel without provoking widespread outrage. Nationalistic critics still denounced bar girls for consorting with American personnel and aping "Western ways," the same line of attack so-called Jeep Girls had been subjected to in China for fraternizing with American personnel during World War II.[70] However, significant anti-American or anti-government backlash did not materialize. Martial law, joint U.S.-ROC efforts to confine R&R to limited spaces and enforce discipline, and the existence of a status of forces agreement that made Taiwan nominally equal to Japan and America's NATO allies all played a role in limiting the resentments over violations of Chinese sovereignty that had sparked previous crises for Chiang's government. As anticipated, the R&R program spurred the development of mass tourism in Taiwan, but it failed to yield the political outcomes that Chiang had aimed for. In late February 1972, around a month before the R&R scheme ended, U.S. president Richard Nixon made his historic trip to Beijing.

・・・・・・

R&R in Taiwan formed part of a larger patriarchal and neocolonial project that underpinned the U.S.-allied war effort in Vietnam. At the program's peak in 1968, 35,000 American personnel participated each month. In Taipei and other Asian destinations, GIs were rewarded for their service with a "once-in-a-lifetime experience" in which U.S. and host-country authorities collaborated to fulfill their Orientalist fantasies.[71] From Washington's perspective, R&R also provided a means to support capitalist economic development in countries of economic and political importance to the United States. The U.S. dollars American servicemen spent on sexual services in Taiwan, Hong Kong, Thailand, Malaysia, Singapore, and the Philippines played a crucial role in stimulating the development of tourism throughout the region. Darrell Houston was right: Uncle Sam was indeed the "biggest panderer in the world," presiding over a transnational prostitution scheme that stretched across the western Pacific. Authoritarian leaders like Chiang, Marcos, and Lee willingly joined in, as R&R dovetailed with their own state-building and economic goals. As scholars have shown, R&R in Asia bolstered dictators and proved good for business.[72]

By the time U.S. forces withdrew from South Vietnam, the R&R program had laid the foundation for the sex tourism industries that have flourished in much of the western Pacific region ever since. R&R during Vietnam built on earlier efforts in South Korea and occupied Japan, where local authorities organized systematic military prostitution to serve American troops and protect native masculinity by shielding "virtuous" women from the U.S. presence. After R&R came to an end, Japanese visitors, many of them men seeking cheap sexual consumption, propped up the sex industry in Taiwan, paralleling efforts by South Korea's government to organize sex tourism targeting Japanese travelers in the 1970s and 1980s.[73] Economic development has reduced prostitution's importance to the contemporary Taiwanese and South Korean economies, but the immense sex industry that still exists in Thailand traces its origins to the R&R program.[74]

The R&R scheme ended nearly fifty years ago, yet as "Fat Leonard" Glenn Francis knew all too well, good times centered on prostitutes and alcohol remain *the* standard leisure experience for U.S. servicemen stationed in the western Pacific. Other legacies of the Vietnam War have faded. The frequency of overseas U.S. military interventions since the early 1990s corroborate George H. W. Bush's 1991 claim about kicking "the Vietnam syndrome once and for all," even if the track record of failure these operations have left behind was not what the president envisioned.[75] And with the U.S. war in Afghanistan approaching its third decade, the term *military quagmire* no longer automatically elicits mental images of Vietnam in the minds of most Americans. However, as the Fat Leonard scandal and the red light districts still surrounding U.S. military bases across the region both attest, the Vietnam War R&R program normalized a conception of militarized masculinity that still endures in Asia.

Notes

1. As of early 2020, U.S. Justice Department investigations have resulted in thirty-three federal indictments and twenty-two guilty pleas. More than sixty admirals were investigated. See "Plea Agreement: *United States of America v. Leonard Glenn Francis*," Case No. 13CR3781, accessed March 3, 2020, https://www.justice.gov/sites/default/files/opa/press-releases/attachments/2015/01/16/francis_plea_agreement_comp.pdf; Craig Whitlock, "The Man Who Seduced the 7th Fleet," *Washington Post*, May 27, 2016.

2. Sam LaGrone, "Paying the Price: The Hidden Cost of the 'Fat Leonard' Investigation," *USNI News*, January 24, 2019.

3. Craig Whitlock, "Admiral, Seven Others Charged with Corruption in New 'Fat Leonard' Indictment," *Washington Post*, March 15, 2017.

4. Zach Fredman, "America's Longtime Foreign Policy in Asia: Booze, Prostitutes and Bribes," *Washington Post*, February 15, 2018.

5. On the "comfort-for-morale formula," see Meredith H. Lair, *Armed with Abundance: Consumerism and Soldiering in the Vietnam War* (Chapel Hill: University of North Carolina Press, 2011), 185–187.

6. Lair, *Armed with Abundance*, 109–110.

7. Zach Fredman, "GIs and 'Jeep Girls': Sex and American Soldiers in Wartime China," *Journal of Modern Chinese History* 13, no. 1 (2019): 76–101.

8. Odd Arne Westad, *Decisive Encounters: The Chinese Civil War, 1946–1950* (Stanford, CA: Stanford University Press, 2003), 101, 140–142.

9. Zhonggong Beijing shi wei dangshi yanjiu shi, *Kangyi Meijun zhuHua baoxing yundong ziliao huibian* (Beijing: Beijing daxue chu ban she, 1989), 127–379.

10. Stephen G. Craft, *American Justice in Taiwan: The 1957 Riots and Cold War Foreign Policy* (Lexington: University of Kentucky Press, 2016).

11. Fredman, "GIs and 'Jeep Girls,'" 76–77, 84–87.

12. Yanqiu Zheng, "A Specter of Extraterritoriality: The Legal Status of U.S. Troops in China, 1943–1947," *Journal of American-East Asian Relations* 22 (2015): 17–44; Hong Zhang, *America Perceived: The Making of Chinese Images of the United States, 1945–1953* (Westport, CT: Greenwood, 2002), 80–111.

13. Craft, *American Justice in Taiwan*, 64–70, 85, 87–89, 150–163.

14. "Agreement between the United States of America and the Republic of China on the Status of United States Armed Forces in the Republic of China," August 31, 1966, in 90th Congress, 1st Session, Committee on Foreign Affairs, ed., *Collective Defense Treaties* (Washington, DC: Government Printing Office, 1967), 446–473.

15. "Shangtao youguan zhuYue Meijun dujia diwei wenti huiyi," November 13, 1965, Waijiao bu dang'an [hereafter WJB], file no.11-07-02-13-05-113, pp. 6–8, Institute of Modern History Archives, Academia Sinica, Taiwan [hereafter IMH].

16. Wan-Chen Yan, *Governing Sex, Building the Nation: The Politics of Prostitution in Postcolonial Taiwan* (Newcastle upon Tyne, UK: Cambridge Scholars Press, 2015), 162–163, 214–215.

17. "Shangtao youguan zhuYue Meijun dujia diwei wenti huiyi," November 13, 1965, WJB, file no.11-07-02-13-05-113, pp. 6–8, IMH; R. Sean Randolph, *The United States and Thailand: Alliance Dynamics, 1950–1985* (Berkeley: University of California Press, 1986), 62–63, 74–75.

18. "Taiwan jingbei silingbu huiyi tongzhi," December 15, 1965, WJB, file no.11-07-02-13-05-113, pp. 30–34, IMH.

19. "Waijiaobu Cai sizhang yu Meiguo dashiguan Lin guishi canshi tanhua jilu," November 26, 1965, WJB, file no.11-07-02-13-05-113, pp. 17–18, IMH.

20. U.S. Embassy, Taipei to North American Department, ROC Foreign Ministry, undated, WJB, file no.11-07-02-13-05-113, pp. 56–57, IMH.

21. "Meijun dujia mian mian guan," *Lianhe bao*, November 13, 1965.

22. U.S. Embassy, Taipei to North American Department, ROC Foreign Ministry, undated, WJB, file no.11-07-02-13-05-113, pp. 56–57, IMH.

23. Cynthia Enloe, *The Morning After: Sexual Politics at the End of the Cold War* (Berkeley: University of California Press, 1993), 145.

24. Hui-Man Lee, "The Face of Free China: Tourism, Cold War and Nation Building, 1945–1979" (PhD diss., University of Exeter, 2012), 23, 117–122.

25. Yen, *Governing Sex, Building the Nation*, 176; Li Guoding, *Wo de Taiwan jingyan: Li Guoding tan Taiwan caijing zhengce de zhiding yu sikao* (Taipei: Yuanliu chubanshe, 2005), 543.

26. Murray Rubenstein, "Lu Hsuilien and the Origins of Taiwanese Feminism," in *Women in the New Taiwan: Gender Roles, and Gender Consciousness in a Changing Society*, ed. Catherine Farris, Anru Lee, and Murray Rubinstein (Armonk, NY: M. E. Sharpe, 2004), 253–254.

27. "Yige xinqi de wenti: tan Meijun lai Hua dujia," *Zhengxin xinwen*, November 22, 1965.

28. Marcos agreed to open the Philippines to R&R on December 14, while Lee okayed the program on March 8, 1966. See Republic of the Philippines Department of Foreign Affairs, Press Release No. 30, December 14, 1965, WJB, file no.11-07-02-13-05-113, p. 65, IMH; "Singapore Oks R-and-R Visits by US Troops," *China Post*, March 9, 1966.

29. "Guofang bu han Waijiao bu bei Meizhou si," May 4, 1965, WJB, file no.11-07-02-13-05-113, p. 147, IMH.

30. "Action Memorandum from the Assistant Secretary for Far Eastern Affairs (Bundy) to Secretary Rusk," August 23, 1965, *Foreign Relations of the United States, 1964–1968, Volume 30, China* (Washington, DC: Government Printing Office, 1998), 193–194.

31. "Procedures for Criminal Proceedings under SOFA," September 21, 1966, WJB, file no. 11-07-02-13-05-032, pp. 207–214, IMH.

32. "Meijun dujia mian mian guan," *Lianhe bao*, November 13, 1965; "Dujia Meijun jiang dao, youye fei yi tigao," *Lianhe bao*, November 20, 1965; "Dujia jun 26 dao, guanguang lvshe da jianjia," *Zhengxin xinwen*, November 21, 1965.

33. "Yi ge xinqi de wenti: tan Meijin lai Hua dujia," *Zhengxin xinwen*, November 22, 1965.

34. "Taiwan R&R Center to Be Closed Soon," *China Post*, March 15, 1972; "Zhu Yue Meijun lai Tai dujia di liu ci xietiao hui yi," April 21, 1967, WJB, file no.11-07-02-13-05-113, pp. 163–167, 212. IMH.

35. John Haydock, "Taiwan: Land of Quiet Pleasure," *Thunder* 2, no. 2 (Winter 1969): 23.

36. "Zhongyang tongxun she cankao xiaoxi 0615 hao," April 8, 1970; "Shangtao Hanguo zhu Yue junren lai Tai dujia qianzheng ji guanzhi deng shiyou huiyi lu," July 8, 1967, WJB, file no.11-07-02-13-05-113, pp. 192–194, 272–273, IMH.

37. Ambassador Walter McConaughy to Minister of Foreign Affairs Chow Shuk'ai, April 10, 1972, WJB, file no.11-07-02-13-05-113, p. 290, IMH.

38. "Meijun lai Tai dujia ming qi tingzhi banli," *Zhongyang ribao*, April 11, 1972.

39. Lair, *Armed with Abundance*, 109–111.

40. Interdepartmental Report: Rest and Recuperation Facilities in Australia for United States and Allied Servicemen in Vietnam, April 26, 1967, NAA: A1313, 1967/3793, Part 1, National Archives of Australia [hereafter NAA], Canberra.

41. *A Holiday from Hell*, directed by Sterling Seagrave (1967; San Francisco, KGO-TV News); "Your R&R Program," August 1968, Claire Brisebois Starnes Collection, box 1, folder 1, The Vietnam Center and Sam Johnson Vietnam Archive, Texas Tech University [hereafter VCA].

42. "Shangtao Hanguo zhu Yue junren lai Tai dujia qianzheng ji guanzhi deng shiyou huiyi lu," July 8, 1967, WJB, file no.11-07-02-13-05-113, pp. 192–194, IMH.

43. Ken White, "R&R in Taipei," Item Number 21610105001, The LRRP/Rangers of the First Cavalry Division during the Vietnam War, VCA.

44. *A Holiday from Hell*.

45. Darrell Houston, "R&R in Taiwan—From Plane to Pad in an Hour Flat," *Seattle Post-Intelligencer*, April 28, 1969.

46. Houston, "R&R in Taiwan."

47. "Zhu Yue Meijun lai Tai dujia di liu ci xietiao hui yi," April 21, 1967, WJB, file no.11-07-02-13-05-113, pp. 163–170, IMH; "26 Bars in Taipei," http://taipeiairstation.blogspot.com/search?q=R%26R.

48. On VD and sex work during the occupation of Japan, see Sarah Kovner, *Occupying Power: Sex Workers and Servicemen in Postwar Japan* (Stanford, CA: Stanford University Press, 2012), 7, 24–48; Robert Kramm, *Sanitized Sex: Regulating Prostitution, Venereal Disease, and Intimacy in Occupied Japan, 1945–1952* (Berkeley: University of California Press, 2017), 127–162.

49. "Zhongguo guomindang zhongyang weiyuan hui zhi Wei Daoming dian," October 26, 1966, WJB, file no.11-07-02-13-05-113, pp. 157–159, IMH.

50. "Zhu Yue Meijun lai Tai dujia di liu ci xietiao huiyi jilu1," April 22, 1967, WJB, file no.11-07-02-13-05-113, pp. 171–173, IMH; Yen, *Governing Sex, Building the Nation*, 172, 179.

51. Yen, *Governing Sex, Building the Nation*, 179–181.

52. Houston, "R&R in Taiwan."

53. Terry Turner, "Rest and Recuperation," *First Team* 3, no. 4 (Autumn 1970): 30–35.

54. Chris Dixon and Jon Piccini, "Destination Downunder: American Servicemen in Sydney, 1967–1972," paper presented at the 2019 Vietnam War in the Pacific World Conference, Sydney.

55. "Activity Tours for R&R Men," *Financial Review*, February 15, 1968, NAA: A1313, 1967/3793, Part 1, NAA; Frank Proust, "Leave Flights from Vietnam to Be Doubled," *Sydney Morning Herald*, January 2, 1968.

56. Houston, "R&R in Taiwan."

57. Houston, "R&R in Taiwan"; Herb Hartley, "Ancient China Meets Mod West in Taipei," *Southern Cross*, August 20, 1969; "Holiday from a War Zone," *Air Cavalry Division* (Spring 1969): 38–44; "Recreation: Five-Day Bonanza," *Time*, December 22, 1967.

58. Yen, *Governing Sex, Building the Nation*, 225–227.

59. "Lin Tingsheng cheng Xingzheng yuan guanguang zhengce shenyi xiaozu dian," December 28, 1968, WJB, file no.11-07-02-13-05-113, p. 254, IMH. On the Chinese cultural renaissance, see Allen Chun, "From Nationalism to Nationalizing:

Cultural Imagination and State Formation in Postwar Taiwan," *Australian Journal of Chinese Affairs* 31 (January 1994): 49–69.

60. Houston, "R&R in Taiwan."

61. "Zhongguo guomindang zhongyang weiyuan hui zhi Wei Daoming dian," October 26, 1966, WJB, file no.11-07-02-13-05-113, pp. 157–159, IMH.

62. "60,000 R&R Men in 1967; TTB Director Airs Hope," *China Post*, March 25, 1968.

63. "Recreation: Five-Day Bonanza."

64. "Zhu Yue Meijun lai Tai dujia di liu ci xietiao hui yi," April 21, 1967; "Guojia anquan ju zhi Waijiao bu dian," October 19, 1967, WJB, file no.11-07-02-13-05-113, pp. 163–167, 197–199, IMH.

65. "Taiwan jingbei zong siling bu zhi Waijia bu dian," April 22, 1967, WJB, file no.11-07-02-13-05-113, pp. 171–173, IMH.

66. "Kebei de 'guanguang' shiye de yi jiao," *Zhengxin xinwen*, July 15, 1968.

67. "R&R Center Man Here Said in Bribery Case," *China Post*, July 15, 1968.

68. "Taiwan jingbei zong siling bu zhi Waijia bu dian," April 22, 1967, WJB, file no.11-07-02-13-05-113, pp. 171–173, IMH.

69. Hartley, "Ancient China Meets Mod West in Taipei."

70. Fredman, "GIs and 'Jeep Girls,'" 78–83; Yen, *Governing Sex, Building the Nation*, 138–139.

71. "Dollars and Sense," MACV Office of Information, September 1968, Claire Brisebois Starnes Collection, VCA.

72. Wen-Qing Ngoei, *Arc of Containment: Britain, the United States, and Anti-communism in Southeast Asia* (Ithaca, NY: Cornell University Press, 2019), 160–161; Yen, *Governing Sex, Building the Nation*, 132; Natasha Hamilton-Hart, *Hard Interests, Soft Illusions: Southeast Asia and American Power* (Ithaca, NY: Cornell University Press, 2012), 119–121; Sheila Jeffreys, *The Industrial Vagina: The Political Economy of the Global Sex Trade* (London: Taylor & Francis, 2008), 116–120.

73. Yen, *Governing Sex, Building the Nation*, 132; Jeffreys, *The Industrial Vagina*, 116–117; Keun-joo Christine Pae, "Spiritual Activism as Interfaith Dialogue: When Military Prostitution Matters," *Journal of Feminist Studies in Religion* 36, no. 1 (Spring 2020): 73–76.

74. Ouyyanont Porphant, "The Vietnam War and Tourism in Bangkok's Development," *Southeast Asian Studies* 39, no. 2 (2001): 157–187.

75. George Bush, "Remarks to the American Legislative Exchange Council," March 1, 1991, American Presidency Project, https://www.presidency.ucsb.edu/documents/remarks-the-american-legislative-exchange-council-0.

9 Taiwanese Economic Assistance to South Vietnam, 1955-1975

JASON LIM

Introduction

In the context of the Cold War, the main narrative of the Vietnam War is a conflict between North Vietnam and its backers the Soviet Union and the People's Republic of China (PRC) on the one hand, and South Vietnam and the United States on the other hand. Less known is about how South Vietnam, in a bid for survival, forged diplomatic relations with countries in East and Southeast Asia and the response of those countries to its diplomatic overtures. Taiwan, officially the Republic of China (ROC), also remains peripheral to research on the Cold War.[1] The ROC is regarded as nothing more than "a pariah state" with the image of "a one-party, US-client, garrison state."[2] Foreign relations of the ROC generates little interest since the country, like South Vietnam, was a recipient of American aid. However, declassified government records held in various archives in Taiwan tell a different story. Our knowledge of the Cold War in East and Southeast Asia can be expanded with the use of these records.

For the noncommunist side of the conflict, the Vietnam War involved more than just South Vietnam and the United States. Australia, South Korea, the Philippines, and Thailand provided military support. Other states offered nonmilitary or limited military support. The ROC sent a small contingent of officers to Saigon as the Republic of China Military Advisory Group, Vietnam. However, the scope of Taiwan's relationship with South Vietnam is wider. This chapter looks at just one area—an overview of the economic relationship from the birth of the Republic of Vietnam (RVN) in 1955 to the end of the Vietnam War in 1975. It focuses on how diplomatic relations were forged and the Taiwanese role in the economic development of the RVN.

Relationship between "China" and "Vietnam"

Throughout its history, Vietnam was colonized four times by various Chinese empires, with the last by the Ming dynasty in the early fifteenth century. The French colonized Vietnam in the nineteenth century and the colony was occupied by the Japanese during World War II. Ho Chi Minh declared Vietnamese independence in Hanoi when the Japanese surrendered in 1945. The returning French did not accept Vietnamese independence and the ensuing war ended with a French defeat at Dien Bien Phu in 1954. The Geneva Conference on Indochina from May to July 1954 saw the division of Vietnam along the 17th parallel—a communist regime in the north led by Ho, and a noncommunist regime in the south with the capital at Saigon. The RVN was proclaimed in Saigon on October 26, 1955.

Both the ROC and the RVN saw themselves as successor states to Chinese and Vietnamese empires, respectively. After the Chinese Communist Party (CCP) proclaimed the founding of the PRC on October 1, 1949, the Kuomintang (KMT) government moved to Taipei, the "temporary capital of the ROC." Although the ROC was strictly just Taiwan and several offshore islands from 1949, it still claimed to be the legitimate government of all of "China." Declassified records in Taipei and Vietnamese newspapers referred to the RVN as "Vietnam," as if North Vietnam did not exist. Both countries were headed by anti-communist leaders who saw economic development as a bulwark against the appeal of communism. The Cold War underpinned one key perspective from both countries: national sovereignty was threatened by the destructive force of communism.

Based on the historical relationship between the Chinese and the Vietnamese, there is a constant theme in the archival records held in Taiwan about how "China" and "Vietnam" had historical, cultural, and economic ties that stretched back millennia. Brantly Womack wrote about how Sino-Vietnamese relations represented a "politics of asymmetry" where both countries shared common interests (including history), but China was the dominant partner.[3] Historical baggage was the basis of twentieth-century ROC-RVN relations. With a sense of cultural superiority, KMT leaders believed it was a duty of the ROC to assist the RVN in its economic development. Since "China" was dominant in that relationship, the ROC saw the RVN as a junior partner in their fight against communism, even though in terms of land area, South Vietnam was about four times larger than Taiwan.

Forging Diplomatic Relations

The ROC and RVN established diplomatic relations on December 17, 1955. Relations did not go well in the beginning due to the economic dominance of the Chinese community in the RVN, which had introduced a policy of cultural assimilation by legislating the compulsory "Vietnamization" of Chinese personal names and the exclusion of ethnic Chinese from several occupations. The RVN government argued that the policy was necessary as part of its nation-building process—the ethnic Chinese had to choose between Chinese or Vietnamese citizenship.

This early antagonism eventually gave way to ideological considerations. Seven months after the proclamation of the RVN and with an ongoing assimilation policy, ROC president Chiang Kai-shek saw the potential of a partner in his plans to counter communist influence and activities in East and Southeast Asia. He appealed to RVN president Ngo Dinh Diem: "The free Asian countries share a common destiny today in the face of the challenge of communism. Like Vietnam, my country is also seeking the most effective measures to achieve collective security and common defense in Asia. . . . I very much hope that our relationship will be further strengthened by more frequent exchange of views and by closer cooperation."[4] Both noncommunist states had "a great deal in common."[5] The KMT government had to balance between assisting the RVN in its nation-building projects and maintaining a controlled criticism of anti-Chinese feelings in that country. The new narrative by the KMT was that anti-Chinese feelings were largely the fault of the former French colonial government who had trusted the Chinese in Vietnam and traded with them, resulting in eventual Chinese domination of the Vietnamese economy and feelings of envy among the Vietnamese.[6]

Despite its concerns about the Chinese in the RVN, Taipei worked toward closer ties with Saigon. The first area of focus was the RVN economy. At the time of its creation in 1954, "South Vietnam held great promise as an economic enterprise" because it could feed its population and needed some agricultural development to create foreign exchange.[7] After a visit to Saigon by ROC foreign affairs minister Yeh Kung-chao in April 1958, the Ministry of Foreign Affairs (MOFA) reported that the ROC could play a major role in the economic development of the RVN. Since the Diem government planned to set up factories and introduce agricultural reform, diplomatic relations could be improved through strengthening economic and agricultural exchanges.[8] The ROC would provide training and assistance because the RVN lacked experts in agriculture.

The MOFA report also questioned the doubts raised by the United States Agency for International Development (USAID) about the economic potential of the RVN.[9] MOFA criticized the Americans for not believing in Diem's plans for industrialization and found it incredible that the Americans considered the opening of factories in the RVN to be a difficult task. To refute the American claim, MOFA noted the work of two Taiwanese who had set up spinning mills in the RVN. The difference in opinion between the Taiwanese and Americans boiled down to working relations with the South Vietnamese. For example, the Foreign Exchange and Trade Review Commission of the Executive Yuan (Cabinet) in Taipei noted that unlike the Americans, the Taiwanese could quickly get used to the working environment in the RVN.[10]

Economic Goodwill Mission

The MOFA report was followed up with the arrival of an economic goodwill mission in Saigon in October 1958. The mission went the length of the country for thirty-six days "to exchange ideas and experience with the [South] Vietnamese Government on the many problems bearing on agricultural and industrial development."[11] The mission recognized that South Vietnam, unlike Taiwan, had the land for large-scale cultivation of rice, rubber, coffee, and coconut, but "what Free China [i.e., Taiwan] lacks in expanse, it has partially made up through the adoption of intensive farming."[12] The mission made suggestions for improvements in rice and sugarcane production, possibilities of the production of crops other than rice and sugarcane, organization of "Farmers' Associations" similar to those in Taiwan, strengthening agricultural experiment stations, and the control and utilization of water resources. The mission also studied plans for the industrialization program in the RVN and the future developments of the textile, sugar, pulp and paper, coal, rubber, chemical fertilizer, rice milling, and pharmaceutical industries.

The RVN government was keen to expand the economy through the introduction of new industries. Early plans were drawn up to build more sawmills and sugar factories.[13] The head of the economic goodwill mission, ROC minister of economic affairs Li Kwoh-ting, noted that the RVN had better conditions to grow sugarcane. Whereas Taiwanese growers required fourteen to eighteen months before the cane was harvested, South Vietnamese growers need not have to wait that long due to more favorable climate conditions.[14] The Taiwan Sugar Corporation sent an eleven-person mission to the RVN in March 1959 for a four-month survey, and the company later planned to build three sugar factories.[15] Taiwan also helped set up cotton processing plants so that the South Vietnamese could process cotton that had been provided by the United States through American aid.[16]

Importance of Economic Ties

In the early 1950s, the main agenda of the KMT government on Taiwan was *fangong dalu* (counteroffensive against the mainland). However, that agenda was no longer realistic even from the perspective of senior ROC military officers. Yang Huei Pang argued that "by the time of the Second Taiwan Straits crisis (1958), for all practical purposes *Fangong dalu* was dead."[17] He noted that from 1958, *fangong dalu* morphed from plans for a military offensive against the CCP to an agenda for the economic, social, and cultural development of Taiwan.

The economic trajectory of Taiwan reflected what Walt Rostow considered to be the route toward an economic "takeoff."[18] Taiwan's First Four-Year Plan (1953–1956) focused on increasing rice production, use of fertilizers, and harnessing hydroelectric power. The Second Four-Year Plan (1957–1960) was a program of import-substitution industrialization. Taiwan could now impart knowledge and experience to aid the RVN. Yeh's visit in 1958, the subsequent MOFA report, and the report of the economic goodwill mission became the reference points for Taiwanese aid to the South Vietnamese. The U.S. State Department and several academics also claimed an economic miracle had occurred in the RVN between 1956 and 1960 and that by 1961, the country was "poised ready to take off."[19]

Diem saw South Vietnamese economic development as a part of the nation-building process, although his economic ideas were criticized by Gabriel Kolko as "an exotic mélange of mandarin anti-capitalism and Catholic feudal ideas and a keen desire for personal power and profit."[20] In his speech before the National Assembly in October 1957, Diem noted that the most urgent task was "the restoration of the means of communications and the maintenance of the existing living standard."[21] He also believed that "the solution of social problems depends upon economic prosperity."[22] Diem worked on new infrastructural and agricultural projects, largely with American economic aid. In 1959, he told reporters that "the future of his country is dependent on highways, airstrips and increased agricultural activity."[23]

He scored a major diplomatic victory when he successfully persuaded the Japanese government to give World War II reparations to Saigon instead of Hanoi. The reparation money worth US$55 million helped fund the Da Nhim hydroelectric project.[24] Yet, as a nationalist, Diem wanted to allay South Vietnamese concerns that the country had become heavily dependent on foreign aid. Although critical of Diem's economic ideas, Kolko noted that "Diem refused to allow American economists to advise him and embarked on economic policies the United States regarded with alarm."[25] As more American military and economic aid poured in, Diem "bitterly resented" how American policy on his country came to be shaped by American aid.[26]

Diem was eager for economic cooperation with other countries so that he was not labeled a collaborator with, or a puppet of, the United States by his critics. He wanted "aid without conditions, without strings attached."[27] To Diem, the Americans were like "great big children—well intentioned, powerful, with a lot of technical know-how, but not very sophisticated in dealing with him or his race, or his country's problems."[28] Diem's agenda was for a "gradual industrialization program consistent with our needs and capacities" where the RVN would produce textiles, sugar, cement, paper, glass, and plastics for local consumption.[29] Several observation trips to the RVN were organized by the ROC. After a short trip to rural South Vietnam by Chang Lien-chun from the Sino-American Joint Commission on Rural Reconstruction (JCRR), Chang proposed irrigation projects to combat drought in central Vietnam, education of farmers in the use of organic fertilizers, fighting epidemics in pigs and chickens, and the planting of intermediary crops.[30] These visits helped the ROC propose the kind of assistance that it could provide. The ROC promised economic assistance with no strings attached since it saw the South Vietnamese as partners in an anti-communist crusade.

Most of the technical assistance provided by the ROC from 1955 to 1975 was for rural South Vietnam, including introduction of new crops, teaching new farming techniques, construction of irrigation systems and hydroelectric power stations, and organizing rural associations for farmers. Future South Vietnamese leaders also saw the need to appear not to be too reliant on American aid. Within the KMT, there was a recognition that interference in another country's domestic affairs could lead to antagonism from that country's population and cited the extensive American aid as a reason for South Vietnamese dislike of the United States.[31]

Economic Assistance and Political Instability

Just before Yeh's visit to Saigon in April 1958, the ROC saw the economic potential of the RVN. It was doing well economically despite receiving American aid, had a steady industrial production, and it was politically stable.[32] As a benefactor of the RVN, political stability was uppermost in the minds of the ROC government. Taipei supported the American policy on Vietnam and urged the Americans not to obstruct Diem's anti-communist work.[33] Yet, the ROC government knew that Diem was an unpopular politician. When discontented officers in the Army of the Republic of Vietnam (ARVN) launched a coup on November 1, 1963, it "did not catch Taiwan by surprise."[34] The value of the RVN as a partner engaged in the anti-communist agenda was so high that the ROC government planned to recognize the new regime immediately after the coup, even though news of Diem's fate had not been officially announced. It sought reassurances from Saigon that it would continue with anti-communist activities and all existing projects spearheaded by Taiwan in the country would continue.[35] Only then did the ROC recognize the new government of the Military Revolutionary Council (MRC) headed by General Duong Van Minh on November 6, one day before the United States did so. The ROC's position remained the same—so long as the MRC remained anti-communist, good relations and cooperation between both countries would be maintained.[36]

The November 1963 coup set a trend that showed the importance of bilateral relations with the ROC. Each time there was a regime change, the new leader would either visit Taipei or send a representative. Two months after Diem was overthrown, a bloodless coup led to a new regime headed by General Nguyen Khanh. Again, the ROC threw its support behind the Khanh government and the new defense minister Tran Thien Khiem paid an official visit to Taipei on behalf of General Khanh in March 1964.[37] Minh also went on a ten-day visit to Taiwan as a special envoy of the MRC in December 1964.[38] When Khanh was removed from power in February 1965, the junta sent Prime Minister Nguyen Cao Ky to Taipei in August. Ky did not ask for any military assistance and focused on securing economic and technical aid.[39] President Nguyen Van Thieu arrived in Taipei on May 30, 1969 for a four-day visit. In every visit to Taipei, the South Vietnamese leaders reaffirmed their anti-communist stand and discussed economic issues with ROC government officials. ROC economic assistance was crucial, and the *Canberra Times* noted its "large agriculture assistance commitment." The ROC was listed as one of the six largest aid countries to the RVN after the United States.[40]

Sino-Vietnamese Economic Cooperation Conferences

The importance of economic ties was underscored by the planning and publicity of the Sino-Vietnamese Economic Cooperation Conference. In January 1960, Diem made an official visit to Taipei, and both sides discussed how regular conferences held alternately in Saigon and Taipei could discuss issues and plans for the future economic development of the RVN. The conference would have four committees based on key issues: industry and mining, agriculture and forestry, communications, and trade. After a general meeting at the opening of the conference, each committee would meet separately to discuss pressing issues and make proposals to both governments.[41] Most negotiations on ROC assistance to the RVN occurred during these conferences.

One perennial issue the conferences tackled was the imbalance of trade in the ROC's favor. In 1956, the RVN's trade with the ROC was small. The former imported 24,147 metric tons of goods from Taiwan, while exports were negligible (see table 9.1). Although imports from Taiwan that year constituted just 2.3 percent of overall imports by the RVN, it was ranked sixth.[42] In 1964, South Vietnamese imports from Taiwan totaled 1,339,000 piastres, but exports to Taiwan was just 25,000 piastres. American aid provided the RVN with the bulk of foreign exchange through the Commercial Import Program (CIP) and the PL-480 Food for Peace Program. Both programs financed the purchase of American goods, including refined petroleum products, machinery, fertilizers, and agricultural products such as rice, wheat, cotton, and tobacco.[43]

Bilateral trade benefited Taipei as one condition for receiving American economic aid was that Saigon could not use the funds to import goods from nineteen industrialized countries that excluded the ROC.[44] The CIP was disbursed so that "Americans told the Vietnamese importers which commodities and how much they could import," resulting in a South Vietnamese overdependence on the United States.[45] Import trade figures increased in 1965 to 1,646,000 piastres, but export figures fell to 17,000 piastres, leading the *Saigon Daily News* to assert that "the Vietnamese war is expected to do to Nationalist China what the Korean War did to Japan economically."[46] During the first conference held in Saigon in December 1960, RVN vice president Nguyen Ngoc Tho suggested that the ROC could buy agricultural products and raw materials from the RVN and that the RVN could purchase manufactured products from the ROC.[47] After two conferences in 1960 and 1962, however, the problem remained unresolved. In May 1963, Taiwan sent two market experts to the RVN to study ways to increase exports. In June, the situation had become so difficult that a Taiwanese official suggested that surplus chemical fertilizers in Taiwan could be exported to the RVN in exchange for rice.[48] Unfortunately, with the coup in November 1963, the RVN had become politically unstable and unable to increase exports.[49]

The trade imbalance increased after Diem was overthrown. The Third Four-Year Plan (1961–1964) in Taiwan emphasized export-oriented industries, energy development, agricultural development, and use of natural resources. In 1964, David Bell, administrator of USAID, said, "Taiwan, which 10 years ago was as heavily dependent on US aid to stay afloat as Vietnam is today, is now reaching a point of economic self-sufficiency and is providing technical assistance to less developed nations."[50]

In June 1965, the United States ended all economic aid to the ROC just as it entered the export-oriented industrialization stage of economic development. Taiwanese exporters targeted the RVN. By August, about 400 Taiwanese businesses applied to join a Sino-Vietnamese Trade Promotion Group organized by the China Productivity and Trade Centre, with steel, machinery, construction materials, and textiles as main export items to the RVN.[51] A survey noted that "the war has made [South] Vietnam Taiwan's third most important export market behind Japan and the United States."[52]

Both countries believed that "the problem is the lack of demand or supply" in trade, an odd way of saying that there remains no solution to the trade imbalance for the RVN. They point out how both the RVN and the ROC exported rice.[53] Both sides then blamed the Americans. The third conference concluded that "since most Vietnamese procurements are made with United States aid funds, complicated procedures are involved."[54] American economic assistance had seen an *increase* in imports by the RVN (though not from Taiwan) although the South Vietnamese insisted that nonessential commodities and locally made goods were banned from importation.[55] After ten years, the RVN still saw itself in the import-substitution phase (the first stage) of economic development toward "takeoff."

In June 1969, industrial and commercial leaders from Taiwan and the RVN met in Taipei to discuss promotion of bilateral trade and strengthening economic cooperation.[56] Again, there was no solution to the trade im-

TABLE 9.1 Trade between Taiwan (ROC) and South Vietnam (RVN), 1956–1972

Year	Imports		Exports	
	Metric tons	VN$ (thousands)	Metric tons	VN$ (thousands)
1956	24,147	147	–	–
1957	43,641	308	950	3
1958	24,018	196	–	–
1959	12,020	214	50	171
1960	23,677	179	10,102	31
1961	219,543	500	20,635	76
1962	337,343	875	1,141	9
1963	477,452	1,311	632	8
1964	508,052	1,339	1,731	25
1965	480,770	1,646	1,090	17
1966	565,466	4,099	2,322	29
1967	768,738	6,439	587	17
1968	525,143	3,670	70	2
1969	362,142	4,203	1,069	5
1970	464,516	3,428	2,136	7
1971	469,407	6,667	515	15
1972	487,332	17,083	3,516	51

Sources: [South] *Viet Nam Statistical Yearbook 1964–65*, 312–315; [South] *Viet Nam Statistical Yearbook 1972*, 140–143.

balance as delegates focused on the RVN expanding trade ties with other countries. During the sixth conference in Saigon in January 1970, Sun Yun-suan, the ROC minister of economic affairs, pointed out that South Vietnamese exports to Taiwan had increased from 1969.[57] However, as table 9.1 shows, the trade imbalance remained unsolved. By the time of the eighth conference on November 3, 1973, bilateral trade was still discussed. The Vietcong then resumed operations, and Thieu announced the resumption of war in January 1974.

Another issue covered by the conferences was the Taiwanese commitment toward granting agricultural and technical assistance to the South Vietnamese. The report of the economic goodwill mission had led to the creation of a permanent mission to the RVN. In December 1959, the first Taiwanese technical team of nine members arrived to assist in the organization of farmers' associations. A team was sent in July 1960 to work on crop improvement and another in November 1960 to work on irrigation. These three teams received financial support from the United States Operations Mission (USOM) in Vietnam and the RVN government with annual renewal contracts signed between the Ministry of Rural Affairs in Saigon and the JCRR in Taipei.[58] The three teams merged into the Chinese Agriculture Technical Mission to Vietnam (CATM/VN) in September 1964. The CATM/VN focused on three main areas—crop and livestock, irrigation and engineering, and rural development. Groups of young Taiwanese who had graduated from technical colleges or vocational schools with field experience were sent to the rural areas of South Vietnam to live and work with the farmers. More than half of the eighty members of the CATM/VN in April 1965 were field agents working in South Vietnam, with another 30 percent of its members assigned to laboratories and experiment stations managed by the RVN government.[59] Taiwanese assistance also included a Chinese power mission whose responsibility was to train power technicians and to work on hydroelectric power projects and power stations in the RVN. Six Vietnamese technicians had been trained on electric power by the Taiwan Power Corporation from March 1962 to February 1963.[60] The Chinese power mission would stay in Vietnam until the early 1970s.

During the sixth conference in January 1970, ROC minister of economic affairs Sun Yun-suan highlighted Taiwanese aid since 1959 in promoting new cultivation methods to its farmers and opening factories producing paper, sugar, monosodium glutamate, and textiles. The ROC was willing to expand its work through electric power, telecommunications, and transport. Pham Vang Ngoc, RVN minister of economic affairs, announced that the Taiwanese would lay 230 kilowatts of electrical lines and build a thermal power plant in Danang.[61] At the end of the seventh conference, plans were made to train South Vietnamese hydraulic engineers and assist in the artificial insemination of pigs and carp spawning. The ROC would set aside scholarship funds to train up to forty South Vietnamese in the cultivation of vegetables and fruits. The ROC agreed to open at least one textile mill and a peanut farm for South Vietnamese war veterans and to continue assisting the South Vietnamese in the sugar and fertilizer industries. Postwar plans by the RVN to rebuild the country would be aided by a loan of NT$2 billion to purchase machinery and train technicians.[62] Following the eighth conference in November 1973, the ROC agreed to provide US$2 million in aid to the RVN, including US$400,000 in grain processing equipment and another US$300,000 to help plan South Vietnamese power needs. The ROC would also donate 250 metric tons of grain and train 232 South Vietnamese technicians in Taipei.[63]

The ROC was also involved in planning "improved villages" for the RVN. In 1965, RVN minister of agriculture Lam Van Tri and ROC minister of economic affairs Li Kwoh-ting discussed an Improved Village Development Program in Vietnam. This program would develop three "improved villages," each of about 300 hectares in size. Each "improved village" would have an operation center and a demonstration farm, and farmers would be trained in new techniques of farming. The ROC would develop irrigation projects in each "improved village" and contribute supplies to the village. These plans were accepted by the delegates during the third conference. Bien Hoa was chosen as a site for an "improved village."[64] Following the sixth conference in January 1970, two improved villages were handed over to the RVN government as plans were made for five more "improved villages" in "secured areas."[65] The importance of the conference, however, declined as the war dragged on (see table 9.2). The Taiwanese and South Vietnamese delegations to the first conference in 1960 were headed by the ROC minister for economic affairs and the RVN vice president. By the time the eighth conference was held in 1973, both delegations were headed by the countries' vice ministers in economic affairs even though the ROC did not reduce technical aid to the RVN. However, Taiwanese experts remained visible in South Vietnamese fields, towns, villages, and cities. During the ninth (and last) conference in 1974, the Taiwanese pledged to strengthen the work of the CATM/VN and to provide a loan of NT$200 million for the purchase of Taiwanese machinery and equipment.[66]

Postwar Plans

After the 1968 Tet offensive, Taiwan's attention turned to the reconstruction of the RVN. Taiwan was into its Fifth Four-Year Plan (1969–1972) with an emphasis on the joint development of agriculture and industry. In his letter to Thieu, ROC vice president Yen Chia-kan wrote about possible Taiwanese contributions and persuaded Thieu that the Fifth Four-Year Plan would have "helpful references for the postwar economic development plans in Vietnam." Yen assured Thieu that there could be technical assistance in fertilizer, cement, paper and pulp, plywood, textile, sugar, marine products, sheet glass, plastic, petroleum exploration, and coal production and exploration. He also promised Taiwanese help in infrastructural development such as railways, highways, harbors, telecommunications, postal services, water supply, and power development. Ongoing Taiwanese assistance in land reform, rice production, agricultural extension, farmers' organizations, animal husbandry, fisheries, forestry, and irrigation would continue.[67]

TABLE 9.2 Sino-Vietnamese Economic Cooperation Conferences

	Period of Discussions and Tours (inclusive of the actual conferences)	Venue	Head of Delegation Republic of China	Head of Delegation Republic of Vietnam
1st	December 18–25, 1960	Saigon	Yang Gi-tzeng, Minister of Economic Affairs	Nguyen Ngoc Tho, Vice President of the Republic of Vietnam
2nd	February 26–March 3, 1962	Taipei	Yang Gi-tzeng, Minister of Economic Affairs	Nguyen Dinh Thuan, Secretary of State
3rd	October 14–October 21, 1965	Taipei	Li Kwoh-ting, Minister of Economic Affairs	Tran Van Kien, Minister of Finance
4th	January 23–February 3, 1967	Saigon	Li Kwoh-ting, Minister of Economic Affairs	Truong Thai Ton, Minister of the Economy
5th	January 13–January 23, 1968	Taipei	Li Kwoh-ting, Minister of Economic Affairs	Truong Thai Ton, Minister of the Economy
6th	January 7–January 13, 1970	Saigon	Sun Yun-suan, Minister of Economic Affairs	Pham Kim Ngoc, Minister of the Economy
7th	September 7–September 15, 1971	Taipei	Sun Yun-suan, Minister of Economic Affairs	Pham Kim Ngoc, Minister of the Economy
8th	October 28–November 3, 1973	Saigon	Yang Chi-chuan, Vice Minister of Economic Affairs	Nguyen Duc Cuong, Vice Minister of the Economy
9th	November 27–December 6, 1974	Taipei	Sun Yun-suan, Minister of Economic Affairs	Duong Kich Nhuong, Minister of Public Works and Communications

On December 21, 1971, a memorandum of understanding was signed for Taiwan to provide urgent agricultural technology to the RVN from January 8 to March 31, 1972. The reason for this memorandum was that funding from USOM to the CATM/VN would terminate on January 7, 1972. The injection of Taiwanese aid would strengthen the development of agriculture, aid agricultural groups and enterprises, production and sale of vegetables, and other short-term projects required by Saigon.[68] The sixth and eighth conferences in 1970 and 1973, respectively, also discussed the possibility of the ROC helping the RVN establish an export processing zone as the latter progresses toward export-oriented industrialization, the next stage of economic development.[69]

With the signing of the Paris Peace Accords on January 27, 1973, that called for a cease-fire between North Vietnam, South Vietnam, and the United States, ROC foreign affairs minister Shen Chang-huan wrote to Vice President Yen about other potential areas for Taiwanese assistance. The seven Sino-Vietnamese Economic Cooperation Conferences organized so far had cost Taiwan NT$40 million. Shen reminded Yen that every year, the ROC would spend about NT$20 million in the RVN. There will be high costs to the long-term assistance to the RVN such as industrial loans of NT$200 million with interest pegged at 4 percent per annum, NT$15.39 million for the CATM/VN, NT$8 million for the Chinese power mission, NT$3.7 million for the Chinese medical team that had been stationed in Vietnam due to the war, and another NT$6.5 million in areas such as agriculture, industry, and public works. Shen, however, was convinced that the ROC could continue the assistance program once the war was over through donations of rice, loans, expansion of the agricultural technical services, development of fisheries, technical cooperation in provision of electric power, engaging in major public works, and provision of jobs to war veterans.[70] Clearly, the ROC wanted to play a major role in the rebuilding of postwar South Vietnam.

An agreement on cooperation in agricultural technology had been signed on January 19, 1973 by ROC ambassador Hsu Shao-chang and RVN foreign minister Tran Van Lam as a follow-up to what had been agreed in the seventh conference in 1971. The CATM/VN would continue to work with the South Vietnamese government on land reforms, the development of animal husbandry and fisheries, and improve agricultural cultivation methods.[71] At the end of the eighth conference in November, Taiwan made an unconditional promise to South Vietnam to rebuild the country when the war ends.⁷² Taiwan undertook to design a master plan for My Tho, a city of 100,000 people located sixty kilometers from Saigon.⁷³

In his "Message to the Nation" marking the eighteenth anniversary of the founding of the RVN in 1973, Thieu emphasized the importance of ensuring a stable food supply "to be self-reliant, self-sufficient and self-developed." He reiterated that increased agricultural production would be "the key helping us to solve the fundamental economic difficulties" confronting the RVN.⁷⁴ However, the resumption of the conflict from January 1974 meant that there was little else the ROC could do other than continue providing technical assistance to the RVN and train South Vietnamese technicians. The South Vietnamese economy started crumbling from 1972 with rampant inflation.⁷⁵ The ARVN also suffered a string of military defeats. At the end of the ninth conference, it was announced that the tenth conference would be held in Saigon in late 1975. However, the writing was on the wall for the RVN. Thieu resigned on April 21 and he fled, with fifteen associates, to Taipei five days later.⁷⁶ Saigon fell to the communists on April 30. The ROC embassy had remained open until April 28, while the RVN embassy in Taipei ceased operations on May 5.

Conclusion

When diplomatic relations were established in 1955, ROC-RVN relations were more important for Taipei than for Saigon. In a publication marking the seventh anniversary of the RVN in October 1962, it noted that "between the Republic of China and Viet-Nam, a fruitful cooperation has been established in various fields, in that of economy, particularly, thanks to the settlement of the problem of Chinese residents in Vietnam as well as to the common policy against communist imperialism."⁷⁷ This was the only reference to Taipei-Saigon ties in the 591-page publication, shoved into a chapter that gave a summary of Saigon's relations with other Asian countries. However, political chaos and war came to the RVN from 1963 just as the importance of Taiwanese aid grew. From the perspective of former ROC minister of economic affairs Li Kwoh-ting, the problem was that military officers got involved with South Vietnamese politics too soon after independence had been achieved in 1955.⁷⁸ However, agricultural and technical assistance from the ROC increasingly made it a key ally for the RVN.

The progress of the ROC from a developing to a developed country was used as a selling point to the RVN. After more than ten years of economic planning and growth, even the United States recognized that the Taiwanese had the capability to help other countries develop their economies.[79] When American aid to the ROC discontinued, it was the United States that suggested it continue with its technical assistance program to the RVN.[80] The ROC did so up to the fall of Saigon in 1975.

Taiwan as the ROC was not a pariah state. It actively involved itself in international affairs in East Asia. It played a minor role in the actual conflict as the main countries supporting the RVN militarily did not request any military assistance from the Taiwanese. The ROC, however, worked behind the scenes to assist the RVN in its economic development, focusing on agricultural reform, industrialization projects, and technology transfer. The economic cooperation conferences, high-level discussions, and correspondence show that both countries wanted the RVN to be an economic success story. The nine conferences were occasions for representatives from both countries to have discussions on changing current policies and proposing plans for the South Vietnamese economy. Most of the discussions resulted in work done with improvement in farming techniques, increase in water supply through irrigation projects, opening of new factories especially in textiles and sugar, provision of electricity, and training of South Vietnamese officials and technicians. The war, however, was a massive distraction for both countries.

Notes

1. I have used the terms *Republic of China* (ROC) and *Taiwan* interchangeably. For the titles of government officials and leaders, I use "ROC" since they were working for that state. Otherwise, I use "Taiwan."

2. John F. Copper, *The Taiwan Political Miracle: Essays on Political Development, Elections and Foreign Relations* (Lanham, MD: East Asia Research Institute and University Press of America, 1997), 10.

3. Brantly Womack, *China and Vietnam: The Politics of Asymmetry* (Cambridge: Cambridge University Press, 2006), 77–92.

4. Letter from President Chiang Kai-shek to President Ngo Dinh Diem, May 10, 1956, Ministry of Foreign Affairs (MOFA) Archives, 0046/12/1, *Zhongyue guanxi* 中越關係, National Archives Administration (NAA).

5. "The President of the Republic to Visit Formosa," *The Times of Viet Nam*, February 22, 1958.

6. Letter from ROC Embassy in South Vietnam to ROC Ministry of Foreign Affairs, January 10, 1957, MOFA Archives, 0046/12/1, NAA.

7. Frances Fitzgerald, *Fire in the Lake: The Vietnamese and the Americans in Vietnam* (Boston: Atlantic-Little, Brown Books, 1972), 433.

8. Report from MOFA to Premier Yu Hong-chun, May 12, 1958, MOFA Archives, 0047/12.21/17, *Ye buzhang fangyue* 葉部長訪越, NAA.

9. Report from MOFA to Premier Yu Hong-chun, NAA.

10. Report from Foreign Exchange and Trade Review Commission of the Executive Yuan, October 15, 1958, MOFA Archives, 020-011004-0014, *Zhongyue maoyi (yi)* 中越貿易（一）, Academia Historica (AH).

11. Economic Good Will Mission of the Republic of China to Vietnam, *Report on Vietnam's Agriculture and Industry* (Taipei: Economic Good Will Mission of the Republic of China to Vietnam, 1958), i.

12. Economic Good Will Mission, *Report on Vietnam's Agriculture*, 1.

13. Li Kwoh-ting 李國鼎, *Li Guoding: Wode Taiwan Jingyan* 李國鼎：我的台灣經驗 [Li Kwoh-ting: My experiences in Taiwan] (Taipei: Yuanliu Chuban, 2005), 460.

14. Li, *Wode Taiwan Jingyan*, 461–462.

15. "Zhongyue jingji hezuo gaikuang" 中越經濟合作概況, undated, p. 2, MOFA Archives, 020-011004-0026, *Zhongyue jingji hezuo huiyi (san)* 中越經濟合作會議（三）, AH.

16. Li, *Wode Taiwan Jingyan*, 462.

17. Yang Huei Pang, "Taiwan and Chiang Kai-shek's *Fangong Dalu*," *Asian Affairs* 45 (2014): 80.

18. W. W. Rostow, *The Stages of Economic Growth: A Non-communist Manifesto* (Cambridge: Cambridge University Press, 1960).

19. Alan Glyn, *Witness to Viet Nam* (London: Johnson, 1968), 173.

20. Gabriel Kolko, *Anatomy of a War: Vietnam, the United States, and the Modern Historical Experience* (New York: New Press, 1994), 90.

21. *President Ngo Dinh Diem on Democracy (Addresses Relative to the Constitution)* (Saigon: Presidency of the Republic of Viet-Nam Press Office, 1957), 27.

22. *President Ngo Dinh Diem on Democracy*, 32.

23. "Viet-Nam Glad to Have Aid of Chiang Forces," typescript of article by Philip Dodd in *Chicago Tribune*, December 30, 1959, MOFA Archives, 0049/12.22/5, *Yuenan Wu Tingyan zongtong fanghua (er)* 越南吳廷琰總統訪華（二）, NAA.

24. William Henderson and Wesley R. Fishel, "The Foreign Policy of Ngo Dinh Diem," *Vietnam Perspectives* 2 (August 1966): 23.

25. Kolko, *Anatomy of a War*, 90.

26. Henderson and Fishel, "Foreign Policy," 26.

27. Nghia M. Vo, *Saigon: A History* (Jefferson, NC: McFarland, 2011), 134.

28. Geoffrey Shaw, *The Lost Mandate of Heaven: The American Betrayal of Ngo Dinh Diem, President of Vietnam* (San Francisco: Ignatius Press, 2015), 61.

29. Bernard B. Fall, *The Two Viet-Nams: A Political and Military Analysis*, 2nd rev. ed. (New York: Praeger, 1967), 299.

30. "Summary Report of Observation Trip to Rural Areas of the Republic of Vietnam," September 1963, MOFA Archives, accession number 020-011004-0024, *Zhongyue jingji hezuo huiyi (yi)* 中越經濟合作會議（一）, AH.

31. *Yuenan zhengchao qifu de fenxi jiqi zhanwang* 越南政潮起伏的分析及其展望, p. 6, October 14, 1964, General Archives 718/353, Kuomintang Party Archives.

32. "Yuenan jingji xiankuang ji jinhou fazhan Dongxiang" 越南經濟現況及今後發展動向, March 12, 1958, MOFA Archives, 020-011004-0014, AH.

33. "Yuenan xinzhengfu cai fangong zhengce chuanwo kaolü chengren" 越南新政府採反共政策傳我考慮承認, November 3, 1963, MOFA Archives, 020-011001-0019, *Yuenan zhengbian jianbao* 越南政變剪報, AH.

34. "China to Recognize New Government in Vietnam," *China News*, November 3, 1963, MOFA Archives, 020-011001-0019, AH.

35. "Taipei to Recognize New Nguyen Gov't in Saigon," *China News*, November 2, 1963, MOFA Archives, 020-011001-0019, AH.

36. "Yuenan xin zhengfu zhi zhengce ji duiwo taidu" 越南新政府之政策及對我態度, November 29, 1963, MOFA Archives, 020-011099-0009, *Yuenan zhengju youguan ziliao* 越南政局有關資料, AH.

37. Letter from Nguyen Khanh to Chiang Ching-kuo, March 12, 1964, Archives of President Chiang Ching-kuo, 005-010100-00083-007, AH.

38. "Yuenan Gongheguo teshi Yang Wenming zuo fanghua" [Republic of Vietnam's special envoy Duong Van Minh arrived yesterday], *Zhongyang Ribao*, December 16, 1964, Archives of President Chiang Ching-kuo, 005-010401-00020-012, AH.

39. "Getting to Know Them," *Time* 86 (August 27, 1965): 19.

40. "Vietnam Aid," *Canberra Times*, August 2, 1965. The six countries were Australia, the ROC, France, West Germany, Japan, and New Zealand.

41. "Zhongyue jingji hezuo gaikuang," p. 1, MOFA Archives, 020-011004-0026, AH.

42. *[South] Viet Nam Statistical Yearbook 1964–1965*, 314. Taiwan was ranked after Indonesia (30.6 percent), Japan (26.5 percent), the United States (20.6 percent), France (8.1 percent), and Tunisia (3.7 percent).

43. Nguyen Duc Cuong, "Building a Market Economy during Wartime," in *Voices from the Second Republic of South Vietnam (1967–1975)*, ed. K. W. Taylor (Ithaca, NY: Cornell University Southeast Asia Program, 2014), 97. For more about the CIP and PL-480, see Kolko, *Anatomy of a War*, 223–230; and Douglas C. Dacy, *Foreign Aid, War, and Economic Development: South Vietnam, 1955–1975* (Cambridge: Cambridge University Press, 1986), 22–37.

44. "Chinese Minister Optimistic about Economic Cooperation with Viet Nam," *The Times of Viet Nam*, December 29, 1960; "Imports from Taiwan Hit All-Time High," *Saigon Daily News*, October 17, 1964.

45. Dacy, *Foreign Aid*, 96.

46. "Taiwan-S.V.N. Trade to Considerably Expand," *Saigon Daily News*, August 30, 1965.

47. "Viet Nam-China Economic Parley Ends," *The Times of Viet Nam*, December 23, 1960.

48. "Outline of Project for the Exchange of Vietnamese Rice with Taiwan Fertilizers," p. 2, June 30, 1963, MOFA Archives, 020-011004-0024, AH.

49. "Zhongyue jingji hezuo gaikuang" 中越經濟合作概況, p. 3, MOFA Archives, 020-011004-0026, AH.

50. "Free China Shows the World It Can Stand Alone Economically," *Saigon Daily News*, October 10, 1964.

51. "400 Taiwan Firms to Participate in Sino-Viet Nam Trade," *Saigon Daily News*, August 28, 1965.

52. Melvin Gurtov, "Taiwan in 1966: Political Rigidity, Economic Growth," *Asian Survey* 7 (January 1967): 42.

53. "A Joint Report of Sino-Vietnamese Economic Cooperation," p. 6, October 14, 1965, MOFA Archives, 020-011004-0027, *Zhongyue jingji hezuo huiyi (si)* 中越經濟合作會議(四), AH.

54. "Sino-Vietnamese Confab to Boost Chinese Export," *China News*, October 14, 1965, MOFA Archives, 020-011004-0027, AH.

55. "Saigon New Trade Pattern Not to Affect Local Export," *China News*, October 19, 1965, MOFA Archives, 020-011004-0027, AH.

56. Zhonghua Minguo Shishi Jiyao Bianwei Hui 中華民國史事紀要編委會, ed., *Zhonghua Minguo Shishi Jiyao (Chugao)* 中華民國史事紀要(初稿), June 24, 1969, 874–875.

57. Zhonghua Minguo Shishi Jiyao Bianwei Hui 中華民國史事紀要編委會, ed., *Zhonghua Minguo Shishi Jiyao (Chugao)* 中華民國史事紀要(初稿), January 10, 1970, 68–69.

58. "A Pictorial Presentation of Highlights of CATM/VN Activities," April 1965, Archives of President Yen Chia-kan, 006-030202-00011-001, *Taiwan nongjituan zai Yuenan gongzuo chengguo* 臺灣農技團在越南工作成果, AH.

59. "A Pictorial Presentation of Highlights," AH.

60. "Zhongyue jingji hezuo gaikuang," p. 2, MOFA Archives, 020-011004-0026, AH.

61. Zhonghua Minguo Shishi Jiyao Bianwei Hui 中華民國史事紀要編委會, ed., *Zhonghua Minguo Shishi Jiyao (Chugao)* 中華民國史事紀要(初稿), January 10, 1970, 68–69.

62. Zhonghua Minguo Shishi Jiyao Bianwei Hui 中華民國史事紀要編委會, ed., *Zhonghua Minguo Shishi Jiyao (Chugao)* 中華民國史事紀要(初稿), September 15, 1971, 709–710.

63. Zhonghua Minguo Shishi Jiyao Bianwei Hui 中華民國史事紀要編委會, ed., *Zhonghua Minguo Shishi Jiyao (Chugao)* 中華民國史事紀要(初稿), November 3, 1973, 751.

64. Minutes of Discussion Meeting between RVN Minister of Agriculture Lam Van Tri and ROC Minister of Economic Affairs Li Kwoh-ting, October 4, 1965, MOFA Archives, 020-011004-0026, AH.

65. "Progress Report on Sino-Vietnamese Economic Cooperation (Jan–Jun 1970)," p. 1, July 31, 1970, MOFA Archives, 020-011004-0032, *Zhongyue jingji hezuo huiyi (jiu)* 中越經濟合作會議(九), AH; "Committee on Land Reform Agriculture and Fisheries Development Final Report," Sino-Vietnamese Economic Cooperation Conference, Sixth Session, Saigon, 1970, MOFA Archives, 020-011004-0032, AH.

66. "Increased Cooperation Slated with RVM [sic] Agriculture, Industry," *Taiwan Trade Monthly of the Republic of China* 13 (January 1975): 29.

67. "Aide Memoire of Possible Areas of Sino-Vietnamese Technical Cooperation in Vietnam's Economic Reconstruction," May 30, 1969, MOFA Archives, 020-011004-0032, AH.

68. Zhonghua Minguo Shishi Jiyao Bianwei Hui 中華民國史事紀要編委會, ed., *Zhonghua Minguo Shishi Jiyao (Chugao)* 中華民國史事紀要(初稿), December 21, 1971, 753.

69. Committee on Trade and Industry Final Report, Sino-Vietnamese Economic Cooperation Conference, Sixth Session, Saigon, 1970, MOFA Archives, 020-011004-0032, AH; Minutes of the Committee on Technical Cooperation, Eighth Sino-Vietnamese Economic Cooperation Conference, Saigon, 1973, MOFA Archives, 020-011004-0036, *Zhongyue jingji hezuo huiyi (shisan)* 中越經濟合作會議(十三), AH.

70. Letter from Minister of Foreign Affairs Shen Chang-huan to ROC Vice President Yen Chia-kan, April 11, 1973, MOFA Archives, 020-011004-0035, *Zhongyue jingji hezuo huiyi (shier)* 中越經濟合作會議(十二), AH.

71. Zhonghua Minguo Shishi Jiyao Bianwei Hui 中華民國史事紀要編委會, ed., *Zhonghua Minguo Shishi Jiyao (Chugao)* 中華民國史事紀要(初稿), January 19, 1973, 109.

72. Zhonghua Minguo Shishi Jiyao Bianwei Hui 中華民國史事紀要編委會, ed., *Zhonghua Minguo Shishi Jiyao (Chugao)* 中華民國史事紀要(初稿), November 3, 1973, 751.

73. Minutes of the Committee on Technical Cooperation, Eighth Sino-Vietnamese Economic Cooperation Conference, Saigon, 1973, MOFA Archives, 020-011004-0036, AH.

74. "Thieu's Message to the Nation," VietNam [sic] Press No. 6484, November 2, 1973, A.9–A.13, November 2, 1973, MOFA Archives, 020-011004-0036, AH.

75. Kolko, *Anatomy of a War*, 489–491.

76. "Thieu, 15 Others Flee to Taiwan," *Canberra Times*, April 28, 1975.

77. *Eight Years of the Ngo Dinh Diem Administration 1954–1962: Published on the 7th Anniversary of the Republic of Vietnam, October 26, 1962* (Saigon: n.p., 1962), 195.

78. Li, *Wode Taiwan Jingyan*, 463.

79. Li, *Wode Taiwan Jingyan*, 464.

80. Li, *Wode Taiwan Jingyan*, 464.

10 The "Vietnamese" Skirt and Other Wartime Myths in Lee Yun-gi's "Trigonometric Functions"

ALICE S. KIM

Introduction: The "Social and Linguistic By-products of ... War"

The cheap, lightweight, often colorfully printed, long flared skirt, widely known as the "Vietnamese" skirt (*wollam chima*), first arose to great popularity in South Korea[1] in the late 1960s and early 1970s—at the intersection of the rapid expansion and structural shift in the Korean textile industry and Korea's decade-long participation in the Vietnam War (1964–1973). The improved quality and diversity of domestically produced textiles in the mid- to late 1960s, including clothing and other apparel and the nascent chemical fibers industry,[2] is an important context for the widespread appeal of the "Vietnamese" skirt, whose popularity had in part to do with the low cost and utility of its new mass-produced, lightweight, easy-to-launder, synthetic fabrics such as nylon, bearing colorful prints and bright solids. In addition, the simple and comfortable form of the skirt, closely resembling the familiar long seamless skirts (*tongchima*) that grew out of the full skirts of premodern Korean costume (*chima jeogori*) as its modernized or reformed versions,[3] contributed to its appeal among older and married women, as well as its application by women of all ages as functional everyday work wear. If in 1971, "the long skirt, also known as the Vietnamese skirt, was the most popular clothing item of the year among mature/married women,"[4] then by 1978, "the Vietnamese skirt" had become so ubiquitous that "there was hardly a housewife who hadn't worn it once or twice."[5]

As indicated by its naming, Korea's participation in the Vietnam War from 1964 to 1973, and the widespread preoccupation with the war that engulfed the Korean population at this time, provides another constitutive context. Contributing the largest contingent of foreign troops after the United States, South Korea dispatched over 300,000 soldiers from 1965 to 1973.[6] In addition to combat troops, tens of thousands of South Koreans also served in Vietnam as military contractors and laborers.[7] As outlined in the infamous Brown memorandum, the South Korean state negotiated enormous benefits from the United States for its participation in the war, from increased securitization and military aid for its own national defenses and the improvement and modernization of the Korean military, to large military construction and logistics contracts for its corporations.[8] More specifically, South Korea benefited from procurement across its various fledgling industries, such as "construction materials, raw blanket material, POL [petroleum, oil, lubricant]" and "supplies, services and equipment for Korean forces in Vietnam" as well as for "'selected types of procurement' for American and Vietnamese forces, and 'a substantial amount of goods' needed by AID for 'rural construction, pacification, relief, logistics, and so forth'" as part of "a $100 million-a-year-market for imported goods and services in South Vietnam" created by the war.[9] With the United States administering and financing Korea's participation, even in the face of skepticism by the South Vietnamese regime, and as a means to alleviate pressure on conscription of American soldiers amid growing anti-war unrest in the United States, the South Korean forces have been primarily characterized as a mercenary force—or "America's rented troops."[10]

The war proceeded under the military dictatorship of Park Chung Hee who came to power in 1961 via military coup, putting an end to the small reprieve (spring) of democracy, which lasted less than a year after student protests toppled the authoritarian leader Syngman Rhee who had been in office since 1948. A little more than a decade after the end of the Korean War (1950–1953), if the Vietnam War was seized upon by the Park regime for its political and economic opportunities vis-à-vis external powers, it also served to quell domestic political unrest behind the strident banner of anti-communist nationalism. Promoted by Park as "a moral repayment of our historical debt to the Free World,"[11] Park's official ideology of the Vietnam War revolved around "the triple alliance of anti-communism, developmentalism, and patriarchy,"[12] orchestrated amid festive send-offs and heroic welcomes, a censored press, and military-produced propaganda newsreels.[13] At the same time, participating under the aegis of U.S. intervention in the Vietnam War, in addition to Cold War ideology, the war became inescapably linked to the phantasmagoria of American wealth and goods, now extending well beyond the U.S. Army post exchanges (PXs) strewn across U.S. military bases in Korea. More broadly, at a "crucial moment" of the need "for [an] export market and hard currency, the Americanization of the Vietnam War created an unprecedented economic boom in the Asia-Pacific region."[14] With over 40 percent of the postwar population suffering from absolute poverty in an ailing economy with widespread unemployment, the "*Wollam* boom" (Vietnam boom), as it came to be called, meant a thirtyfold increase in pay to serve in Vietnam instead of military service at home[15] as well as the possibility of "three hot meals a day,"[16] unattainable at home for some of the most destitute. In addition to the increase in pay, access to the American PX afforded soldiers with small lump-sum down payments to use on their return home as many soldiers leveraged PX goods as investments to resell in Korea for a considerable profit.[17] The "return boxes," or more accurately crates, that each soldier was allowed to bring back from their military tour were filled with army clothing and other household items, dishes, and afghans, American and Japanese electronics and household appliances such as cameras, radios, televisions, and refrigerators, not to mention leftover C rations, instant coffee mixes, and so forth, all items hard to come by in Korea at the time.[18]

The "Vietnamese" skirt was not, however, among the trove of foreign goods that trickled back with the soldiers, laborers, or contractors from the late '60s to early '70s, much of which were sought-after American and Japanese commodities. Although its origins in the rapidly improving Korean textiles industry at this time can be seen to put it squarely within the larger gambit of the economic boom created by the war, or the "*Wollam* boom," the "Vietnamese" skirt did not originate in Vietnam or have any direct or obvious links to the war.[19] Why, then, was this new, cheap, comfortable, widely popular long flared skirt—both produced and consumed on a mass scale in Korea at the time—called a "Vietnamese skirt"? Among a litany of names, such as the "elastic-banded skirt" (*gomujulchima*),[20] the "creased skirt" (*jureumchima*), "the seamless skirt" (*tongchima*), or even the "long skirt" taken from its English loan word (*rongseukeoteu*),[21] why does it take on the name "Vietnamese skirt" by early 1970? What exactly was the term "Vietnamese" in the Vietnamese skirt pointing to anyway? Was it so named because it was "patterned after the Vietnamese *áo dài*" as some commentators allege?[22] Or was it because returning veterans from the war would buy these popular skirts from local or general markets as gifts for their wives or mothers, as claimed by others?[23] Was it referring, then, to the idea of or some relation to Vietnam, the country lying southeast of Korea, or to Koreans' experience of the Vietnam War? If Vietnam, as erroneously imagined in the popular Korean song of the 1960s "Vietnam's Moonlit Night" as the "Far South Island Nation" is any indication, it would appear that there was not much of a difference between the two.[24]

It is against this background of speculative origins and loose resemblances arising from the overlapping contexts of South Korea's early industrialization and participation in the Vietnam War that the late South Korean author and translator as well as Vietnam War veteran Lee Yun-gi takes up the naming of the "Vietnamese skirt" as a topic in need of demythologization. In his short story titled "Trigonometric Functions" ("*Samgak hamsu*," 2003), Lee ultimately posits that there is no "Vietnamese skirt" in Vietnam, situating it instead as one among a series of baleful "social and linguistic byproducts of the war" (175). Identifying the "Vietnamese skirt" as part of a series of other similarly strange and incongruous "Vietnamese" appellations, Lee suggests that although it was undoubtedly part of the South Korean "Vietnamese" imaginary that took shape during Korea's participation in the war, its links to Vietnam were as illusory and distorted as the links between this "Vietnamese" imaginary and the historical, geographical, and cultural reality of Vietnam. As the demystification of the "Vietnamese skirt" helps brings into focus the general pattern of distortions that characterize "Korea's Vietnam," Lee's short story becomes a site to both decipher the mechanism of these myths and misconceptions as well as redress the troubling distortions harbored therein.

The late author Lee Yun-gi (1947–2010) was also a prolific and award-winning translator, who returned to writing after a long career in translating. This complementary craft can be seen not only in his interest in the use of language as a subject of investigation but also in his acuity in linguistic and semiological analysis, and precision in deciphering the mythic distortions of "Vietnam." At the same time, the publication of Lee's short story in the spring of 2000 in the serial monthly *Dongseo munhak*, later reprinted in an anthology of his short fiction in 2003, *Noreui nalgae* (Wings of melody), was concurrent with a major turning point in the public discourse on the "Vietnam question" in Korea, triggered by a series of articles on war crimes committed by South Korean troops in the Vietnam War, which ran over the span of a year in the progressive news daily *Hankyoreh* and *Hankyoreh 21*. Coincidentally, the Pulitzer-winning Associated Press report on civilian atrocities by U.S. troops in the Korean War at No Gun Ri also broke at the same time. The revelatory testimonies by Vietnamese survivors and South Korean veterans provide an important backdrop for the testimony-like narratives of the Vietnam War that comprise Lee's text as a whole, as well as the consistent and pronounced affect—of discomfort, unease, shame, embarrassment, incredulity, and indignation—that guides them. Narrated as part of a larger framework of stories of redress and responsibility based on personal recollections and testimony as a veteran of the war, this autobiographically based short story incorporates the reckoning of war's "social and linguistic by-products" (175) as an integral part of the reappraisal of Korea's Vietnam.

Deciphering the "Vietnamese" Myth

In "Trigonometric Functions," Lee Yun-gi introduces the "Vietnamese skirt" as one among a series of new terms linked to the rise of a particular usage of the "Vietnamese" modifier in South Korea during its participation in the Vietnam War. As the narrator recounts in conversation with his friend Harold Baker, an American anthropologist,

> just after the Vietnam War, there was a time when the pre-noun determiner [*gwanhyungsa*] "Vietnam/ese" [*wollam*][25] became popular in South Korea. Vietnamese fish [*wollam bungeo*], Vietnamese skirt [*wollam chima*], Vietnamese toilet [*wollam hwajangsil*], Vietnamese poker [*wollam ppung*]. . . . As you know the pre-noun determiner is a part of speech [in Korean grammar] that modifies or specifies the noun that follows it. However, I also recall a feeling of grave discomfort as to the usage of the classifying function of this "Vietnamese" modifier.[26]

Take for example, the term "Vietnamese fish," which came to circulate as a nickname for the bluegill, a fish much disliked among South Korean fishermen. The bluegill, he informs us, first populated Korean rivers and streams as part of U.S. imported fish-aid in the early 1970s, and quickly became a bane to fishermen as the carnivorous species indiscriminately ate up native fish populations that Koreans enjoyed.[27] This bluegill, henceforth associated with "the feeling of displeasure, that which was unlucky, or stood for a bad omen," came to be called "Vietnamese fish" at this time—that is, without having any relation to Vietnam (177). This is all the more discomfiting to the narrator as he recalls "the rich marine life of Vietnam's abundant streams and rivers" where "such a small fish like the bluegill would not even be considered 'game'" (178). Quite to the contrary, he declares, "Vietnam is a place where all you have to do is lower your fishing pole into the water to see large catfish or mullet weighing 4–5 kilograms swim up to the surface" (178). In short, he exclaims, "I have never seen 'Vietnamese fish' in Vietnam!" (178).

The narrator recollects with similar "unease" the term "Vietnamese skirt" (*wollam chima*), used to refer to the new long flared skirt that became quite popular in South Korea at this time (178). The "Vietnamese skirt," he states, designated "a makeshift seamless skirt (*tongchima*) or pants (*tongbaji*), something that could be made without any design or sewing ability, which anyone could make by fitting an elastic waistband on top of a long seamless skirt" (178). Yet, this makeshift seamless skirt or pants, he points out, resembled nothing like the Vietnamese *áo dài* that he had admired in Vietnam:

> The *áo dài*, composed of underpants made with wide legs at the bottom hemlines for breathability and paired with a silk top dress that is a one-piece but with open slits on the sides, is an elegant and beautiful costume and does not come even close to something that could be made in such a makeshift manner. I had the impression that the *áo dài* was no different than the Korean *chima jeogori* (skirt and blouse) or the Japanese *kimono*, having evolved beautifully over a long period of time. (178)

Thus, highlighting the gap between the integrity of the Vietnamese *áo dài* and the "makeshift" character of the "Vietnamese skirt" in Korea, which appeared an empty, even debased, caricature in comparison—the narrator implores, "So, let's think about it. What kind of impression Koreans will have of the Vietnamese the moment when such a makeshift seamless skirt is called the 'Vietnamese skirt'" (179). Or, as he delineates from each of its analogues, when the ill-omened "bluegill is called 'Vietnamese fish'" (178); when "the wide natural plain with no end in sight on a mountain-hiking trail" is called "a Vietnamese toilet" (180); or "when a card game with seemingly illogical or inane rules is called 'Vietnamese poker'" (181). It would appear that the "grave discomfort" over the "'Vietnamese' modifier," with which he began, had to do with the troubling distortions entailed "in the usage of the classifying function of the 'Vietnamese' modifier," and the generally debased representations of "Vietnam" and "Vietnamese culture/people" that took shape from it among the Korean public at this time (176).

With this account of the "Vietnamese skirt," Lee turns a critical eye toward the naming of the skirt to reveal the ideological construct lurking within. In identifying it as one among a chain of values derived from the same "Vietnamese" modifier, he situates it within a system of interdependent values whose identity/meaning is dependent on the existence of the other values that constitute the system. In doing so, he highlights, on the one hand, how the "Vietnamese" modifier was coming to fix a range of everyday objects in Korea from fisheries aid to women's fashion with negative connotations, social derision, and judgments of inadequacy or lack, while on the other hand, how the very terms and objects being fixed by this "Vietnamese" modifier had little or no relation to Vietnam or Vietnamese culture. That is, he puts into relief the distortions characterizing the "classifying" or naming function of the "Vietnamese" modifier to show how it was simultaneously disfiguring and overwriting the concept of Vietnam with a whole new set of meanings to form a new "Vietnamese" imaginary.

Thus, in much the same manner as French cultural critic and semiologist Roland Barthes sought to demystify the mythologies of French mass culture by a mixture of semiological analysis and ideological critique,[28] Lee proceeds to expose the mythology of Korea's "Vietnam" by deciphering the myth-like operation of the naming function of the "Vietnamese" modifier. He does this by highlighting the incommensurability between the debased sociocultural abstractions standing in for the "Vietnamese" modifier (as mythic signifier) in each of the mythic values—"Vietnamese skirt," "Vietnamese fish," "Vietnamese toilet," "Vietnamese poker"—and the integrity of Vietnam and Vietnamese culture that he reconstitutes through testimony of his personal recollections of Vietnam as a veteran of the war. That is, he focuses on the *meaning* of the signifier "Vietnamese" that has been robbed by myth and with it the integrity of Vietnam, by underlining the various social, geographical, linguistic, cultural bases of distortions that its "parasitical form"[29] imposes on it. In the process, he restores the dignity that is robbed of Vietnamese society and culture in its disfigurement in myth. For example, in calling attention to the difference between the "makeshift" "Vietnamese skirt" and the "elegant" Vietnamese *áo dài*, he emphasizes not only that the two bore little resemblance but more importantly that the *áo dài* belonged to a whole different order or category of dress—weighted with the history of a society's development, if not its unique cultural and aesthetic identity, much in the same manner as "the Korean *hanbok*, or the Japanese *kimono*" (178). Unmasking the myth of the "Vietnamese skirt" thus entails both reconstituting and underscoring the integrity of the history and culture of the Vietnamese costume as part of the meaning of "Vietnamese" that has been stolen from it, as well as highlighting the distortion that amounts to a form of cultural or ethnonational denigration entailed in the mythic signification of the "Vietnamese skirt" in particular and as one value of the mythical "Vietnamese" concept driving the larger system in its repetition through different signifying forms in general.

Lee's discussion of the "Vietnamese fish" reveals a similar pattern in which the image of Vietnam's fertile streams and rivers are summoned to reconstitute the integrity of Vietnam's physical and natural landscape that the myth has stolen from it, while again pointing to its unjust disfigurement. The "Vietnamese toilet" presents a slight variation but serves the related purpose of restoring the dignity of Vietnamese people. He explains that it is true that during the war, he had seen Vietnamese people in central Vietnam where he was stationed using nature's "open air toilet" (179). He admits having used it himself many times. "In the context of wartime, when it was often an unmanageable task to safeguard one's residence," he goes on to explain, "this is not difficult to understand" (179). What is troubling, rather, and fills him with deep "embarrassment," akin to the "discomfort" and "unease" that characterized his recollection of the myths of the "Vietnamese skirt" and "Vietnamese fish," is the "utter heedlessness of the usage of the term among Korean hikers to refer to lack of toilet facilities" (179). And last, the myth of "Vietnamese" poker is also one where the force of the myth subsides through the recovery of its wartime context. "Vietnamese" poker, derided for the inanity of its design, "designated a card game in which three people are each dealt a card and upon turning the card over, the person with the middle value wins the game" (180). However, insofar as the game is contextualized as parody of the political situation of South Vietnam "lodged in between the U.S. and the National Liberation Front of North Vietnam" (180), the mythic signification of inanity or idiocy is largely neutralized.

Barthes's definition of myth as a "second-order semiological system," or a kind of "metalanguage" constructed atop an already existing system is useful in bringing into focus Lee's analysis because the form of the "Vietnamese" modifier likewise harbors a "double system."[30] In Lee's analysis, as in the signification of myth, "the relation which unites the concept of the myth [its message or the ideological content of the second-order system] to its meaning [the 'body' of the first-order system that serves as the form or signifier of the second-order message] is essentially a relation of deformation."[31] However, unlike Barthes's classic examples of myth taken from French mass culture, the myth of Korea's "Vietnam," perhaps due to its postcolonial origins, literally wears its name (mythical concept/ideological content) on its sleeve. In other words, here we are not dealing with a single signifier with two aspects (meaning and form) but rather two signifiers brought together or superimposed in the process of naming.

Although Lee's analysis focuses on the distortions relating to the meaning of "Vietnam" in particular, we can also see in this process that the history of the popular Korean skirt is also emptied out, its own history and identity erased, in order to function as the stripped-down, disfigured body-as-form of the mythic signifier of the impoverished "Vietnamese" skirt. The skirt restored to the fullness of its history might speak thus:

> I am a product of the expansion and transformation of the textile industry in Korea in the mid to late 1960s, characterized by rising exports as well as domestic consumption, leading to the widespread availability of inexpensive, lightweight chemical fabrics like nylon, that made me so appealing as one of the first ready-to-wear clothing items for masses of Korean women. I mark an important turning point in the export-oriented industrialization of the textile industry and the shift in the domestic chemical industry from light to heavy industry, aided by the economic boom created by the "Americanization of the Vietnam War,"[32] and serving as handmaiden to Korea's celebrated heavy and chemical industrialization program, that holds center stage in the miracle myth of Korean development. As such I also bear witness to the super-exploited Korean female and male workforce that labored in the garment industry, as well as the domestic, informal, and other forms of marginalized and unrecognized labor of the many women who wore me. I thus mark a significant period of early industrialization in Korea with reference especially to the experience of countless laboring Korean women.

However, as the *form* of the Korean myth of "Vietnamese-ness," all of this is brushed aside so as to stand in as a mythic version of the "Vietnamese" skirt. It is a process where Vietnam is reimagined by the Korean forms that give meaning to it, but in the process of their superimposition, it entails the concealment of the Korean object—which must itself become a mere gesture, robbed of its own history and proper name in order to stand in for the specific ideological motivations of Korea's mythic "Vietnamese" imaginary—just as the historically rich meaning of Vietnam, containing "a whole system of values,"[33] is emptied out to be overwritten by it.

It is in essence the same mechanism behind the naming of "Vietcong" or *beteukong* in Korean, another English loanword, picked up from their

American allies as a nickname for the North Vietnamese National Front for the Liberation of the Southern Region, also known as the National Liberation Front (NLF). Taken from an abbreviated form of Viet Nam Cong San, which translates as "Vietnamese communist/commie," in a derogatory fashion, "Vietcong" is burdened with the same negative appraisals and concealments of the "Vietnamese" modifier to disfigure the political identity of the NLF, and thus the politics of Vietnamese communism and the larger totality of the Vietnam War. Making use of Lee's mode of reconstituting the integrity of "Vietnam," we might say that the anti-communist caricature of "Vietcong" bears little to no resemblance to the full meaning of the NLF that understands the war as an extended anti-colonial war of national independence.[34] Mirroring the juxtaposition and distortion of Korean and Vietnamese forms in the "Vietnamese" myths detailed above, "Vietcong" likewise functions by simultaneously presenting and obscuring from view, by way of mutual disfigurement, the many possible forms of identification and mutual recognition between the two postcolonial nations.

It is through the ideologically motivated *mythical concept* (the signified), Barthes tells us, that "a whole new history is implanted in the myth," leaving the meaning of the first-order sign "drained of its contingency."[35] As Lee exposes this "Vietnamese" form as an imposter standing in as an "alibi"[36] of the mythic concept of Vietnamese-ness as an impoverished, "backward" caricature of Vietnam, he highlights these distortions as taking shape vis-à-vis Korea's particular experience of the Vietnam War, especially pertaining to those of "the general public who were never there" (176). It is "quite obvious," he asserts, "that without an ounce of concrete information about Vietnam during the war, Koreans were affixing the 'Vietnamese' modifier to all sorts of vague caricatures and negative connotations" (180). What is naturalized in myth was Korea's imagined relation to Vietnam through the experience of the Vietnam War. Embodied in the term "Vietnamese" was the process by which the geography, culture, and politics of Vietnam in all its historical contingency—including its long history of cultural development, colonial occupations, or even a shared Sinocentric past—was being filtered through the narrow, highly specific lens of Korea's Vietnam War. As Koreans were coming to see Vietnam through the haze of anti-communist ideology and state propaganda amid active censorship of wartime coverage as well as the material desires and economic benefits surrounding the war amid the dire postwar economic situation in Korea, a

Vietnam on its own terms—or one that could be recognized and identified with by Koreans—was nowhere in sight.

Contextualizing the "Vietnamese" Myth in Korea's Vietnam

As the "Vietnamese" skirt formed a value of the "Vietnamese" modifier in unmasking the myth of Vietnamese-ness, this narrative of demystification is positioned within Lee's text like a value within a larger field of personal recollection and testimony linked to redress and responsibility in the face of Korea's Vietnam. The short story consists of two additional narratives based on the personal recollections of the narrator as a South Korean soldier—the disclosure of his responsibility for the death of another soldier, alongside that of the destruction of the beaches and surrounding waters of a fictional city called Hoi Nan—both arising from the consequences of his and his brigade's actions during the war. The narrator's reckoning of the "Vietnamese" myth is thus contextualized within the text's broader theme of coming to terms with and taking responsibility for South Korean involvement in the destruction and violence inflicted on Vietnam during the war, as well as contending with its social, cultural, psychological, and environmental consequences. With the consistent affect of "discomfort," "shame," and "sadness" that envelops all of the narratives alike, the distortions of the "Vietnamese" myth mirror the destruction of Hoi Nan in important ways serving at times like the manifest meaning to the deeper trauma latent in Hoi Nan.

These recollections and thoughts are recounted as a series of conversations with Harold Baker, an American anthropologist, with whom he shares an interest in Southeast Asian history and culture. The text begins with a call from Baker, who teasingly addressing the narrator as "Mr. Killer," informs him that he had returned from Vietnam with the pictures he requested (167). Baker had invited him to visit Hoi Nan with him for a conference, where both the narrator and Baker's older brother had been stationed during the war in their respective Korean and U.S. military installations. Although the narrator refused the invitation, same as Baker's brother had, he asked for pictures of the city, where, thirty years ago, he had spent fourteen months during the war. He "wanted to see the small, beautiful city . . . and its beaches again," he maintains, "not because he missed it, but because he was filled with an unbearable disquiet about it" (168).

If the mythic distortions of "Vietnam" were the "linguistic byproducts of the war" (175), then the death and destruction in and of Hoi Nan comprises its main theater. It is the tale that both opens the text and that which occupies its deepest interior, wherein he recounts the death of a newly arrived soldier to his brigade in an accidental explosion, owing in part, he claims, to his own personal negligence. Stationed along the beaches of Hoi Nan, he had ordered the new soldier to add more oil to the waste drum that the brigade had buried in the sand as a makeshift latrine. Yet, he had neglected to specify the type of oil, leading to the fatal explosion, at the spark of a match. He confesses, with recourse to a popular morality tale among South Korean students about responsibility for the death of another arising from one's inaction, that according to "Wangdo's principle," he was responsible for his death (183). "While I have never been convicted as a murderer in a court of law," he avows, "I am a murderer according to 'Wangdo's principle'" (183).

However, this story of the death of the soldier is at the same time a story of the death of Hoi Nan. It doubles as the story of the narrator and his brigade's wartime destruction of its "boundless, white sandy beaches" on which they were stationed, as a result of burying inhumerable barrels of waste and oil into the sand. As he looks upon the pictures Baker had brought back, he is "overcome with shame" (188). Seeing how the beaches of Hoi Nan "had turned into a garbage dump," he finds himself confronted with "the sad process of confirming" his role in "the death of the beach, the sea that held it, and the city that held the sea" (188–189). He is further disheartened by a report issued by the Vietnamese environmental authority, which anticipates "little chance of recovery" for the "tragic destiny" of "the contaminated, barren waters" of present-day Hoi Nan and its surrounding areas (188). As detailed in the report, "because of the leaching water of the thousands of barrels of waste- and diesel oil–filled drums that the Korean brigade buried on the beach" (188) and "the wastewater of the industrial area that was erected in the area after the war which further accelerated pollution," "the majestic giant turtles that used to inhabit the nearby island" like the onceplentiful fish "can no longer be seen in its vicinity," just as "people disappeared from its seemingly boundless coastline of white sand beaches over thirty years ago" (189). Finding himself confronted not only with the death of the soldier but also of "having killed Vietnam," its beaches and greater ecosystem, he declares, "Although we may not have intended to kill it, according to 'Wangdo's law,' it is because of us that it is dead" (189).

There is, then, within the context of the larger text, another side to the narrator's Vietnam—albeit a more discomfiting, painful, and benighted one residing at the deepest interior of the text. For alongside the narrator's recollections of Vietnam's beautiful beaches, its fertile waters, and elegant costumes—a culture full and respectable with abundant nature and an elegant long-evolved culture that the narrator recovers to counter the disfigurements of the "Vietnamese" myth—are also his recollections of how he and his brigade had desecrated these beautiful lands, along with the many lives and forms of life that have disappeared with it. There is also this experience of Vietnam, mirroring the distortions of the myth in their actions as participants of war, of having transformed "the abundant streams and rivers [that once] abounded with large catfish" into the "contaminated, barren waters" of its present. Permeated with the sense of "disquiet," "shame," "remorse," and "sadness" throughout—much like the "discomfort," "unease," and "embarrassment" above—the consistent affect that binds these narratives together inflects the recollection of what he refers to as "my Vietnam"—that is, experienced through the "identity of a South Korean soldier" (169)—into an image both divided within itself, as one that is beset by resounding echoes, perhaps unintended but tragic and disquieting nonetheless in its consequences and by-products.

Demythologizing Korea's Vietnam in the Twenty-First Century

The late 1990s into the early 2000s, when this short story was published, formed a key turning point in the public discourse on the "Vietnam question" in South Korea. Starting in 1999, a series of articles published in the progressive newspaper *Hankyoreh* and its weekly *Hankyoreh 21* made public for the first time in the national media allegations of atrocities committed by Republic of Korea (ROK) soldiers in the Vietnam War. The allegations, based on the research of a Korean graduate student studying in Vietnam, made use of official Vietnamese documents, supported by eyewitness accounts of Vietnamese survivors and South Korean war veterans.[37] The ensuing testimony of the ROK marine commander Kim Ki Tae in early 2000 in particular as to overseeing multiple incidents of civilian massacres in October and November 1966 opened the floodgates to other similar testimonies by South Korean veterans. Coincidentally, these reports overlapped with the Pulitzer Prize–winning Associated Press reportage on the July 1950 civilian massacre at No Gun Ri by U.S. troops during the Korean War, which like the South Korean war crimes in Vietnam had remained strictly censored by the successive military regimes in Korea from 1961 to 1987. As Charles Armstrong, who first introduced the unfolding of "Korea's Vietnam" to an English-speaking audience, noted, it was not the case that such atrocities were unknown in Korea before this time, but up until then, the "brutality of ROK troops in Vietnam remain[ed] largely anecdotal," lacking any "systematic investigation of atrocity claims in Korea."[38] As reflected in the testimonies compiled in the report on No Gun Ri fifty years after the fact, this was doubly true for the war crimes of both U.S. and ROK troops in the Korean War.

The 2000s inaugurated the truth and reconciliation era, which became the primary framework for systematically investigating wartime atrocities among other human rights violations in Korea. The Truth and Reconciliation Commission, which was formally established in 2005 as an independent body, has made some important achievements investigating and documenting Korean War atrocities and abuses. For example, the commission's findings on the illegal mass executions by the South Korean government of alleged leftists who were enrolled in the National Guidance League for rehabilitation by the Syngman Rhee government in 1950, have, in addition to "setting the Korean historical record straight," led to the implementation of a number of steps to help recover the dignity of victims and their families who have suffered discriminatory treatment as "traitors," "antistate criminals," or "Reds," including property confiscation, barriers to education and employment, and social ostracism.[39] Although many of the recommendations have been stalled by the conservative Lee Myung-bak and Park Geun-hye regimes from 2008 to 2017, such as reparations and the rewriting of history textbooks, measures that have been enacted following from publicized testimonies, memorials, and changes to the public record, including an official state apology made by President Roh Moo Hyun to the league's victims and families in January 2008 before leaving office, have led to "changing views regarding past tragedies . . . in many local communities and neighborhoods."[40]

The case of Vietnam War atrocities by South Korean troops, however, currently remains outside of the scope of the commission, and the South Korean government has yet to issue a formal apology while denying access to related government documents. Reinvigorated calls for both have mounted from South Korean civil society in recent years, optimistic in the face of the new Moon Jae-in administration in 2017, breaking up the long decade of conservative right-wing regimes. In April 2018, the People's Tribunal on War Crimes by South Korean Troops during the Vietnam War was organized in which its civil court, headed by former South Korean supreme justice Kim Young Ran, demanded "the South Korean government to compensate for the plaintiffs' losses (Vietnamese survivors), launch an investigation into South Korean atrocities committed between 1964 and 1973, and correct all forms of memorial pertaining to South Korean participation in the Vietnam War."[41] Although not legally binding, the tribunal garnered broad public attention, covered by all the main news networks.[42] In April 2020, the first reparations claim against the South Korean government was filed by MINBYUN (Lawyers for a Democratic Society) on behalf of Nguyen Thi Thanh, the survivor of a massacre in Phong Nhi.[43]

Lee's short story, with its personal testimonial format and global ethos of "setting the . . . record straight"[44] and taking responsibility for the "deep wound" Koreans have "inflict[ed] . . . on the Vietnamese people" (181), helps usher in a new stage of Korean discourse on its participation in the Vietnam War. This change in discourse is moreover part of a broader shift toward reckoning with the many distortions and myths of Korea's postcolonial past that situates the issue of South Korean atrocities in Vietnam in conjunction with those of the South Korean military during the Korean War as with U.S. military interventions in the region. As the narrator promptly differentiates his "Vietnam," experienced through the "identity of a South Korean soldier," from "the anthropological object of Baker's 'Vietnam'" (169) of his American interlocutor, Lee points to Korea's experience of Vietnam as part of a social history of two inextricable brutalizing wars in the region, which is undoubtedly part of a broader geopolitical history of the global Cold War,[45] but the specificity and experience of which—as reflected in the unique forms and inflections of its myths and countermyths—can hardly be reduced to it. The chorus-like refrain framing the text's narrative—"What right do Koreans have to inflict such a deep wound on the Vietnamese people?" (174, 175, 181)—Lee contends, also begs the question, "What right do Americans have to inflict such a deep wound on Koreans?" (175). This Vietnam is inevitably haunted by the specters of U.S. imperialism in the region and especially the Korean War—what Lee refers to as the "tragic triangular relation of war and industry that lodges itself deep within the space between people and nature" (189). The "trigonometric functions" structuring "the relations between U.S., South Korea and Vietnam" (188) that underlie Lee's narratives also thus underlie the scope and mission of the truth and reconciliation framework ushered in at this time. Insofar as the narrator's confirmation of his responsibility for "killing" the soldier of his brigade as well as the nature and culture of Vietnam is offered as "a prelude to the story of Americans in Korea" (188), Lee's reckoning of the usage of the "Vietnamese" modifier in Korea is framed as much to also "pry open" the "unjustly distorted view of Koreans harbored by Americans during the Korean War," as in the "openly debased representations of Koreans" circulating in U.S. media in "the American TV series MASH" (175). Thus, the lingering violence of these distortions that function like the root source of his "grave discomfort" also leads him to reckon with the wounds of his own doing and those inflicted by his larger society.

Although Lee's testimony-like text echoes the method and ethos of the *Hankyoreh* exposés that gripped the nation, written in the short fiction format, it is uncertain to what extent Lee's stories of the death of the soldier and the city might be true, or from where they might originate. In an interview with *Hankyoreh 21*, while participating in the Korea-Vietnam Peace Marathon in 2004, Lee reveals that the fictionalized city of Hoi Nan in his story was based on Tuy Hoa, a city on the central coast of southern Vietnam where he was stationed during the war but not much else.[46] However, the force of Lee's text lies not in its truth value, as the truth and reconciliation testimonies must, but rather in signaling the important new shift in consciousness on an old subject matter, thematizing in method and ethos as well as message this new orientation.

In this, it continues in the "soldier-writer" tradition of Vietnam War narratives, which appeared in the late '80s–'90s, such as Hwang Suk-yong's *Shadow of Arms* (1985–1988), Ahn Jung-hyo's *White War* (1989), and Park Young-han's *River at Song-ba* (1992). As Jinim Park has argued, these earlier works of fiction "demarcat[ed] a [new] epoch in the history of Korean literature," making up "the first narratives that questioned and resisted the prevailing ideology in Korean society of the period: the Cold War ideology."[47] With their critical gaze fixed on the mercenary role of Korean soldiers, these writers turned to examining Vietnam as an "economic rather than ideological war," explored through themes of identity loss, ambivalence, and racial discrimination amid colonizer-colonized relations and the hierarchy of nations, in the face of their identification with the Vietnamese people, including "Vietcong enemies."[48] As these writers approached "the Vietnamese situation as a mirror to reflect Korean reality," they came to ultimately recognize South Korea's own colonized position under U.S. imperialism as well as the Vietnam War as an American neocolonial expansionist war and not a war against communism, as most explicitly examined in Hwang's *Shadow of Arms*.[49]

Lee's text follows in this tradition of ideological critique, but it also reflects the revisionist impulses of the early 2000s and the evolving understanding of Korea's Vietnam War experience in light of present realities. If earlier texts thematized Koreans awakening to U.S. imperialism through the Vietnam War, Lee's text signals a shift to deciphering the varied forms and enduring effects, consequences, and by-products of such official state or neo-colonial ideologies and taking responsibility for them. Reflected in the two intersecting narratives of distortion and destruction of Korea's Vietnam, the formal mechanism of such "linguistic byproducts of . . . war" (175) offers a heuristic for decoding the broader pattern of brutality and violence, including forms of social suppression as well as personal repression that characterize this experience. As we saw earlier, the full history of the skirt, the fish, the open-air toilet, and the card game, which like "Vietnam" were also deformed in myth, not only functioned as debased phantasms of Vietnamese society but also served to disguise, in plain sight, the fact that these ideologems point to the everyday reality of postwar Korea. Lee's text highlights both the superimposition and concealment of shared Korean and Vietnamese experiences to refocus the critique closer to home, from anti-imperialist critique to the postcolonial critique of the South Korean state and its myths and mystifications of the national developmentalist and anti-communist ideologies of the South Korean state: underneath the distortions of the skirt and the fish are not only the obscured image of Korea's strivings for development amid the burden of its own perceived "backwardness" in the face of American military and economic might across the region, but also Korea's experience of industrialization pitted side by side with a state-organized mercenary force, as the geopolitics of Korea's own reality of the "division system"[50] that may be glimpsed behind the repressed unconscious of the ludicrous card game, forms a lingering part of what might be called Korea's collective unconscious. Lee's short story thus points us to the need for reckoning with the myths of Korea's Vietnam as part of the distortions of the larger myths of Korean development, focusing on their concrete overlaps, within an inescapable geopolitical perspective.

Notes

I would like to thank Dr. Lee Sin Jae for his helpful discussions and materials on Korea's participation in the Vietnam War. I am also grateful to the volume editors, anonymous reviewers, fellow participants in the Vietnam War in the Pacific World conference at Macquarie University in 2019, and Dr. Laam Hae for their helpful comments on my earlier drafts.

1. Hereafter referred to as Korea and South Korea interchangeably.

2. Yung Bong Kim, "The Growth and Structural Change of Textile Industry," in *Macroeconomic and Industrial Development in Korea*, ed. Chong Kee Park (Seoul: Korea Development Institute, 1980), 185–276.

3. On the evolution of *tongchima* and change in women's clothing in the mid-'60s, see Soojin Kim, "Yeoseonguibogui byeoncheoneul tonghae bon jeontonggwa

geundaeui jendeojeongchi - haebang ihu~1960nyeondae chobaneul jungsimeurot," *Peminijeumyeongu* [Feminism research] 7, no. 2 (2007): 281–320.

4. "Jirihanbokjungeul siwonhago anjeonhage," *Gyeonghyang Sinmun*, July 28, 1971.

5. "Momppeeseo cheongbajikkaji," *Donga Ilbo*, August 17, 1978.

6. Frank Baldwin, "America's Rented Troops: South Koreans in Vietnam," *Bulletin of Concerned Asian Scholars* 7, no. 4 (1975): 34.

7. As outlined by Kil J. Yi, "in 1965, before Korea's first [combat] division arrived in South Vietnam, only 93 South Korean civilians were employed by American and Korean contactors . . . [yet] when the Korean commitment increased to 50,000, 10,204 Koreans gained employment in South Vietnam. . . . This number increased to 25,120 in 1970." Kil J. Yi, "The U.S.-Korean Alliance in the Vietnam War: The Years of Escalation, 1964–68," in *International Perspectives on Vietnam*, ed. Lloyd C. Gardner and Ted Gittinger (College Station: Texas A&M University Press, 2000), 164.

8. See, for example, Yi, "The U.S.-Korean Alliance in the Vietnam War," 159; Baldwin, "America's Rented Troops," 36–40. For a discussion of the links between South Korea's involvement in the Vietnam War and Korean industrialization, see, for example, Jung-en Woo, *Race to the Swift: State and Finance in Korean Industrialization* (New York: Columbia University Press, 1991); and Jim Glassman and Young-Jin Choi, "The Chaebol and the US Military-Industrial Complex: Cold War Geopolitical Economy and South Korean Industrialization," *Environment and Planning A: Economy and Space* 46, no. 5 (2014).

9. Yi, "The U.S.-Korean Alliance in the Vietnam War," 164, 162.

10. Baldwin, "America's Rented Troops," 34.

11. Joungwon Alexander Kim, "Korean Participation in the Vietnam War," *World Affairs* 129, no. 1 (1966): 28.

12. Youngju Ryu, "Korea's Vietnam: Popular Culture, Patriarchy, Intertextuality," *Review of Korean Studies* 12, no. 3 (September 2009): 119.

13. For the social context of the deployment of Korean soldiers, see Eun Seo Jo, "Fighting for Peanuts: Reimagining South Korean Soldiers' Participation in the Wollam Boom," *Journal of American-East Asian Relations* 21 (2014); for army newsreels, see Namhee Han, "Incomplete Pictures: Mediated Immediacy in the South Korean Newsreel, the Frontline in Vietnam," in *The Cold War in Asian Cinemas* (New York: Routledge, 2019).

14. Yi, "The U.S.-Korean Alliance in the Vietnam War," 162.

15. Kim, "Korean Participation in the Vietnam War," 31.

16. Jo, "Fighting for Peanuts," 70.

17. Jo, "Fighting for Peanuts," 73–74.

18. Jo, "Fighting for Peanuts," 73–74; Also, information gathered from the Academy of Korean Studies Vietnam War veteran oral history archives, as well as from author interviews conducted on return boxes with two groups of Vietnam War veterans at the Gwanak region veterans' community center and at the Seocho Veterans Community Center on December 10, 2019.

19. Although not direct or obvious, its relation to large exports of "Other Chemical Products" from Korea to Vietnam during the war, making up 40.87 percent of all

Korean exports of the category for the years 1966–1967 might be seen as a significant relation, which overlaps the category of man-made fibers and related components of the chemical fibers industry. See Seji Naya, "The Vietnam War and Some Aspects of Its Economic Impact in Asian Countries," *Developing Economies* 9, no. 1 (1971): 43, table V.

20. "Uisikju 23(yeon) eotteoke dallajyeonna," *Donga Ilbo*, August 15, 1968.

21. "Jirihanbokjungeul siwonhago anjeonhage," *Gyeonghyang Sinmun*, July 28, 1971.

22. "Momppeeseo cheongbajikkaji," *Donga Ilbo*, August 17, 1978.

23. Hanguktonggyejinheungwon (Korean Statistics Promotion Institute), "Yunbokui miniseukeoteu 'sinseonhan chunggyeok' ieonneundett," *Sports Korea*, August 22, 2009.

24. See Jo, "Fighting for Peanuts," 84, who points out that the lyrics were later corrected to "Far far away nation" after it dawned on the songwriter-singer that Vietnam is not an island nation.

25. *Wollam* in Korean is the phonetic derivation in the Korean alphabet of corresponding Sino-Korean ideographs used to represent/signify "Vietnam."

26. Lee Yun-gi, "Samgak Hamsu," in *Noreui nalgae* (Seoul: Minumsa, 2003), 176. All translations are mine. In reference to the Korean author, Lee Yun-gi, I use his surname followed by his given name, per Korean custom.

27. See, for example, corroboration for this claim in "'Wollambungeo' seolchyeo 'hangangbungeo' momsal," *Joongang Ilbo*, May 22, 1991, https://news.joins.com/article/2565277. According to this and other related news articles on the topic, although the bluegill appears to be indigenous to the United States, it was imported via Japan in 1969 by the Fisheries Ministry.

28. Roland Barthes, *Mythologies*, trans. Annette Lavers (New York: Hill & Wang, 1972).

29. Barthes, *Mythologies*, 117.

30. Barthes, *Mythologies*, 114–115, 123.

31. Barthes, *Mythologies*, 122.

32. Yi, "The U.S.-Korean Alliance in the Vietnam War," 162.

33. Barthes, *Mythologies*, 118.

34. For a close study on this topic through the history of the People's Army of Vietnam, see Greg Lockhart, *Nation in Arms: The Origins of the People's Army of Vietnam* (Sydney: Allen & Unwin, 1989).

35. Barthes, *Mythologies*, 119.

36. Barthes, *Mythologies*, 123.

37. Han Gil Jang, "People's Tribunal on War Crimes by South Korean Troops during the Vietnam War," *Asia-Pacific Journal Japan Focus* 17, no. 1 (2019): 5.

38. Charles Armstrong, "America's Korea, Korea's Vietnam," *Critical Asian Studies* 33, no. 4 (2001): 533.

39. Dong Choon Kim, "Korea's Truth and Reconciliation Commission: An Overview and Assessment," *Buffalo Human Rights Law Review* 19 (2013): 110, 113.

40. Kim, "Korea's Truth and Reconciliation Commission," 114.

41. Jang, "People's Tribunal on War Crimes," 5.

42. Jang, "People's Tribunal on War Crimes," 5.

43. "[Interview] Continuing the Fight for Victims of Civilian Massacres during the Vietnam War," *Hankyoreh*, May 24, 2020.

44. Kim, "Korea's Truth and Reconciliation Commission," 113.

45. On the reconceptualization of the Cold War as a global Cold War, with particular reference to the Vietnam War, see Heonik Kwon, *The Other Cold War* (New York: Columbia University Press, 2010), 35–36.

46. "[Interview] Ttuihoa, nae cheongchunui tsinhwayeo," *Hankyoreh 21*, February 4, 2002, https://news.naver.com/main/read.nhn?mode=LSD&mid=sec&sid1=001&oid=036&aid=0000004299.

47. Jinim Park, "The Colonized Colonizers: Korean Experiences of the Vietnam War," *Journal of American–East Asian Relations* 7, no. 3 (1998): 225.

48. Park, "The Colonized Colonizers," 222, 226.

49. Park, "The Colonized Colonizers," 225, 232.

50. See Paik Nak-chung's conceptualization of the "division system" in Paik Nak-chung, "The Double Project of Modernity," *New Left Review* 95 (September–October 2015): 68–73.

11 The American-Led Military Coalition in Vietnam
Interests, Incentives, and Interpretations
••
DAVID L. ANDERSON

The American war in Vietnam was fought by a military coalition of seven countries: the United States, the Republic of Vietnam (RVN), the Republic of Korea (ROK), Australia, New Zealand, Thailand, and the Philippines. At the peak of U.S. deployment in South Vietnam in 1969, the troop strengths were 543,400 United States, 897,000 RVN, 48,869 ROK, 11,586 Thailand, 7,672 Australia, 552 New Zealand, and 189 Philippines. Joining the American and RVN troops battling the Vietcong (VC) and North Vietnamese Army (NVA) were 68,889 soldiers from five Asia-Pacific nations. These free world military assistance forces, or third-country forces, were under the operational control of the U.S. Military Assistance Command, Vietnam (MACV) at brigade level or higher, while the RVN armed forces (RVNAF) retained command of its own troops. The RVNAF reached 1,048,000 in 1972 as a result of Vietnamization, when the U.S. and third-country forces approached zero. Even with more than one million men listed in the RVNAF at the end of 1972, the force at Saigon's disposal was far less than the 1.5 million available in the military coalition contesting Hanoi in 1969.[1]

These third-country nations deployed military members to the RVN for reasons of their own national interests. Some studies of "more flags"—President Lyndon Johnson's term that came to identify his persistent quest for troops to fight alongside Americans—start with the notion of buying allies or even with the tendentious characterization of coalition partners as mercenaries or as a "coalition of the unwilling."[2] Today in an age of private military companies, sometimes termed corporate warriors, the term *mercenary* has a meaning that is distinctly different from what occurred in Vietnam, which was the incentivizing of governments to employ their forces in a military coalition. Each of the five participants who joined with the United States in military defense of the RVN followed its own national trajectory. Australia and New Zealand paid their own troops and reimbursed the United States for military equipment and materiel. Poorer nations that responded needed financial assistance to participate and negotiated for and accepted U.S. payments and subsidies. Coalitions are of two types: those between equal states—such as the U.S.-British-Soviet alliance of World War II—and those between greater and lesser powers. In the second case, the state with the greatest economic power usually dictates the plan, and the American-led coalition in Vietnam clearly fits this model.[3]

National security strategy defends the welfare of a nation as broadly defined by geography, borders, economic resources, trade relationships, citizen safety, proximate threats, core social values, and historical traditions. Each of the participants in the American-led coalition in Vietnam came with its own particular set of interests. Through a combination of force and diplomacy, the United States has historically sought to deter its enemies not only through armed might and economic leverage but also through alliances, treaties, negotiations, and appeals to reason. Soft power is real power and makes policy more than cynical transactional calculations of self-interest. Even the pragmatist Machiavelli acknowledged that it is better to be loved than feared. Too much faith in friendship can be dangerous or disappointing, but without some level of trust and empathy, diplomacy can falter and leave only force and its dangerous uncertainties to shape actions.[4]

U.S. economic aid and military protection are hard realities in American alignments with most countries, which are almost always less wealthy and armed than the United States. Soft power advocates assume, however, that values, culture, long-term attitudes, and preferences make a difference. As John Lewis Gaddis notes about the origins of the Soviet and American empires after World War II, the first was by imposition and the second by invitation. American allies welcomed the security, economic benefits, and defense of democracy that Washington offered and feared the record of oppression that the communist state represented.[5]

These soft power and hard power containment strategies were applicable to Western Europe, where the legacy of an invasion threat remained from World War II and the Soviet army's postwar occupation of Eastern Europe, but President Dwight Eisenhower and later President Johnson found their application challenging in fashioning Cold War coalitions in Southeast Asia. In 1954, as communist-led forces of the Democratic Republic of Vietnam (DRV) threatened to break the colonial grip on Indochina of America's North Atlantic Treaty Organization (NATO) ally France, Eisenhower faced a fundamental decision: Should he send U.S. combat forces to the region or limit America's response to military and economic assistance to South Vietnam, which remained beyond Hanoi's control at the moment? He authorized Secretary of State John Foster Dulles to undertake "united action" with U.S. allies to deter the DRV.[6]

Although sensitive to the desire for independence among the peoples of Southeast Asia, the Eisenhower administration chose to classify the containment of global communist expansion in Southeast Asia as a "have to" choice that preempted the "want to" option of condemning French colonialism. As the Kennedy, Johnson, and Nixon administrations would also maintain, Eisenhower and Dulles believed that the global threat represented by aggressive and repressive communist regimes in Moscow and Beijing required the United States and its allies to stand together against it.

Allied coalitions are common practice in international security policy, and Washington anticipated the appearance of an anti-communist coalition in Vietnam as in Korea. American policymakers considered Vietnam to be another "testing ground where the Free World had to use its strength against the forceful expansion of communism."[7] They drew a parallel between USSR and People's Republic of China (PRC) support of North Korea and their support of North Vietnam. It was not surprising and even seemed obvious that the United States would seek multilateral help in fashioning its Vietnam policy.

With the key battle between France and the DRV under way at Dien Bien Phu, Eisenhower made explicit the strategic importance of Southeast Asia. He publicly advanced his domino theory that if Hanoi succeeded in gaining control of all of Vietnam, the result would be a chain reaction ending with puppet regimes of the USSR and PRC throughout Southeast Asia. The White House viewed the stakes as high enough to merit military intervention in support of France but wanted congressional backing of this move. Senator Lyndon Johnson was among the legislators who pressed the White House to seek European allies before entering the military fray in French Indochina. Recalling that in Korea, 90 percent of the men and money came from the United States, Johnson cautioned Dulles that "in Indochina we ought to know first who would put up the men."[8] Eisenhower's personal appeal to British prime minister Winston Churchill for united action proved unsuccessful. Washington's major international partners—especially Great Britain—believed the ends were too muddled and the means too expensive to join in a rescue of the beleaguered French garrison. There was no intervention, the DRV forces took Dien Bien Phu, and Paris reached a cease-fire agreement with Hanoi at Geneva in July 1954.

At a hastily convened conference in Manila in September 1954, the Eisenhower administration moved to make the Geneva-created cease-fire line at the 17th parallel a global containment frontier, not unlike the 38th parallel in Korea. A treaty signed at the Manila meeting created the Southeast Asia Treaty Organization (SEATO), which included the United States, Great Britain, France, the Philippines, Thailand, Pakistan, Australia, and New Zealand. SEATO was no NATO, despite the intentional rhyme of the names. It provided for consultations with no mutual-defense obligations from any signatory to commit forces in the region. It was a diplomatic deterrence strategy that Washington realized had not existed before Chinese entrance into the Korean conflict. Dulles believed that SEATO was a "no trespassing" sign, one that might have prevented the invasion in Korea and could now warn Hanoi against aggression against South Vietnam.[9]

Nations chose to join or not join SEATO for diverse reasons. Nonaligned states such as India and Indonesia, though invited, declined participation. Britain and France were lukewarm to the idea. Both countries focused their resources on the Soviet threat in Europe, and Paris was mired in another anti-colonial war in Algeria. Still, these European powers had sufficient interests in Southeast Asia and valued their strategic and historic ties to the United States enough to agree to join. The weak and unstable governments in South Vietnam, Laos, and Cambodia were not signatories, but an attached ambiguous protocol listed them as included in the "treaty area."[10] SEATO never functioned as a defensive alliance and remained largely a device for the United States to buy time to develop South Vietnam, but four Asia-Pacific SEATO members—Australia, New Zealand, Thailand, and the Philippines—played a role in Washington's more flags initiative.

President Johnson remarked on April 23, 1964, that "I would hope that we would see some other flags in [South Vietnam] . . . and that we could all unite in an attempt to stop the spread of communism in that area of the world, and the attempt to destroy freedom."[11] He specifically desired the presence of soldiers other than Americans in Vietnam to demonstrate the legitimacy of U.S. objectives and to bolster Saigon's morale. Unlike Eisenhower's primarily diplomatic maneuver with SEATO, Johnson wanted a military coalition willing to join the United States in the use of force.

SEATO members Britain and France along with other major allies, such as West Germany and Japan, rejected repeated U.S. requests for troops. "All European and some Asian allies saw, in a way that Americans never seemed to," according to George Herring, "the dubiousness of the U.S. cause in Vietnam."[12] Most of them provided only rhetorical affirmations of containment, limited trade with South Vietnam, or nonpolitical humanitarian aid for war victims. Charles de Gaulle's government in Paris sharply criticized the war and advocated the "neutralization" of all of Indochina. Britain had been a cochair of the Geneva Conference, and London urged negotiations, rather than combat. For obvious reasons, West German leaders strongly endorsed the U.S. containment strategy, but their obsession was German reunification, and they would make no move that risked a serious break with London or Paris.

Herring argues that diplomatic isolation from European allies contributed to the U.S. defeat in Vietnam and contrasted to Hanoi's steady support from Moscow and Beijing. Johnson claimed that U.S. credibility in backing allies was at stake, but Fredrik Logevall contends that a more credible position with America's NATO partners was to end U.S. military intervention. Eugenie Blang finds that European officials disagreed with U.S. escalation of the Vietnam War, but because their individual interests dictated different approaches to Washington, they never fashioned a united front toward Johnson on the issue. Geopolitically, the violence and instability in Vietnam was simply too far removed from Europe to pose a proximate threat to NATO.[13]

Without SEATO or NATO as a vehicle for an American coalition to support the RVN, Johnson's more flags became an ad hoc agreement among multiple partners to achieve specific short-term objectives.[14] After the U.S. experience in Iraq and Afghanistan, a 2016 U.S. Army monograph on multinational force integration argued that "the Vietnam War provides an example of multinational partnership in modern warfare, where the US Army was part of a multinational force conducting decisive action in a unified effort towards a strategic objective."[15] Although this coalition's purpose was the survival of an independent Republic of Vietnam, the RVN itself lacked the manpower, wealth, and institutional infrastructure to mount its own defense. It was failing as a nation, and the United States assumed the task of rescuing it from fatal collapse. Johnson was prepared for unilateral U.S. action, if necessary, but he preferred a joint effort of nations threatened by a DRV victory. In political scientist Marina Henke's terms, the United States was the "pivotal state" that cared "most about the deployment and success of a particular military operation and thus [would] provide the bulk of the means to cover such payments" as necessary for the mission.[16]

The largest contributor of troops to the coalition was the RVN itself. It had the most to lose in the war but little to offer its supporters. What assistance Saigon obtained from third countries was acquired through direct U.S. negotiations with those governments. The survival of a particular regime, including that of President Nguyen Van Thieu after 1965, was not the coalition's connecting link. Even the United States had intervened in Vietnam as part of a global strategy that had little to do with internal Vietnamese politics. Washington viewed South Vietnam as a salient that must be defended to contain communist expansion emanating from Moscow and spreading to Asia through Beijing. The RVN was only an incidental interest for Australia, New Zealand, and Korea, who fought not for Saigon but in keeping with their established practices of protecting their regional interests and constructing their national defense with allies. Australia's and New Zealand's participation in the coalition was in large part to maintain their alliance with Washington at a time when their traditional ally Great Britain was ending its historic role as stabilizer in Southeast Asia and the Southwest Pacific. The ROK was an ally of the United States, not the RVN, and relied on good relations with Washington for its security.[17]

Not a SEATO member, the ROK provided the decidedly largest contingent of military personnel to the coalition after the United States and the RVN. Both Washington and Seoul viewed the wartime arrangement as mutually beneficial. Washington gained a strong containment partner in Vietnam and the Asia-Pacific region at a time when other nations were not stepping up as hoped. In military terms, the two nations' armies had two decades of joint operations and training that had created confidence and trust on both sides. While jealously preserving control of their own troops, the two commands cooperated effectively in the field. In the arrogance typical of U.S. leadership at the time, Secretary of Defense Robert McNamara informed Johnson in 1966 that Seoul had requested "about $600–$700 million worth of cumshaw [a term of Chinese origin for bribes] . . . in order to send a division."[18] Despite the patronizing remark, the "cumshaw" was a good economic deal for an administration that was trying to fight a war without going to Congress for money and trigger political debate on the war. Johnson's aide Jack Valenti remarked that the cost of two ROK divisions was "cheap—for the equipping of Koreans is at the ratio of 5–1 to 10–1 for the same equipment of the same number of Americans. Moreover, the Koreans are competent jungle fighters—and ready to fight."[19]

President Park Chung Hee wanted to demonstrate reciprocity for American defense of the ROK, but his nation was one of the world's poorest countries and required economic assistance to participate. From 1965 to 1973, U.S. supply of military hardware, direct cash subsidies, and loans reached into the billions of dollars. One ROK official quipped that Seoul was "digging for gold in the jungles of Vietnam."[20] Park's government acquired a mercenary image, but the generous U.S. aid packages came in large part from Johnson's haste. He was so eager for allies to convince Congress of the legitimacy of the war effort that he offered inducements above and beyond what might have been necessary. Since 1954, Johnson had maintained that even the powerful United States should not have to stand alone as the world's policeman. He sometimes told Secretary of State Dean Rusk to play coy in negotiations for coalition support but be prepared to pay if required.[21] Park used the foreign exchange and hard currency from the incentives Johnson offered to jump-start ambitious economic development programs. From 1963 to 1973, South Korea's gross domestic product quadrupled. In addition, as a member of the American-led coalition, the ROK was, for the first time in its history, not just a recipient but a provider of military assistance, and it has participated in global security operations ever since.[22]

Park's critics have complained about his mercenaries, but Korean veterans have defended themselves in memoirs and gained through their efforts (widely supported by the public) combat disability benefits. There are reports of alleged ROK atrocities in Vietnam, kept secret for many years, that South Korean soldiers killed sixty-nine defenseless civilians at Phong Nhi and Phong Nhat in 1968. These accounts echo those of American troops killing civilians at My Lai the same year. These horrific and often-denied events are important reminders that modern warfare is brutal and deadly and that civilian populations suffer. Whether these terrible costs are the price of any war or they are somehow emblematic of particular wars, commanders and soldiers are always morally, legally, and historically accountable for their actions.[23]

Thai leaders were well aware of Seoul's hard bargaining with Washington. In Henke's analysis of coalition building, Thailand was a "critical contributor" to U.S. efforts in Southeast Asia. As one of the most visible dominoes to which Eisenhower had referred and the only mainland Southeast Asian state in SEATO, it had diplomatic value in terms of legitimizing the war against the DRV and shoring up morale in the RVN. Its ruling generals exhibited little anxiety for the fate of Saigon's politicians but wanted U.S. military aid to augment their own domestic political power. Thailand's proximity to Vietnam made it almost indispensable for U.S. airpower, communications, and intelligence. It was also an accessible reservoir of fighters for the ground war in Vietnam. For their part, Thailand's leaders wanted assurances that the United States was a reliable long-term ally and that it understood Bangkok's concern was not Vietnam but Laos and the threat posed by the communist Pathet Lao. Both the Kennedy and Johnson administrations publicly reassured Thailand of U.S. backing, and Washington ultimately gained Bangkok's acceptance of eight air bases, a deep-water port, ammunition depots, and long-distance communication terminals in the country. Thailand committed a full division of ground forces and, by exploiting the Johnson administration's obvious craving for Asians in the combat ranks, demanded and got full American funding for training, equipping, supplying, and paying its troops plus an increase in overall military assistance of $60–$75 million per year. Although this transaction appeared "mercenary," Thailand lacked the money to self-finance its participation and could not afford to subsidize the United States with money as well as with men and land use for bases.[24]

The Philippines was a member of SEATO and had a historic connection to the United States as a former colony and home of major U.S. air and naval bases. Also, its leaders were anti-communist and wary of Beijing's regional ambitions, but they required considerable coaxing to join the coalition. The country faced little security danger from the mainland Southeast Asian conflict, but Manila hoped to play a key role through SEATO in a robust Pacific defense system. Despite heavy diplomatic pressure from Washington, including missions to Manila by Secretary Rusk and Vice President Hubert Humphrey, President Ferdinand Marcos resisted sending the Philippine Civic Action Group (PHILCAG), a 2,300-man engineering unit, to South Vietnam until September 1966. The Philippine congress rightly protested that their poor country's meager budget could not support the expense of involvement in Vietnam. To obtain even a token show of support for the American war effort, Washington paid the full costs and made what Henke terms a side deal with an additional $80 million in economic assistance to the Philippines. Controversy persistently plagued the deployment because of domestic criticism that Marcos was too politically dependent on and too closely tied to the Americans. As the war sparked mounting international censure and as congressional hearings in Washington revealed how much assistance had greased the wheels of the arrangement, Marcos withdrew PHILCAG in November 1969 to appease his domestic critics.[25]

Among the SEATO nations responding to Johnson's call for more flags, Australia and New Zealand came closest to the United States in strategic assessments as well as historical and cultural identification. These neighboring Southwest Pacific nations self-funded their participation and approached the challenge of the Vietnam War in their own ways. They both had a strategic interest in stability in Southeast Asia and a desire to maintain and encourage Washington's interest in their defense. Following U.S.

endorsement of Australia's and New Zealand's military contribution to counterinsurgency warfare to contain Indonesian ambitions in Malaysia, Canberra sent a small number of military advisers to Vietnam in 1964. After Johnson committed U.S. combat divisions to South Vietnam in 1965, Australia deployed a two-regiment task force and supporting elements responsible for securing the entire province of Phuoc Tuy. Australian Labor Party leader Gough Whitlam quipped that Prime Minister Harold Holt's "slogan is not 'All the way with LBJ,' but 'Further than LBJ.'"[26]

New Zealand had much smaller national defense resources than did Australia. Although Prime Minister Keith Holyoake and much of the population in New Zealand never desired any substantial involvement in the Vietnam War, Wellington deployed a token force in 1965 of 119 men, mostly in an artillery battery, and in 1967 the number grew to slightly more than 500 with the attachment of two Royal New Zealand infantry companies to the Australian task force. Neither Hanoi nor Beijing posed any imminent threat to New Zealand, and most of its citizens with knowledge of the conflict believed the Saigon regime was doomed by ineptitude and little anti-colonial credibility compared to the DRV. Consequently, Wellington precariously balanced supporting the U.S. desire for an alliance-based strategy against limiting its participation as much as possible for financial and political reasons. Holyoake played the role of "dovish hawk" and rejected both the "hawk" and "dove" labels for his and New Zealand's position on the war.[27]

Australia, New Zealand, and the United States experienced persistent tension in their Southeast Asian policies between a perceived need to contain world communism and a democratic impulse to acknowledge the anti-colonial motives of radical nationalist movements. Strategists in the three countries were not blind to this dichotomy, but Canberra and Wellington followed Washington's lead and assessed that America's vast power made the dilemma manageable. The seeming success of counterinsurgency warfare in Malaysia (Malaya), where Australia and New Zealand had joined with Great Britain, also made the defeat of communist rebels seem possible, without careful consideration of how Vietnam differed from Malaysia. Policy architects accepted the possibility of a domino effect with a communist victory in Vietnam aided by the PRC, and all underestimated the cost and difficulty of trying to counter it.[28]

New Zealand's official historian, Roberto Rabel, has used the term *cultural province of Britain* to describe his country.[29] He notes local and Indigenous influences in the Southwest Pacific, but as former British

Commonwealth nations, Australia and New Zealand are English-settler nations that have at times had common strategic interests and shared "normative sentiments" in a community of common values. This cultural affinity can be extended to include the United States, itself an English-settler nation. John Murphy has argued that Robert Menzies, Harold Holt, and other architects of Australia's alignment with the United States in Vietnam shared with Americans an "orientalism" that romanticized and patronized Vietnamese culture and created "an imagined boundary between West and East, between the democracies and threatening communism."[30] Australia and New Zealand passed through phases in their Vietnam War experience that paralleled those in American society and strategic thinking. In each country, a majority of the public accepted the formation of a military coalition against the DRV to contain communism, to block presumed Chinese ambitions, and to honor historical connections of friendship and joint security.[31]

In October 1966, Johnson staged a successful public relations summit in Manila with the leaders of the other six coalition countries. Bland pronouncements and photo opportunities conveyed the desired image that the United States did not stand alone in Vietnam. A year later, the public face and the private confidence in the effort was fading. The costs in lives, money, and domestic discord were rising for all the partners. In the summer of 1967, Johnson sent Clark Clifford and General Maxwell Taylor on a special mission to gain more troop support, especially from Australia. None of the nations visited during the trip agreed to supply more troops. Leaders in Australia, New Zealand, and Thailand made clear they did not see their vital interests at stake. As historians Jonathan Coleman and J. J. Widén have concluded, Clifford's tour with Taylor "buried" the domino theory that he had once accepted and promoted.[32]

Following the Communists' Tet offensive in early 1968, the United States and its coalition partners began to reexamine Southeast Asian strategy. The public in New Zealand had always exhibited unease with a role in the war, and Australian opponents of the war had become increasingly outspoken over time. Even the less democratic regimes in Manila and Seoul faced domestic political limits to their commitments. War frustration helped elect Richard Nixon U.S. president. While negotiating a compromise with Hanoi, Nixon began his Vietnamization policy in 1969, a withdrawal of U.S. forces in rapid stages while preparing the RVNAF to fight alone. His military chiefs briefly harbored a false hope that some of the coalition members might keep forces in the RVN, but only Thailand did so for a time. The small Philippine contingent was gone by 1969, and Australia, New Zealand, and South Korea paced their own withdrawals with those of the United States in 1970–1972.[33]

The war polarized the politics of the United States, Australia, and New Zealand. Anti-war sentiment in the three countries did not alone bring an end to their military engagement, but protest movements conditioned the political process to accept negotiation and withdrawal when government strategists decided national security no longer required the cost and sacrifice of the conflict.[34] In 1970, Australian polls revealed that the public was evenly divided for and against the merits of the war. Despite that level of tension—especially over Canberra's implementation of conscription in 1964—there is evidence that popular support remained for general alignment with the United States and that unease with the methods and appearance of the protesters was common.[35]

The way the American war ended had a lasting effect on its coalition partners. The so-called Nixon Doctrine declared in 1969 that "military defense . . . will be increasingly handled by, and the responsibility for it taken by, the Asian nations themselves."[36] Although intended for the RVN, this statement and the unilateral U.S. decision to withdraw forces quickly without consulting its third-country allies created understandable disquiet in the Asia-Pacific region, even before Saigon's ultimate collapse in 1975. A particularly humiliating moment for Australia's prime minister William McMahon came in 1971 when, just days after he had attacked his Labor Party opponents as "pawns of the giant Communist power in the region," Nixon suddenly announced he would be visiting Beijing.[37]

Each nation joined the coalition based on its interests and resources. The ROK, Thailand, and the Philippines were poor nations that required financial reimbursement. They received generous financial benefits that suggested mercenary motives but also reflected the hasty excessiveness of Washington's offers. These countries valued connection with the United States before Johnson's appeal for more flags and his offers of incentives. From the beginning and without prompting, Seoul viewed itself as a military ally of the United States in the containment of Asian communism based on two decades of shared defense efforts. With armed violence on its borders, Thailand could not remain indifferent to the Vietnam conflict and sought security in providing bases and troops to support the U.S.-led battle against Hanoi. The Philippines had little to offer on its own and was geographically distant from the fighting, but the Marcos government believed the islands' historical links to the United States required cooperation with

Washington. Australia and New Zealand accepted no payments for their help and avoided any implication of being mercenaries. Both nations had long-established security doctrines of defending their nations with strong allies—originally Great Britain and then the United States. Australia was forthcoming with offers of assistance, and New Zealand was cautious, but both generally agreed with Washington's assessment that an aggressive China and its allies and an ambitious Indonesia should be restrained within the Asia-Pacific region. By the early 1970s, however, the urgency of the perceived Chinese threat had lessened, the instability in Indonesia had passed, and Saigon was being left on its own. The national interest assessments and wartime calculations for the coalition members, including the United States, had changed.

In the years after the Vietnam War, all the contributing partners pursued greater self-reliance and independence from the United States. Building up their economic and defense structures and nurturing regional and other relations took on greater importance, as Washington was seen as a less reliable partner. Australia, New Zealand, the ROK, Thailand, and the Philippines had entered the wartime coalition in pursuit of their own goals and continued to chart their own courses. They all maintained friendly relations with the United States while fashioning and maturing their own national security strategies.[38] Foreign policy realists like to recall Lord Palmerston's famous dictum that "we have no eternal allies, and we have no perpetual enemies. Our interests are eternal and perpetual, and those interests it is our duty to follow." In that same parliamentary speech, however, the British statesman also acknowledged that "when we find other countries marching in the same course, and pursuing the same objects as ourselves, we consider them as our friends."[39] Interests, friendship, and enmity do not exist in isolation, and during and after the Vietnam War, interests and friendships between the United States and its Asia-Pacific partners remained central to everyone's own national security calculations.

Notes

1. The Philippines' peak strength came in 1966 at 2,061, and the ROK had 50,003 in 1968. See Robert Larsen and James Lawton Collins Jr., *Allied Participation in Vietnam* (Washington, DC: Department of the Army, 1975), 23; David L. Anderson, *The Columbia Guide to the Vietnam War* (New York: Columbia University Press, 2002), 286–288.

2. Jonathan Coleman and J. J. Widén, "The Johnson Administration and the Recruitment of Allies in Vietnam, 1964–1968," *History* 94 (October 2009): 504;

Robert Blackburn, *Mercenaries and Lyndon Johnson's "More Flags": The Hiring of Koreans, Filipino, and Thai Soldiers in the Vietnam War* (Jefferson, NC: McFarland, 1994), 32.

3. Travis J. Hardy, "Coalition Warfare," in *Encyclopedia of Military Science*, ed. G. Kurt Piehler and M. Houston Johnson V (Los Angeles: Sage, 2013), 337–338.

4. The author served in the U.S. Army in the RVN, shared a defensive perimeter with ROK troops, and went on rest and recreation (R&R) in Australia. He personally experienced genuine camaraderie and friendship from the soldiers and citizens of these partner nations.

5. John Lewis Gaddis, *We Now Know: Rethinking Cold War History* (Oxford: Oxford University Press, 1997), 52; Joseph Nye Jr., *Soft Power: The Means to Succeed in World Politics* (New York: Public Affairs, 2009).

6. Gary R. Hess, "With Friends Like These: Waging War and Seeking 'More Flags,'" in *The War That Never Ends: New Perspectives on the Vietnam War*, ed. David L. Anderson and John Ernst (Lexington: University Press of Kentucky, 2007), 57.

7. Larsen and Collins, *Allied Participation in Vietnam*, 1.

8. Quoted in William Conrad Gibbons, *The U.S. Government and the Vietnam War: Executive and Legislative Roles and Relationships,* Part 1, 1945–1960 (Princeton, NJ: Princeton University Press, 1986), 193.

9. David L. Anderson, *Trapped by Success: The Eisenhower Administration and Vietnam, 1953–1961* (New York: Columbia University Press, 1991), 71.

10. Hess, "With Friends Like These," 58–59; "Southeast Asia Collective Defense Treaty (with Protocol)," September 8, 1954, United Nations Treaty Series, https://treaties.un.org/doc/publication/unts/volume%20209/volume-209-i-2819-english.pdf.

11. Lyndon B. Johnson, The President's News Conference, April 23, 1964, The American Presidency Project, https://www.presidency.ucsb.edu/node/239184.

12. George C. Herring, "Fighting without Allies: The International Dimensions of America's Defeat in Vietnam," in *Why the North Won the Vietnam War*, ed. Marc Jason Gilbert (New York: Palgrave, 2002), 79.

13. Herring, "Fighting without Allies," 77–78, 91–92; Fredrik Logevall, *Choosing War: The Lost Chance for Peace and the Escalation of the War in Vietnam* (Berkeley: University of California Press, 1999), 182, 373, 388–389; Eugenie M. Blang, *Allies at Odds: America, Europe, and Vietnam, 1961–1968* (Lanham, MD: Rowman & Littlefield, 2011), 189–192.

14. Hardy, "Coalition Warfare," 337.

15. Michael H. Liscano Jr., *Multinational Force Integration: The ROK Army's Integration with the US Army in the Vietnam War* (Fort Leavenworth, KS: United States Army Command and General Staff College, 2016), 63.

16. Marina E. Henke, "Buying Allies: Payments in Multilateral Military Coalition-Building," *International Security* 43 (Spring 2019): 130.

17. Sean Fear, "Saigon Goes Global: South Vietnam's Quest for International Legitimacy in the Age of Détente," *Diplomatic History* 42 (June 2018): 436; Peter G. Edwards, *A Nation at War: Australian Politics, Society and Diplomacy during the Vietnam War, 1965–1975* (St. Leonards, Australia: Allen & Unwin, 1997), 20–25.

18. U.S. Department of State, *Foreign Relations of the United States, 1964–1968*, vol. 4, *Vietnam 1966*, doc. 26, January 17, 1966, https://history.state.gov/historical documents/frus1964-68v04/d26 (hereafter FRUS).

19. FRUS, 1964–1968, vol. 26, *Indonesia; Malaysia-Singapore; Philippines*, doc. 322, January 4, 1966, https://history.state.gov/historicaldocuments/frus1964-68v26/d322; Liscano, *Multinational Force Integration*, 64; Hess, "With Friends Like These," 68, 70.

20. Quoted in Fear, "Saigon Goes Global," 435. For funding figures, see Daniel Oh, "The Two Koreas and the Vietnam War," Wilson Center Digital Archive, accessed June 5, 2019, https://digitalarchive.wilsoncenter.org/resource/modern-korean-history-portal/the-two-koreas-and-the-vietnam-war.

21. Colman and Widén, "Johnson Administration," 495.

22. Glenn Baek, "A Perspective on Korea's Participation in the Vietnam War," *Asan Institute for Policy Studies Issue Brief* 53 (April 10, 2013), https://www.jstor.org/stable/resrep08116; Nicholas Evan Sarantakes, "In the Service of Pharaoh? The United States and the Deployment of Korean Troops in Vietnam, 1965–1968," *Pacific Historical Review* 68 (August 1999): 425–449, https://www.jstor.org/stable/4492337.

23. James Griffiths, "The 'Forgotten' My Lai: South Korea's Vietnam War Massacres," CNN, February 23, 2018, https://www.cnn.com/2018/02/23/asia/south-korea-vietnam-massacre-intl/index.html; David L. Anderson, "What Really Happened?" in *Facing My Lai: Moving beyond the Massacre*, ed. David L. Anderson (Lawrence: University Press of Kansas, 1998), 1–17.

24. Hess, "With Friends Like These," 64–65; Blackburn, *Mercenaries*, 111–113; Larsen and Collins, *Allied Participation*, 25; Henke, "Buying Allies," 137–138.

25. Hess, "With Friends Like These," 63–64; Blackburn, *Mercenaries*, 80–94.

26. John Murphy, *Harvest of Fear: A History of Australia's Vietnam War* (Boulder, CO: Westview, 1994), 152. See also Larsen and Collins, *Allied Participation in Vietnam*, 88–93, 99; Blackburn, *Mercenaries*, 124–129.

27. Roberto Rabel, *New Zealand and the Vietnam War: Politics and Diplomacy* (Auckland: Auckland University Press, 2005), 350–353; Larsen and Collins, *Allied Participation in Vietnam*, 105–109.

28. Peter Edwards, "Some Reflections on the Australian Government's Commitment to the Vietnam War," in *Australia's Vietnam War*, ed. Jeff Doyle, Jeffrey Grey, and Peter Pierce (College Station: Texas A&M University Press, 2002), 13–14.

29. Rabel, *New Zealand*, 4.

30. Murphy, *Harvest of Fear*, 277. See also Dan Halvorson, "From Commonwealth Responsibility to the National Interest: Australia's Post-war Decolonization in South-East Asia," *International History Review* 40 (2018): 874. This cultural affinity was visible to the author, as an American soldier on R&R in Sydney in 1970.

31. Rabel, *New Zealand*, 348–349; Carl Bridge, "Australia and the Vietnam War," in *The Vietnam War*, ed. Peter Lowe (Basingstoke, UK: Macmillan, 1998), 186.

32. Coleman and Widén, "Johnson Administration," 504; Clark Clifford with Richard Holbrooke, *Counsel to the President: A Memoir* (New York: Doubleday, 1991), 440–441, 448–449; FRUS, 1964–1968, vol. 5, *Vietnam 1967*, doc. 270, August 5, 1967, https://history.state.gov/historicaldocuments/frus1964-68v05/d270.

33. Edwards, *Nation at War*, 303–304; Fear, "Saigon Goes Global," 451.

34. Melvin Small, *Antiwarriors: The Vietnam War and the Battle for America's Hearts and Minds* (Wilmington, DE: Scholarly Resources, 2002), 1, 162–163; Peter Pierce, "'Never Glad Confident Morning Again': Australia, the Sixties, and the Vietnam War," in Doyle et al., *Australia's Vietnam War*, 66–68; Rabel, *New Zealand*, 355–356.

35. Bridge, "Australia and the Vietnam War," 191–194; Jeffrey Grey, "Protest and Dissent: Anti-Vietnam War Activism in Australia," in Doyle et al., *Australia's Vietnam War*, 60–62.

36. Richard Nixon, "Informal Remarks in Guam with Newsmen," July 25, 1969, The American Presidency Project, https://www.presidency.ucsb.edu/node/239667.

37. Murphey, *Harvest of Fear*, 270.

38. Edwards, *Nation at War*, 343; Rabel, *New Zealand*, 355, 362; Ronald Bruce Frankum Jr., *The United States and Australia in Vietnam, 1954–1968: Silent Partners* (Lewiston, NY: Edwin Mellen, 2001), 288–289; Bridge, "Australia and the Vietnam War," 194–195; Hess, "With Friends Like These," 70–71.

39. Lord Palmerston, House of Commons Debates, March, 1, 1848, https://api.parliament.uk/historic-hansard/commons/1848/mar/01/treaty-of-adrianople-charges-against.

12 LBJ's Hessians?

Korean Troops' Dispatch to Vietnam

CHRISTOPHER LOVINS

South Korea (hereafter simply "Korea") was the largest allied contributor to America's war effort in Vietnam, maintaining 50,000 troops in South Vietnam for the majority of the war and suffering casualties of approximately 5,000 dead and 16,000 wounded. These troops continue to be disparaged as mercenary soldiers both in Korea and in the United States because of the enormous aid packages Korea received from its American patron in exchange for the dispatch of first one and then a second division of frontline combat troops to Vietnam. They have also been characterized as a "bribe" to ensure the United States would not withdraw troops stationed protecting Korea. This chapter argues that the characterization of Korean troops in Vietnam as mercenaries is inappropriate and serves to distract from and obscure our understanding of Korea's involvement in the war. It also argues that although the Park Chung Hee government did take advantage of America's offers of aid in exchange for boots on the ground and that Park was deeply concerned about the possibility of American withdrawal from Korea, neither of these was the primary impetus behind Park's decision to involve Korea in the war. Rather, Park was most concerned with shoring up his legitimacy at home, which was intimately tied to his ability to improve Korea's economy and to demonstrate American support for his regime. Park had seized power through a military coup in 1961 and only after enormous U.S. pressure resigned his commission and won election as president in 1963. The next year, Park was in negotiations to dispatch troops. Sending Korean soldiers to Vietnam guaranteed the U.S. support for his regime that he desperately needed to retain power in the face of significant opposition within Korea. The United States also got what it wanted in the end: the stable, wealthy, militarily strong, and democratically governed South Korea of today.

In the United States, studies of the war have explored virtually every aspect of American involvement in the war, but the role of U.S. allies is not widely considered. To find such scholarship, one must look at specialists on the country in question; nearly all of the scholarship on Korean participation in the war I was able to find in English-language scholarship was written by Korean scholars who work in that language. (Two important exceptions will be discussed below.) Failing that, one then looks at the scholarship within the country. In Korea, understanding of the Vietnam War and Korea's participation in it is obscured by the politics of suffering—namely, the sufferings of those young men who were forced, as the narrative goes, to fight in it—despite most veterans' positive attitude toward their service in Vietnam. Overlooking that the majority of soldiers who served in Vietnam volunteered to do so,[1] those Korean authors critical of Korean involvement in the war largely deflect blame on the United States, emphasize Korean suffering, and deploy that suffering for political ends. Even professional historians of the war in Korea largely replicate popular attitudes, stifling meaningful dialogue.[2] To take just one example, Jin-kyung Lee argued in 2009 that the war both revitalized a Korean nationalized masculinity that had been weakened by the country's subordination to the United States and cemented Korea's development into a "subimperial" nation subservient to global American capitalism. As for the war's portrayal in popular culture, even the most critical Korean fiction dealing with the war replicates this nationalized, racialized masculinity, contrasting the racially inferior, effeminate Vietcong with the robust, masculine Republic of Korea (ROK) soldiers.[3]

The Mercenary Question

The view of Korean soldiers as mercenaries is most forcefully and influentially articulated by Robert M. Blackburn in his provocatively titled 1994 monograph *Mercenaries and Lyndon Johnson's "More Flags": The Hiring of Korean, Filipino and Thai Soldiers in the Vietnam War*. Blackburn argues that Lyndon B. Johnson (LBJ) extended the initially nonmilitary, symbolic aid provided by U.S. allies, intended to demonstrate the righteousness of the American cause in Vietnam through the "more flags" campaign, into actual boots on the ground. He carefully examines Johnson's intense concern that the U.S. war in Vietnam not be viewed in terms of U.S. unilateralism by means of allied support of the war effort, or even just of South Vietnam generally, regardless of the timing, source, goal, or effectiveness of that support. Secretary of State Dean Rusk, reporting on aid to Vietnam from allies, included aid programs that began before U.S. involvement in the war and counted promises of forthcoming support as support now. By June 1965, even *personal assurance of support* by any political leader was regarded as receiving "support" from that country.[4] It was only by these means that the Johnson administration could tout that thirty-four countries supported the U.S. war effort. By December 1964, out of the thirty-four countries specially targeted by more flags, only six—Australia, New Zealand, the Philippines, South Korea, Taiwan, and Thailand—offered significant support. Five of those six later sent combat troops to fight in Vietnam; Taiwan's offer was rejected for fear of provoking China. For Blackburn, however, only two of those countries were true allies of the United States. The other three merely sent mercenaries.

Surely, in our present era we must pause at the realization that these "true allies" are the two predominantly white countries of Asia, while the "Third World combat troops [hired] as an American mercenary force," to use Blackburn's own words, were from nonwhite populations.[5] He takes pains throughout the book to reiterate this point, seemingly to condemn LBJ's disgraceful means of shoring up support for an unjust war. However, it does have the perhaps unintended side effect of portraying whites as motivated by such lofty intangibles as patriotism, ideology, or strategic considerations while America's Asian "allies" are just in it for the money. Gerald Waite, himself a Vietnam veteran, published an article in 2014, drawn largely from Blackburn's work, that explicitly describes Australia and New Zealand as "true allies." Korea, on the other hand, was "in fact mercenary in [its] involvement in Vietnam" and was "probably overcompensated" for the support it provided.[6] Yet, as Nicholas Evans Sarantakes has pointed out, the United States gave in to Korea's supposedly excessive demands because its government failed to understand that there was no danger Park would refuse to send troops. The Johnson administration's combined ignorance and eagerness allowed Park to rake them over the coals to get an agreement they would have gotten anyway. Then, naturally, the precedent of major U.S. concessions had been set, allowing a repeat of this when it was time for dispatch of a second combat division.[7] Blackburn did not use the term *true allies*, but it is implicit throughout his monograph in the constant reminders that Thai, Korean, and Filipino soldiers were mercenary. Waite's article includes a postscript defending the actual soldiers themselves from the stain of the mercenary label. However, it is clear that in both Blackburn's and Waite's work, the label is intended to tarnish the American government's conduct of the war and perhaps even its very involvement in Vietnam. By implication, then, the governments of Thailand, Korea, and the Philippines are also tarnished, while those of Australia and New Zealand escape unscathed.

Moral connotations aside, how well does "mercenary" describe Korea's involvement? Despite writing that "by definition, a mercenary fights only if he or she receives pay for their skills" and that "the only relevant consideration in the definition of mercenary is simply whether a person's military service was dependent on the receipt of financial benefits,"[8] Blackburn generally uses the term to mean a soldier who fights (1) in a foreign country (2) for a reason not connected to his or her own country's national interests and (3) receiving pay or other benefits from a third country. One could define mercenary in this way, but it is not the definition used by the Geneva Conventions, which states in part, "A mercenary is any person who . . . (e) is not a member of the armed forces of a Party to the conflict; and (f) has not been sent by a State which is not a Party to the conflict on official duty as a member of its armed forces."[9] Certainly, the case can be made that Korea was no less "a Party to the conflict" than the United States itself was. Yet, even if we ignore this, its soldiers were in fact "on official duty as a member of [Korea's] armed forces." Although it broke more than ten years after *More Flags*'s publication, the controversy over U.S. use of mercenary soldiers in the Iraq War clearly centered on their status as private contractors rather than members of the military—America's or anyone else's. That they were receiving pay from the American government and not some other, and whether they were fighting in a conflict directly connected to their country's political interests, were not of particular interest to anyone. So Blackburn's definition does not seem very useful to us in connection with the general understanding of what the term *mercenary* entails.

Blackburn's reliance on declassified U.S. government documents means he also overestimates the value of the increased wages earned by those Koreans who served in Vietnam. Eun Seo Jo notes that these men were required to remit an average of 88.5 percent of these wages to the Korean government. Hence, those who served in Vietnam were seeking a way out of poverty, not a path to luxury. Jo also notes there were many motivations for service beyond monetary benefit. Many Koreans bought into the so-called domino theory and thus believed that fighting communists in Southeast Asia was in fact defending their own country. Others desired to demonstrate South Korea's increasing strength after its century of humiliation at the hands of Western powers and Japan, while still others simply thought war was the manly thing to do.[10] Waite claims that the Korean command operated independently from the U.S. command because the United States "did not want them seen as mercenary in nature."[11] Certainly, it did not, but another interpretation is simply that Korea, and perhaps the United States as well, sought independent operation because this was the armed forces of an independent country, as Min Yong Lee has argued.[12] Moreover, as pointed out by Choi Dong-Ju, during the Cold War, a superpower offering financial support for an ally to send military assistance to another ally was not unheard of. Indeed, the Soviet Union bankrolled Cuba's involvement in the civil war in Angola, as Cuba lacked the financial muscle to do so on its own.[13] Throughout the Korean involvement, the troops were completely dependent on U.S. logistical support and close air support, as South Korea lacked the resources to project power beyond the Korean Peninsula during the Vietnam War.

The Coup and the Dispatch

But perhaps we are arguing legalese here. Even if Korean soldiers in Vietnam do not meet the legal definition of mercenary as defined by the Geneva Conventions, the fact remains that Korea received enormous financial benefits from its participation in the war. Its soldiers were paid, equipped, and transported to Vietnam at U.S. expense, while those of Australia and New Zealand were not. So Korean involvement was still a dollars-for-bodies arrangement, right?

In May 1961, a group of military officers overthrew the democratic government of South Korea and established an authoritarian council of military officers. The central figure was Major General Park Chung Hee. Park's relationship with the United States did not start well. Without authorization, the American chargé d'affaires and the commander of U.S. forces in Korea both immediately condemned the coup and called on forces loyal to the government to suppress it; the State Department ex post facto authorized these actions. U.S. intelligence reported throughout the rest of 1961 that Park's new government lacked popular support and faced enormous economic challenges. At the same time, Park traveled to Washington to meet John F. Kennedy and offered to send troops to assist the United States. Kennedy was gratified but declined, noting that the time was not right; his focus was on Korea restoring diplomatic relations with Japan.[14] The following year, 1962, was not much better, with only 22 percent of Koreans reporting in a newspaper survey that things were better under the military junta than they had been before; 26 percent reported things were worse.[15] In 1964, when Ambassador Winthrop G. Brown relayed the Johnson administration's request for noncombat troops, Park expressed his desire to support the United States to the extent the ROK's resources allowed and then offered, unprompted, to send two divisions of combat troops. Brown declined, noting that "this was not that kind of war." Park approved the dispatch of noncombat troops but a half hour later.[16]

As a dictator in the "free world," Park was constantly concerned with his legitimacy and how U.S. actions affected it. Like his predecessor Syngman Rhee, Park's "need for good relations [with the United States] as a symbol of legitimacy, both domestically and internationally," gave the United States considerable leverage.[17] The United States pressed Park and the other members of the military junta to establish a civilian government and move toward democracy. Ambassador Samuel Berger recommended in June 1963 that the United States help keep the opposition strong enough to take over from the junta, should this become necessary. He continued to stress that the United States should not support Park unconditionally, yet with the dispatch of combat troops to Vietnam, this is precisely what happened.[18] Although Park did resign and earn election as a civilian president in October 1963, he remained willing to use military force and other nondemocratic means to ensure his policies were carried out. Ambassador Robert Komer told McGeorge Bundy in March 1964 that Park's government was "in danger" and that the United States should "tolerate a little more dictatorship" to keep it in power.[19] In the run-up to the Korean presidential election of 1967, Park's legitimacy and prestige received a significant boost from two meetings with Secretary of State Dean Rusk, two with Vice President Hubert Humphrey, and one with Johnson himself, all courting Park to maintain his troops in Vietnam.[20] Faced with alleged voting irregularities when Park won reelection, the United States had no alternative but to accept the results, rendered unable to challenge the man who put 50,000 troops into the war effort.[21] Rather than moving toward democracy as America insisted, Park's government became increasingly dictatorial, particularly after 1972 when Park instituted a new constitution effectively making himself president for life. Despite America's official position of neutrality on Park's running for a previously barred third term as president, Korean newspapers portrayed the situation as though the United States supported a third term, undoubtedly under Park's instructions.[22] The United States accepted all of Park's dictatorial excesses until Jimmy Carter's human rights policies came into direct conflict with them and the Vietnam War was a memory.

The difference Korean troops made in Vietnam is revealed in American treatment of Park on his first two visits to the United States; in 1965, with Korean boots on the ground in Vietnam, Park was feted by Johnson far more than Kennedy's rather more distant reception in 1961, including travel on Air Force One.[23] In an interesting twist on Blackburn's and Waite's view of Korean troops in Vietnam, Johnson told Park in May 1965 that he "feels that Korea has been the greatest assistance in helping to bring pressure to bear so that other countries like Australia and New Zealand would come in[to the war]."[24] Conversely, Tae Yang Kwak has argued, from both documents and personal interviews with surviving high-ranking ministers of Park's government, that Park used the dispatch to effect changes in U.S. policy since he was still concerned with any U.S. attempt to cede its responsibilities to Korea over to Japan, despite his successful normalization of relations with Japan in the face of popular opposition.[25] The dispatch further strengthened the alliance forged in blood—shifting it from a purely military alliance to a more political one—and the ensuing U.S. commitment to his regime permitted Park to easily transition from de facto to formal dictatorship in 1972.[26] In addition to the economic benefits, Korea also received an exaggerated U.S. guarantee of security as a reward for sending troops to Vietnam.[27] Investors were reassured by this additional guarantee, encouraging further stimulation of the fledgling Korean economic miracle.[28] Korean troops' fighting in Vietnam also spurred the American government to inaction on the "Koreagate" scandal, an influence-peddling scheme in which the Korean government allegedly funneled bribes through Korean businessman Tongsun Park in exchange for support in Congress. U.S. intelligence agencies learned of and informed authorities of these activities by 1971 at the latest, but the executive branch refused to act for fear of jeopardizing the continued presence of the Korean divisions.[29] Once Korean troops in Vietnam were no longer relevant, Jimmy Carter began to press Park on his regime's human rights record, significantly reducing Park's legitimacy at home.[30] The dispatch of troops also served to drum up nationalistic support in the face of the deeply unpopular normalization of relations with Japan. Forced to use martial law to disperse protesters against the normalization, Park needed something to restore his patriotic credentials, and committing Korean troops to fight communism elsewhere in Asia alongside the United States provided that. The Korean people generally supported the service of Korean troops in Vietnam and were proud of it, even politicians and other leaders opposed to Park.[31] His opposition in the National Assembly boycotted the sure-to-pass vote on the dispatch, but it was known that many of them actually approved of it.[32] Thus, it was a public relations loss for them since Park could portray them as boycotting the vote out of personal and partisan spite rather than substantive objections.

The dollars-for-bodies view also obscures the deep reluctance on Park's part to agree to Johnson's request for yet a third combat division, despite the outrageous amounts of aid offered. He delayed making a decision for nearly a year, and then any hope Johnson had was scuttled by the U.S. response to the *Pueblo* crisis. In January 1968, North Korea seized the American intelligence-gathering ship USS *Pueblo* and imprisoned its crew for a year. Johnson's decision not to retaliate and to negotiate directly with North Korea for the release of these hostages, bypassing Park, damaged his image among the Korean people. This, combined with Johnson's refusal to permit ROK retaliation for North Korea's attempt to assassinate Park and his family (the Blue House raid), reduced Park's willingness to further weaken Korea's own defenses.[33] The third division was never sent.

"Blood Money" as a Continuation of Existing Aid

Another way to examine the problem of the mercenary characterization even in spirit, if not in form, is the necessity of funding. The implication behind Blackburn's and Waite's characterization of Australia and New Zealand as "true allies" (though again, only Waite uses that specific term) is that they sent combat troops to Vietnam out of genuine friendship to the United States, while Korea only did so for selfish financial gain. Like the Hessians of old, Korean soldiers were not in a land far from home to fight for duty, honor, or country but for mere dollars. However, this view overlooks two crucial points. First, neither Australia nor New Zealand *needed* financial aid from the United States. These were both developed economies providing their people with a high standard of living. The commander in chief of Pacific forces reported to Washington that offering to pay all costs of any allied troops sent to Vietnam would have no effect on support for the more flags campaign; those already expected to contribute would still do so, and those who had declined would not change their minds for this reason.[34] The difference between Australia and New Zealand declining American financial assistance and Korea accepting the same was a matter of means, not desire. Further, this focuses only on monetary gain. As Blackburn himself notes, Australia and New Zealand cared not a fig for South Vietnam or its people. They sent troops as a quid pro quo with the United States for the latter's diplomatic muscle being deployed on their behalf against an upstart

Indonesia.³⁵ Australia's motivation was certainly no more about supporting the United States than Korea's was and was arguably less. It was, rather, about a realist calculation of potential threats to itself.³⁶ Given the other nonfinancial benefits Park's government also received from the dispatch of troops, it is problematic to single out economic and military aid as marking a country's dispatch of troops as "mercenary," invalidating all the other considerations among the countries involved. For example, Brown cabled Bernstein in September 1965 to remind U.S. leaders that Korea's motives for involvement were both tangible and intangible and that both were seen as reasonable by Koreans and by Brown himself, especially since Koreans viewed Japan as having benefited economically from Korea's own destructive civil war.³⁷ Military assistance programs did not just involve funds. In an interview in the 1990s, Park's minister of defense at the time of the dispatch, Kim Seong-eun, remarked that the Vietnam War was a chance not just to modernize the Korean military but also to give its men real-world experience operating this equipment³⁸ and thereby to increase Korean defense readiness. Indeed, the embassy reported to the State Department in March 1965 that Park was eager to send troops because he "want[ed] ROK to play a greater role in East Asia" and that the troops' dispatch might boost Koreans' national confidence and sense of equal partnership with the United States. The mercenary view portrays Korean soldiers as signing up for service in Vietnam for the extra pay earned, which ignores both that there were other factors—the embassy cited a "sense of adventure," Koreans' pride in fighting communism, and the debt to the United States for the Korean War—and that the embassy encouraged the use of volunteers, as sending mostly conscripts would prove unpopular.³⁹ Two weeks later, however, the embassy told the State Department that Korea was "in no position to play important international role or to give economic or military assistance" since its economy was weak, it was an anti-communist enclave surrounded by communist states, and relations with Japan had only just been restored.⁴⁰ Korea could neither protect itself at home nor provide men to fight abroad with the resources it had.

Plus, the economic, political, and military relationship between Korea and the United States was complicated and intertwined, and the financial windfall Korea reaped through its involvement in Vietnam can be seen as the extension of existing American aid programs. Ambassador Brown reported to the State Department that "many Koreans seem to take for granted that US [will be] footing bill" for ROK troops in Vietnam.⁴¹ The ROK had been receiving aid since its inception, and one goal that Park shared with every U.S. administration was ending the American aid program. That meant an economy and military that could stand up to North Korea alone and at least delay a Chinese attack until U.S. forces could arrive in strength.[42] The lion's share of aid received for the dispatch went toward modernizing and upgrading Korea's military, which was already a key U.S. goal. Korea was the largest recipient of funds from the Military Assistance Program (MAP), about half of the total,[43] or $216 million in 1968.[44] Ambassador Komer remarked on the "MAP theory of buying cheap infantry," referring to the lesser expense of financing allied military strength compared with deploying U.S. forces.[45] The Joint Chiefs reported to Secretary of Defense Robert McNamara that continued MAP support of Korea was necessary because of its importance in the Cold War and for its own military self-sufficiency. Specifically,

> the Department of Defense recognizes the contributions to Free World security being made by the Republic of Korea, and the ROK need for support under MAP. . . . The basic principle of the MAP Transfer Program [is] to encourage a country to shoulder more of the operations and maintenance cost of its defense burden. . . . Through it a greater portion of the MAP can be devoted to investment purposes. . . . As stipulated in the Military Assistance Manual, AID will support approximately two-thirds of the ROK defense budget, and the ROK defense budget should be permitted to increase to allow for the MAP Transfer. . . . The Military Assistance Manual provides that AID will underwrite approximately two-thirds of the cost of a cost-of-living pay adjustment.[46]

The United States was, then, already paying Korean soldiers through existing aid programs, before it even became involved in the Vietnam War.

Korea even came to accept the U.S. belief that the war must be won. If economic benefits were the only or even just the primary goal, it would be in Korean interests to prolong involvement in Vietnam as long as possible. However, the American government recognized that Park remained a soldier committed to victory. In March 1968, the prime minister of Korea, Jeong Il-gwan, told Ambassador William J. Porter that if the United States failed in Vietnam, it was an equal loss for Korea.[47] At the same time, Brown warned Rusk that a doubling of ROK forces in Vietnam would give Korea a seat at the strategic planning table from which it would insist on prosecuting the war to total victory.[48] On the other hand, once it became clear the United States was leaving Vietnam, Korea was determined to do so as well, according to its own schedule. In February 1970, despite the drawdown of American forces in Vietnam and the reduction of American troops in Korea, the Joint Chiefs of Staff reiterated that it was vital Korean troops remain in Vietnam. A year later, Secretary of Defense Melvin Laird reported that South Korea's planned unilateral withdrawal of 17,000 troops from Vietnam was not connected to U.S. withdrawal from Korea and so it should be encouraged, but Richard Nixon rejected this advice and demanded both ROK divisions remain.[49] In September and again in November 1971, the United States pressured South Korea to keep its troops in Vietnam through 1972, particularly in the shadow of Park's insistence that Korea maintain its own independent withdrawal schedule and its operational autonomy.[50] Nevertheless, 12,000 troops were withdrawn over U.S. objections.[51] Even in the middle of 1972, with the end of U.S. involvement less than a year away, Nixon asked Park to cooperate with U.S. forces to open the Kontum Pass.[52]

The communist side also paid close attention to the developing dispatch of Korean troops, and they were not idle. U.S. intelligence suggested the communists would respond to the dispatch of one Korean division by stepping up their propaganda against the United States—focusing on their imperialist use of Asians to fight other Asians—pressuring the Soviet Union for more aid to North Vietnam, and a minor North Korean dispatch of troops to Vietnam, that is, either technicians or anti-aircraft personnel.[53] North Korea did just that and also sent pilots who fought U.S. pilots in the war.[54] The communists also attempted to punish South Korea for getting involved in the war. Director of Defense Research and Engineering John Foster reported to Secretary McNamara that the goal of North Korean agitation against South Korea and United States in the late 1960s was to prevent the further dispatch of Korean troops to Vietnam. At the same time, U.S. forces in Korea commander Charles Bonesteel reported on North Korean efforts to "divert . . . efforts from Vietnam," and Secretary Rusk later reported the North Korean goal as either blocking additional deployment of Korean troops to Vietnam or scaring Park into withdrawing some or even all of them.[55]

A Strong, Independent South Korea Was an American Goal

Finally, the implication of the "mercenary" claim is that Korean soldiers were paid for their services at U.S. expense. American taxpayers funded the misadventure of the Vietnam War, and the aid to Korea was a part of this colossal waste of blood and treasure. And certainly, Vietnam was a costly war in virtually every possible way—to the United States and its allies, to the communist bloc, and above all, to the people of Vietnam. But judged according to America's overriding policy goal in the case of Korea, the dispatch of Korean troops to Vietnam and its accompanying benefits, both tangible and intangible, were a resounding success. From the creation of the ROK in 1948 down to the present, if the United States could not have a unified Korea, then it wanted a South Korea that was stable, wealthy, democratic, and a close U.S. ally in Asia. And this goal was achieved, in no small part due to Korea's involvement in the war. In 1954, Acting Secretary of State Walter Smith told the Korean embassy that a strong and stable Korea was "basic to US policy in [the] Far East."[56] On June 5, 1961, the Presidential Task Force on Korea reported to President Kennedy that U.S. goals in South Korea included democracy and "self-sustaining economic progress," but thus far, U.S. policy and aid had failed to achieve appreciable progress toward either.[57] At this time, the United States paid 95 percent of Korea's defense cost, yet those defenses were still considered inadequate to defend against communist attack, even in a limited war. Therefore, development of the Korean economy could not be effected by a major reduction of the military, enormously complicating modernization in Korea.[58] In January 1962, the National Security Council reported U.S. goals as democratic government, a military that could defend the country with minimal U.S. assistance, a strong economy, and a continued pro-U.S. attitude. It also reported that the ROK forces were enough to stop a North Korean invasion (though not one with Chinese help), but only because they were entirely provided and maintained by the United States. These forces could be reduced by approximately one-third if the rest were modernized, which would be acceptable to the Korean government only if it were both gradual and accompanied by economic aid.[59] This is essentially what happened, mediated by the dispatch of Korean combat troops to Vietnam. Ambassador Brown noted that a "strong and stable Korea is important anchor for our security interests in Far East,"[60] while Park Chung Hee told Johnson that although Korean forces were part of America's anti-communist forces that would fight alongside them, "at the same time they were dependent on U.S. assistance."[61] Years later, Secretary Laird reported to President Nixon that Park had told him, "The current ROK stability and development successes are direct functions of the aid and assistance offered by the US since World War II. The ROKs are trying to develop self-reliance, and thereby relieve the burden on the US."[62] According to a study made by the State Department (with input from the Department of Defense, the Central Intelligence Agency [CIA], and others), U.S. goals for Korea included "to increase ROK ability to defend itself; [and] (5) to promote South Korea's economic development and political stability."[63] Ambassador Brown reported to the State Department that even as of April 1965, the Korean military "is not now adequately MAP supported and pay and allowances are heavy drain on limited budgetary resources which will be increasingly needed for local costs of economic development program."[64] The dispatch changed all that. Four years after the dispatch, a 1969 draft study by the Interagency Korean Task Force reported that "ROK contributions to the SVN [South Vietnam] conflict . . . have served to shift Korea's relationship with the US from dependence toward partnership" and that "improvements in military capabilities have been confirmed by the strong performance of the two ROK divisions in Vietnam; the country's first expeditionary force provides evidence that ROK forces might well assume a larger defense role at home." The CIA's intelligence estimate of Korea at the end of 1970 reported that "its participation as an American ally in the Vietnamese war has given it a sense of pride and self-confidence which may prove as important as the more tangible military and economic benefits that participation has brought." For the military specifically, the report stated that Korea's "officer and noncommissioned officer corps has received leadership and combat experience in Vietnam. Moreover the younger officers now coming into leadership positions are better trained, and seem . . . more imbued with professionalism, than were their predecessors."[65] Five years after U.S. withdrawal from Vietnam, a U.S. House of Representatives subcommittee report concluded that the military aid given to Korea as a result of its involvement in Vietnam in turn "freed South Korea from the burden of heavy defense spending," which was indispensable for its rapid economic development in the 1960s and 1970s.[66] The wealthy, democratic South Korea of today owes its existence in part to the benefits of its involvement in the Vietnam War, and it remains a close U.S. ally into the third decade of the twenty-first century.

Notes

1. In this chapter, "volunteers" means those who volunteered to serve in Vietnam. All Korean men, then as now, owed military service. The military set a quota for volunteers for Vietnam service; the remainder were assigned. Thus, the combat forces sent to Vietnam were a mix of those who requested this duty and those who were stuck with it.

2. Remco Breuker argues this point. See Remco Breuker, "Korea's Forgotten War: Appropriating and Subverting the Vietnam War in Korean Popular Imaginings," *Korean Histories* 1, no. 1 (2009): 36–59. For just a few examples of this focus on Korean veterans' suffering, see Choi Ho Rim, "'Wolnamjeon chamjeon yongsa' eui jeonjeokji gwangwang gwa jeonjaeng gieok eui jaeguseong," *Bikyo munhwa yeon'gu* 16, no. 2 (2010): 71–114; Choi Jung Gie, "Han'gukgun Beteunamjeon chamjeon, eotteoge gieok doego itneun ga? Gongsikjeogin gieok gwa daehang gieok eui chai reul jungsimeuro," *Minjujueui gwa ingweon* 9, no. 1 (2004): 65–98; Kim Juhyeon. "Wolnamjeon hubangi (1970–1975) gwihwan seosa e damgin 'Han'gungmin doegi' eui (bul)," *Eomullonjib* 70 (2017): 295–329; Park Jin-Im, "Han'guk soseol e natanan Beteunam jeonjaeng eui teukseong gwa chamjeon Han'gukgun eui jeongcheseong," *Han'guk hyeondae munhak yeon'gu* 14 (2003): 111–139.

3. Jin-kyung Lee, "Surrogate Military, Subimperialism, and Masculinity: South Korea in the Vietnam War, 1965–73," *Positions* 17, no. 3 (2009): 655–682.

4. Robert M. Blackburn, *Mercenaries and Lyndon Johnson's "More Flags": The Hiring of Korean, Filipino and Thai Soldiers in the Vietnam War* (Jefferson, NC: McFarland, 1994), 135.

5. Blackburn, *More Flags*, 25.

6. Gerald Waite, "Outsourcing a War: What You Get for Your Mercenary Dollar," *International Journal on World Peace* 31, no. 4 (2014): 96.

7. Nicholas Evan Sarantakes, "In the Service of Pharaoh? The United States and the Deployment of Korean Troops in Vietnam, 1965–1968," *Pacific Historical Review* 68, no. 3 (1999): 439.

8. Blackburn, *More Flags*, 146, 148, 132.

9. International Committee of the Red Cross, *Protocol Additional to the Geneva Conventions of 12 August 1949, and Relating to the Protection of Victims of International Armed Conflicts (Protocol I), 8 June 1977*, Article 47, https://ihl-databases.icrc.org/applic/ihl/ihl.nsf/4e473c7bc8854f2ec12563f60039c738/9edc5096d2c036e9c12563cd0051dc30.

10. Eun Seo Jo, "Fighting for Peanuts: Reimagining South Korean Soldiers' Participation in the Wŏllam Boom," *Journal of American–East Asian Relations* 21, no. 1 (2014): 69–71, 79–80.

11. Waite, "Outsourcing a War," 93.

12. Min Yong Lee, "The Vietnam War: South Korea's Search for National Security," in *The Park Chung Hee Era: The Transformation of South Korea*, ed. Byung-Kook Kim and Ezra F. Vogel (Cambridge, MA: Harvard University Press, 2011), 415.

13. Choi Dong-Ju, "Han'guk eui Beteunam jeonjaeng donggi e gwanhan jaegochal," *Han'guk jeongchihak hoebu* 30, no. 2 (1996): 269.

14. *Foreign Relations of the United States, 1961–1963*, Volume XXII, Northeast Asia, 1961–1963, ed. Edward C. Keefer, David W. Mabon, Harriet Dashiell Schwar, and Glenn W. LaFantasie (Washington, DC: Government Printing Office, 1996), Documents 247 and 256. Also note 2 in the former document.

15. Hong Seuk-Ryule, "1960nyeondae Han-Mi gwan'gye wa Bak Jeong-heui gunsa jeonggweon," *Yeoksa wa hyeonsil* 56 (2005): 289.

16. *Foreign Relations of the United States, 1964–1968*, Volume XXIX, Part 1, Korea, 1964–1968, ed. Karen L. Gatz and David S. Patterson (Washington, DC: Government Printing Office, 2000), Document 28.

17. United States Congress, *Investigation of Korean-American Relations: Report of the Subcommittee on International Organizations of the Committee on International Relations, U.S. House of Representatives* (Washington, DC: Government Printing Office, 1978), 22.

18. Hong, "Han-Mi gwan'gye wa Bak Jeong-heui gunsa jeonggweon," 275, 295.

19. *Foreign Relations of the United States, 1964–1968*, Volume XXIX, Part 1, Korea, 1964–1968, Document 7.

20. Hong, "Han-Mi gwan'gye wa Bak Jeong-heui gunsa jeonggweon," 286.

21. Hong, "Han-Mi gwan'gye wa Bak Jeong-heui gunsa jeonggweon," 293.

22. United States Congress, *Investigation of Korean-American Relations*, 31.

23. Glenn Baek, "Park Chung-hee's Vietnam Odyssey: A Study in Management of the U.S.-ROK Alliance," *Korean Journal of Defense Analysis* 25, no. 2 (2013): 153; Kwanpyo Bae, "The Vietnam War, Korea's Opportunity for More Reliable Security Assurances," *Korean Journal of Defense Analysis* 27, no. 3 (2015): 374.

24. *Foreign Relations of the United States, 1964–1968*, Volume XXIX, Part 1, Korea, 1964–1968, Document 48.

25. Baek, "Park Chung Hee's Vietnam Odyssey," 149; Tae Yang Kwak, "Han'guk eui Beteunam jeonjaeng chamjeon jaepyeongga," *Yeoksa bipyeong* (2014): 204.

26. Kwak, "Han'guk eui Beteunam jeonjaeng chamjeon jaepyeongga," 202; Hong, "Han-Mi gwan'gye wa Bak Jeong-heui gunsa jeonggweon," 288.

27. Tae Yang Kwak, "The Nixon Doctrine and the Yusin Reforms: American Foreign Policy, the Vietnam War, and the Rise of Authoritarianism in Korea, 1968–1973," *Journal of American–East Asian Relations* 12, no. 1/2 (2003): 36.

28. Richard Stubbs, *Rethinking Asia's Economic Miracle: The Political Economy of War, Prosperity and Crisis* (Basingstoke, UK: Palgrave Macmillan, 2005), 134.

29. United States Congress, *Investigation of Korean-American Relations*, 5–6, 35.

30. Sun-won Park, "Belief Systems and Strained Alliance: The Impact of American Pressure on South Korean Politics and the Demise of the Park Regime in 1979," *Korea Observer* 34, no. 1 (2003): 94, 100–102.

31. Hong, "Han-Mi gwan'gye wa Bak Jeong-heui gunsa jeonggweon," 285.

32. *Foreign Relations of the United States, 1964–1968*, Volume XXIX, Part 1, Korea, 1964–1968, Document 58.

33. Baek, "Park Chung-hee's Vietnam Odyssey," 156–158; Sarantakes, "In the Service of Pharaoh?" 445–446.

34. Blackburn, *More Flags*, 25.

35. Blackburn, *More Flags*, 124–130.

36. Choi, "Han'guk eui Beteunam jeonjaeng donggi e gwanhan jaegochal," 277.

37. *Foreign Relations of the United States, 1964–1968*, Volume XXIX, Part 1, Korea, 1964–1968, Document 59.

38. Choi, "Han'guk eui Beteunam jeonjaeng donggi e gwanhan jaegochal," 273.

39. *Foreign Relations of the United States*, 1964–1968, Volume XXIX, Part 1, Korea, 1964–1968, Document 37.

40. *Foreign Relations of the United States*, 1964–1968, Volume XXIX, Part 1, Korea, 1964–1968, Document 37, 68n3.

41. *Foreign Relations of the United States*, 1964–1968, Volume XXIX, Part 1, Korea, 1964–1968, Document 56.

42. *Foreign Relations of the United States*, 1969–1976, Volume XIX, Part 1, Korea, 1969–1972, ed. Daniel J. Lawler, Erin R. Mahan, and Edward C. Keefer (Washington, DC: Government Printing Office, 2009), Documents 46 and 80.

43. *Foreign Relations of the United States*, 1961–1963, Volume XXII, Northeast Asia, 1961–1963, Document 238.

44. *Foreign Relations of the United States*, 1964–1968, Volume XXIX, Part 1, Korea, 1964–1968, Document 192.

45. *Foreign Relations of the United States*, 1964–1968, Volume XXIX, Part 1, Korea, 1964–1968, Document 2.

46. *Foreign Relations of the United States*, 1964–1968, Volume XXIX, Part 1, Korea, 1964–1968, Document 19.

47. *Foreign Relations of the United States*, 1964–1968, Volume XXIX, Part 1, Korea, 1964–1968, Document 186.

48. *Foreign Relations of the United States*, 1964–1968, Volume XXIX, Part 1, Korea, 1964–1968, Document 187.

49. *Foreign Relations of the United States*, 1969–1976, Volume XIX, Part 1, Korea, 1969–1976, Document 97.

50. *Foreign Relations of the United States*, 1969–1976, Volume XIX, Part 1, Korea, 1969–1976, Documents 101, 106, 114, and 145.

51. United States Congress, *Investigation of Korean-American Relations*, 35.

52. *Foreign Relations of the United States*, 1969–1976, Volume XIX, Part 1, Korea, 1969–1972, Documents 51 and 144.

53. *Foreign Relations of the United States*, 1964–1968, Volume XXIX, Part 1, Korea, 1964–1968, Document 35.

54. Kwak, "The Nixon Doctrine and the Yusin Reforms," 37.

55. *Foreign Relations of the United States*, 1964–1968, Volume XXIX, Part 1, Korea, 1964–1968, Documents 138, 146, and 177.

56. *Foreign Relations of the United States*, 1952–1954, Volume XV, Part 2, Korea, 1952–1954, ed. Edward C. Keefer and John P. Glennon (Washington, DC: Government Printing Office, 1984), 1887.

57. Papers of John F. Kennedy. Presidential Papers. National Security Files. Countries. Korea. General, June 5, 1961, Task Force Report. JFKNSF-127-011. John F. Kennedy Presidential Library and Museum, 4, 12.

58. Papers of John F. Kennedy. Presidential Papers. National Security Files. Countries. Korea. General, June 5, 1961, Task Force Report. JFKNSF-127-011. John F. Kennedy Presidential Library and Museum, Appendix E, 11–13.

59. Papers of John F. Kennedy. Presidential Papers. National Security Council Meetings, 1962: No. 496. January 18, 1962 [1 of 5 folders]. John F. Kennedy Presidential Library and Museum, 1, 38–40.

60. *Foreign Relations of the United States, 1964–1968*, Volume XXIX, Part 1, Korea, 1964–1968, Document 39.

61. *Foreign Relations of the United States, 1964–1968*, Volume XXIX, Part 1, Korea, 1964–1968, Document 51.

62. *Foreign Relations of the United States*, 1969–1976, Volume XIX, Part 1, Korea, 1969–1972, Document 101.

63. *Foreign Relations of the United States*, 1969–1976, Volume XIX, Part 1, Korea, 1969–1972, Document 27.

64. *Foreign Relations of the United States, 1964–1968*, Volume XXIX, Part 1, Korea, 1964–1968, Document 39.

65. *Foreign Relations of the United States*, 1969–1976, Volume XIX, Part 1, Korea, 1969–1972, Document 80.

66. United States Congress, *Investigation of Korean-American Relations*, 7; Kwak, "Han'guk eui Beteunam jeonjaeng chamjeon jaepyeongga," 224.

13 Strengthening the Regime

Singapore, the United States, and the War in Indochina

S. R. JOEY LONG

Southeast Asian regimes faced external and internal challenges as they engaged in state building, economic development, and domestic power consolidation during the 1960s and 1970s.[1] As Cold War tensions intensified and war raged in Vietnam, Southeast Asia's noncommunist regimes had to address the likelihood that the Indochinese dominoes might fall, communist power in Southeast Asia might grow, and domestic left-wing groups might be emboldened to challenge their rule.[2] Scholars argue that these anxieties fed into other complex reasons for the high-handed moves noncommunist Southeast Asian governments undertook to crush their opponents and consolidate political power.[3] Still others note that a number of Southeast Asian regimes intervened extensively in their economies to develop their societies and buttress their hold on power.[4] External powers such as the United States further supported the rule of several Southeast Asian regimes, assisting characters such as Ferdinand Marcos to maintain their political positions.[5]

This chapter examines the attempt by Singapore's postcolonial regime to strengthen its rule in the city-state. The People's Action Party (PAP) government pursued that endeavor against the context of the Cold War, rapid sociopolitical change across Southeast Asia, and American moves to cultivate Asian support for its war in Indochina. Subscribing to the domino theory (the fear that if Vietnam fell to communism, the rest of noncommunist Southeast Asia would likewise be overrun by communists), Singaporean policymakers expressed public and private support for the U.S. involvement in Vietnam. The endorsement won them not only American goodwill. It also won them economic and security benefits. Scrutinizing the interactions between Singapore and the United States could yield important insights into how states on the periphery of the Vietnam War exploited the Cold War and regional tensions to advance their interests.

Singapore's international history has drawn some scholarly attention in recent years. Ang Cheng Guan contends that Singaporean officials feared

Hanoi's ambitions and welcomed the U.S. intervention in Vietnam. Ang does not, however, investigate the war's impact on domestic developments in Singapore. He cursorily refers to a study undertaken by economist Lim Chong Yah and suggests that the conflict had negligible effect on Singapore's political economy.[6] Lim's analysis, while judicious, was informed essentially by public sources. It also did not assess the nature and outcomes of the broader Singapore-U.S. interactions.[7] Daniel Chua does that, characterizing the Singapore-U.S. relationship as one marked by intimacy and distance. The Lee government championed nonalignment, but it also supported the American efforts in Vietnam, fearing that communist gains in Indochina would undermine Singapore's security in the long run.[8] In contrast, Wen-Qing Ngoei argues that Singapore was more pro-American than nonaligned during the Cold War. Singapore joined other noncommunist Southeast Asian states in supporting the U.S. containment of China and the Vietnamese revolution. In doing so, Singapore helped sustain U.S. influence and power in Southeast Asia.[9] Although Chua's and Ngoei's studies shed new light on Singapore's foreign relations history, they do not explore extensively the impact of U.S. economic and foreign policies on the Lee government's narrower domestic and regional interests.

This chapter details that aspect of the Singaporean-U.S. relationship. It argues that the Singaporean government exploited the Cold War to advance its regime interests. Understanding that Washington sought its support for the war in Indochina, Singapore cultivated and engaged the United States to obtain weapons and investment. The inflow of American military equipment and capital enhanced the Singaporean regime's capacity to defend its interests against adversarial neighbors, further its development strategies, distribute rewards to supporters, neutralize or win over detractors, and consolidate its control of the city-state. At the same time, a close and cordial Singapore-U.S. relationship obtained. Thus, even as Washington retreated from Vietnam, its defeat did not lead to the significant diminution of U.S. power in Southeast Asia. Rather, the Vietnam War years actually saw the continued advancement of American influence in other parts of the subregion such as Singapore.

Context of the Singapore-U.S. Relationship

The relationship between independent Singapore and the United States did not get off to a good start. Shortly after Singapore separated from Malaysia on August 9, 1965, Singapore's prime minister Lee Kuan Yew publicly berated

Washington. At a news conference on August 31, 1965, Lee attacked the U.S. government while responding to a journalist's question about the future of the British bases on the island. He complained that the U.S. Central Intelligence Agency had attempted to subvert his government in 1960. He also criticized the high-handed way American officials had treated his wife when she attempted to obtain medical assistance in the United States. Capping off his rant, Lee declared that if the British vacated the bases in Singapore, he would permit Moscow rather than Washington to use the installations.[10]

Lee's tirade occurred against the backdrop of Singapore's tumultuous separation from Malaysia and Indonesia's confrontation policy toward its neighbors. A constituent state of Malaysia between September 1963 and August 1965, Singapore left the federation after PAP officials in Singapore and Alliance Party leaders in Kuala Lumpur failed to resolve their economic and sociopolitical differences. After the separation of the two states, Singaporean policymakers harbored fears that Kuala Lumpur might isolate Singapore economically or exploit the city-state's dependence on Malaysia for a large part of its water needs to act against Singapore's interests.[11]

Besides Malaysia, Singaporean officials also worried about Jakarta's intentions. In 1963, Indonesia's Sukarno condemned Malaysia's formation and launched a diplomatic and military offensive against the new state. The September-October 1965 coup d'état in Indonesia, which politically marginalized Sukarno, should have eased the concerns of Singapore's leaders. However, religious and sociopolitical groups, backed by the Indonesian army, murdered hundreds of thousands of Chinese Indonesians for allegedly supporting the communist cause, sending a chill through the mainly ethnic Chinese Singaporean leadership. It seemed that hostile countries in the south and north surrounded and threatened the security of the ethnic Chinese majority city-state.[12]

American analysts noted Singapore's concerns. In 1965, they assessed that the Malaysia-Singapore relationship "will be clouded by strong antagonism between their leaders and by mutual suspicions between Malays and ethnic Chinese." PAP leaders also ostensibly feared that with confrontation's impending end, more uncertainties might follow. Jakarta and Kuala Lumpur might gang up against Singapore. Deterring them were the Australian, British, and New Zealander troops stationed in the city-state. However, London was finding the financial burden of maintaining its forces in Southeast Asia to be increasingly less bearable. It might withdraw its forces, leaving a power vacuum that Singapore's regional adversaries could exploit.

Even worse from the American viewpoint was the prospect of the communist powers moving into that vacuum. Lee's highly charged August 1965 news conference did not allay American anxieties.[13]

The question for U.S. officials in 1965 and early 1966 was whether Lee Kuan Yew was prepared to improve Singapore's ties with Washington. The Johnson administration could do with more Asian support for its military intervention in Indochina. However, the early signs were ambivalent. In a conversation with U.S. ambassador James Bell in August 1965, Lee did not directly endorse the American efforts in Vietnam.[14] In another exchange with U.S. senator Edward Kennedy who visited Singapore after touring South Vietnam, Lee stated he would not tolerate any American attempts to "pressure him or 'bully' him or buy him off" to support U.S. activities in Asia.[15]

Despite Lee's vitriol, U.S. officials observed that the Singaporean prime minister seemed to privately accept that American forces could function to protect the security of regional noncommunist regimes like his. Lee, in fact, stated that his government did not have a strong military to defend it against foreign threats and could do with some external assistance.[16] Sharing their concerns with American diplomats, Lee and other PAP leaders also expected the United States to help them develop Singapore economically. They wanted Washington and other Western countries to open their markets for Singapore's manufactures. By gaining access to the markets of the developed world, industrializing Singapore's economy, creating jobs (10 percent of the working population were unemployed), and generating wealth, PAP leaders could take all the credit for advancing the economic growth of the city-state and raising the living standards of Singaporean citizens. The PAP would then be able to triumph at the polls. Minister for Defense Goh Keng Swee thus "called on the Western countries [principally the United States, United Kingdom, Australia, and New Zealand] to help Singapore by opening their markets."[17]

Given the Singaporean desires for security assurances and economic development, the Singapore-U.S. relationship gradually thawed. PAP politicians understood that to consolidate the regime's authority, the city-state had to be made economically and political viable. Returning to Malaysia on Kuala Lumpur's terms was not an option. Being undercut by the opposition at the polls was unacceptable. Lee and his people were accordingly prepared to talk to the Americans about some form of cooperation. In January 1966, so were American officials. Assistant Secretary of State for East Asian and Pacific Affairs William Bundy took the lead in engaging Lee.

He was drawn to the prime minister after reading a number of Lee's speeches on Vietnam.[18] Singapore also recently permitted the first group of 100 American soldiers serving in Vietnam to spend their recreation leave in the city-state.[19] In March 1966, Bundy called on Lee in Singapore. They discussed Singapore-U.S. trade relations. The conversation also touched on Vietnam, with Lee advising the Americans to strengthen South Vietnamese resilience against communist attacks. Following the visit, Bundy concluded that Lee had become "more mellow." The change in Lee's attitude "may have opened the way to a more serious and deep relationship than we have ever had."[20]

Bundy was right. In April 1966, the U.S. consulate general in Singapore was raised in status to an embassy.[21] Bundy's assurance to Lee that Washington would consider expanding Singapore-U.S. trade relations paved the way for the relationship to thaw further. In June 1966, Lee publicly lauded the American efforts in Indochina, stating that Washington was buying time for noncommunist states like Singapore to develop.[22] A month later, his government crushed an opposition-led "Aid Vietnam against U.S. Aggression" campaign in Singapore, arresting demonstrators for disrupting public order.[23] By September 1966, U.S. officials were sure that the PAP government "supports our objectives" in Vietnam. They recognized, nonetheless, that the PAP government had to operate "within limitations imposed by its internal political environment and desire to avoid an overt pro-U.S. stance."[24] However, they also wanted to engage the PAP government more extensively. They could do with more Asian leaders supporting the American cause in Asia.

By 1967, the U.S. intervention in Vietnam was not making much headway. Members of the U.S. Congress were openly critical of the war. Large-scale anti-war demonstrations broke out in New York and San Francisco in April. Approval ratings for the Johnson presidency dropped to an all-time low. The war also undermined the president's capacity to advance his Great Society programs. Partly to combat the negative opinion and partly to engage an articulate Southeast Asian leader to champion the administration's cause in Southeast Asia, Secretary of State Dean Rusk recommended in May that Johnson invite Lee to Washington for an official visit. Persuaded that Lee could help shape domestic American opinion of the war, Johnson approved the visit.[25]

Lee welcomed the invitation. His government faced significant challenges. In July 1967, Britain announced it would withdraw its forces from Southeast Asia by the mid-1970s. U.S. officials discerned that Lee planned to seek and obtain U.S. assurances that Washington would remain engaged in Asia and act as a security umbrella for small states like Singapore. Lee also wanted Singapore-U.S. trade relations to expand: "for economic survival, an independent Singapore must expand its exports to the United States and attract American capital to develop new export industries."[26] Whether Washington would address Lee's concerns was one matter. However, the prime minister correctly noted that he would be of use to the Johnson administration. "America was getting such bad press," Lee observed, "that they were relieved when someone not a client state stood up to voice support for their unpopular policy."[27] Lee accepted Johnson's invitation and eventually visited the White House in October 1967.

The meeting between Lee and Johnson marked a high point in Singapore-U.S. relations. They discussed economic and security issues, with Johnson assuring Lee that U.S. forces would hold the line against communist expansion in Southeast Asia. Lee also engaged key U.S. officials, academics, business leaders, journalists, think tank analysts, and university students. A senior U.S. official observed that Lee consistently said "helpful things about Viet-Nam and the President," and "that the visit was a considerable success."[28] On his return to Singapore, even Lee's cabinet colleagues "were disturbed that I sounded too pro-American, defending Johnson's intervention in Vietnam."[29] Still, the two sides had come to an understanding. Singaporean leaders viewed Washington as a key economic and security actor that could further the regime's economic interests and preserve regional stability. The Americans, conversely, regarded Singapore as a friendly Asian state that could shore up support in the United States and Southeast Asia for U.S. policy toward Vietnam. As relations turned, American and Singaporean officials sought to build on the new understanding to enhance Singapore-U.S. economic and security cooperation.

Security Cooperation

Singaporean leaders welcomed closer defense relations with the United States, but they did not want a formal alliance relationship. They understood that their political opponents would attack the PAP for being an American stooge. Lee's cabinet colleagues were, in fact, concerned about his pro-American speeches. They feared that Lee might "alienate our grassroots Chinese speaking base." This base, which was increasingly stirred up politically by China's Cultural Revolution, might abandon the PAP if its leaders expressed support for Washington in the Cold War. Following his 1967 visit to Washington, therefore, Lee had to publicly criticize the Johnson government to calm his party's supporters. Besides its domestic supporters, the Lee administration likewise did not wish to alienate the neighboring states. Indonesia could harass and undermine the PAP regime if Singapore formally aligned itself with Washington. Nonalignment was thus the PAP government's declared foreign policy position.[30]

Although Singaporean leaders championed nonalignment, they understood that the city-state needed a military force and the help of friendly powers to further its security. Mired in their domestic problems, Afro-Asian states were unlikely to assist or defend Singapore against an external threat. Britain had also declared in 1967 and 1968 its intentions to withdraw its forces from Southeast Asia. The Lee government worried that neighboring states might be emboldened to directly undercut its interests. Malaysia could use Singapore's dependence on Johor for freshwater (a supply the separation agreement guaranteed) to pressure the city-state to return to the federation on Kuala Lumpur's terms. To give Malaysian politicians pause and enforce its rights, Singapore needed its own armed forces. Between 1965 and 1967, therefore, Singapore's parliamentarians passed legislation to create a professional military force and a mass citizen army manned by conscripts. Singaporean officials also looked to foreign powers for military hardware and training assistance.[31]

The Lee government approached the Americans for equipment because Britain was reluctant to develop Singapore's military. The British did not want Malaysian politicians to think they were aiding one ex-colonial state against the other. Singaporean planners, conversely, found the United States willing to sell weapons to the city-state. Although Israel, which had answered Singapore's call for training assistance after India and Egypt rejected the city-state's overtures, was another major supplier of weapons, the American military industry signed significant arms deals with the PAP government. For instance, Singapore bought refurbished AMX-13 light tanks from Israel, but it purchased much of its other hardware from the United States.[32]

Reviewing a range of basic assault weapons, the Lee administration decided to buy the American-manufactured AR-15 Armalites (also known as the M16) for its military. It assessed that smaller-built Asians would find the smaller AR-15 to be less cumbersome to carry than the FN FAL, which was then in use in Singapore. The smaller but no less powerful rifle could enhance Singaporean soldiers' mobility.[33] In early 1966, the Lee government informed the U.S. embassy in Singapore it intended to procure 23,000 American-made AR-15 rifles. Unsure of Lee's political proclivities, State Department and Pentagon officials were initially reluctant to facilitate the deal. Following the Bundy-Lee meeting and Lee's engagement of U.S. officials, however, the Americans acted. In June 1966, the State and Defense Departments finally sanctioned the sale.[34]

Despite the State and Defense Departments' support, Singapore initially faced problems procuring the rifles. Seoul balked at the deal, claiming it would deny South Korean soldiers serving in Vietnam from being adequately armed.[35] The U.S. Congress charged that the Johnson administration "was selling rifles needed by our forces and our allies in Viet-Nam to a 'neutralist' country, which might in turn sell them to North Viet-Nam." Defending the deal, the Pentagon assured that the sale would not undermine allied operations in Vietnam. Singapore had also pledged it would not re-export the rifles to any country without the U.S. government's consent.[36] Despite the assurances, it was only after October 1967 that Colt Industries, which manufactured the rifles, could deliver the weapons to Singapore. During his 1967 visit to the United States, Lee convinced U.S. congressmen he was an Asian leader they could trust and support. Persuaded that Lee's public statements also helped the American cause in Vietnam, U.S. officials pushed for the sale to proceed.[37] By July 1968, the AR-15 completely replaced the FN FAL as the basic assault weapon of the Singaporean volunteer and conscript soldier.[38]

After obtaining the rifles, though, the Singaporean government decided in late 1968 to amend the sales agreement for "nationalistic and security reasons." It informed Washington that Singapore planned to build a facility to manufacture the assault rifles. It wanted American assistance. It would turn elsewhere for know-how if the United States refused to help Singapore. U.S. officials assessed the request and determined that Washington should not alienate one of its key backers in Asia.[39] Such considerations also bore heavily on the mind of the American ambassador to Singapore, Francis Galbraith. He stated that Washington should sanction the request.[40] With the Nixon administration's support after 1969, Singapore finally obtained a license to manufacture the AR-15s locally. Initially in collaboration with Colt Industries and then on its own, the Singaporean government–linked company Chartered Industries would churn out 30,000 of the semiautomatic rifles annually from its factory in Singapore.[41]

Besides the assault rifles, the Lee government was able to procure other weapons from the United States. These included V-200 amphibious armored cars, M-113 armored personnel carriers, the supersonic Northrop

F-5 aircraft, and the subsonic Douglas A-4 Skyhawk.[42] Singapore also attempted to acquire flame-throwers, but Washington rejected its request "because of the tremendous adverse publicity and propaganda concerning flame-throwers and napalm weapons that the U.S. Government would not now release these to any other government."[43] Still, the Singaporean government continued to look to U.S. suppliers for other military hardware. Rather than British or French equipment, it was convinced of the reliability of U.S. weapons because they had ultimately been "tested in Viet-Nam."[44]

It is instructive to note what Lee recounts in his memoirs as the intent and significance of Singapore's military acquisitions during the 1960s and early 1970s. Suharto's ascension to power in Indonesia had stabilized Indonesia-Singapore relations. Lee's fear was that intemperate leaders in Malaysia might dislodge the moderate leadership from power and "decide to send the [Malaysian] army marching down to take Singapore back into the Federation forcibly." If Malaysia's perception of Singapore's military in 1966 was that "it was all a joke," its view drastically changed by 1969. Apart from the refurbished AMX-13 tanks and the U.S.-made V-200 armored cars which the government paraded in public, the sight of Singaporean soldiers equipped with the latest assault rifles seem to have deterred what Lee called the Malay Ultras in Malaysia from engaging in any adventurist actions against Singapore. Lee believed the ultras provoked the May 1969 racial riots in Malaysia and planned to create trouble in Singapore. However, the island's armed forces gave them pause.[45]

American observers agreed.[46] The weapons advanced Singapore's security. They also helped preserve the PAP's hold on power. Some groups in Malaysia, after all, viewed Lee and his colleagues as separatists who should be removed from government. They also wanted Singapore returned to the federation. But American weapons as well as those acquired from Israel ensured Malaysia's so-called ultras could not further their aspirations. By cultivating relations with the Americans, Lee and his colleagues were able to obtain benefits from America that helped protect their regime against potential external adversaries.

Economic Interactions

If U.S. weapons sharpened Singapore's deterrent edge against external threats and strengthened the PAP regime, the extensive American involvement in the city-state's economy between 1965 and 1975 helped enhance the PAP's capacity to preserve its rule against domestic political rivals. In 1965,

U.S. analysts noted that the PAP government needed to generate robust economic growth in Singapore to shore up grassroots support for the party. But Singapore's entrepôt trade, which constituted some 20–30 percent of gross national product, confronted challenges. Malaysia and Indonesia, which previously exported commodities to Singapore to re-export to overseas markets, were directly exporting their products to foreign markets. A declining Britain could not be expected to sustain its defense spending in Singapore—expenditures that comprised 20–25 percent of the city-state's gross national product. Singapore's industrial production, which formed 14 percent of the gross national product, had to expand. Without a large domestic market, however, Singapore had to gain access and sell its manufactures to foreign markets. The move would help its industries to grow and create jobs for the restive population. The PAP regime could take credit for raising the country's living standards and undercut its political opponents' appeal. Conversely, the opposition parties "would profit if Lee finds it impossible to meet the basic economic and political needs of the Singapore people."[47]

Minister for Defense Goh Keng Swee identified the United States as a key export market. In November 1965, Goh stated that Singapore's industries would benefit from having greater access to U.S. consumers. He also reasoned that it would be in America's "political and strategic interests" to support Singapore's economic development. A stable and viable Singapore could help enhance capitalism's appeal and undercut communism's allure in Asia.[48]

Apart from obtaining greater access to the American market, the PAP government also worked to keep U.S. investors happy in Singapore and attract U.S. investment to the city-state. In 1965, Minister for Finance Lim Kim San announced that Singapore would reward foreign investors with tax deductions if they parked their capital in the city-state. Foreign companies could also freely repatriate their profits and capital. In 1966, the Singaporean government lightened the tax burden on foreign companies by lowering the taxes on export profits, heartening American businessmen who cheered the move.[49] It cut bureaucratic red tape to make business transactions more efficient. It spent heavily to develop the city-state's infrastructure and improve its communication network. It created an industrial park on the western part of the island to accommodate factories and industry. It established technical and vocational schools to train skilled workers who could support the foreign companies' businesses.[50] On March 25, 1966, Singapore and Washington also signed an investment guarantee agreement that protected U.S. investments in Singapore.[51] Some five months later, they signed another agreement on cotton textiles. Singapore was permitted to export 35 million square yards of cotton textiles annually to the United States, making the city-state's cotton industry more attractive to investors.[52]

Besides employing various incentives to appeal to American investors, Singaporean officials including Lee Kuan Yew also courted them directly. In September 1966, the PAP government established a trade promotion agency in New York City, with the stated "purpose of attracting United States manufacturers to invest in manufacturing enterprises in Singapore."[53] Lee and his officers wanted to dispel the notion that Singapore did not welcome American investors. Lee had ironically created that impression when he lashed out at Washington in 1965 for attempting to subvert his government. As Singapore-U.S. relations thawed, Lee sought to change minds. Besides exposing his fears of communist expansion in Southeast Asia, his statements supporting Lyndon Johnson's war in Vietnam also conveyed the idea to U.S. businesspeople that Lee and his government were not anti-American. Johnson's public endorsement of Lee in October 1967 furthered the Singaporean cause. Lee built on Johnson's support and his reputation as a pro-business Singaporean politician to cultivate American investors during his trip to the United States. He addressed business executives in Chicago, informing them his government would protect their capital as they operated from Singapore to expand into the regional markets.[54]

If at first there was a trickle of American investors coming to Singapore, there would be a deluge from 1966 and 1967. Many were drawn to the city-state's pro-business policies. Others such as the oil companies Caltex, Esso, and Mobil saw opportunities to expand their refinery and redistribution businesses in Asia. The U.S. military's decision to procure petroleum products from the region for the war in Vietnam incentivized them to establish or enhance their existing facilities in Singapore. From the city-state, they competed to win U.S. government procurement orders.[55] Drawn by the expanding aircraft repair and refurbishment businesses in the region, other companies such as Grumman and Lockheed also moved to lease hangar and building space in Singapore. They likewise competed for U.S. defense contracts to service aircraft damaged in the Vietnam War.[56]

By 1970, the American investment in Singapore amounted to some US$200 million, with the bulk of that money parked in the oil refining, oil support, banking, and electronics industries.[57] By 1972, U.S. investments swelled to US$450 million.[58] The number of American firms also rose from 60 in 1967 to 260 in 1972, with their output growing in value from US$33 million in 1968 to an estimated US$100 million in 1970. Local workers that American businesses employed increased from 1,500 in 1968 to 10,000 in 1972. The hiring helped to reduce the number of unemployed in Singapore—an accomplishment that the PAP regime justifiably took credit.[59]

Besides procuring products and services from American companies in Singapore, the U.S. government also did business with local industries. From 1967 through 1970, it purchased US$7.1 million worth of fuel oil, agricultural and forestry products, prefabricated and portable buildings, automobile repair services, motor scooters, and bicycles from Singaporean companies to support the military efforts in Vietnam.[60] It further spent US$1 million annually in Singapore to repair ships damaged in the conflict. Benefiting from the American contracts was Sembawang Shipyard—a Singaporean government–linked company. Chaired by PAP politician Hon Sui Sen, the company developed its business rapidly, went on a hiring spree, and directly helped to lower Singapore's unemployment numbers.[61] In all, the military procurements, which amounted to 15 percent of Singapore's national income, helped the city-state to develop economically.[62]

Finally, Singapore's service industry also benefited from American spending in the region. Official figures show that the number of American visitors to Singapore rose from 21,554 in 1964 to 90,883 in 1969. American servicemen constituted about 7–8 percent of that number and spent S$17.3 million (11 percent of the total tourist expenditure) annually in the city-state.[63] For the Americans, Singapore was "a good leave town." For the Lee regime, they were consumers who contributed to Singapore's economy. To ensure that the American soldiers did not become a political liability, the PAP government stopped the press from reporting on their numbers or visits. The U.S. embassy also helped, counseling American troops to dress in civilian rather than military attire when walking the streets of Singapore. Opposition politicians were ultimately unable to exploit the rest and recreation arrangement to attack the PAP for supporting an unpopular war in Vietnam.[64]

American investments and expenditures, in sum, helped Singapore's economy to grow strongly between 1965 and 1975. Its per capita income increased from US$450 in 1965 to US$2,500 in 1975. In 1972, PAP politicians also declared that Singapore no longer had unemployment problems. The economic achievements vindicated the PAP's policies and discredited its political opponents' criticisms. The PAP further won over detractors who either disavowed their associations with opposition groups or turned to actively support the Lee regime.[65] So impressive were the government's economic accomplishments that PAP leaders were reelected in September 1972 to another five-year term by a landslide. U.S. observers assessed that "the continued infusion of sizable amounts of American and other foreign capital [into Singapore] combined with the hard work of its citizenry" ensured that the Lee regime's hold on power was unchallengeable.[66]

The Lee government's support for Washington's Asia policy, then, had enabled it to win the favor of U.S. officials, attract American capital, grow the Singaporean economy, and weather the domestic challenges to its rule. The PAP administration did its part by developing the infrastructure, adopting pro-business policies, and reforming the educational system to create the conditions that would appeal to American and other investors. Still, Lee and his colleagues played their cards in the Cold War game well. They reaped the rewards and entrenched themselves as the dominant political group in Singapore.

Conclusion

When Lee Kuan Yew declared that the U.S. intervention in Vietnam bought time for Southeast Asians "to strengthen themselves so that they can stand on their own feet," he was not merely referring to sovereign states in the subregion being given time by the United States to strengthen themselves against an advancing communist tide. Lee was also referring to the help rendered by Washington in enhancing the capacity of regimes like his to defend themselves against other potential external aggressors, and consolidate their domestic authority and legitimacy.[67]

The Lee administration confronted external as well as domestic challengers to its rule. It had to hedge against political uncertainties in Jakarta and Kuala Lumpur, fearful that hostile Indonesian and Malaysian politicians might take power and impose their will on Singapore. Lee faced the probable end of his political career if Singapore was compelled to merge again with Malaysia on Kuala Lumpur's terms. He also believed that political life in Singapore was a zero-sum game. The PAP's opponents were likely to unleash the full force of the government on Lee's political organization if they won a general election. Lee's immediate priorities were, therefore, to develop a credible military deterrent, strengthen his regime, and consolidate the rule of the PAP in Singapore. To those ends, the Lee government engaged the United States to build up Singapore's armed forces and advance its economic development.

Desirous of Asian leaders who would back the American cause in Vietnam, U.S. officials were drawn to Lee and his articulate opinions about the Vietnam War. Lee could be exploited to rally U.S. domestic support for the presidency. Yet, American policymakers also understood that Singaporean leaders sought U.S. assistance in addressing the economic and military needs of the Southeast Asian state. Singaporean appeals to American investors to sink their capital into Singapore were not controversial and were essentially supported. Singaporean requests for American-made weapons generated more debate, with Congress becoming involved in the AR-15 sale. However, the U.S. government ultimately endorsed the transactions.

The outcomes of the Singaporean courtship of American capital and military deals are noteworthy. Apart from creating jobs in Singapore, the American investments in the city-state also expanded Singapore-U.S. trade especially in manufactures. American businesses took advantage of Singapore's low labor costs to manufacture their products and export them to the United States. Between 1965 and 1973, the value of Singapore-U.S. trade increased tenfold from S$372 million to S$3,401 million, making the United States the second largest trading partner of Singapore.[68] The relationship between the Singaporean and U.S. defense establishments also intensified as the city-state looked to the United States for weapons and other equipment. Ultimately, the American presence in Southeast Asia did not significantly diminish even as Saigon capitulated to the North Vietnamese forces in 1975. A multidimensional Singapore-U.S. economic and security relationship had obtained.

Notes

I thank the Lyndon B. Johnson Foundation for awarding me a Moody Research Grant, which facilitated my research at the Lyndon B. Johnson Library. I also gratefully acknowledge the School of Humanities and Social Sciences at Nanyang Technological University for awarding me a start-up grant, which funded my research at the National Archives in College Park, Maryland. My thanks as well to the Department of History, National University of Singapore, and the Department of Security Studies and Criminology, Macquarie University, for financially supporting my participation in the Vietnam War in the Pacific World conference at Macquarie University in 2019.

1. Clive Christie, *Ideology and Revolution in Southeast Asia 1900–1980* (Richmond, UK: Curzon, 2001).

2. Ang Cheng Guan, "The Domino Theory Revisited: The Southeast Asia Perspective," *War and Society* 19 (May 2001): 109–130.

3. Harold Crouch, *The Army and Politics in Indonesia* (Ithaca, NY: Cornell University Press, 1978); David A. Rosenberg, ed., *Marcos and Martial Law in the Philippines* (Ithaca, NY: Cornell University Press, 1979).

4. Jacques Bertrand, "Growth and Democracy in Southeast Asia," *Comparative Politics* 30 (April 1998): 355–375.

5. Albert Celoza, *Ferdinand Marcos and the Philippines: The Political Economy of Authoritarianism* (Westport, CT: Praeger, 1997).

6. Ang Cheng Guan, "Singapore and the Vietnam War," *Journal of Southeast Asian Studies* 40 (June 2009): 353–384.

7. Lim Chong Yah and Ow Chwee Huay, "The Singapore Economy and the Vietnam War," in *The Singapore Economy*, ed. You Poh Seng and Lim Chong Yah (Singapore: Eastern Universities Press, 1971), 352–369.

8. Daniel Chua, *US-Singapore Relations, 1965–1975: Strategic Non-alignment in the Cold War* (Singapore: NUS Press, 2017).

9. Wen-Qing Ngoei, *Arc of Containment: Britain, the United States, and Anticommunism in Southeast Asia* (Ithaca, NY: Cornell University Press, 2019).

10. U.S. Consulate General, Singapore (hereafter USCGS), to Department of State (hereafter DOS), September 4, 1965, Record Group 59: General Records of the DOS Central Foreign Policy Files (hereafter RG59), Box 2651, National Archives, College Park, Maryland (hereafter NACP).

11. U.S. Embassy, Malaysia (hereafter USEM), to DOS, August 24, 1965, *Foreign Relations of the United States, 1964–1968*, Vol. 26, *Indonesia; Malaysia-Singapore; Philippines* (Washington, DC: Government Printing Office, 2000), 589–591 [hereafter *FRUS, 1964–1968*, with volume and page numbers].

12. Michael Leifer, *Singapore's Foreign Policy: Coping with Vulnerability* (London: Routledge, 2000), 10–42.

13. NIE, December 16, 1965, *FRUS, 1964–1968*, 26:592–601.

14. USCGS to DOS, August 16, 1965, *Declassified Documents Reference System* (hereafter *DDRS*), CK3100135742.

15. USCGS Memorandum, November 1, 1965, *DDRS*, CK3100135753.

16. Tim Huxley, *Defending the Lion City: The Armed Forces of Singapore* (St Leonards, Australia: Allen & Unwin, 2001), 1–23.

17. USCGS to DOS, December 19, 1965; Memorandum of Conversation (hereafter Memcon), December 30, 1965, RG 59, Box 741, NACP.

18. DOS to USEM, January 29, 1966, *FRUS, 1964–1968*, 26:602.

19. Lee Kuan Yew, *From Third World to First: The Singapore Story: 1965–2000* (Singapore: Times Editions, Singapore Press Holdings, 2000), 504.

20. Bundy to Rusk, March 14, 1966, *FRUS, 1964–1968*, 26:605.

21. "Singapore to Have Full Ties with U.S.," *Straits Times*, April 5, 1966.

22. U.S. Embassy, Singapore (hereafter USES), to DOS, June 19, 1966, RG59, Box 2651, NACP.

23. USES to DOS, July 10, 1966, RG59, Box 2651, NACP.

24. Ropa to Rostow, September 19, 1966, *DDRS*, CK3100130100.

25. Rusk to LBJ, May 2, 1967, *DDRS*, CK3100021278.
26. Hughes to Rusk, August 9, 1967, *FRUS, 1964–1968*, 26:618–620.
27. Lee, *From Third World to First*, 505.
28. Wright to Jorden, November 28, 1967, National Security File, Country File (hereafter NSFCF), Box 282, Lyndon Johnson Library, Austin, Texas (hereafter LBJL).
29. Lee, *From Third World to First*, 510; Memcon, December 11, 1967, RG 59, Subject File of the Office of Indonesia, Malaysia and Singapore Affairs, 1965–1974 (hereafter SFOIMSA), Box 5, NACP.
30. Memcon, December 11, 1967, RG 59, SFOIMSA, Box 5, NACP.
31. CIA Report, October 6, 1967, NSFCF, Box 281, LBJL; Huxley, *Defending the Lion City*, 6–14.
32. Lee, *From Third World to First*, 29–31.
33. Huxley, *Defending the Lion City*, 128.
34. Rusk to USCGS, February 25, 1966; USES to Rusk, June 3, 1966 and June 13, 1966; DIA Memorandum, June 20, 1966; RG59, Box 3, NACP.
35. "U.S. Sells 23,000 M16 Rifles to S'pore," *Straits Times*, March 7, 1967; "Singapore Will Get Those Rifles Says Bundy," *Straits Times*, March 18, 1967.
36. "U.S. Military Sales," October 12, 1967, NSFCF, Box 282, LBJL.
37. Galbraith to Bean, July 26, 1967, RG 59, SFOIMSA, Box 5, NACP.
38. DIA Summary, July 1, 1968, RG59, SFOIMSA, Box 2, NACP.
39. Cavanaugh Note, December 11, 1968, RG 59, SFOIMSA, Box 4, NACP.
40. Galbraith to Bundy, June 24, 1968, RG 59, SFOIMSA, Box 4, NACP.
41. "S'pore to Make M16 Rifles within Two Years," *Straits Times*, October 26, 1969.
42. Memcon, May 20, 1968, RG 59, SFOIMSA, Box 1, NACP; "Foreign Military Sales," March 25, 1969, RG59, SFOIMSA, Box 3, NACP; Bean to Brown, August 6, 1969, RG 59, SFOIMSA, Box 7, NACP.
43. McGhee to Galbraith, October 10, 1968, RG 59, SFOISMA, Box 4, NACP.
44. Cross to Bean, April 16, 1970, RG 59, SFOIMSA, Box 8, NACP.
45. Lee, *From Third World to First*, 40–41.
46. Bennet to Green, August 31, 1970, RG 59, SFOIMSA, Box 7, NACP.
47. NIE, December 16, 1965, *FRUS, 1964–1968*, 26: 596–598.
48. USCGS to DOS, December 19, 1965, RG59, Box 741, NACP.
49. USCGS to DOS, November 30, 1965; USES to DOS, December 30, 1966, RG59, Box 741, NACP.
50. You Poh Seng and Lim Chong Yah, eds., *Singapore: Twenty-Five Years of Development* (Singapore: Nanyang Xingzhou Lianhe Zaobao, 1984).
51. USCGS to DOS, April 3, 1966, RG59, Box 2651, NACP.
52. USES to DOS, September 3, 1966, RG59, Box 2651, NACP.
53. USES to DOS, July 12, 1966, RG59, Box 906, NACP.
54. Attachment to Wright to Rostow, November 28, 1967, NSFCF, Box 282, LBJL.
55. USES to DOS, July 22, 1966, RG59, Box 1032, NACP; Galbraith Memorandum, October 27, 1966, RG59, Box 906, NACP.
56. Bennett to Green, September 25, 1970, RG59, SFOIMSA, Box 2, NACP.

57. Bennett to Green, August 31, 1970, RG59, SFOIMSA, Box 7, NACP.
58. "Singapore Study," April 22, 1972, RG 59, SFOIMSA, Box 10, NACP.
59. "Singapore," undated, RG 59, SFOIMSA, Box 10, NACP.
60. Green to Monteiro, March 31, 1970, RG 59, SFOIMSA, Box 7, NACP.
61. Memorandum for Kissinger, August 3, 1971, RG 59, SFOIMSA, Box 8, NACP.
62. CIA Report, October 6, 1967, NSFCF, Box 281, LBJL.
63. Lim and Ow, "The Singapore Economy."
64. Galbraith to Bundy, July 7, 1967, RG 59, SFOIMSA, Box 5, NACP.
65. O'Neill to Heimann, March 6, 1972, RG59, RG 59, SFOIMSA, Box 10, NACP; Edwin Lee, *Singapore: The Unexpected Nation* (Singapore: ISEAS Publishing, 2008), 273.
66. President's Foreign Policy Report Draft, undated, RG 59, SFOIMSA, Box 9, NACP.
67. Memorandum for LBJ, October 14, 1967, NSFCF, Box 282, LBJL.
68. You and Lim, *Singapore*, 34.

14 Buying Time?

The Vietnam War and Southeast Asia

MATTIAS FIBIGER

The mid- to late 1960s witnessed the rise of a curious argument about the Vietnam War. As early as January 1965, a full two months *before* the Americanization of the war, the indefatigable *New York Times* columnist C. L. Sulzberger argued that "We have lost most of the space in South Vietnam; but we can still buy time—time to reinforce the anti-Communist position in Thailand, Malaysia and the Philippines."[1] Others soon began echoing Sulzberger's argument. Singaporean prime minister Lee Kuan Yew claimed in July 1966 that the war, now in full swing, was "buying time" for the rest of Southeast Asia to build up its political, military, economic, and psychological defenses against communism.[2]

This argument—call it the "buying time thesis"—proved remarkably durable. As recently as January 2019, the *Wall Street Journal* published an op-ed by William Lloyd Stearman, who served on the National Security Council staff under four Republican presidents, claiming that "U.S. intervention in Vietnam achieved a strategic victory by saving Southeast Asia—albeit not Vietnam—from communism."[3] By rhetorically transmuting the American failure in Indochina into triumph, Stearman and other latter-day advocates of the buying time thesis endeavor to rescue the Vietnam War from decades of popular and historiographical derision. Not only was the war a "noble cause," as U.S. president Ronald Reagan called it, but it was also a constructive one.[4]

Its revisionist utility does much to explain the buying time thesis's enduring purchase on the public imagination. So too does its inherent plausibility, for a cursory comparison of Southeast Asia in 1965 and 1975 reveals the region became far more prosperous, more united, and more secure. When the Johnson administration Americanized the war in Vietnam, the region was mired in poverty, beset by bitter antagonisms, and home to powerful communist movements. Ten years hence, the situation had changed markedly. The Suharto regime had presided over a politicide of approximately half a million Indonesians and decimated the Communist Party of Indonesia (PKI)—until then the world's largest nonruling communist movement. Insurgencies continued to smolder in the Philippines, Thailand, and Malaysia, but nowhere did they pose an immediate or existential threat to national stability. Meanwhile, the region's noncommunist states had resolved their disputes over territory and ideology and banded together to form the Association of Southeast Asian Nations (ASEAN), which became a vehicle for renewed diplomatic interconnectivity, a hub for increased economic integration, and an instrument for newfound security cooperation. Among the five ASEAN countries, gross domestic product (GDP) per capita measured in constant dollars increased on average 63 percent in the decade after 1965.

If the effect is certain, the cause is not. Advocates of the buying time thesis have failed to marshal convincing evidence for the claims that American intervention in Vietnam led directly to the destruction of Southeast Asian communist movements, the formation of ASEAN, or the region's dramatic economic growth.

But neither have detractors of the buying time thesis convincingly rebutted these claims. The most compelling refutation of the thesis comes from Robert McMahon, who points out it is guilty of conflating intentions and outcomes.[5] His is an important argument, but it is also something of a dodge, focusing on the fallacious, post hoc, ergo propter hoc reasoning marshaled by proponents of the thesis rather than delving into the empirical realities of the Vietnam War as a regional conflict. McMahon's refutation thus reveals the extent to which the buying time thesis has consistently vexed historians—much more so than its less sophisticated cousin, the domino theory. By suggesting that the "fall" of Vietnam would mechanistically and inevitably lead to the "fall" of Cambodia and Laos and then the rest of Southeast Asia, the domino theory rendered the region's states "lifeless entities that automatically fall one way or the other, depending on which way their neighbor falls," in the words of the Indonesian diplomat Soedjatmoko. The buying time thesis added to the domino theory elements of temporality, agency, and contingency—in short, a more sophisticated sense of history.[6]

To answer definitively what would have transpired in Southeast Asia had the United States not intervened in Vietnam is an impossible counterfactual: the variables are too numerous, the time period too protracted. Analyzing the buying time thesis is made all the more difficult by the fact that its proponents have put forward at least two different ways in which the Vietnam War allegedly bought time for Southeast Asia. The first suggests that the war afforded anti-communist Southeast Asian leaders the time necessary to subdue domestic communist movements. As Henry Kissinger put it, "America failed in Vietnam, but it gave the other nations of Southeast Asia time to deal with their own insurrections."[7] The second suggests that the war focused Vietnamese, Chinese, and Soviet energies on the struggle over South Vietnam, buying time for the other states of Southeast Asia to build up their defenses against an inevitable communist offensive. Walt W. Rostow articulated this variant of the buying time thesis in a self-serving review of Robert McNamara's mea culpa of a memoir, *In Retrospect*: "In short, we certainly lost the battle—the test of will—in Vietnam; but we won the war in Southeast Asia because South Vietnam and its allies for ten years were 'holding aggression at bay'—the phrase used on 12 July 1966 by President Johnson speaking to the Alumni Council. And that was what it was all about."[8]

Of course that was *not* what it was all about.[9] There is little evidence that internal communist subversion or external communist aggression posed immediate threats to Southeast Asia beyond Indochina at the moment of the Americanization of the Vietnam War. Nevertheless, the buying time thesis remains worthy of historical analysis. This chapter unveils new evidence, including archival documentation from across Southeast Asia, to reevaluate the buying time thesis. It suggests that there is *some* truth to the claims that the Vietnam War strengthened Southeast Asia's noncommunist states, stimulated the region's economic growth, and led to the creation of ASEAN— all of which left the region more stable and secure. In other ways, though, the war was a source of instability. It led the United States to funnel vast quantities of military and economic aid to dictatorial regimes whose repression of loyal political opposition fueled a resurgence of disloyal opposition in the form of communist, Islamist, and separatist insurgencies. The economic growth the war fueled reinforced emerging systems of oligarchy that diminished opportunities for ordinary Southeast Asians to promote peaceful political change. And the war ensured that regional cooperation was based on rigid sovereigntist principles that impeded ASEAN's ability to solve long-term problems. Ultimately, the buying time thesis masks the complexity of the Vietnam War and its contradictory legacies for Southeast Asia.

● ● ● ● ● ●

Communism posed little threat to Southeast Asia when President Lyndon B. Johnson Americanized the war in Vietnam. And American officials knew as much. One intelligence estimate prepared by the Central Intelligence Agency (CIA) in early 1964 admitted that most crises in the region were "the product of causes other than Communist scheming."[10]

Much had changed since the end of World War II, when a revolutionary wave crested across Southeast Asia. In the Philippines, Malaysia, and Singapore, communists won renown as the most steadfast opponents of the Japanese occupation, which endowed them with considerable nationalist legitimacy at the dawn of the era of decolonization. But colonial and neocolonial governments waged counterinsurgency campaigns and engaged in other forms of political repression that blunted communist momentum by the mid-1960s.[11] In Thailand, by contrast, the Communist Party of Thailand (CPT) was hobbled by weak and disunited leadership. It quickly lost ground to the indigenous Free Thai Movement as the exemplar of nationalist opposition to the Japanese occupation. A series of field marshals, aided by substantial American largesse, then violently suppressed the CPT and all manner of political opposition in the postwar era. Only in Indonesia did communists ascend to the commanding heights of national politics. President Sukarno cultivated the PKI to counterbalance the power of the conservative army as he erected an authoritarian system of Guided Democracy. The delicate triangular equilibrium of Indonesian politics survived until the mid-1960s, when Sukarno's health waned and his impressive political talents dulled. At the moment American marines first came ashore at Da Nang, both the PKI and the army were maneuvering to secure their position in a post-Sukarno Indonesia. The country was poised not for a communist takeover but for a dramatic conflict—and given the army's enduring monopoly on violence, it was a conflict the communists were ill-positioned to win.[12]

The notion that the Vietnam War was necessary in order to buy other Southeast Asian states time to crush indigenous communist movements therefore begins from mistaken assumptions. Across the region, communists generally found refuge only in what the geographer Willem van Schendel and the political scientist James Scott call Zomia, the upland portion of the Southeast Asian massif whose rugged terrain has historically rendered it impenetrable to the states that arose in the region's lowlands and thus attractive to "runaway, fugitive, maroon communities . . . fleeing the oppressions of state-making."[13] (Zomia refers only to mainland Southeast Asia, but the same principle applies to the region's maritime world: only in relatively inhospitable environments, including remote islands and dense jungles, did armed communist movements find sanctuary.) Admittedly, the ruling states of Southeast Asia varied in capacity and legitimacy, and none could count itself entirely immune to political or economic instability. But nowhere, with the possible exception of Indonesia, were communists positioned to take advantage of that instability.

If indigenous communist movements were largely impotent by 1965, what of Vietnamese expansionism, or even Soviet or Chinese aggression? By concentrating Vietnamese, Soviet, and Chinese attention and resources on the struggle over South Vietnam, did the United States buy time for other Southeast Asian states to build up their defenses against communism?

Historical experience, national chauvinism, and wartime exigency impelled Vietnam's communist leaders to carve out a sphere of influence that included Cambodia and Laos. And Vietnamese communists were hardly averse to demonstrations of wider revolutionary solidarity. For instance, North Vietnam accommodated the Malayan communist leader Chin Peng during his retreat to China in 1960; so too did Hanoi offer to host a radio station to beam communist propaganda into Malaysia in 1964—though the offer went nowhere after Beijing refused to put up the funds.[14] In general, however, Vietnamese communists refrained from providing succor to communist insurgencies beyond Indochina. Proponents of the buying time thesis might protest that the conflict over South Vietnam militated against the diversion of precious resources to other revolutionary fronts. But even after the communist takeover of South Vietnam in April 1975, Vietnamese communist internationalism remained conspicuously limited. What impresses most about Hanoi's acts of revolutionary solidarity is not their breadth but their modesty. Communist Vietnam offered rhetorical support to left-wing movements across Latin America, Asia, the Middle East, and Africa, befitting its reputation as the giant slayer of the international communist movement. Only rarely, though, did Hanoi move beyond rhetorical to material assistance. Except for a token dispatch of two dozen advisers to train Sandinista rebels in the early 1980s, Vietnam mostly denied the appeals of Third World revolutionary movements for material aid in the decade after 1975.[15] In other instances, Vietnam offered material assistance to revolutionary groups in Nicaragua and El Salvador, but this entailed the shipment of captured American M-16 rifles—hardly a notch in the column for the buying time thesis since this assistance was *enabled by* the Vietnam War.[16]

The Soviet Union and China possessed both means and motive to undermine Southeast Asia's noncommunist states. The Sino-Soviet split, brewing since the mid-1950s, burst into the open in the 1960s. Determined to assert leadership of the international communist movement, Moscow and Beijing each poured considerable energy and resources into the developing world.

At the moment of the Americanization of the Vietnam War, however, both communist giants were also on the verge of tectonic geopolitical reorientations that foreshortened their ambitions in Southeast Asia.

In Moscow, a collective leadership in which Leonid Brezhnev gradually achieved preeminence assumed power in 1964. Brezhnev accelerated Soviet support for national liberation movements and radical nationalist regimes across the globe, but the Soviet Union's agenda in Southeast Asia remained relatively tame in comparison to its offensives in Africa and the Middle East.[17] Most of the region's communist parties had aligned themselves with China in the deepening Sino-Soviet rift, and the Kremlin was skeptical of the ability of the region's communist movements to seize state power. Moscow thus worked to court rather than undermine Southeast Asia's noncommunist states—an effort emblematized by Brezhnev's 1969 proposal for a collective security arrangement in Asia.[18] The Soviet Union had become a status quo rather than revisionist power in the region.

Meanwhile in Beijing, Mao Zedong began funneling ever-greater sums of money and matériel to national liberation movements across the Third World. But Mao was on the cusp of plunging China into the Great Proletarian Cultural Revolution, which would paralyze the Foreign Ministry's operations in Beijing and prompt the recall of all but one of China's ambassadors and two-thirds of its diplomatic personnel stationed overseas. The capability of the People's Republic to conduct basic diplomacy subsequently deteriorated.[19] Yet even amid the turmoil of the Cultural Revolution, China managed to dispatch tens of thousands of workers to the Zambian copper belt to construct the Tazara railway and crates of weapons to Palestine to support the anti-Zionist cause. Moreover, Chinese leaders remained enamored of the strategy of using rear-base areas to support guerrilla movements in neighboring countries. Whatever Chinese intentions, a revolutionary thrust into Southeast Asia would have met considerable obstacles. Widespread anti-Chinese sentiment across much of the Nanyang impeded China's ability to cultivate clients in the region. And beyond Indochina, noncommunist Southeast Asian states generally claimed greater legitimacy than their South Vietnamese counterpart.[20] Archival limitations preclude definitive conclusions, but the available evidence suggests the Chinese threat in Southeast Asia was neither immediate nor overwhelming. The CIA concluded that, among communist parties in ASEAN states, only the CPT received material aid from China in the decade following 1965.[21]

The Vietnam War belied the taming of Chinese and Soviet ambitions in Southeast Asia. Vietnamese revolutionaries relied on the support of both

Moscow and Beijing throughout the period of American involvement in Vietnam. Chinese military aid to Vietnam escalated dramatically in 1965 and remained high for the following decade.[22] Reliable figures of Soviet aid to Vietnam are more elusive, though CIA estimates suggest Soviet aid consistently exceeded Chinese aid even without accounting for the aid furnished by Soviet satellites in Eastern Europe.[23] But these aid figures masked a deeper reality. Moscow and Beijing provided North Vietnam with such vast quantities of aid primarily to check the other's influence and establish a dominant position within the international communist movement, for which the Vietnam War harbored profound symbolic importance. Indeed, both Moscow and Beijing, anxious to cultivate burgeoning relationships with Washington, leavened their aid to Hanoi with appeals to accept a negotiated settlement that fell short of Vietnamese communists' maximalist objectives.[24]

The conclusion is inescapable: when the Johnson administration chose to Americanize the war in Vietnam, neither indigenous communist movements nor Vietnamese, Soviet, or Chinese aggression posed an immediate threat to Southeast Asia's noncommunist states. Time need not have been bought at all.

· · · · · ·

If the buying time thesis is suspect as a justification for the Vietnam War, whether in advance or in retrospect, it remains a useful jumping-off point for an analysis of the war's effects. Indeed, the relationship between the Vietnam War and Southeast Asia has long suffered from historiographical neglect.[25] As it happened, the war brought massive changes to the wider region. Nowhere is this more evident than the growing strength of Southeast Asia's noncommunist states.

The relationship between the Vietnam War and the strength of Southeast Asia's non-communist states is indirect. The American military machine's actions in Indochina had little, if any, bearing on the ability of governments outside of Indochina to command the loyalty of their populations, to extract and mobilize resources, or to suppress challenges to their authority. However, the American war effort in Vietnam did elicit a corresponding expansion of U.S. military and economic aid to the anti-communist states of Thailand, Malaysia, Singapore, Indonesia, and the Philippines—an expansion that would have been unthinkable absent the war raging nearby. As Graph 14.1 shows, measured in constant dollars, U.S. aid trebled between 1965 and 1969, when American troop levels in Vietnam reached

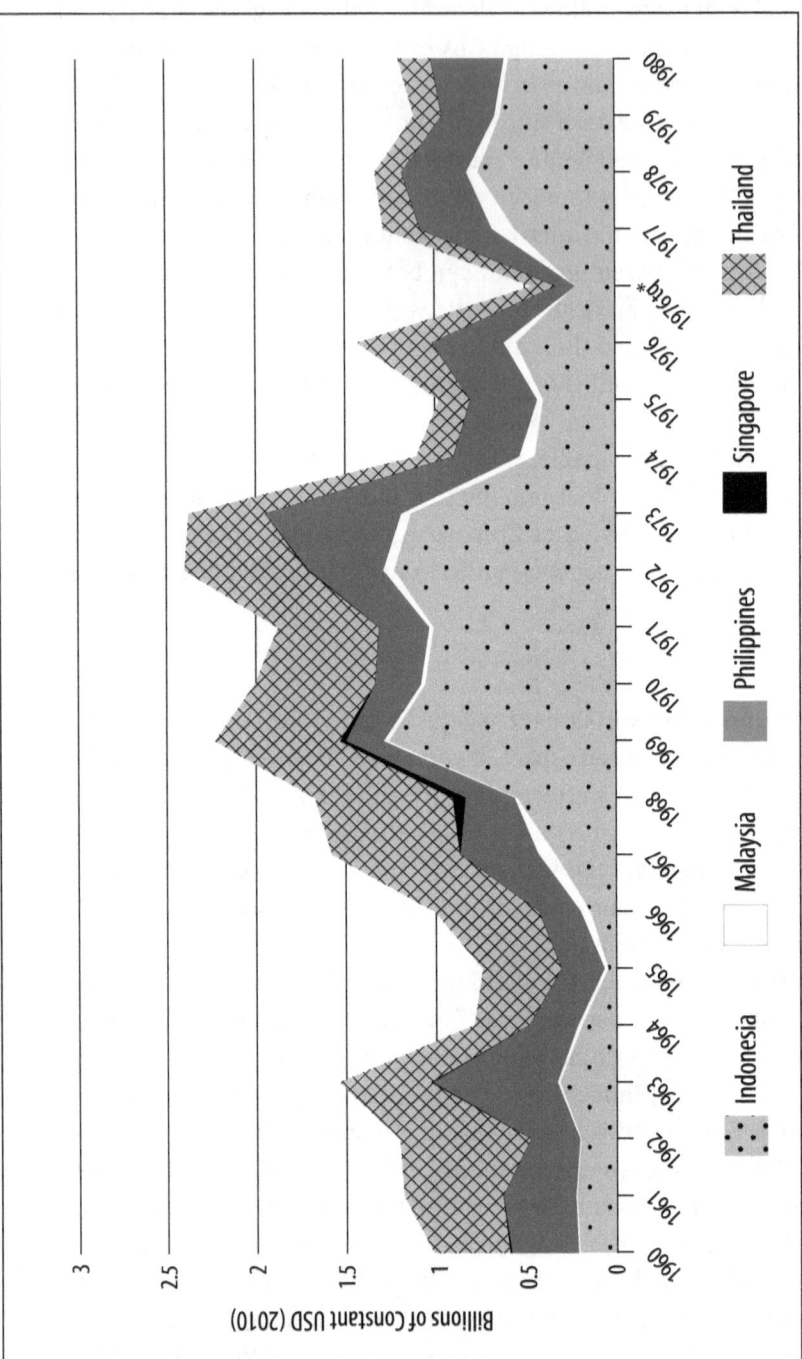

GRAPH 14.1 U.S. military and economic aid to ASEAN states, 1960–1980

*In 1976, the U.S. fiscal year shifted from July 1–June 30 to October 1–September 30, necessitating a three-month transition quarter between fiscal years 1976 and 1977.

Source: Data compiled by author from United States Agency for International Development, "U.S. Overseas Loans and Grants: Obligations and Loan Authorizations, 1945–2018," https://explorer.usaid.gov/prepared/us_foreignaid_greenbook.xlsx.

their peak. And U.S. aid to the five ASEAN states largely sustained that remarkably high level until 1973, when the Paris Peace Accords ushered an end to direct American involvement in Vietnam. The massive increase in aid brought conflicting legacies for the region. It helped build autonomous, capacious states capable of securing national territories and implementing developmental agendas. At the same time, it enabled the construction and consolidation of exclusionary, coercive regimes that narrowed or eliminated legitimate channels of political contestation. Facing foreshortened opportunities for peaceful political change within existing national institutions and ideological frameworks, many opponents of dictatorial rule turned to revolutionary discourses and armed resistance. Communist, Islamist, and separatist insurgencies flourished.

The United States supported the rise of the New Order in Indonesia. It offered token aid as Suharto turned back the September 30th Movement—an apparent putsch launched by leaders of the PKI in coordination with elements of the Indonesian military—and embarked on a politicide in which approximately 500,000 Indonesians were killed.[26] American military and economic aid figures escalated dramatically over the next several years. Meanwhile, the Paris Club and the Inter-Governmental Group on Indonesia, institutions in which the United States wielded preponderant influence, organized moratoria on the repayment of Indonesia's sovereign debt and issued new loans worth hundreds of millions of dollars. American and international aid enabled Suharto to consolidate his domination of the Indonesian state and expand its coercive and developmental capacities.

Economic aid was most important. Before the last American troops left Vietnam, the United States delivered more than $1 billion in economic assistance to Indonesia. Most of that money went toward financing the New Order's five-year development plans, called Repelita. Repelita I, active from 1969 to 1974, depended on international aid for 60 percent of its expenditures. It aimed to overcome inflation, jump-start rice production, increase exports, and rehabilitate physical infrastructure.[27] Given that only about 20 percent of the archipelago's roads and 40 percent of its ports were in good repair in 1969, huge sums of money were required to promote the country's economic recovery.[28] Even after the explosion of oil revenues in the last quarter of 1973, the Suharto regime still relied upon international aid for its domestic economic development programs. Repelita II, active from 1974–1979, envisioned international aid accounting for 30 percent of its expenditures.[29] Far more ambitious than its predecessor, the second five-year development plan proposed an expansive effort to meet the educational, housing, employment, and health needs of ordinary Indonesians as well as a significant expansion of the Indonesian military and the construction of raw material processing facilities. Massive deliveries of American economic aid enlarged the capacity of the Indonesian state to formulate and implement its developmental agenda. As Graph 14.2 reveals, until the oil crisis left the Indonesian state awash in petrodollars, foreign aid regularly constituted roughly 30 percent of a rapidly expanding government budget.

Military aid was critical as well. Even though the dollar amount of military aid was comparably small, the on-the-books figure understated its significance. The Pentagon valued the weapons, equipment, and training it provided to Indonesia at bottom-barrel prices, offered used military equipment deemed "excess stock" from the Indochina theater at depreciated prices, and accepted token payment for Foreign Military Sales items in Indonesian rupiah rather than American dollars. Although establishing a more accurate estimate of the value of American military aid to Indonesia is a gargantuan task beyond the scope of this chapter, such vast quantities of equipment rebuilt the Indonesian armed forces and did much to replace the $1.1 billion worth of Soviet military equipment delivered to Indonesia under Sukarno.[30] American aid also enabled Suharto to maintain a bloated military establishment whose manned strength hovered around 300,000 soldiers, a number Indonesian and international observers alike considered far greater than necessary to meet the country's defensive needs.[31] According to the annual budgets prepared by the Indonesian government—whose comprehensiveness is admittedly open to dispute given the prevalence of so-called off-budget financing arrangements—the military's share of routine government expenditures hovered around 25 percent in the early 1970s.[32] The cornerstone of Suharto's authority, Indonesia's massive military establishment would have been unsustainable without American aid.

International aid enabled Suharto to eliminate his political opposition and consolidate his authority. Most important was securing his dominance of the Indonesian military. Resistance to Suharto's authority remained widespread in the officer corps of the navy, marines, and air force in the wake of the September 30th Movement.[33] Because these branches relied overwhelmingly on old, Soviet-supplied equipment, they opposed Suharto's reorientation of Indonesia toward the West; and because they emphasized the projection of power outside Indonesia's borders, they opposed Suharto's reorientation of the military toward internal security and development. As General Sumitro, a key ally of Suharto, remembered, "All of the other armed forces branches, the Navy, the Air Force, and the Police Force

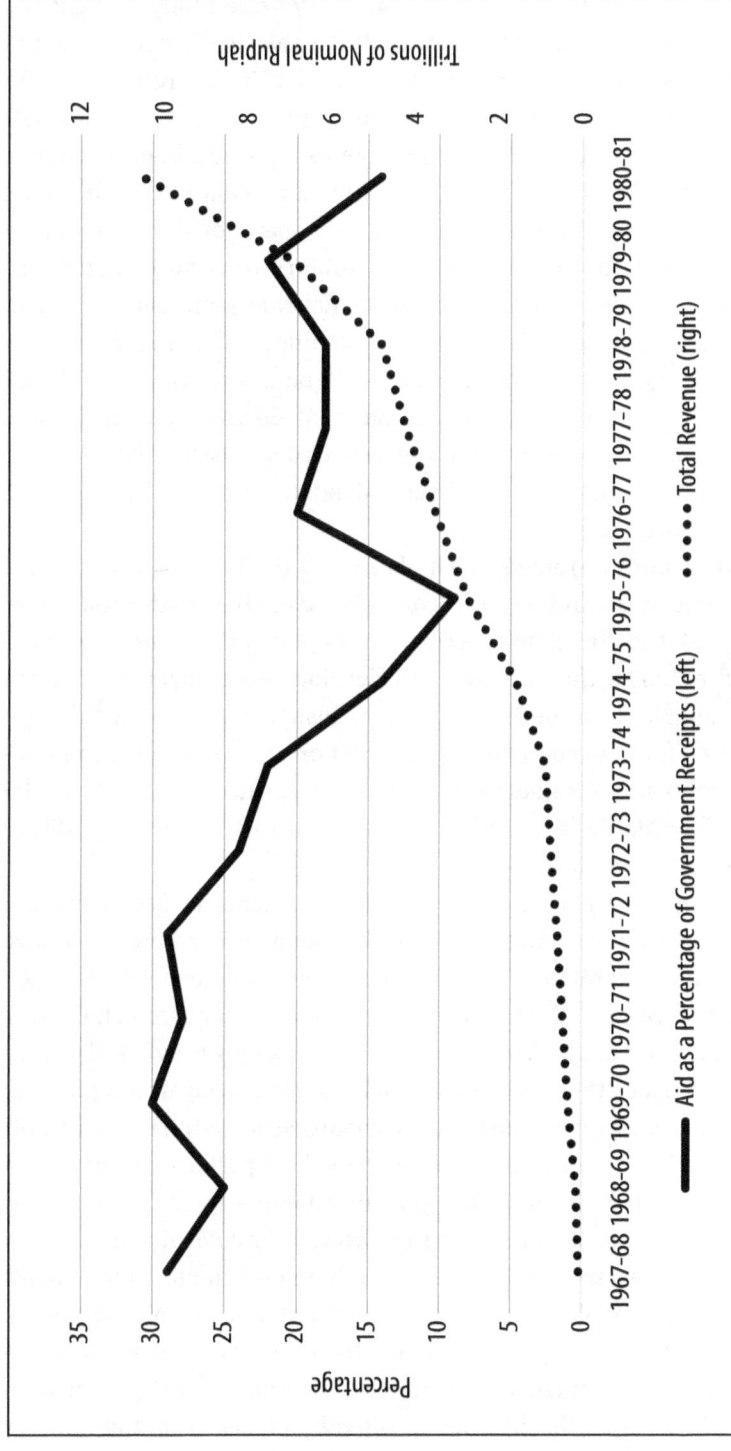

GRAPH 14.2 International aid and Indonesian government revenue, 1967–1981

Source: Data compiled by author from Government of Indonesia, *Nota Keuangan dan Rancangan Anggaran Pendapatan dan Belanja Negara* (Jakarta: Departemen Keuangan, 1969–1980).

treated the Army like an enemy. At worst they were ready to fight the Army, at least they were suspicious of it."[34] But the steady degradation of rival branches' equipment in the face of the Soviet Union's refusal to offer spare parts to an Indonesian military increasingly linked to the West left the air force, navy, and marines vulnerable to Suharto's blandishments. (Audits conducted in 1969 revealed that only 20 percent of the air force's planes and 40 percent of the navy's vessels were operational.)[35] In 1969, Suharto at once reorganized the Indonesian military to eliminate each service's operational independence, kicked recalcitrant generals upstairs to ambassadorships, purged the military of his opponents, and channeled American military equipment to the air force and navy.[36] Once the United States loosened the purse strings on international aid and rendered Indonesia's political parties less relevant to the New Order's coalitional logic, Suharto brought his civilian rivals to heel and mobilized the military behind his own quasi-party, Golkar.[37]

Similar dynamics unfolded in Thailand and the Philippines: massive amounts of American military and economic aid enabled authoritarian regimes to shrink the domestic constituencies upon which state power depended and enhance the coercive and developmental capacities of the states they inhabited. In the Philippines, for instance, American aid regularly accounted for between 25 and 50 percent of a rapidly expanding military budget following President Ferdinand Marcos's declaration of martial law in 1972.[38] In Malaysia and Singapore, by contrast, American military and economic aid were largely unimportant.

The Vietnam War thus contributed to the emergence of developmental authoritarian states in Southeast Asia. And although these states may have preserved political stability in the short term, they also generated instability in the long term. As authoritarian governments suppressed challenges to their power, opponents of dictatorial rule increasingly gravitated toward insurgency. Consider the story of Abdullah Sungkar, who would go on to found Jema'ah Islamiyah, which would become one of Southeast Asia's most fearsome terrorist networks. Sungkar described his path to militancy in a 1982 trial, excoriating the Suharto regime for suppressing the more moderate Islamic political parties he once supported.[39] Or consider the story of one Filipino, who remembered that he and other noncommunist opponents of the Marcos regime joined the Maoist New People's Army (NPA) because, faced with the threat of imprisonment and torture, they "had no place else to go. They were all threatened with arrests. Their names were on the military lists and their families had been visited by people from the military who instructed the parents to turn them in. The colleges had been ordered to blacklist them. That was their situation."[40] Amid the Marcos regime's rounding up of suspected radicals, a new verb entered Manila's lexicon: *mamundok*, which literally means "to go to the mountains" but was almost always used to connote joining the NPA's guerrilla war.[41]

・・・・・・

In the quarter century after 1965, the economies of East and Southeast Asia expanded more than twice as quickly as the economies of other world regions. Most of that growth owed to the remarkable—"miraculous," it came to be called—performance of eight economies along the southeastern rim of Asia's communist world: Japan, South Korea, Taiwan, Hong Kong, Indonesia, Singapore, Malaysia, and Thailand. These countries grew not only more prosperous but also more equal. Shared prosperity resulted in significant improvements in almost all quantifiable indicators of human welfare, from life expectancy to poverty to the number of people living without necessities such as food, water, and shelter.[42] And trade followed growth. Intra-ASEAN trade accounted for only 6.3 percent of the total trade of the organization's member states in 1967; by 1979, that figure had expanded to 14.9 percent.[43] Economic change lifted huge numbers of Asians out of poverty, knit the region together, and diminished the appeal of revolutionary movements.

The Vietnam War served as an engine of economic growth in Southeast Asia. It fueled the growth of vast export markets—in the United States and in South Vietnam, as Graph 14.3 displays—at the precise moment that several ASEAN states began dismantling import-substitution schemes in favor of export-oriented industrialization. Southeast Asian states thus accrued foreign exchange and attracted foreign investment, which enabled them to import sophisticated machinery, jump-start industrial production, and ascend the global value chain. Some Southeast Asian governments dispatched troops to Vietnam, the cost of which was borne by the United States under what one American senator dubbed a "mercenary" scheme.[44] The war also promoted tourist industries in major metropolitan areas across the region, especially in Hong Kong, Bangkok, and Taipei, the most popular destinations for American soldiers on rest and recreation leave, but also in Tokyo, Manila, Kuala Lumpur, Penang, Singapore, and Seoul. And of course the American military and economic aid delivered to Southeast Asian states in massive amounts during the Vietnam War helped newly empowered states implement developmental agendas.

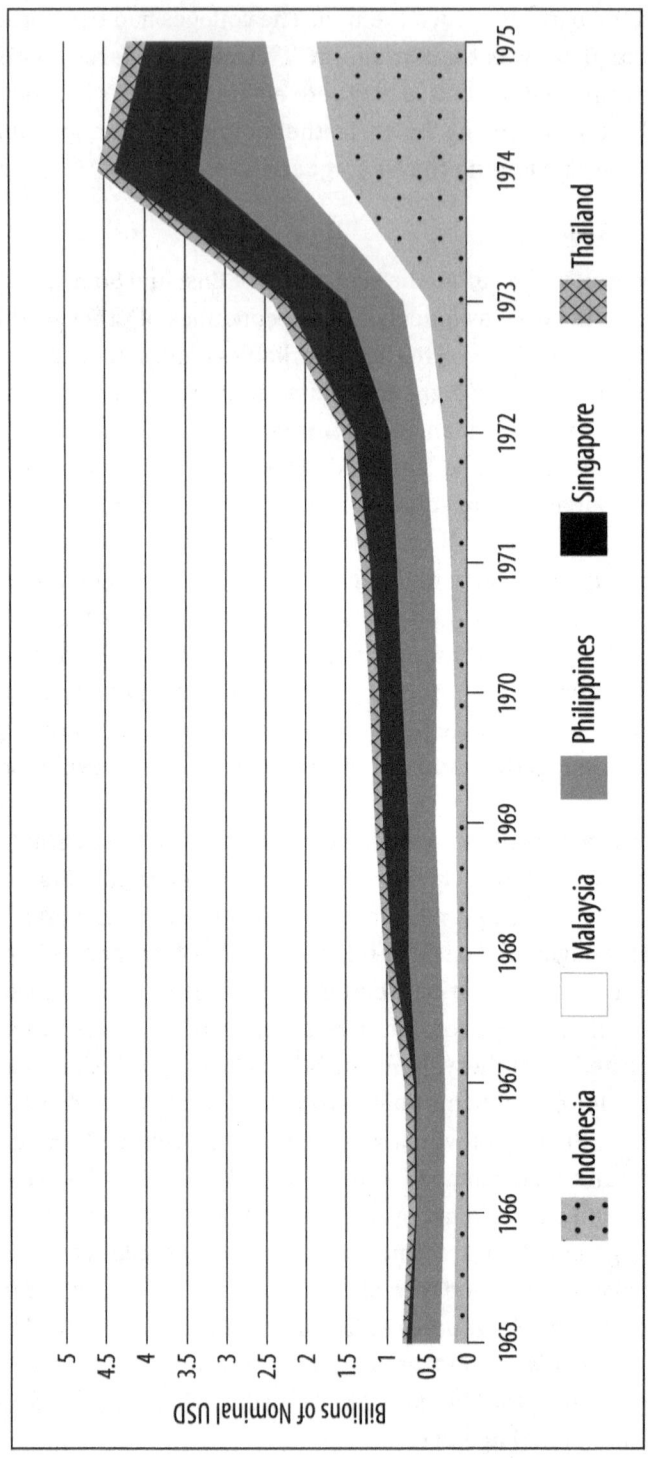

GRAPH 14.3 ASEAN exports to the United States and South Vietnam, 1965–1975

Source: Data compiled by author from International Monetary Fund, Directions of Trade Yearbook (Washington, DC: International Monetary Fund, 1966–1976).

No Southeast Asian country reaped as many economic benefits from the Vietnam War as Singapore. Singapore's exports to South Vietnam rose from $22 million in 1964 to $146 million in 1969—by which time South Vietnam was Singapore's third-largest export market. A large portion of this expansion owed to the city-state's position as the region's hub for the processing and export of petroleum and the war-related demand for fuel for military aircraft, helicopters, tanks, transport vehicles, and naval vessels.[45] Already in 1967, the CIA estimated that 15 percent of Singapore's gross national income derived from American military procurements related to the war in Vietnam.[46] The war benefited Singapore in other ways as well. Large numbers of American soldiers visited the city-state on rest and recreation leave, and by 1969 approximately 1,600 GIs arrived each month and spent about $300 each.[47] The inflow of American soldiers proved a boon to Singapore's nascent tourism industry, which earned the city-state only $23 million in 1965 and more than $332 million in 1975. The city-state's naval repair facilities also became a key port of call for American ships, more than fifty of which docked in Singapore each year, allowing the Singaporean government to weather the withdrawal of British forces whose presence previously accounted for one-fifth of Singapore's GDP.[48] Nascent manufacturing industries grew alongside the war in Vietnam. For instance, Chartered Industries of Singapore, an arms manufacturing company established in 1967, got off the ground by producing ammunition for Australian troops in Vietnam and, eventually, a locally produced version of the M-16 rifle.[49] More broadly, growing prosperity made Singapore an attractive destination for foreign direct investment, which increased from $16 million in 1965 to $681 million in 1975.[50] Several multinational firms established outposts in the city-state during the war. By the time the flag of the Provisional Revolutionary Government was raised over Saigon in April 1975, Singapore attracted almost half of all foreign direct investment entering Asia.[51] This had a knock-on effect in the wider region, as Singapore became a key source of foreign direct investment into Indonesia, Malaysia, the Philippines, and Thailand.

Although Singapore was unique among its Southeast Asian peers in the extent to which it benefited from war-related procurement, other ASEAN states also won economic gains as a result of the Vietnam War. Thailand became the logistical hub for U.S. bombing operations. Americans built seven air bases in the country's northeast and central regions beginning in 1961 and dozens of smaller bases throughout the country. Tens of thousands of Thais were employed in the construction and operation of the bases as well as the roads, bridges, and ports surrounding them, affording these workers opportunities to develop skills that would drive economic development going forward. More broadly, American aid financed the construction of transportation infrastructure that knit Thailand together and enabled the creation of economies of scale.[52] Bangkok became a can't-miss destination for young, unmarried American servicemen on rest and recreation leave, and the money they spent accounted for almost 30 percent of all tourist spending in Thailand. These visitors fueled the growth of Thailand's massive tourism industry—including its sex tourism industry, as brothels, massage parlors, and go-go bars proliferated, almost always with the cooperation of Thai government officials who regarded them as profitable sources of foreign exchange and corrupt accumulation.[53] The Johnson administration's "more flags" program also paid some 40,000 Thai soldiers and sailors to serve in Vietnam, where in addition to engaging in combat, they shopped for American goods at military post exchanges and imbibed a consumer culture that they helped disseminate upon their return to Thailand.[54] Although the war was not the sole engine of economic change in Thailand, its effects were manifold and substantial. Researchers at the *Economist* estimated that U.S. military spending accounted for 60 percent of the increase in the country's gross national product between 1964 and 1967.[55]

Indonesia and the Philippines benefited less than Thailand. Neither archipelagic state saw its exports to the United States or South Vietnam rise as a result of war-related demand. (The growing value of Indonesian exports to the United States reflected the quadrupling of world oil prices, a phenomenon related to conflict in the Middle East rather than Southeast Asia.) But both countries squeezed some economic gain from the war. They received considerable amounts of American military and economic aid, which signaled they could count on the support of the United States and enhanced their creditworthiness in the eyes of international lenders. The combination of aid and loans enabled Suharto and Marcos to dramatically expand public investment during the Vietnam War.[56] For instance, flush with international capital, the National Economic and Development Authority of the Philippines planned to build 25,000 kilometers of road, irrigate 500 million hectares of agricultural land, hang 2,500 kilometers of power lines, and construct 75,000 classrooms.[57] Finally, as with Thailand, the Philippines dispatched a brigade of 2,300 engineers to South Vietnam whose salaries were paid by the United States, a sum that came to $36 million. Although much of the Philippines' Vietnam War dividend was siphoned away to the private accounts of Marcos and his cronies, the war doubtless furthered the country's economic development.

Of all the countries in Southeast Asia, Malaysia benefited least from the Vietnam War. It received little in the way of U.S. military or economic aid, and its exports to the United States and South Vietnam remained limited. But even here, the war brought some benefits. In December 1971, an attaché at the American embassy in Kuala Lumpur sent a note to a deputy secretary in the prime minister's office, informing him of surplus equipment from Vietnam that could be used to further Malaysian economic development programs, including land reclamation and port construction schemes.[58] After the collapse of Cambodia and South Vietnam in the spring of 1975, Prime Minister Tun Abdul Razak told his commanders that he saw a "golden opportunity" to secure surplus weapons and equipment from the Indochina theater.[59] He seized the opportunity: Kuala Lumpur received an additional $65 million in military credits between 1976 and 1979.[60]

Precisely allocating the sources of economic growth in a region as diverse as Southeast Asia over a period of ten years is a nigh impossible proposition. There are no simple lines of cause and effect, only a tangled mass of endogeneity. However, we need not establish precise estimates for the percentage points added to GDP, nor the millions of dollars generated in foreign direct investment. More important for our purposes is to recognize the undeniable fact that the Vietnam War *did* contribute to the region's growing prosperity.

Modernization theorists suggested that economic growth would generate pressures for democratization among ascendant middle classes.[61] But Southeast Asia's newfound prosperity seemed to legitimize rather than undermine authoritarianism. Upwardly mobile classes generally rallied behind their governments, whether because they opened access to patronage arrangements, as in Indonesia and Malaysia, because they ensured public safety, as in the Philippines, or because they delivered public goods, as in Singapore. Only in Thailand and Indonesia did a movement led by middle-class students mount a meaningful challenge to governmental authority. However, Southeast Asia's economic takeoff also tended to reinforce systems of oligarchy. Regnant elites siphoned away much of the region's newfound wealth. In Thailand, for instance, politically connected speculators leveraged easy access to credit and bought up land around the American-financed highways that radiated from the center of the country to its borders with Laos and Cambodia, reaping substantial profits for themselves and casting many former landowning subsistence farmers into precarious forms of tenancy.[62] Similar stories played out across the region.[63] The expansion of oligarchic power enabled by the Vietnam War sowed seeds of instability that would not sprout for many years to come.

· · · · · ·

At the moment of the Americanization of the Vietnam War, Southeast Asia was mired in conflict. Malaya and Singapore were briefly united in the new state of Malaysia in 1963 and then separated in 1965, their messy divorce in part the product of racial tensions between the ethnic Chinese majority of Singapore and the ethnic Malay majority of Malaya. Indonesia under Sukarno's revolutionary leadership was waging a campaign of *Konfrontasi* against the creation of Malaysia, and border skirmishes and terrorist attacks threatened to erupt into a broader regional conflict. The Philippines refused to recognize Malaysia in order to preserve its irredentist claim to the state of Sabah on Borneo. Malaysia, the Philippines, and Thailand nursed anxieties that Indonesia sought to unify the entire Malay world within a "Greater Indonesia" that threatened their sovereignty. These cross-cutting ideological, territorial, personal, and ethnic conflicts contributed to the collapse of two attempts at regional agglomeration, the Association of Southeast Asia (1961) and Maphilindo (1963). So endemic did regional conflict seem to Southeast Asia that scholars and statesmen alike began speaking of the region as "the Balkans of the Orient."[64]

The year after the collapse of South Vietnam, the heads of state of Indonesia, Malaysia, the Philippines, Singapore, and Thailand gathered in Bali to sign the Treaty of Amity and Cooperation and the Declaration of ASEAN Concord. The documents pledged ASEAN member states to noninterference in the internal affairs of other member states and cooperation on social, political, economic, and cultural matters. The assembled heads of state also agreed to the establishment of an ASEAN Secretariat in Jakarta. Although disagreements among ASEAN states remained over issues like free trade and relations with the communist states of Indochina, the Bali Summit marked an undeniable step forward for regional integration and a striking contrast with the Southeast Asia of only a decade earlier. The Vietnam War *did* play a role in the creation of ASEAN, though not in the way proponents of the buying time thesis claim.[65]

When ASEAN's founding foreign ministers gathered in Bangkok in August 1967, doubts about the endurance of American power in Southeast Asia had already become commonplace. Thailand, Indonesia, and the Philippines were especially anxious about what they saw as an impending American withdrawal from the region. Similar concerns wracked Southeast Asia's British clients, Malaysia and Singapore. Although the policy would not be formally announced until January 1968, already in 1967 members of Prime Minister Harold Wilson's administration had begun making noises about a forthcoming military retrenchment from positions "east of Suez," which would abrogate the Anglo-Malaysian Defense Agreement that covered both Malaysia and Singapore. A shared fear of international abandonment, stimulated in part by the Vietnam War, provided an impetus for the creation of ASEAN. "Events are beginning to show the diminishing value of reliance on one's friends," Philippine foreign minister Carlos Romulo remarked in 1969.[66] However, other factors unrelated to the Vietnam War were equally important in allowing ASEAN governments to paper over their disagreements and establish a new regional body. Most notable in this regard were leadership changes in several Southeast Asian states—foremost among them Suharto's ouster of Sukarno in Indonesia and Marcos's replacement of Diosdado Macapagal in the Philippines.[67]

The Vietnam War did not only inspire fear of American abandonment. It also reinforced the idea that internal divisions within Southeast Asia invited external interventions in the region. Only by ensuring "their stability and security from external interference in any form," as the Bangkok Declaration heralding the creation of ASEAN proclaimed, could Southeast Asian states prevent events in Vietnam from recurring across the region. Marcos gave voice to this realization in a speech to the fourth ASEAN Ministerial Meeting in 1971, noting that the nations that banded together in 1967 were "known by all to have been hapless victims of some of the world powers, thought of by some as a veritable testing ground for contending ideologies, [and] feared by a few to be the probable arena of future armed clashes." As a result, he continued, "we were finally conscious of the need to create a harmonious stability in the region."[68] The notion that unity would build resilience found its most visible recognition in the Zone of Peace, Freedom, and Neutrality (ZOPFAN) Declaration, which the five ASEAN states promulgated in November 1971. The ZOPFAN Declaration affirmed that ASEAN member states would "secure the recognition of, and respect for, South East Asia as a Zone of Peace, Freedom and Neutrality, free from any form or manner of interference by outside Powers."[69]

The gradual American withdrawal from Vietnam, accompanied by a steep reduction in overall American aid to ASEAN states, reinforced the drive for regional unity in Southeast Asia. ASEAN ministers met in Kuala Lumpur in February 1973 to consider the implications of the final

American withdrawal from Vietnam. The meeting saw the first endorsement of the Indonesian ideas of national and regional resilience as the foundation on which Southeast Asian states could ensure the peace and stability of the region.[70] Likening ASEAN to a chain, only as strong as its weakest link, Indonesian foreign minister Adam Malik explained that if one member state proved vulnerable to subversion or infiltration, other member states would have to divert precious resources away from development and toward defense, which would in turn hinder their ability to meet the aspirations of their peoples and render them more vulnerable to instability. Only by ensuring the ability of all ASEAN member states to preserve internal security and promote economic development could regional stability be maintained. ASEAN also moved toward informal, diffuse cooperation on security matters, animated by Indonesia's national resilience framework.[71] For instance, through the annual Kista (Special Course) training programs, military and political officials from each ASEAN country began gathering annually to study the threats facing the region.[72]

Jusuf Wanandi, chief of the Centre for Strategic and International Studies (CSIS) in Jakarta, a think tank linked to the Suharto regime, remembered that "ASEAN had been established in 1967 to withstand the dominoes likely to fall to communism after Vietnam. The socio-economic 'front' of ASEAN was just a cover for the strategic build-up of a force that could withstand communist pressure in the region."[73] Wanandi's reminiscence suggests two insights. First, it confirms that growing regionalism was in part a product of the Vietnam War. Second, it reveals that the regionalism that took root in Southeast Asia was of a decidedly limited nature, focusing on cultural, social, and economic cooperation and foreswearing formal security cooperation. The Vietnam War instilled the lesson that national and regional divisions invited foreign intervention. ASEAN therefore concerned itself above all else with preserving sovereignty and unanimity, which rendered the organization largely incapable of solving problems that emerged within Southeast Asia. ASEAN's fecklessness in the face of the Rohingya genocide is only the latest manifestation of the limitations embedded in the institution by the Vietnam War.

· · · · · ·

The Vietnam War's legacies for Southeast Asia are thus more complex than the buying time thesis allows. The war contributed to the creation of strong states, to the growth of regional prosperity, and to the formation of ASEAN.

But it also contributed to the rise of authoritarian governments, to the deepening of oligarchy, and to the weakness of regional sentiment. Even if it allowed for these subtleties, the buying time thesis suffers from a final, fatal flaw. At the heart of the buying time thesis is a metaphor of *transaction*: what is gained equates to what is lost. Whatever its intellectual worth, then, by implying that the Vietnam War's salutary effects in Southeast Asia somehow cancel out its massive human and environmental cost in Indochina and beyond, the buying time thesis reveals itself as morally bankrupt.

Notes

1. "The Loss of Options in Vietnam," *New York Times*, January 11, 1965.
2. "Asian's Thanks Show Fulbright Owes Apology," *Boston Globe*, July 27, 1966; see also "Lee Kuan Yew," *Harvard Crimson*, October 23, 1967.
3. "America Lost Vietnam but Saved Southeast Asia," *Wall Street Journal*, January 27, 2019.
4. Ronald Reagan, "Peace: Restoring the Margin of Safety," August 18, 1980, http://www.reagan.utexas.edu/archives/reference/8.18.80.html.
5. Robert McMahon, "What Difference Did It Make? Assessing the Vietnam War's Impact on Southeast Asia," in *International Perspectives on Vietnam*, ed. Lloyd Gardner and Ted Gittinger (College Station: Texas A&M University Press, 1999).
6. Soedjatmoko, "South-East Asia and Security," *Survival* (October 1969): 302, 304.
7. Henry Kissinger, "Vietnam: A Noble Goal but a Flawed Strategy," *International Herald Tribune*, April 8, 1985.
8. W. W. Rostow, "Vietnam and Asia," *Diplomatic History* 20, no. 3 (June 1996): 469–470.
9. See, among others, Fredrik Logevall, *Choosing War: The Lost Chance for Peace and the Escalation of War in Vietnam* (Los Angeles: University of California Press, 1999).
10. Special National Intelligence Estimate, Short-Term Prospects in Southeast Asia, February 12, 1964, https://www.cia.gov/library/readingroom/docs/DOC_0000919245.pdf.
11. See, among many others, Benedict Kerkvliet, *The Huk Rebellion: A Study of Peasant Revolt in the Philippines* (Los Angeles: University of California Press, 1977); Richard Stubbs, *Hearts and Minds in Guerrilla Warfare: The Malayan Emergency 1948–1960* (New York: Oxford University Press, 1989).
12. Ruth McVey, *The Rise of Indonesian Communism* (Ithaca, NY: Cornell University Press, 1965), 323–346.
13. James Scott, *The Art of Not Being Governed: An Anarchist History of Upland Southeast Asia* (New Haven, CT: Yale University Press, 2009), ix.
14. Chin Peng, *My Side of History* (Singapore: Media Masters, 2003), 442–449.
15. Lien-Hang T. Nguyen, "The Vietnam Decade: The Global Shock of the War," in *The Shock of the Global: The 1970s in Perspective*, ed. Niall Ferguson,

Charles Maier, Erez Manela, and Daniel Sargent (Cambridge, MA: Belknap, 2010), 168–171.

16. See Merle Pribbenow, "Vietnam Covertly Supplied Weapons to Revolutionaries in Algeria and Latin America," *Cold War International History Project*, https://www.wilsoncenter.org/publication/vietnam-covertly-supplied-weapons-to-revolutionaries-algeria-and-latin-america.

17. Jeremy Friedman, *Shadow Cold War: The Sino-Soviet Competition for the Third World* (Chapel Hill: University of North Carolina Press, 2015), 101–148.

18. Leszek Buszynski, *Soviet Foreign Policy and Southeast Asia* (Surry Hills, Australia: Croom Helm, 1986); "Asian Defence—Communist Style," *Far Eastern Economic Review*, July 3, 1969.

19. Barbara Barnouin and Yu Changgen, *Chinese Foreign Policy during the Cultural Revolution* (New York: Kegan Paul International, 1998), 1–27; Melvin Gurtov, "The Foreign Ministry and Foreign Affairs during the Cultural Revolution," *China Quarterly* 40 (October–November 1969): 65–102; Central Intelligence Agency, "Mao's Red Guard Diplomacy: 1967," June 21, 1968, https://www.cia.gov/library/readingroom/docs/polo-21.pdf.

20. See, for instance, Liu Hong, *China and the Shaping of Indonesia, 1949–1965* (Singapore: NUS Press, 2011).

21. Central Intelligence Agency, "Intelligence Report: Peking's Support of Insurgencies in Southeast Asia," April 1973, https://www.cia.gov/library/readingroom/docs/polo-37.pdf.

22. See Shao Xiao and Xiaoming Zhang, "Reassessment of Beijing's Economic and Military Aid to Hanoi's War, 1964–75," *Cold War History* 19, no. 4 (2019): 549–567.

23. "Soviet and Chinese Aid to Vietnam," May 15, 1974, https://www.cia.gov/library/readingroom/docs/DOC_0000309268.pdf; Ilya Gaiduk, *The Soviet Union and the Vietnam War* (Chicago: Ivan R. Dee, 1996), 218.

24. See Odd Arne Westad, Chen Jian, Stein Tønnesson, Nguyen Vu Tung, and James Hershberg, eds., "77 Conversations between Chinese and Foreign Leaders on the Wars in Indochina, 1964–1977," *Cold War International History Project Working Paper Series*, no. 22 (May 1998): 132, 182–183.

25. Exceptions include Wen-Qing Ngoei, *Arc of Containment: Britain, the United States, and Anticommunism in Southeast Asia* (Ithaca, NY: Cornell University Press, 2019); Ang Cheng Guan, *Southeast Asia and the Vietnam War* (New York: Routledge, 2010).

26. See Bradley Simpson, *Economists with Guns: Authoritarian Development and U.S.-Indonesia Relations, 1960–1968* (Stanford, CA: Stanford University Press, 2008), 171–206; Geoffrey Robinson, *The Killing Season: A History of the Indonesian Massacres, 1965–66* (Princeton, NJ: Princeton University Press, 2018), 118–147.

27. Government of Indonesia, *Rentjana Pembangunan Lima Tahun 1969/70–1973/74* (Jakarta: Departemen Penerangan, 1969), 36.

28. John M. Allison, "Indonesia: The End of the Beginning?" *Asian Survey* 10, no. 2 (February 1970): 150.

29. Government of Indonesia, *Rencana Pembangunan Lima Tahun Kedua 1974/75–1978/79* (Jakarta: Departemen Penerangan, 1974), 6–15.

30. Taomo Zhou, "China and the September 30th Movement," *Indonesia* 98 (October 2014): 41.

31. Interagency Study Group Report: U.S. Military Assistance to Indonesia, February 24, 1971, NSDM-107, H-223, National Security Council Institutional ("H") Files, Richard Nixon Presidential Library.

32. See the issues of Government of Indonesia, *Nota Keuangan dan Rancangan Anggaran Pendapatan dan Belanja Negara* (Jakarta: Departemen Keuangan, 1969–1980).

33. Telegram, Jakarta to State, January 6, 1969, POL 23 INDON 1/1/67, Central Foreign Policy Files, 1967–1969, Record Group 59 (hereafter RG 59), United States National Archives (hereafter USNA).

34. Soemitro, *Soemitro: Dari Pangdam Mulawardam sampai Pangkopkamtib* (Jakarta: Pustaka Sinar Harapan, 1994), 203.

35. Harold Crouch, *The Army and Politics in Indonesia*, rev. ed. (Ithaca, NY: Cornell University Press, 1988), 240.

36. Airgram, Jakarta to State, April 8, 1971, POL-1 INDON-US 2/16/70, Subject Numeric Files, 1970–1973, RG 59, USNA; "Kesedjahteraan Pradjurit Akan Langsung Ditangani," *Kompas*, February 2, 1970; Sudomo, "Perintah Harian Kepala Staf Angkatan Laut Berkenaan Dengan Serah Terima Djabatan Kepala Staf Angkatan Laut," December 16, 1969, in *Himpunan Amanat Kepala Staf Angkatan Laut (Periode 16 Desember 1969–31 Desember 1970)* (Jakarta: Markas Besar Angkatan Laut, 1971), 3; "Susunan Personalia Baru Dilingkungan Hankam," *Kompas*, November 11, 1969; "Kilasan Hidup para Kepala Staf Angkatan," *Kompas*, October 12, 1969; Julius Pour, *Laksamana Sudomo: Mengatasi Gelombang Kehidupan* (Jakarta: Gramedia Widiasarana Indonesia, 1997), 217–221.

37. Jusuf Wanandi, *Shades of Grey: A Political Memoir of Modern Indonesia, 1965–1998* (Jakarta: Equinox Publishing, 2012), Kindle location 1563; Risalah Petunjuk-Petunjuk dan Putusan-Putusan Presiden pada Sidang Dewan Stabilisasi Politik dan Keamanan Nasional, March 12, 1974, Folio 567, Sekretariat Wakil Presiden Sri Sultan Hamengku Buwono IX 1973–1978, Arsip Nasional Republik Indonesia.

38. *Worldwide Military Expenditures and Arms Transfers, 1965–1974* (Washington, DC: Arms Control and Disarmament Agency, 1976), 42; *U.S. Overseas Loans and Grants: Obligations and Loan Authorizations, 1945–2013* (Washington, DC: United States Agency for International Development, 2015).

39. Berita Acara Persidangan Abu Bakar Ba'asyir dan Abdullah Sungkar, No.1/Pid.Subv/1982/P.N. Smh, CD 1: Ba'asyir-1—From Trial 1982–1st of Bap 2003, Indonesian Terrorism Documents, Rare and Manuscript Collections, Cornell University Rare and Manuscript Library.

40. Quoted in William Chapman, *Inside the Philippine Revolution* (New York: Norton, 1987), 101.

41. Kabataang Makabayan, Be Resolute! Unite and Oppose the Murder, Maiming and Mass Arrest of Fellow Students and Countrymen! February 2, 1970, Philippine Radical Papers, Box 8, Aklatan ng Unibersidad ng Pilipinas Diliman.

42. World Bank, *The East Asian Miracle: Economic Growth and Public Policy* (New York: Oxford University Press, 1993), 1–26.

43. See the data in International Monetary Fund, *Directions of Trade Yearbook* (Washington, DC: International Monetary Fund, 1967–1979).

44. *Hearings before the Subcommittee on United States Security Commitments Abroad of the Committee on Foreign Relations, United States Senate, Ninety-First Congress, First Session, Part 1: September 30, October 1, 2, and 3, 1969* (Washington, DC: Government Printing Office, 1969).

45. Richard Stubbs, *Rethinking Asia's Economic Miracle*, 2nd ed. (London: Palgrave, 2018), 113–114.

46. Directorate of Intelligence Weekly Summary Special Report: Singapore on the Eve of Lee Kuan Yew's Visit to the US, October 6, 1967, https://www.cia.gov/library/readingroom/docs/CIA-RDP79-00927A006000070008-3.pdf.

47. Study of Non-Embassy U.S. Government Presence in Singapore, November 1969, POL 15-1 Ambassador's Correspondence 1969, Box 3, Subject Files of the Office of Indonesia, Malaysia, and Singapore Affairs, 1965–1974, RG 59, USNA.

48. Daniel Wei Boon Chua, *US Singapore Relations, 1965–1975: Strategic Non-Alignment in the Cold War* (Singapore: NUS Press, 2017), 176–179.

49. David H. Capie, *Small Arms Production and Transfers in Southeast Asia* (Canberra: Australian National University Strategic and Defence Studies Centre, 2002), 79–80.

50. International Monetary Fund, *Balance of Payments Yearbook Volume 22: 1965–1969* (Washington, DC: International Monetary Fund, 1971), 4; International Monetary Fund, *Balance of Payments Yearbook Volume 28: 1969–1976* (Washington, DC: International Monetary Fund, 1977), 522.

51. Hafiz Mizra, *Multinationals and the Growth of the Singapore Economy* (New York: Routledge, 1986), 6.

52. For the growing interconnectedness of the national economy, see Porphant Ouyyanont, *A Regional Economic History of Thailand* (Singapore: ISEAS Yusof-Ishak Institute, 2017).

53. Boonkong Huncangsith, "Economic Impact of the U.S. Military Presence in Thailand, 1960–1972" (PhD diss., Claremont Graduate University, 1974), 46; Wantanee Suntikul, "Thai Tourism and the Legacy of the Vietnam War," in *Tourism and War*, ed. Richard Butler and Wantanee Suntikul (New York: Routledge, 2013), 98–99.

54. See Robert M. Blackburn, *Mercenaries and Lyndon Johnson's "More Flags": The Hiring of Korean, Filipino, and Thai Soldiers in the Vietnam War* (Jefferson, NC: McFarland, 1994); Richard Ruth, *In Buddha's Company: Thai Soldiers in the Vietnam War* (Honolulu: University of Hawai'i Press, 2011).

55. Economist Intelligence Unit, "The Economic Effects of the Vietnamese War in East and Southeast Asia," *QER Special*, no. 3 (November 1968): 11.

56. James K. Boyce, ed., *The Philippines: The Political Economy of Growth and Impoverishment in the Marcos Era* (Honolulu: University of Hawai'i Press, 1993), 262; International Monetary Fund, *Balance of Payments Yearbook Volume 28: 1969–1976* (Washington, DC: International Monetary Fund, 1977), 489.

57. Gerardo Sicat, *New Economic Directions in the Philippines* (Manila: National Economic and Development Authority, 1974), 150–166.

58. Letter, Crawford to Thong, December 16, 1971, Surplus Equipment in Vietnam–1987/0029239–W/E/06/B/28/d/2, Arkib Negara Malaysia (hereafter ANM).

59. Minit Mesyuarat Membeli Senjata dan Alat Kelengkapan Perang Amerika yang Berlebih dari Peperangan Vietnam dan Khmer, May 9, 1975, American Aid and Credit Sales–KP/Laut/1275 Vol. 2–W/E/04/B/06/b/2, ANM.

60. Memorandum, Scowcroft to Rockefeller, March 1976, Vice President's Trip to East Asia, March–April 1976 (3), Box 20, National Security Adviser–NSC East Asian and Pacific Affairs Staff Files, Gerald Ford Presidential Library; Cheah Kong Lee, Pembelian Kelengkapan melalui Tunai/Pinjaman, December 21, 1976, American Aid and Credit Sales–KP/Laut/1275 Vol. 2–W/E/04/B/06/b/2, ANM.

61. Seymour Martin Lipset, "Some Social Requisites of Democracy: Economic Development and Political Legitimacy," *American Political Science Review* 59, no. 1 (March 1959): 83–85.

62. See Benedict Anderson, *The Spectre of Comparisons: Nationalism, Southeast Asia, and the World* (New York: Verso, 1998), 147.

63. See Paul Hutchcroft, *Booty Capitalism: The Politics of Banking in the Philippines* (Ithaca, NY: Cornell University Press, 1998); Richard Robison, *Indonesia: The Rise of Capital* (Sydney: Allen & Unwin, 1986); Richard Robison and Vedi Hadiz, *Reorganising Power in Indonesia: The Politics of Oligarchy in the Age of Markets* (New York: RoutledgeCurzon, 2004); Jomo K. S. and Edmund Terence Gomez, *Malaysia's Political Economy: Politics, Patronage and Profits* (New York: Cambridge University Press, 1999); Christopher Tremewan, *The Political Economy of Social Control in Singapore* (London: Palgrave Macmillan, 1996).

64. Charles A. Fisher, "Southeast Asia: The Balkans of the Orient? A Study of Continuity and Change," *Geography* 47, no. 4 (November 1962): 347–367.

65. Marvin Ott, "Our Belated Victory in Vietnam," *Washington Post*, April 24, 1994.

66. Ross Terrill, "Bangkok-Manila," *Atlantic Monthly*, July 1969, 26.

67. See Alice Ba, *(Re)Negotiating East and Southeast Asia: Region, Regionalism, and the Association of Southeast Asian Nations* (Stanford, CA: Stanford University Press, 2009), 48–53.

68. Ferdinand Marcos, "New Directions for ASEAN," in *New Directions for ASEAN: Fourth Meeting of the Foreign Ministers of the Association of South East Asian Nations, Manila, 12–13 March 1971* (Manila: Department of Foreign Affairs, 1971), 7–8.

69. ASEAN Secretariat, "Zone of Peace, Freedom and Neutrality Declaration," November 27, 1971, https://www.pmo.gov.my/wp-content/uploads/2019/07/ZOPFAN.pdf.

70. "Joint Press Statement: The ASEAN Foreign Ministers Meeting to Assess the Agreement on Ending the War and Restoring Peace in Vietnam and to Consider Its Implications for Southeast Asia, Kuala Lumpur, February 15, 1973," https://asean.org/?static_post=joint-press-statement-the-asean-foreign-ministers-meeting-to

-assess-the-agreement-on-ending-the-war-and-restoring-peace-in-vietnam-and-to-consider-its-implications-for-southeast-asia-kuala-lumpur-15-f.

71. Boni Ray Siagian, ed., *Eighth Year Cycle of ASEAN: With Forewords/Messages of ASEAN Foreign Ministers* (Jakarta: ASEAN National Secretariat of Indonesia, 1976), 181; see also Dewi Fortuna Anwar, "National versus Regional Resilience: An Indonesian Perspective," in *Southeast Asian Perspectives on Security*, ed. Derek da Cunha (Singapore: Institute of Southeast Asian Studies, 2000), 88.

72. See Ngandani, "ASEAN and the Security of Southeast Asia: A Study of Regional Resilience" (PhD diss., University of Southern California, 1982).

73. Wanandi, *Shades of Grey*, Kindle locations 2879–2885.

15 From Resident to Refugee
The Exodus from Southern Vietnam in the Late 1970s

LISA TRAN

The exodus of refugees from Vietnam in the aftermath of U.S. withdrawal in 1975 has been generally filtered through the lens of the Vietnam War and Cold War geopolitics. As a result, the storyline has centered on the fall of Saigon and shifts in Vietnam's relationship with China. For the people who fled Vietnam during the latter half of the 1970s, however, the end of the war and the breakdown of Sino-Vietnamese relations served as a backdrop rather than pivotal moments in their life drama.

To be sure, the communist takeover of South Vietnam and the skirmishes between China and Vietnam contributed to the refugee flow, with the number of refugees skyrocketing to unprecedented levels beginning in 1978. Worthy of note is that the majority of people leaving Vietnam during this period were ethnic Chinese.[1] Observers of the shifting alliances of Cold War geopolitics have noted the connection between tensions in Sino-Vietnamese relations after the Vietnam War and the sudden rise in the number of ethnic Chinese leaving Vietnam beginning in 1978. Although they differ in the relative importance they attach to certain events, scholars note the role of the following in contributing to the breakdown of Sino-Vietnamese relations: conflicting interests in Cambodia, clashes along Vietnam's border with China, Vietnam's alliance with the Soviet Union, and rapprochement between China and the United States.[2] Discussions of these regional and international realignments in the post–Vietnam War era have noted the implications for ethnic Chinese living in Vietnam.

Within the context of deteriorating Sino-Vietnamese relations following the end of the Vietnam War, many observers assumed that the Vietnamese government was persecuting and expelling its Chinese residents.[3] The ethnicity of the refugees became politicized as the war of words between Beijing and Hanoi erupted into a border war in early 1979. Beijing led the charge, presenting itself as the protector of overseas Chinese, a move that undermined the authority of Southeast Asian governments over their

Chinese population. Beijing's self-appointed role as defender of overseas Chinese assumed a primordial connection rooted in a shared ethnicity. This confirmed the worst fears of Vietnam and other Southeast Asian countries with significant Chinese populations, which tended to conflate ethnicity with loyalty. During this period of intensive nation building in Southeast Asia, the ethnic identity of Chinese often impeded their political integration into the nation and made them politically suspect.

Yet, most Chinese residents in the southern half of Vietnam, in both word and action, expressed little interest in the People's Republic of China (PRC). The political reality of communist China overshadowed the nostalgic imaginings of an ancestral land. When Vietnamese communists assumed control of South Vietnam in 1975, most Chinese residents in the south moved away from, not toward, China.[4]

For Chinese residents in the southern part of Vietnam, the new communist government's domestic agenda rather than foreign policy created conditions that made remaining in Vietnam intolerable. In late March 1978, the Vietnamese government returned to policies introduced in the south in 1975 with renewed vigor: confiscation of assets, currency reform, and the movement of people from urban areas to new economic zones in the countryside.[5] Although these policies had a disproportionately negative effect on ethnic Chinese, who dominated industry and trade, the goal of the policies was economic leveling, not ethnic persecution, as Kathleen Gough and Barry Wain pointed out.[6] The Vietnamese government went after those who owned commercial and industrial assets; ethnic Chinese were targeted because they owned most of those assets.

Yet, much of the scholarship misses this important distinction and tends to interpret the *implications* of economic policies on ethnic Chinese as evidence of the Vietnamese government's *intent* to persecute the Chinese as an ethnic group. Even those scholars who acknowledge that distinction tend to dismiss its relevance. For example, Michael Godley cited statements from Vietnamese government representatives who refuted accusations that the government's policies constituted "an anti-Chinese campaign" by emphasizing the role of "class struggle" in ending "capitalist trade" and "exploitation." In response, Godley remarked, "Be that as it may, Cholon was a Chinese city and any activity easily took on racial overtones."[7] That Godley interpreted "racial overtones" as evidence of ethnic persecution is suggested by his statement that "there can be no question that Chinese residing in Vietnam today suffer persecution."[8] More than a quarter of a century later, Sucheng Chan wrote in a similar vein, "Between 1978 and 1989, several developments affected the outflow of refuge-seekers from Vietnam: that country's persecution of its ethnic Chinese residents."⁹ Yet, in the section titled "Punitive Measures against the Ethnic Chinese," Chan's discussion of these punitive measures—relocation to new economic zones, another round of currency exchange, crackdown on smuggling along the northern border with China—does not show how they were ethnically motivated.¹⁰ As Chan remarked earlier in a discussion of the new economic zones, "middle-class people—both ethnic Chinese and Vietnamese—who feared they might be penalized because of their class backgrounds began to escape by sea."¹¹ Class antagonism, rather than ethnic cleansing, motivated the Vietnamese government's policies.

In southern Vietnam, then, ethnicity made Chinese residents economic, not political, targets. Interviews and narratives of Chinese residents who left southern Vietnam as refugees in the late 1970s reveal that Chinese refugees were troubled by the economic rather than political implications of communist control and linked ethnicity to economic discrimination rather than political persecution. The perspectives of ethnic Chinese refugees offer a counterweight to Cold War narratives that tend to conflate the political and economic aspects of communism, or if they separate them, to privilege politics over economics. The refugee narratives from which this chapter draws offer alternative understandings of communism that are rooted in the unique histories and experiences of ethnic Chinese who had earlier migrated from China to Vietnam and then fled Vietnam in the late 1970s.

Ethnic Chinese in South Vietnam

Chinese migration to Vietnam dates back centuries. Among the refugees I interviewed, a few traced their roots in Vietnam back several generations. The majority, however, were descendants of the wave that left southeastern China and settled in Vietnam in the 1930s and 1940s, a period when China was being torn asunder by foreign invasion and civil war. All my interviewees were born in Vietnam, with the oldest among them born in the 1940s. They lived in Saigon and Cholon, the Chinatown district, and speak various local dialects, most notably Teochiu and Cantonese. Most are proficient in Mandarin and Vietnamese. All left Vietnam by boat in the late 1970s and spent time in refugee camps in Thailand, Malaysia, Indonesia, and Hong Kong before being resettled in the United

States, Canada, Australia, and New Zealand. At the request of my interviewees, I have not disclosed details that may reveal their identities.

As a result of the political division of Vietnam in 1954, Chinese residing in the northern and southern halves of the country had different experiences.[12] As armed conflict resumed, their links to China, relationship to the Vietnamese government and community, and view of the war were shaped by their location. This chapter focuses on ethnic Chinese in the south, and more narrowly, those residing in Saigon and Cholon, which together had the greatest concentration of Chinese in Vietnam.

Ties to China

For Chinese residents in South Vietnam, distance, time, and ideology weakened connections to mainland China. In the late 1970s, China represented not a safe haven to return to but the political embodiment of the communism from which they now hoped to escape. China's inward orientation throughout the 1950s and 1960s reduced the migrant flow between China and South Vietnam, and news from China during these tumultuous decades usually came from people fleeing China. Not surprisingly, none of my interviewees expressed a desire to find safe haven in China.

Among my interviewees were descendants of Chinese who emigrated from Shantou in the southeastern province of Guangdong to Saigon in the 1930s and 1940s. In one family, an oft-told story features the Chinese communists as the antagonists. The matriarch of the family had remained in Shantou, where the family still owned land. As one of her grandsons, who was born in Saigon, related, "The communists said my grandmother has land to rent, so she is guilty. They locked her up in a barn. They told kids to throw rocks at her. As a result, she died."[13] This story, passed down through the generations, shaped this family's reaction to the political reunification of Vietnam under communist rule. Stories like these filled Chinese immigrants and their descendants with a sense of foreboding as they watched events unfolding in Vietnam after 1975.

Similarly, an account from a Chinese woman born in Vietnam demonstrates how family stories of life in China during the political ascendancy of the Chinese Communist Party in the 1940s colored her views of the communists in Vietnam. Her father had left southeastern China in the 1940s "when he heard rumors of people being captured."[14] Having grown up hearing stories of how her relatives and their acquaintances fled China as the country came under the control of the Chinese Communist Party, she came to associate communism with persecution and loss. Little wonder, then, that when the communists assumed control of southern Vietnam, the woman feared a repeat of what the previous generation had experienced in China before they left for Vietnam. When asked what communism meant to her, she responded, "It was what my father had escaped from in China."[15]

Another branch of the migrants who left Shantou settled in Saigon in 1936. As a descendant recounted, his parents left Shantou and moved to Saigon shortly after their marriage. With financial backing from his grandfather, a merchant turned landowner in Shantou, his father opened a grocery store in Saigon. The business became so successful that he opened a second store a decade later. Everything changed after the communists assumed control of the south. As he explained, "Then [after 1975] the communists took everything. They came to our stores and took everything. We had nothing to sell. They came to our house. They lived with us. They were there to monitor us."[16] In recounting his family history, the interviewee drew parallels between what the communists were doing in Vietnam after 1975 to what the communists in China had done earlier. As he reflected, "My grandfather worked hard to buy land [in China]. Then the communists came and took it all away. My father worked hard to build his grocery business [in Vietnam]. Then the communists came and took it all away."[17] From the perspective of this man, the communists in Vietnam seemed no different from the ones in China. Just as his parents had fled communism in China, he prepared his family to escape it when it reached southern Vietnam. For families who had emigrated from China in the years before the Chinese Communist Party assumed control, the Vietnamese government's rhetoric of socialist transformation foreshadowed a future they had already sought to escape in the past.

Relationship to Vietnam

The label "Hoa" to refer to ethnic Chinese residents in Vietnam reflects both the long history of Chinese settlement in Vietnam and the enduring identity of the Chinese as a distinctive ethnic group. Some Chinese residents rarely left Cholon, generally regarded as Vietnam's largest Chinatown. Language also contributed to a sense of Chinese identity. For my interviewees, a local Chinese dialect that reflected their ancestral connection to a village in China was their first language. Cantonese operated as the language for social exchange in the wider Chinese community, and Mandarin was taught in Chinese language schools. Most learned Vietnamese by interacting with the larger community. Those with formal schooling recalled that Vietnamese was the language of instruction in secondary school; for the most part, primary education was taught in Chinese.

Although Chinese residents in Vietnam preserved their cultural ties to China, many severed their political ties to the mainland. After the establishment of the PRC in 1949, most Chinese in Vietnam associated themselves with Taiwan, now headed by the Kuomintang (KMT), the political party that had previously controlled the mainland. The KMT shaped the political content of the curriculum in Chinese language schools in South Vietnam, supplying instructional materials and teaching resources produced by its Overseas Chinese Affairs Committee in Taipei.[18]

In the mid-1950s, the South Vietnamese government sought to strengthen its political hold over its Chinese residents. As a result of directives issued in 1955 and 1956, most ethnic Chinese in the south became Vietnamese citizens. One decree declared all Chinese born in Vietnam to be Vietnamese citizens. Another barred noncitizens from certain industries. Since Chinese residents dominated most of these industries, many of them became naturalized citizens in order to keep their businesses. As the son of an owner of a grocery store remarked, "We had no choice. If we didn't become Vietnamese citizens, we would lose our store."[19] An estimated half a million Chinese residents in the south naturalized between 1955 and 1958.[20] Some who wished to remain Chinese nationals and retain their businesses circumvented the law by transferring ownership to a Vietnamese partner.[21]

After assuming control of the south in 1975, the Vietnamese communists reneged on their promise, made in the 1950s, to allow Chinese residents in the south to choose the country of their citizenship.[22] In 1976, the Vietnamese government declared that citizenship would be based on status before 1975, thereby upholding the South Vietnamese government's policy toward Chinese residents.[23] Hence, the majority of ethnic Chinese in southern Vietnam were categorized as Vietnamese citizens and not Chinese nationals.

Views of the War

For my interviewees, residence in Saigon and Cholon insulated them from the fighting. When asked to describe life in the 1960s, the oldest among my interviewees, who would have been in their twenties at the time, responded with some variation of "everything was normal." They recalled hearing the sound of distant gunfire and seeing American soldiers around, but this information only came forth in response to specific questions. None of my interviewees had any direct experience of the war. One woman stated that she did not even know what the war was about and had no idea about the role of the communists in the war. Her only experience with the war was limited to knowing that her less-well-off friends and classmates had to go to the battlefield because they could not afford to pay for alternative forms of military service. Laughing at what she saw as her naïveté at the time, she recalled her initial enthusiasm when the communists entered Saigon:

> Because before we don't know what's VC [Vietcong], it doesn't affect us. I saw my friends, my schoolmates, they don't have money, so they have to go to the military, so when they said no more war happened, 1975, 4/30, April 30, OK, they come. I'm so happy, because no more, my friends don't need to go to the war, so I go outside, hey, welcome, you guys come, the soldiers from the north side, because I don't know what's the meaning of the war, why they come, we don't know at all at that time. I just know that no more war happened.[24]

Similarly, another woman remembered feeling joyful when she heard news that the war had ended. Like the woman above, she associated the war with the draft and expressed relief that the end of the war meant that men would no longer be drafted for military service. As she reflected, "The war was occurring in the countryside but had not arrived at Saigon. We heard the United States will stop fighting and that north and south will stay as it is. On hearing the end of the war, everyone was happy thinking there was peace. At the time my husband was about to be drafted. So everyone was happy for the signing. But after the departure of the American soldiers, North Vietnam came in."[25] The reference to North Vietnam signaled the transfer of South Vietnam to communist control, a turn of events that would have monumental consequences. For this woman and many other residents of South Vietnam, the moment when the war became real was, ironically, when it came to an end.

Although my interviewees referred to April 30, 1975, as "liberation," they used the communist term for that day to identify a historical event and not to celebrate the emancipatory effects of the communists' military victory. As one woman described that day, "Nineteen seventy-five, liberation, the northern communists win the war. Americans . . . they go away. And north side, the VC, they come to south side. . . . They control all."[26] The juxtaposition of "liberation" and "control" draws out the contrast between communist propaganda and the economic reality that would soon unfold. As the woman continued, "After 1975, a few days later, everything changed. They start to change money. No matter how much money you have, they give you $200. All your money is of no value."[27] What mattered to this woman, who came from a well-to-do family and owned a factory manufacturing plastic goods, was not the change in government but the change in currency that wiped out her wealth. Another ethnic Chinese refugee from Vietnam echoed the same sentiment: "The Communists, they changed the dollar bill, and no business, no salary, so every people, the living, is very hard to keep living."[28] An account from another Vietnam-born ethnic Chinese follows a similar storyline. This woman's family migrated in 1941 "because China became Communist, then my parents left China, came to Vietnam."[29] They settled in Cholon, where her father opened a textile business. Echoing the same sense of loss as those mentioned above, she explained, "April 30, 1975, the country taken by communists. Then they take all my business. In Saigon, there was no war, just in the far away. But then the Communists took all my business, and took my saving account, took all the money, took all the goods, many, many, and let our family go outside the house, and took our house."[30] As the new government rolled out its policies, many residents in the south began to plan their escape.

The Decision to Flee

Many residents in southern Vietnam were already thinking of fleeing before the communists consolidated their control over the south. In the panic sparked by the U.S. withdrawal, some seized the chance to be evacuated with American personnel. Those associated with the Americans or the South Vietnamese government were included in evacuation plans. About 130,000 Vietnamese were airlifted out of Saigon and resettled in the United States.[31]

Some of those eligible to be evacuated decided to remain. A Chinese policeman rushing to prepare his wife, son, and daughter to leave was pressured to abandon his plan by other family members. As he recounts, "My mother was against it. She threatened to kill herself if I left."[32] His wife related that her elder sister warned that their two-year-old daughter might not survive the journey.[33] Faced with family pressure, the man decided to remain in Vietnam for the time being. Another man had the opportunity to leave at the time of the U.S. withdrawal but ultimately decided to stay because he could not take his wife, two daughters, and infant son with him.[34] Having missed the window of opportunity opened up by the U.S. evacuation, these two men and others hoping to escape looked for alternative ways to leave the country.

For others, however, the decision to leave came after it became clear what living under communism meant. For one Chinese woman who adopted a wait-and-see attitude after the political unification of Vietnam, life under communism became increasingly intolerable. In 1978, she made plans to escape, explaining that "because of the communists, that's why I have to go. I have to go because I cannot live under communism anymore."[35] A number of interviewees reported having to share their living quarters with communists, making them feel as if they were under surveillance. One woman surmised that "it was a way for them to keep an eye on us."[36] Some said they felt pressured to go to the new economic zones in the countryside. As one woman speculated, "That way, they got your entire house."[37] Business owners complained about having their shops and factories closed, and their inventories confiscated. The owner of an electrical shop said, "One to two months after liberation, they [the communists] asked businesses to provide an accounting of stock to the government. The stock was confiscated for their [the government's] own use, but [the government] did not pay for these."[38]

Robbed of their livelihood and dependent on food rations, many searched for ways to support themselves. An entrepreneurial Chinese woman turned to brokering deals for those who wanted to exchange jewelry for U.S. currency. She had an epiphany after she was caught by local officials. "After they catch me, they let me go. That time, I realized what is communism. . . . They take your business. No more freedom. You have to go."[39] The woman presented the choices facing her in dire terms: "I decided to escape. Even if I die in the sea, I still have to go. Because they are communist. I start to know. They took all my money. They catch me. So everything is bad for my family if I have to stay in Vietnam. I don't have interest in Vietnam anymore. I have to go out [of the country]. . . . If I don't escape, I would die. No future. No business. Nothing."[40] A recurring theme in refugee narratives was economic despair caused by the loss of livelihood. Facing economic uncertainty exacerbated by shifting government policies and without the ability to shape their future in Vietnam, many sought to escape.

Ethnicity and Politics

Explanations for the jump in refugee numbers beginning in the spring of 1978 that assume the ethnic persecution of Chinese residents in Vietnam continue to be influential despite the lack of empirical evidence. The origins of that view can be traced to Beijing's allegations during its battle of words with Hanoi in the summer of 1978. That the geopolitical clash between Beijing and Hanoi centered on ethnic Chinese in Vietnam and that explanations of ethnic persecution were so readily accepted by the United States and its allies show how ethnicity came to be politicized as geopolitical alliances shifted after the Vietnam War.

Despite its moral rhetoric, Beijing's allegations of ethnic persecution of Chinese nationals in Vietnam were economically motivated. As the Chinese Communist Party loosened government control of the economy in the late 1970s, it used ethnicity as a political tool to attract investment from overseas Chinese. Within this context, Chinese ethnicity was conflated with Chinese nationalism. Yet, narratives of Chinese residents in the south who left Vietnam by boat reflect no identification with the Chinese nation. To them, the PRC represented communism, an ideology, system, and way of life from which they now sought to escape.

With few exceptions, however, the assumption that Chinese residents in Vietnam were persecuted because of their ethnicity has gone unchallenged and is identified, whether implicitly or explicitly, as the reason for the mass movement of ethnic Chinese from Vietnam beginning in 1978.[41] Yet, the theme of ethnic persecution cannot explain some of the inconsistencies that emerge in accounts of the movement of Chinese residents from Vietnam. On the one hand, characterizing this exodus as an "expulsion" gives the Vietnamese government an active and coercive role in pushing Chinese *out* of the country. On the other hand, the Vietnamese government was accused of failing to patrol its borders to keep people *in* the country, which would indicate that Chinese residents were leaving the country illegally rather than being expelled.

Moreover, the Vietnamese government was trying to assimilate Chinese residents with its naturalization campaign, which further weakens the expulsion theory. Indeed, if Vietnam intended to purge itself of its Chinese population, it would not have accepted the predominantly ethnic Chinese refugees fleeing Pol Pot's Cambodia.

Finally, the presence of ethnic Vietnamese among the boat people who confessed to using false documents identifying them as ethnic Chinese to gain passage on boats suggests that people regardless of ethnicity wanted to get out of Vietnam.[42] Reports that ethnic Vietnamese had to pay more than ethnic Chinese to get out of the country weakens the interpretation of the refugee movement as a forced expulsion.[43] The Vietnamese government may have wanted to rid itself of its Chinese residents, but people, both Chinese and non-Chinese, also wanted to leave Vietnam. Considered in this light, the different fees charged based on ethnicity had a more detrimental effect on those of Vietnamese ancestry.

This is not to say that people were not persecuted or that they did not feel persecuted in Vietnam. The point is that Chinese ethnicity was not the basis for state-sanctioned, systemic persecution as widely assumed. What was state sanctioned and systemic was the imprisonment of those affiliated with the former South Vietnamese government. An ethnic Chinese man who had served as a police officer in South Vietnam was sentenced to three months in a reeducation camp. As he explained, "Officers with two stripes or more were sent away for longer periods."[44] An ethnic Vietnamese man who had been an official in the South Vietnamese government and an officer in the South Vietnamese army spent almost six years in reeducation camps.[45] These men were sent to reeducation camps because of their affiliation with the South Vietnamese government; ethnic Chinese were not specifically targeted, and ethnic Vietnamese were not exempt.[46]

If ethnicity was not a causal factor, then how else might we understand the role of ethnicity in shaping the refugee movements out of Vietnam in the late 1970s? The assumption of a shared ethnic identity among Chinese communities in Vietnam has glossed over the disparate histories and experiences of Chinese residents in North and South Vietnam before they were politically unified. Han Xiaorong's work on ethnic Chinese in North Vietnam highlights the importance of paying attention to those differences. This chapter complements Han's studies by focusing on Chinese residents in South Vietnam and argues that the refugee movements southward were motivated by a different set of causes than the northward movement.

In southern Vietnam, Chinese ethnicity was associated with the capitalist system rather than the Chinese nation. Hanoi's defense that its policies targeted those with property is substantiated by refugee accounts that identify the loss of property as a motivating factor to leave Vietnam. Yet, Hanoi's view of its Chinese residents as a privileged class of exploiters was eclipsed by views of the ethnic Chinese as a persecuted minority. Rather than emphasize one or the other, perhaps the key is to explore the intersection of class and ethnicity and analyze its implications for governments and people alike.

Notes

1. The term "ethnic Chinese" is used to refer to people who trace their ancestry to China, which includes groups beyond the Han majority conventionally associated with Chinese ethnicity.

2. Pao-Min Chang, "Some Reflections on the Sino-Vietnamese Conflict over Kampuchea," *International Affairs* 59 (Summer 1983): 381–389; André Gunder Frank, "Kampuchea, Vietnam, China: Observations and Reflections," *Contemporary Marxism* 12–13 (Spring 1986): 107–119; Nicholas Khoo, "Revisiting the Termination of the Sino-Vietnamese Alliance, 1975–1979," *European Journal of East Asian Studies* 9, no. 2 (2010): 321–361; Kosal Path, "China's Economic Sanctions against Vietnam, 1975–1978," *China Quarterly* 212 (December 2012): 1040–1058.

3. See, for example, Charles Benoit, "Vietnam's 'Boat People,'" in *The Third Indochina Conflict*, ed. David W. P. Elliott (Boulder, CO: Westview, 1981), 139–162; C. Y. Chang, "Overseas Chinese in China's Policy," *China Quarterly* 82 (June 1980): 281–303; Pao-Min Chang, "Peking, Hanoi, and the Ethnic Chinese of Vietnam," *Asian Affairs* 9 (March–April 1982): 195–207; Hugh Deane, "The Chinese Flight from Vietnam," *Contemporary Marxism* 12–13 (Spring 1986): 75–80; W. E. Willmott, "The Chinese in Indochina," in *Southeast Asian Exodus: From Tradition to Resettlement: Understanding Refugees from Laos, Kampuchea and Vietnam in Canada*, ed. Elliot L. Tepper (Ottawa: Canadian Asian Studies Association, 1980), 69–80.

4. Some Chinese residents in the south did migrate north to cross the border into China, but refugee testimonials indicate that many of them regarded China as a country of first asylum rather than final resettlement. Even among those from the north who crossed the border into China, there were some who sought to relocate elsewhere. Many made their way to Hong Kong, where they had to convince officials they had come directly from Vietnam rather than China. Until 1989, boat people from Vietnam were treated as prima facie refugees while boat people from China were repatriated. See Sucheng Chan, ed., *Stories of War, Revolution, Flight, and New Beginnings* (Philadelphia: Temple University Press, 2006), 181–189; Xiaorong Han, "Spoiled Guests or Dedicated Patriots? The Chinese in North Vietnam, 1954–1978," *International Journal of Asian Studies* 6, no. 1 (2009): 29–34.

5. Ramses Amer, "Vietnam's Policies and the Ethnic Chinese since 1975," *Sojourn* 11, no. 1 (1996): 79–81.

6. Kathleen Gough, "The Hoa in Vietnam," *Contemporary Marxism* 12–13 (Spring 1986): 86; Barry Wain, *The Refused: The Agony of the Indochina Refugees* (New York: Simon & Schuster, 1981), 78.

7. Michael Godley, "A Summer Cruise to Nowhere: China and the Vietnamese Chinese in Perspective," *Australian Journal of Chinese Affairs* 4 (July 1980): 38.

8. Godley, "A Summer Cruise," 37. As evidence, Godley points to what he describes as "circumstantial evidence": the Vietnamese government's relocation of large numbers of ethnic Chinese and the exodus across the border to China and out to sea (Godley, "A Summer Cruise," 38). Relocation in and of itself, however, is not evidence of persecution; otherwise, the U.S. government's internment of its residents of Japanese ancestry during World War II, which the Vietnamese govern-

ment compared its actions to, should be similarly judged (Benoit, "Vietnam's 'Boat People,'" 139). With regard to the exodus by land and sea, Godley's suspicion that it occurred with "the concurrence and, perhaps, 'assistance' of the entire security apparatus" was widely acknowledged by the international community and supported by refugee testimonials. See, for example, Australia, *Report from the Senate Standing Committee on Foreign Affairs and Defence on Indochinese Refugee Resettlement—Australia's Involvement* (Canberra: Australian Government Publishing Service, 1982); Chan, *Stories of War*, 161; Eleanor Herz Swent, *Asian Refugees in America: Narratives of Escape and Adaptation* (Jefferson, NC: McFarland, 2011); Wain, *The Refused*. Yet, these testimonials give no indication that Chinese felt they had been persecuted or expelled from Vietnam because of their ethnicity.

9. Chan, *Stories of War*, 71.

10. Chan, *Stories of War*, 71.

11. Chan, *Stories of War*, 67. More than two decades earlier, the Australian journalist Barry Wain had also attributed the stream of boat people to the Vietnamese government's recent economic policies, noting that Chinese residents "were happy to leave Vietnam in much the same way as were middle-class ethnic Vietnamese" (Wain, *The Refused*, 78).

12. Han, "Spoiled Guests"; Lewis M. Stern, "The Overseas Chinese in Vietnam, 1920–75: Demography, Social Structure, and Economic Power," *Humboldt Journal of Social Relations* 12 (Spring/Summer 1985): 1–30.

13. Interview conducted by author. C01-77-10. Personal collection.

14. Interview conducted by author. D01-77-01. Personal collection.

15. Interview conducted by author. D01-77-01. Personal collection.

16. Interview conducted by author. A03-78-01. Personal collection.

17. Interview conducted by author. A03-78-01. Personal collection.

18. E. S. Ungar, "The Struggle over the Chinese Community in Vietnam, 1946–1986," *Pacific Affairs* 60 (Winter 1988): 605.

19. Interview conducted by author. A02-78-02. Personal collection.

20. Ungar, "The Struggle," 606. It is difficult to determine what percentage this would have been of the Chinese population in the south. Figures for the Chinese population in Vietnam vary widely, depending on the criteria used for who gets included. Official records generally used nationality rather than ethnicity to calculate the Chinese population, so they only reflect the number of Chinese nationals (Ungar, "The Struggle," 606n29). *Le annuaire statistique* counted 703,120 Chinese in Vietnam in 1955. Figures from the 1957 census pegged the number of Chinese residents in Saigon and Cholon at 130,000. According to the May 1961 edition of the *Annual Statistical Bulletin* published by the U.S. Operation Mission to Vietnam (later renamed the U.S. Aid to International Development for the Republic of Vietnam's Joint Economic Affairs Office), 8,971 Chinese nationals lived in Saigon as of 1960. This suggests that the vast majority of ethnic Chinese who congregated around the Saigon-Cholon district were Vietnamese citizens. Estimates for all of South Vietnam are less reliable. An undocumented source gave estimates of 1,357,000 and 1,500,000 Chinese in South Vietnam in 1952, with 500,000 of that number concentrated in Cholon. Another undocumented source estimated

500,000–800,000 Chinese in South Vietnam in 1958 (Stern, "The Overseas Chinese," 10). As with the figures for Saigon-Cholon, the sharp drop in numbers suggests that Chinese who acquired Vietnamese citizenship by birth or naturalization were being counted as Vietnamese. To be sure, some Chinese left Vietnam but not in great enough numbers to account for the dramatic dip. Of the 50,000 Chinese who applied for permission to return to Taiwan in 1957, only 3,000 actually left (Stern, "The Overseas Chinese," 11). Given the socialist experiments and campaigns to stifle political dissent being carried out by the communist leadership in China throughout the 1950s, it is not likely that many ethnic Chinese in South Vietnam would have sought to return to China.

21. Stern, "The Overseas Chinese," 11–12.
22. Han, "Spoiled Guests," 22.
23. Amer, "Vietnam's Policies," 81.
24. Interview conducted by author. E50-78-10. Personal collection.
25. Interview conducted by author. D01-77-05. Personal collection.
26. Interview conducted by author. E50-78-01. Personal collection.
27. Interview conducted by author. E50-78-01. Personal collection.
28. Swent, *Asian Refugees*, 126–127.
29. Swent, *Asian Refugees*, 187.
30. Swent, *Asian Refugees*, 189.
31. For a discussion of the refugee movement during this first phase, see Yen Le Espiritu, *Body Counts: The Vietnam War and Militarized Refugees* (Berkeley: University of California Press, 2014).
32. Interview conducted by author. A01-78-30. Personal collection.
33. Interview conducted by author. A10-78-10. Personal collection.
34. Interview conducted by author. D10-77-01. Personal collection.
35. Interview conducted by author. E51-78-01. Personal collection.
36. Interview conducted by author. A10-78-01. Personal collection.
37. Interview conducted by author. A12-78-01. Personal collection.
38. Interview conducted by author. D05-77-01. Personal collection.
39. Interview conducted by author. E55-78-01. Personal collection.
40. Interview conducted by author. E55-78-01. Personal collection.
41. See, for example, Laura Madokoro, *Elusive Refuge: Chinese Migrants in the Cold War* (Cambridge, MA: Harvard University Press, 2016), 190.
42. See, for example, Madokoro, *Elusive Refuge*, 198; Willmott, "The Chinese in Indochina," 112.
43. "Unwanted Citizens," *Canberra Times*, January 7, 1979.
44. Interview conducted by author. A07-78-07. Personal collection.
45. Joanna C. Scott, *Indochina's Refugees: Oral Histories from Laos, Cambodia and Vietnam* (Jefferson, NC: McFarland, 1989), 36.
46. For additional accounts of refugees who had been sent to reeducation camps, see Chan, *Stories of War*, 173; Scott, *Indochina's Refugees*, 71–105.

16 Vietnamese Refugee Status, Habeas Corpus, and Hong Kong, 1988–1997

JANA K. LIPMAN

In July 1989, hundreds of Vietnamese who had fled their country by boat found themselves behind barbed wire in Hong Kong. Unlike thousands of Vietnamese before them, they were not granted automatic refugee status and instead faced "individual asylum screenings." Hong Kong immigration officials would determine on a case-by-case basis whether they were "refugees" fleeing political persecution or not. If they convinced the officer, they would be "screened in" and resettled in the United States, Australia, Canada, or Western Europe. If the officer believed they fled for economic reasons, they would be "screened out," held in a Hong Kong detention center on appeal and, for most, ultimately repatriated back to Vietnam. The stakes were high.

The recent arrivals were understandably anxious. One asked, "How can the United Nations let us be forced back? What about Human Rights?" Another individual challenged a United Nations High Commissioner for Refugees (UNHCR) official, "Have you ever lived under a communist regime? They are liars, you cannot trust them." His or her final sentence brought home an even grimmer precedent: "Look at the T.A.M. [Tiananmen Square Massacre]."[1] In Hong Kong, these words held particular weight.

Between 1988 and 1997, the Vietnamese who sought asylum in Hong Kong became an outsized population, and their detention triggered significant controversy and human rights activism.[2] After a relative lull in the mid-1980s, more than 52,000 Vietnamese entered Hong Kong between 1988 and 1989.[3] Because the Hong Kong government detained incoming Vietnamese in closed camps, often indefinitely, their fates became intertwined with Hong Kong's political status, habeas corpus, and the rule of law after 1997.

When analyzing the relationship between the U.S. war in Vietnam and the Pacific, I argue that the resulting regional refugee crisis persisted in

Southeast Asia and Hong Kong for more than a generation. The unprecedented numbers of Vietnamese entering Malaysia, Thailand, Indonesia, the Philippines, China, and Hong Kong after 1975 created stresses and opportunities for regional players, and host sites first improvised and then negotiated how best to assert their own authority and priorities in the face of growing numbers of Vietnamese on their shores. Vietnamese landed in colonies like Guam and Hong Kong, countries like Japan and the Philippines with clear ties to the United States, and others like Indonesia and Malaysia with their own colonial histories and agendas. Throughout it all, the specific politics of the sites that hosted Vietnamese camps mattered.[4]

In this chapter, I will focus on Hong Kong in the mid-1990s and legal debates over habeas corpus. This chapter will briefly introduce the key challenges facing Hong Kong's Vietnamese policy in the 1970s and 1980s and explain how anxieties about the Vietnamese intersected with anxieties about Hong Kong's shift to Chinese sovereignty. The United Kingdom, Hong Kong, and Chinese governments all hoped to shutter the camps and repatriate all the "screened out" Vietnamese before 1997; however, the prominence of long-term detention in Hong Kong alongside Vietnamese individuals' ability to gain legal counsel created a paradox for Hong Kong politicians. How long could the Hong Kong government hold Vietnamese? If Vietnamese could be held indefinitely in closed camps, could Hong Kong Chinese lose their civil liberties? Would habeas corpus, a bedrock British legal principle, still hold after 1997? These questions about human rights and habeas corpus were not abstract but played out through the lives and legal cases of Vietnamese in Hong Kong.

Refugees to Asylum Seekers:
Vietnamese in Hong Kong, 1980–1988

Between 1975 and 1988, approximately 100,000 Vietnamese entered Hong Kong, and the UNHCR ensured that all received refugee status and resettlement in a third country. Initially, Hong Kong had hosted "open camps," which offered relatively liberal conditions and the ability to work in Hong Kong's active economy. The UNHCR and Western media outlets lauded Hong Kong's generosity (particularly compared to Thailand and Malaysia), and because many of the incoming Vietnamese spoke Cantonese, they more easily found jobs during their short stays before being resettled. This changed in 1982, when the Hong Kong government shifted to a policy of "closed camps." The goal was deterrence. It did not want Vietnamese entering Hong Kong indefinitely. Although the incoming numbers stabilized in the 1980s, the United States, Australia, Canada, and the United Kingdom became more restrictive, resettling only a minority of those in the camps. The result was a growing "long stayer" population in Hong Kong. Throughout the 1980s, Hong Kong's patience wore thin, especially, as Vietnamese lingered in camps without resettlement placements for years on end.[5]

This time period coincided with the 1984 Sino-British Joint Declaration.[6] Prime Minister Margaret Thatcher and Chinese officials agreed that Great Britain's lease on Hong Kong, Kowloon, and the New Territories would cease in 1997. Senior Chinese officials wanted the camps closed and the Vietnamese gone before July 1, 1997. Lu Ping, a senior Chinese official said as much on his visit to Hong Kong in 1988. He stressed that the "boat people" could "never become permanent inhabitants" after 1997.[7] This point of view found a friendly audience in Hong Kong. Hong Kong had been accepting all incoming Vietnamese as "refugees," but it also had a firm policy of returning unauthorized Chinese border crossers back to China as "illegal immigrants." For the majority of Hong Kong's Chinese population, this practice seemed unfair and paradoxical. Although one should never underestimate general xenophobia and hostility to migrant populations, Hong Kong's anger at the incoming Vietnamese focused on the inequities between Chinese and Vietnamese migrants.

Hong Kong politicians decided to take action. Despite initial resistance within the British government, Hong Kong unilaterally denied Vietnamese de facto refugee status after June 15, 1988 and instead instituted a "screening" process. It then insisted that Vietnamese who did not meet its threshold of being "refugees" would be repatriated back to Vietnam. There would no longer be a presumption of refugee status and resettlement in the West. The UNHCR was very hesitant about Hong Kong's new and controversial directive, but it eventually embraced the practice of individual asylum determination.

The UNHCR organized a conference in Geneva for June 1989 to nail down the Comprehensive Plan of Action (CPA), which was a joint agreement governing Hong Kong, Southeast Asian first asylum countries, resettlement countries, donor countries, and Vietnam. The CPA would put the UNHCR's imprimatur on the new logic: Vietnamese arriving in first asylum countries (including Hong Kong) would no longer be de facto refugees. Instead, they would face individual screening by immigration authorities. Those deemed "refugees" would be resettled in third countries. Those deemed not to be refugees would be repatriated to Vietnam.[8]

Even though most Hong Kong people backed this more restrictive policy, in some instances, it made Hong Kong residents uneasy. If Hong Kong was willing to carry out an aggressive repatriation campaign, the precedent might have ramifications for Hong Kong people who found themselves at odds with China's communist government. As one writer for the *South China Morning Post* explained, "If the people of Hong Kong are seen to support such inhumane treatment for the refugees as forced repatriation, then they should not expect anything better for themselves with concern of 1997 under Chinese communist sovereignty and the loss of their British nationality."[9] This author's words called into question the paradox of Hong Kong shutting its shores to refugees, just when its residents might be seeking escape.

Several Hong Kong students made similar parallels between the British negotiations with China and the British government's push for Vietnamese repatriation. "Hong Kong people have had their future and their nationality negotiated away for them by Britain." They believed this was similar to Britain's decision to "negotiate the lives and future of the Vietnamese refugees in their care." In both instances, Hong Kong Chinese and Vietnamese had little control over their futures and were resigned to lives under communist governments.[10] These students ultimately believed Hong Kong and the United Kingdom should do more for the Vietnamese. However, this was a minority opinion—far more people in Hong Kong favored harsher policies and repatriation.[11]

The UNHCR could not have anticipated that the June 1989 Geneva conference on the CPA would occur just two weeks after the Chinese crackdown on democracy activists and the Tiananmen Square massacre on June 4, 1989. There was clearly no causative relationship between the two, and I found few documents in the UNHCR archives that acknowledged the chaos and controversy over the Chinese crackdown. However, the timing of the two events made the urgency about refugee status and human rights far more acute. A UNHCR desk officer wrote to Geneva that Hong Kong's animosity against the Vietnamese was being exacerbated by the "dramatic rise in feelings of domestic insecurity in the territory [Hong Kong] resulting from June 4 events [Tiananmen Square massacre] and subsequent developments in China."[12] He believed the Vietnamese were a veritable "scapegoat" for local anxieties that emanated from Hong Kong's uncertain future and Chinese authoritarianism demonstrated through the crackdown.

Between 1988 and 1997, Hong Kong held thousands of Vietnamese in closed camps run by the Hong Kong Correctional Services Department, which were increasingly characterized by their prison-like conditions. After numerous starts and stops, Hong Kong established a robust, and often forcible, repatriation program, and in response, Vietnamese organized militant protests and fierce legal campaigns. In 1995, there were still approximately 10,000 Vietnamese in Hong Kong. With the 1997 handover approaching, the Vietnamese in camps raised key questions about human rights, detention, and the rule of law in Hong Kong.

Habeas Corpus: "A Victory for People in Hong Kong as Much as the People Detained"

With the accelerated repatriations, thousands of Vietnamese continued to argue that they met the criteria to receive refugee status, and they refused the offer of "voluntary" repatriation. With desperate clients, many who seemed to have little chance of release, Hong Kong–based human rights lawyers began filing habeas corpus petitions. These activist lawyers argued that Hong Kong was holding individuals in closed camps indefinitely, with no chance of repatriation or release, and that this violated the principle of habeas corpus. This was a powerful argument and one that tapped into Hong Kong's British colonial history. As a Crown colony, England's common law traditions and its statutes, which included the Habeas Corpus Acts of 1679 and 1816, governed Hong Kong. Habeas corpus protected individuals from indefinite detention and limited the king's power, and this check on executive power has been central to the modern understanding of Western, liberal democracies. In question was whether Hong Kong residents would be protected by habeas corpus after the return to Chinese sovereignty in 1997. Great Britain negotiated the transition to Chinese sovereignty through the Basic Law, which along with the 1991 Bill of Rights, included provisions against "unlawful detention."[13] However, Hong Kong human rights lawyers argued that the closed camps were holding Vietnamese asylum seekers contrary to habeas corpus protections, with potential consequences for all Hong Kong people.

In 1995, Refugee Concern Hong Kong, a nonprofit organization led by expatriate lawyer Pamela Baker, filed habeas corpus petitions on behalf of three Chinese Vietnamese families who held Republic of China (Taiwanese) residency papers. This was a tricky case. The clients were Chinese Vietnamese, a minority population in Vietnam, of whom more than 250,000 left the country in 1978 and 1979, some by sea, leading to the "boat people crisis" in Malaysia, Thailand, Indonesia, and Hong Kong, and some by land to southern China.[14]

Despite this exodus, a Chinese Vietnamese community remained in Vietnam, and members of this group continued to leave for Hong Kong in the late 1980s and early 1990s. Refugee Concern's habeas corpus clients were among this number. Like 90 percent of Vietnamese who arrived in Hong Kong after the CPA, they failed their initial asylum hearings and were slated for repatriation. However, a subset of these Chinese Vietnamese carried Republic of China (Taiwan) travel papers and rejected claims to Vietnamese citizenship.[15] This created a conundrum. When Hong Kong tried to repatriate them, Vietnam refused to accept these individuals, stating they had no responsibility to resettle non-nationals, in this case individuals claiming to be Taiwanese. The Hong Kong government dismissed this argument, insisting that the Chinese Vietnamese *were* Vietnamese and that Vietnam needed to accept them.[16] The individuals themselves continued to claim that they were refugees and deserved resettlement. As Phung Hoan testified, "In Vietnam I was persecuted because I was a foreign national, ethnic Chinese and considered to be politically suspect. We face further persecution if we return."[17]

Hong Kong and Vietnam remained at a standstill, and Taiwan refused to engage with the controversy. As a result, the Hong Kong government continued to detain these families at the Whitehead Detention Centre, a closed camp known for violence, protests, tear gas, abuse, and poor living conditions. Because neither Vietnam nor Taiwan would claim them, this group of Chinese Vietnamese with Republic of China travel papers faced indefinite detention.

This set a lawsuit in motion. Refugee Concern claimed Hong Kong detained Tan Te Lam, Phung Hoan, Ly Hue My, their spouses, and their children in violation of habeas corpus. Their lawyer, Peter Graham, argued that Hong Kong had detained his clients in closed camps for more than four years since the Refugee Status Review Board had rejected their refugee claims. This was an "extraordinary" amount of time, which far exceeded any "reasonable period" to hold someone against their liberty. By taking up these cases, Refugee Concern did not argue against all repatriations or the screening process per se, but rather it made a more limited argument against detaining people who might never be repatriated. Pamela Baker argued, "After they are screened out, they are held pending their removal. But if that proves impossible or even very difficult that does not entitle you to lock them up for the rest of their lives."[18] Refugee Concern's "landmark habeas corpus case" rested on Vietnam's intransigence against accepting non-nationals. It argued that if Vietnam would not accept them back, Hong Kong could not continue to detain them with no timeline or plan for release.[19]

At first, advocates were successful in court. Justice Brian Keith found in their favor. He agreed that the presence of Taiwanese documents meant that it was unlikely that Vietnam would accept these individuals, and as such, Hong Kong could not hold the families indefinitely. He ordered the three families released immediately.[20] He added that the length of detention, sometimes topping five years was "truly shocking."[21] The Hong Kong government disagreed. If it could not hold Vietnamese in the closed camps, its entire policy since 1988 was at risk of falling apart. It believed if Vietnamese asylum seekers were released into the community, they would lose leverage, and then Vietnam would never accept those who were "screened out." In fact, the government needed repatriation accelerated, not slowed, in order to empty the camps before 1997. The government quickly appealed the case. At the appellate level, the Hong Kong court overturned Justice Keith's decision and ordered that the plaintiffs be redetained.[22]

The result was a showdown in London. During the trials in Hong Kong, the English-language *South China Morning Post* had not emphasized how the case might have significant ramifications for Hong Kong beyond the fates of the three Chinese Vietnamese families. However, once in London, lawyers explained how the case could affect all Hong Kong people. The lead attorney, Rob Brook, argued that the "case was important for the future of civil liberties for everyone in Hong Kong after 1997," and he feared that Hong Kong's appellate court wanted to create a "dangerous" precedent that would allow the government to hold people "in administrative custody indefinitely."[23] Dr. Nihal Jayawickrama, a senior lecturer at Hong Kong University elaborated. "Habeas corpus is not available in China. With regard to what's happening across the border, it's something we should guard very jealously. . . . We should not in any way restrict its applicability or narrow down its scope."[24] When speaking to the press, Brook emphasized this point and complained that journalists and politicians had not been attentive enough to the long-term consequences of these Vietnamese cases. "Administrative detention after 1997 is going to be an issue because it's been such a problem in China. Any administration which says indefinite administrative detention is acceptable at this point in history is very, very worrying."[25]

In March 1996, the Privy Council ruled in favor of the Vietnamese. It deemed the length of detention "truly shocking" and affirmed Justice Keith's initial decision. In other words, Hong Kong could not keep individuals locked up "just because no country would take them in."[26] The Privy Council explained its decision as one steeped in common law tradition and "the standards of the civilized society Hong Kong aspires to be."[27] This nod to English law and protection of individual liberty may not be surprising, but its call to Hong Kong's "civilized" aspirations were somewhat ironic. Britain had ruled Hong Kong for over a century with very few concessions to representative government, and it was negotiating Hong Kong's future with China at this very moment. Despite these contradictions, the plaintiffs' lawyers celebrated their win. The test case had succeeded, and as a result, Hong Kong had to release more than 200 Chinese Vietnamese with Taiwanese papers who had been waiting in limbo with no hopes of resettlement in a third country or repatriation back to Vietnam. Most were transferred to "open camps," where they could come and go as they pleased and find employment in Hong Kong.

Refugee Concerns' lawyers also were explicit about the implications for Hong Kong's future and the importance of habeas corpus writ large. Lawyer Rob Brook said, "It's a victory for people in Hong Kong as much as the people detained. It shows that the courts are prepared to step in and supervise the Government's powers of administrative detention and that's a very important protection coming up to the handover."[28] Another lawyer, Gerard McCoy, said, "At the end of the day it comes down to how long you can lock someone up who has not committed a crime. This is a very clear affirmation from Hong Kong's highest court that administrative detention is alien to our system unless strictly controlled according to law. It is a reiteration of the guarantee for freedom for the future. It has a general application post-1997. If you are detained by the PLA [People's Liberation Army] or any authority and [it] does not comply with the time limitations, you can apply for habeas corpus."[29] In other words, the Chinese Vietnamese cases inadvertently, yet importantly, created the groundwork and reiterated the importance of habeas corpus for Hong Kong people through the transition to Chinese sovereignty.

Hong Kong's Legislative Council, 1996–1997: "The Bill Casts a Shadow upon the Rule of Law"

However, the story did not end there. Hong Kong was a Crown colony, and historically the British-appointed governor selected both the Executive Council (ExCo) and Legislative Council (LegCo) members from the administrative elite and business sectors. This means that even though LegCo may sound like a representative, democratic body, for most of its history, it was not. With 1997 looming, Britain faced pressure to implement more democratic structures as a hedge against Chinese communist control and protect Hong Kong's economic system. It also initiated a process of "localization" to transpose imperial, British laws into Hong Kong's legal system under China.[30] In addition, the British colonial government initiated new reforms, first, allowing for indirect elections by members of district boards and professional constituencies to constitute half of LegCo's seats, and second, by launching the first direct elections for LegCo seats in 1991. Then, in 1995, there were territory-wide elections for LegCo seats, although again, many were filled through indirect elections.[31] Although by many measures these were modest moves toward democratization, they represented a sea change in Hong Kong's political culture.

By the mid-1990s, LegCo had become a dynamic body, which included outspoken members who championed democratic traditions and who had significant interest in solidifying habeas corpus in Hong Kong. At the same time, more conservative members of LegCo believed that the Privy Council's ruling interfered with Hong Kong's immigration policies and carefully calibrated plans for repatriation and closing the camps. The *South China Morning Post* noted the irony. In other circumstances, an editorial proclaimed, Hong Kong people would rejoice at the affirmation of habeas corpus, but with the Vietnamese cases, it did not.[32] LegCo was divided. Some members believed Hong Kong needed to enshrine habeas corpus in its statutes; however, other LegCo leaders wanted to do so while eliminating the Vietnamese claims to this very same right. In other words, the fight moved from the courts to Hong Kong's late-colonial political system.

The government next proposed a new bill that would circumvent the release of additional Vietnamese from the closed camps despite the Privy Council's decision. It claimed Hong Kong should not release Vietnamese who had been in limbo for years *unless* the Vietnamese government explicitly refused to accept them as repatriates, something the Vietnamese government rarely did. Peter Lai, secretary of security, argued that Vietnam might still take back these individuals, and the government needed to use detention as leverage. If the Vietnamese asylum seekers were released, the pressure would be off, and Vietnam would feel no obligation to accept them. They would become Hong Kong's problem.[33]

Other Hong Kong politicians opposed this work-around, and argued that these attempts to narrow Vietnamese claims to habeas corpus would ultimately backfire. LegCo member Lee Cheuk-yan was a prominent labor and democracy activist, who as a youth leader had traveled to Tiananmen Square in 1989 to demonstrate Hong Kong people's support for the protests.[34] He was opposed to any exceptions or bureaucratic "fixes" that might give the government more power to detain people: "There is no need to give the Government such discretionary powers which will pose a threat to our rights. . . . The bill casts a shadow up on the rule of law."[35] The Hong Kong Human Rights Monitor, a local nongovernmental organization, objected to the attempt to buck the Privy Council's decision, characterizing it as a "knee jerk exercise of political expediency," which intended to further marginalize "vulnerable individuals who are not looked on with favour by the administration and many in Hong Kong."[36] In the United States, the *Wall Street Journal* saw the irony (and problem) of Hong Kong legislating away its rights to basic British legal protections, including the limits on the government's ability to detain individuals. "What makes this decision so intriguing is that the so-called loophole is actually a protection that the people of Hong Kong themselves may dearly need after 1997. Basically, legislators are being asked to legalize arbitrary, indefinite detention. What a nice present that would be for Beijing. Today the boat people, tomorrow Hong Kong trade unionists and democratic members of LegCo itself." The op-ed concluded, "But if they decide that their only policy option in this case is a law against the rights of Vietnamese boat people, they must be prepared to wake up one day and find that law turned on themselves."[37]

Despite this principled, if legalistic rhetoric, local popular opinion solidified against the Vietnamese in May 1996, after a major uprising in the Whitehall Detention Centre. This included a violent confrontation between the Hong Kong Corrections Service Department and the Vietnamese slated for repatriation, complete with tear gas, homemade weapons, and dozens of injuries.[38] With the Vietnamese finding dwindling support in Hong Kong, LegCo passed the "loophole legislation" by three votes. Circumventing the Privy Council's decision, LegCo voted that the government only needed to release Vietnamese "formally rejected for repatriation by Hanoi."[39] Since most affected Vietnamese were on lists labeled only "pending" (not "rejected"), in practice, the Hong Kong government asserted its power to detain the Vietnamese. The public debate over this question indicated how Hong Kong's frustration with Vietnamese camps coincided with anxieties over the transition to Chinese sovereignty, but in this instance, the desire to detain the Vietnamese outweighed concerns over a potentially troubling precedent.

Next, in 1997, LegCo debated the Supreme Court (Amendment) Ordinance, which sought to explicitly include habeas corpus protections in Hong Kong after the July 1 reversion.[40] Habeas corpus was a matter of English common law, so ostensibly protected through the Basic Law, but many LegCo members feared this would not be sufficient after July 1, 1997. LegCo wanted to get a statute on the books. The goal was to safeguard the civil liberties of Hong Kong people and guarantee habeas corpus even under Chinese authority. However, there was still the sticky subject of the remaining Vietnamese in the Whitehead Detention Centre and High Island. In its first reiteration, the bill tried to have it both ways: protect habeas corpus *and* remove "illegal immigrants" from the territory. Specifically, the habeas corpus law presented before LegCo initially contained language that would allow authorities to remove a person from Hong Kong even after a habeas corpus petition was filed. The bill stated that the government "must take all reasonable steps" to ensure the person in habeas proceedings was not removed and it included an exception under the High Court. This proposed language fell far short of habeas corpus's protections.[41] Supporters of this framing argued that the government needed to be able to deport illegal immigrants expeditiously. The bill's authors implied that this provision would only be used to remove migrants, but the language left the door open for the government to "remove" any individual in habeas proceedings out of the territory.

LegCo member Margaret Ng objected to the attempted immigration detention exception. She had been elected to LegCo in 1995 by the legal profession's constituency, and she became a diligent and relentless advocate for the rule of law.[42] She argued this language would obliterate the very aims and goals of having habeas corpus sanctified in Hong Kong law, and it was all because the government wanted the ability to detain and remove migrants it deemed undesirable. She argued that once an individual filed a habeas claim, they could not be deported or "removed" until their claim had been heard. She explained, *"Habeas Corpus* is the fundamental protection of the liberty of individuals, and that remedy should not be compromised simply because of the fear of possible abuse by illegal immigrants."[43]

In a long op-ed in the *South China Morning Post*, Ng claimed the way the bill was written was "fundamentally wrong" and "undermine[d]" the "whole aim" of protecting habeas corpus for Hong Kong people after July 1. She explained that the bill's limitations were due to the government's desire to remove the Vietnamese. Her analysis is worth quoting at length:

> The fact that the detaining authorities can remove the person somewhere outside Hong Kong without letting anyone know where he is removed to is horrifying. . . . These officials are able to advance such an argument because their minds are trained on Vietnamese boat people who happen, currently to be the largest group of people applying for writs of habeas corpus. To these officials, to be able to remove these Vietnamese applicants out of Hong Kong must be the speediest and most convenient way of dealing with the situation, not least because a large number can be dealt with at one go. Once they are gone, there is no need to argue the rights or wrongs of their earlier detention.
>
> But whether this is the proper or improper way to deal with Vietnamese migrants, these officials ought to realise that the provisions in this legislation will affect a far wider range of people. It is not only Vietnamese migrants who are vulnerable to removal from Hong Kong. So are people who are subject to extradition. So are people who are wrongfully treated as people without the right to land or right of abode. After July 1, this last category of people may well be greatly increased and more various.[44]

Ng homed in on the consequences of the proposed legislation. It was clear to her anyway that Hong Kong could not have it both ways. Refugee Concern lawyer Gladys Li concurred and backed Ng's critique. She argued that the administration's proposal was a "radical departure from the current law," and she characterized the proposal as "shameful" and "scaremongering."[45] The proposed law could not safeguard the rights of habeas corpus into Hong Kong's jurisdiction, while still trying to oust its detained Vietnamese population. The bill sought a speedy end to the Vietnamese problem, but it left open fears over extradition for others who might be without migration documents.

Those who supported the attempt to simultaneously protect habeas corpus for Hong Kong people and to remove and detain unwanted migrants argued that immigration procedures were distinct from habeas corpus. They parsed the difference between the right to habeas corpus and administrative detention under immigration law, where the goal was removal from Hong Kong. Richard Hoare, director of administration, argued that if Councilor Ng's provisions were baked into the law, it would provide undocumented migrants unprecedented abilities to contest their detention and delay removal, perhaps indefinitely. "This would extend the scope and effect of habeas corpus and would allow would-be illegal immigrants to take advantage of the legal proceedings to stay in Hong Kong for a longer period of time, thus posing a greater burden on taxpayers and on the community at large." The government insisted that the bill as originally written would provide new safeguards for Hong Kong's population while also maintaining immigration control.[46]

Ultimately, LegCo disagreed with immigration officials. It passed new habeas corpus legislation right under the wire, just days before the ceremonial July 1 handover. Ng's vision won out, at least formally. After debate, the final ordinance stated that once a writ of habeas corpus was issued, the person must *not* be moved from Hong Kong. This was a clear win for LegCo's democratic proponents. This final bill would not allow the director of immigration to remove an individual until all legal proceedings had concluded. The English Habeas Corpus Acts of 1679 and 1816 would remain the law in Hong Kong.[47]

Conclusion

Ironically, for the Vietnamese who remained in Hong Kong, 1997 did not bring the rupture or fear they anticipated. Approximately 2,500 Vietnamese remained after the handover. The Chinese government did not proactively deport them, and the majority remained in open camps, such as Pillar Point and New Horizons. After July 1, 1997, the Hong Kong government allowed these unsettled Vietnamese to remain, but it did not grant them blanket residency status. This population contained a mixture of Chinese Vietnamese, Vietnamese who had been "screened in" as refugees but who never received a resettlement placement, and Vietnamese who had been "screened out" but who Vietnam refused to accept via repatriation because of health problems, illness, and drug addiction. Most lived in Pillar Point, which allowed Vietnamese to go in and out throughout the day, but social workers noted that many in the camp were addicted to drugs and had serious medical problems.

By 2000, the government provided the remaining 1,400 Vietnamese at Pillar Point Hong Kong identity cards, but this was not the same as permanent residency or citizenship. Some married to gain residency, while others remained essentially stateless. Many believed they faced regular discrimination in Hong Kong, and others worried about their economic security. For example, one person was grateful for the identity card but worried about being able to pay the HK$4,000 monthly rent with only odd jobs. Another teen who had spent most of their life in the camps added, "My parents regret we are stateless. We don't belong to any country." In the present, their stories are generally forgotten. Occasionally, the Hong Kong English-language press publishes a retrospective of the camps or a human interest feature on a Chinese Vietnamese marriage, but these post–1997 experiences remain footnotes at best.[48]

These stories should cause us to pause and reflect on the ramifications of a war in the Pacific region more than twenty years after said war "ended" and the ways in which Vietnamese triggered debates over human rights and habeas corpus that remain in Hong Kong today. The presence of Vietnamese in Hong Kong in the late 1980s and 1990s were tangible reminders of how the war reverberated far from the battlefield and diplomatic relations. Moreover, the politics and geopolitical specificities of Hong Kong mattered.

In Hong Kong, fears over the 1997 handover and the Tiananmen Square massacre intersected in powerful ways with Vietnamese asylum procedures and detention. On the one hand, Hong Kong Chinese politicians used their policies vis-à-vis the Vietnamese as a way to stake out an independent position from the United Kingdom, the UNHCR, and China. It sought to control Hong Kong's borders, limit and deter Vietnamese arrivals, and ultimately repatriate them on their own terms. In most instances, Hong Kong Chinese leaders (including civil service employees and LegCo members) succeeded. Hong Kong's insistence on its ability to manage the Vietnamese (and expel them) was one of the few ways that Hong Kong was able to exert control over its future, in a political context where the United Kingdom and China made major decisions, often without the consultation of Hong Kong's majority Chinese population. At the same time, activist lawyers and LegCo members pointed to the inherent contradictions of holding Vietnamese indefinitely at the very moment Hong Kong politicians hoped to safeguard human rights norms, the rule of law, and habeas corpus.

For Vietnamese caught in Hong Kong, their lives had become entangled with these international and local geopolitics, and their routes led in unanticipated directions far outside the well-known narrative of Vietnamese migration or the Cold War. In this case, their escape from a communist country did not mean that they had escaped detention. More notably, their arrival in Hong Kong provoked questions about detention, habeas corpus, and the rule of law for both the Vietnamese *and* Hong Kong's general population. It also meant, ironically, that many of those who had been able to evade repatriation nonetheless hoped to leave Hong Kong. As one fifty-year-old Vietnamese man still in Hong Kong in 1997 insisted, "We don't want to live under the communists. That's why we fled Vietnam."[49]

Notes

Thank you to Brian Cuddy and Wen-Qing Ngoei for their insightful comments, and thank you to Christopher C. Munn for going above and beyond and sharing his expertise.

1. Questions and Statements by Vietnamese Asylum Seekers in Hong Kong, July 1989, United Nations High Commissioner for Refugees Archive, Geneva (UNHCR) Fonds 11, Series 3, 840.HKG Press.

2. Leonard Davies argued Vietnamese refugees received more attention than almost any other issue in the Hong Kong press, and his book went on to republish numerous articles, op-eds, and letters to the editor from the English-language *South China Morning Post* and *Hong Kong Standard*. Leonard Davies, *Vietnamese Asylum Seekers in Hong Kong* (New York: Palgrave Macmillan, 1991).

3. Sucheng Chan, ed., *The Vietnamese American 1.5 Generation* (Philadelphia: Temple University, 2006), 90.

4. Jana K. Lipman, *In Camps: Vietnamese Refugees, Asylum Seekers, and Repatriates* (Oakland: University of California Press, 2020).

5. For scholarship on the Hong Kong camps, see John Chr. Knudsen, *Chicken Wings: Refugee Stories from a Concrete Hell* (Bergen, Norway: Magnat Folag, 1992); W. Courtland Robinson, *Terms of Refuge: The Indochinese Exodus and the International Response* (London: Zed Books, 1998); Yuk Wah Chan, ed., *The Chinese/Vietnamese Diaspora: Revisiting the Boat People* (New York: Routledge, 2011); Yến Lê Espiritu, *Body Counts: The Vietnam War and Militarized Refugees* (Berkeley: University of California Press, 2014); Carina Hoang, "From Both Sides of the Fence: Vietnamese Boat People in Hong Kong, 1975–2000" (PhD diss., Curtin University, 2018) and http://vietnameseboatpeople.hk/oral-history/ (accessed March 1, 2019); Lipman, *In Camps*, chaps. 4 and 5.

6. John M. Carroll, *A Concise History of Hong Kong* (Lanham, MD: Rowman & Littlefield, 2007), 179–188.

7. Stanley Leung, "Lu Ping Goes Walkabout in Kowloon City," *South China Morning Post*, September 14, 1988, UNHCR 100.HKG.SRV, Refugee Situations, Folder B.

8. Robinson, *Terms of Refuge*; W. Courtland Robinson, "The Comprehensive Plan of Action for Indochinese Refugees, 1989–1997: Sharing the Burden and Passing the Buck," *Journal of Refugee Studies* 17, no. 3 (2004): 319–333; Alexander Betts, "Comprehensive Plan of Action: Insights from CIREFCA and the Indochinese CPA," UNHCR Working Paper No. 120, January 2006, https://www.unhcr.org/en-us/research/working/43eb6a152/comprehensive-plans-action-insights-cirefca-indochinese-cpa-alexander-betts.html.

9. Letter from John Davison, May 16, 1989, UNHCR Fonds 11, Series 3, 391.89, International Conference on Indochinese Refugees, Folder E.

10. Hong Kong University Students' Letter, May 17, 1989, UNHCR Fonds 11, Series 3, 100 HKG.SRV Refugee Situations, VN Refugees in Hong Kong, Folder C.

11. Chan Kwok Bun, "Hong Kong's Response to the Vietnamese Refugees: A Study in Humanitarianism, Ambivalence, and Hostility," *Southeast Asian Journal of Social Science* 18, no. 1 (1990): 107–109.

12. UNHCR HK to Geneva, Vieira de Mello, August 16, 1989, UNHCR Fonds 11, Series 3, 100 HKG.SRV Refugee Situations, VN Refugees in Hong Kong, Folder D.

13. Yash Ghai, *Hong Kong's New Constitutional Order: The Resumption of Chinese Sovereignty and the Basic Law* (Hong Kong: Hong Kong University Press, 1997), 382.

14. Chan, *1.5 Generation*, 71–77; Xiaorong Han, "Exiled to the Ancestral Land: The Resettlement, Stratification and Assimilation of the Refugees from Vietnam in China," *International Journal of Asian Studies* 10, no. 1 (2013): 25–46; Xiaorong Han, "From Resettlement to Rights Protection: The Collective Actions of the Refugees from Vietnam in China since the Late 1970s," *Journal of Chinese Overseas* 10 (2014): 197–219.

15. See Alvin Bui, "Working Paper: Vietnamization and Regionalization: The Hoa, the Republic of Vietnam and the Republic of China," Vietnamese Studies Symposium, Boston University, May 2021.

16. "Policy on Detention Defended," *South China Morning Post*, January 7, 1995; "Hosts Countries Pitching In," *South China Morning Post*, January 25, 1995; Lindy Course, "125 Viets Seek Freedom," *South China Morning Post*, January 27, 1995; "Bid to Return Viets to Camp," *South China Morning Post*, March 25, 1995.

17. Emma Batha, "Viets in Privy Council Appeal," *South China Morning Post*, January 29, 1996.

18. "Viets Set for Privy Council," *South China Morning Post*, January 29, 1996.

19. "Boat People in Limbo for 4 Years," *South China Morning Post*, January 5, 1995.

20. "Host Countries Pitching In."

21. Scott McKenzie, "Appeal on Viet Ruling Due," *South China Morning Post*, January 26, 1995.

22. "Bid to Return Viets to Camps"; Scott McMenzie, "120 Viets Face Being Returned to Camps," *South China Morning Post*, April 14, 1995.

23. "Viets Set for Privy Council."

24. "Viets Set for Privy Council."

25. "Viets Set for Privy Council."

26. Emma Batha, "Boat People Ruling Spells Freedom for Many More," *South China Morning Post*, March 28, 1996.

27. Emma Batha, "Hopes Raised for Custody Rights after 1997," *South China Morning Post*, March 29, 1996.

28. Batha, "Hopes Raised."

29. Batha, "Hopes Raised."

30. Ghai, *Hong Kong's New Constitutional Order*, 366.

31. For more on debates over democratic reforms in the 1990s, see Carroll, *Concise History of Hong Kong*, 197–203.

32. "Comforting Decision," *South China Morning Post*, March 29, 1996.

33. Scott McKenzie and Chris Yeung, "Bid to Counter Privy Council's Viet Ruling," *South China Morning Post*, April 3, 1996.

34. Jennifer Creery, "It's the Same Dictatorship," *Hong Kong Free Press*, June 4, 2019, https://www.hongkongfp.com/2019/06/04/dictatorship-veteran-activist-lee-cheuk-yan-keeping-flame-tiananmen-protests-alive/.

35. Fung Wai-Kong, "Viet Bill 'Tarnishes' Reputation on Rights," *South China Morning Post*, April 25, 1996.

36. Fung, "Viet Bill."

37. "Row Your Own Boat," *Wall Street Journal*, April 24, 1996.

38. "Breakout, Riots Fuel Resentment," *South China Morning Post*, May 12, 1996.

39. "Viet Deal Passes despite Criticism," *South China Morning Post*, May 23, 1996.

40. Draft Bill, Supreme Court (Amendment) Ordinance 1997, Hong Kong. Again, a special thank you to Christopher Munn for locating these documents.

41. Draft Bill, Supreme Court (Amendment) Ordinance 1997, Hong Kong.

42. "In Full: Hong Kong Barrister Margaret Ng's Mitigation Plea before She Was Sentenced over a Peaceful 2019 Demo," *Hong Kong Free Press*, April 16, 2021, https://hongkongfp.com/2021/04/16/in-full-hong-kong-barrister-margaret-ngs-mitigation-plea-given-before-she-was-sentenced-over-a-peaceful-2019-demo/.

43. LegCo Official Records of Proceedings, June 25, 1997, 835–851.

44. Margaret Ng, "Our Freedoms Must Be Writ Large," *South China Morning Post*, May 9, 1997.

45. Gladys Li, Letter to the Editor, "Bill to Erode Protection of Individual Liberty," *South China Morning Post*, June 7, 1997.

46. R. J. F. Hoare, Letter to the Editor, "Bill Aims to Ensure Safeguards Continue," *South China Morning Post*, May 18, 1997.

47. "New Version," *South China Morning Post*, June 26, 1997.

48. Diana Lin, "Goodbye to Pillar Point," Radio Television Hong Kong (RTHK), 2000; "Leaving Vietnam," Hong Kong Stories, RTHK, 2010 (available through the online RTHK archive at the University of Hong Kong).

49. Emma Batha, "'Stateless' Family Eyes New Home Overseas," *South China Morning Post*, June 1, 1997.

17 Moving beyond the Past

Vietnamese Serving in the Australian Defence Force

....

NATHALIE HUYNH CHAU NGUYEN

The top graduate at the Australian Defence Force Academy (ADFA) in 2013 was a second-generation Vietnamese, Midshipman Nam Nguyen, the winner of the Commander in Chief Medal and the Megan Ann Pelly Perpetual Memorial Award.[1] Nguyen's maternal and paternal grandparents came from northern Vietnam and formed part of the one million refugees who moved from the communist north to the republican south following partition in 1954. His paternal grandfather became an interpreter for the Republic of Vietnam Armed Forces (RVNAF) and was interned in the reeducation camp system for seven years after the end of the Vietnam War in 1975. The family was Catholic. Nguyen's father escaped from Vietnam as a boat refugee in 1983 and reached Malaysia before resettling in Australia in 1984. He sponsored his girlfriend to Australia in 1990, and their son was born in 1991. Nguyen was named after Nguyen Khoa Nam, one of the five South Vietnamese generals who committed suicide on April 30, 1975, the day that Saigon fell. Nguyen's father admired the general and wanted "to remind his son that he is Vietnamese."[2] In an oral history interview in 2017, Nguyen explains that he learned about the general he was named after as he was growing up but when asked whether it was a heavy burden to bear as a child, he responded, "Not really, I didn't think about it much, no."[3] Although his family history and heritage culture were important in shaping his life and career choices, his words indicate that the past does not weigh unduly on him.

Apart from an article by Bao Vu on Radio Australia's *Australia Network News*, directed at the Asia-Pacific region, the fact that the valedictorian of Australia's prestigious tri-service academy was a Vietnamese Australian was not noted by any of the Australian newspapers. Interestingly, however, this story was picked up by *Kompas*, the largest daily newspaper in neighboring Indonesia. *Kompas* provides a condensation of Vu's original article and highlights three facets: Nguyen's Vietnamese heritage, the importance of this achievement for the Vietnamese community in Australia, and Nguyen's assertion that although Vietnam was his parents' homeland and he is of Vietnamese descent, "in his heart, his homeland is Australia."[4] Nguyen's negotiation of his Vietnamese family history and heritage alongside his service in Australia's armed forces reflects the experiences of other second-generation Vietnamese personnel. Drawing on an oral history project conducted in Australia, this chapter examines the narratives of second-generation Vietnamese serving in the Australian Defence Force (ADF).[5] As noted by Robert Perks and Alistair Thomson, oral history scholarship highlights "the complexity of the oral history relationship, the richness of oral testimony, and the extraordinary variety of ways of interpreting the past."[6] I argue that the narratives reveal not only the ways in which second-generation Vietnamese Australian personnel have interpreted their family histories and heritage culture and the role of the past in their decision to enlist in the military but also the advantages conferred to them by flexible bicultural identities.

Vietnamese Veterans in Australia

The Vietnamese community is the largest refugee community in Australia. From 1,000 people in 1975, the Vietnamese community grew to 277,400 people in 2016 or 1.2 percent of the Australian population.[7] Vietnamese refugees formed the "first and most difficult test case" of the abolition of the White Australia policy[8] and had a high profile in the media and in public discourse particularly in debates on Asian immigration.[9] In one of the most significant diasporas of the late twentieth century, more than two million Vietnamese left their homeland in the two decades following the end of the Vietnam War. The scale of this exodus was unprecedented as was the international response. Vietnamese were resettled in fifty countries worldwide.[10] The exodus was driven by widespread state repression in postwar communist Vietnam, including the internment of one million people in reeducation camps, the forced displacement of another million people to New Economic Zones in rural areas, curtailment of individual and religious liberties, and discrimination directed against three specific groups: first, those associated with the former South Vietnamese government; second, ethnic Chinese; and third, Amerasians.[11] Military personnel and civil servants of the former South Vietnam and their families were labeled *nguy* (puppet) and marginalized by the new socialist state. Many were interned in the gulag while their families were evicted from their homes and sent to the New Economic Zones. By 1979, more than 700,000 Vietnamese had fled their country.[12] The oral histories of Vietnamese refugees reflect not only on issues of memory and commemoration in the aftermath of war but also on the shaping of stories following state-perpetrated violence and forced migration.

In Australia, veterans of the former RVNAF have marched on Anzac Day since 1981.[13] The large numbers marching in the 1980s were notable for such a new refugee community. They revealed the Vietnamese veterans' pride in their service and their gratitude that they were given the opportunity to remember their country and their cause at a public commemorative event in Australia. For these veterans, their war service represents a vital part of their identity, one that is remembered on a personal and communal level through a range of commemorative practices including membership of service associations, interactions with other veterans, and recording their experiences in service magazines and unit histories.

Australia has formally recognized the service of RVNAF veterans. As allied veterans, they are entitled to an Australian service pension and full membership of the Returned and Services League of Australia (RSL). These entitlements were conferred in 1980 as part of the Repatriation Acts Amendment Act (No. 2) 1979 under the Fraser Liberal government, and even though there was some political controversy surrounding their application, particularly in the lead-up to the Veterans Entitlement Bill 1985 under the Hawke Labor government in 1985–1986,[14] these entitlements highlight issues of integration and belonging for members of a minority community and point to the ways in which Australia, as a resettlement country, contends with experiences of loss and trauma among minority communities. Australia's recognition of the former military status of Vietnamese veterans is not only a means of validating their service but also of acknowledging their place in Australian war and migration history and of incorporating them into the Australian veteran community. This formal recognition is all the more symbolic in light of first, the exclusionary practices of the postwar Vietnamese state; second, the RVNAF's erasure in postwar Vietnam; and third, the RVNAF's absence from much of Vietnam War historiography. Australia has enabled these veterans to embrace their previous identities as South Vietnamese military personnel and concurrently adopt new identities as Vietnamese Australian veterans. Due to the refugee nature of the Vietnamese community in Australia, the allegiances of Vietnamese Australian veterans do not entail complications such as split transnational loyalties. The veterans' attachment to Vietnamese values and Vietnamese culture is divorced from the postwar Vietnamese state. Veterans can therefore assert their pride in being Vietnamese and in having served in the RVNAF while affirming their sense of belonging to a new homeland, Australia.

This situation differs from that of RVNAF veterans in the United States. Although the Vietnamese American community is the largest Vietnamese community overseas, Vietnamese veterans there have not benefited from a similar level of recognition. The contrast between Australian and American attitudes toward RVNAF veterans is underlined by Tran Dang Vinh, a veteran of the Vietnamese Air Force in Australia, who notes,

> They [the Australians] regard us as Australians, as former members of the Australian Armed Forces and we enjoy the same statutory rights and the same benefits as other Australians. That's an honour for all Vietnamese veterans living in Australia. Those resettled in the United States and elsewhere, they all say that those of us in Australia are very lucky. And I say, "Yes, it's the lucky country." They regard us as equals, not as second-class citizens like in America.[15]

The conflicted interpretations of the Vietnam War and of U.S. involvement in the war, and the absence of official U.S. acknowledgment of RVNAF veterans are echoed in the mixed feelings expressed by Vietnamese American service personnel.[16] As Long Bui posits, "How do individuals of the South Vietnamese geopolitical diaspora reconcile their duties to honor, protect, and serve America when America failed to do the same for South Vietnam during the Vietnam War?"[17] These fraught deliberations are not replicated in the Australian context. Although it is clear that the involvement of Australia and the United States in the Vietnam War differed vastly in scale, I contend that Australia's recognition of RVNAF veterans—and by extension of South Vietnam, a former ally—has been instrumental in engendering a sense of belonging among first-generation Vietnamese and enabling constructive bicultural identities among the second generation. Bui also notes that there are "no statistics on the number of Vietnamese American soldiers in the U.S. military,"[18] which is somewhat surprising as the U.S. military publishes statistics on the proportion of Asians in its armed forces, and Karin De Angelis and David Segal were able to provide analysis on levels of Asian representation in the U.S. military with Filipinos comprising the largest Asian American group in the active enlisted force followed by Koreans and Indians.[19]

Although first- and 1.5-generation Vietnamese refugees enlisted in the ADF in the 1980s and 1990s,[20] Australian Department of Defence statistics relating to Vietnam-born or Vietnamese-heritage personnel are only available from 2002.[21] They reveal a steadily rising number of Vietnamese in the ADF between 2002 and 2018, particularly among the second generation, whose numbers rose from 142 in 2002 to 388 in 2018.[22] With a total of 457 Vietnamese personnel including 72 women out of 83,284 ADF personnel overall including the reserves, Vietnamese personnel make up 0.55 percent of the ADF. This may seem underrepresented compared to the size of the Vietnamese community in Australia; however, it is significantly offset by the fact that the majority are second generation and the second generation represent approximately a quarter of the Vietnamese community in Australia.

Vietnamese Australian personnel were interviewed as part of a pilot project that I conducted on Vietnamese in the ADF in 2017–2018. They knew that I was a Vietnamese Australian academic whose parents had arrived in Australia as political refugees after the fall of Saigon in 1975, although I am a member of the 1.5 generation as I was a child refugee at the time. My point of entry to the ADF was Lieutenant Nam Nguyen in 2017. My initial contact with Nam[23] was made possible through a family connection who was able to provide Nam's details because they attended the same Catholic church as Nam's family. Once I had established that initial contact, Nam then reached out to other Vietnamese Australian personnel in the ADF, and those who were interested in taking part in the project then contacted me directly. Interviewees referred me to colleagues or friends, and I also made fortuitous contact with a medical doctor in Melbourne who was a former squadron leader in the Royal Australian Air Force and who in turn referred me to his sister, a former major in the Australian Army. The population of Vietnamese Australian ADF members is small enough that this approach was effective in drawing in for qualitative interviews a diverse range of subjects for whom ADF service was an important part of their identity. I interviewed thirteen male and female current and former ADF personnel from all three services, the Australian Army, the Royal Australian Navy (RAN), and the Royal Australian Air Force (RAAF) including the reserves in four states and territories: the Australian Capital Territory, New South Wales, Queensland, and Victoria. I will now examine the narratives of three second-generation Vietnamese personnel and their individual negotiations of and reflections on their family histories, heritage culture, and service in the Australian military.

The Narratives

The first narrative is that of Anne Nguyen,[24] a captain and Australian Army reservist for over ten years. Her parents were boat refugees who left Vietnam in 1977 and reached camps in Singapore and Indonesia before resettling in Sydney in 1978. Anne was born later that year. She comes from a South Vietnamese Protestant family. Anne's paternal grandparents both served in the RVNAF, her grandfather as a noncommissioned officer and her grandmother as an officer and military nurse. Her maternal grandfather migrated to Vietnam from China and established a business in South Vietnam. Anne did a bachelor of arts degree at the University of Sydney, majored in psychology, and became a registered psychologist. She joined the ADF as a direct entry captain in 2007. In 2008, she was deployed to the Middle East. She recalls,

> My paternal grandfather was a warrant officer, and my grandmother a military nurse. They were often posted to various locations. When my father was eight, his mother died along with his younger brother in a horrific car accident.
>
> My parents were among the first boat refugees to arrive in Australia in the late 1970s. They left for reasons that were partly economic and partly persecutory. My mum said that there were guards living in her house, taking information and collecting data, and making sure that communist policies were being implemented.
>
> I think early on I knew what I wanted to do in terms of career, which was psychology. I knew that I had a long road ahead of me in terms of trying to get to that point and commit to education and training. Along the way, I felt a strong need to be able to utilize my clinical training in terms of working with the Vietnamese population. There weren't many counselors when I was growing up, and I'm sure it would have been really helpful to have that in terms of someone who actually understood where you came from culturally or could actually speak the language. I was keen to also be involved in some way with the military.
>
> They were employing part-time psychologists in the army. I was quite keen to give back to the community and the country that had actually been very supportive of me. I also had a strong interest in humanitarian work—I was looking at Doctors Without Borders, but they weren't really utilizing psychologists at that stage.

> My fear was being in a difficult political environment and not having the means to protect myself or others. So I thought this way of getting through the army was the best of both worlds in terms of being able to do humanitarian work but also with the safety and security of being able to defend myself or defend others.

In all, Anne had three deployments overseas, the second to the Solomon Islands in 2009, and the third to the Middle East again, this time with Special Operations Command in 2016. The assignment with Special Operations was the one that she found the most rewarding as she felt that her work as a psychologist was truly valued. Anne notes that to remain in the active reserve, personnel have to serve twenty days every year, but while in Special Operations, her service went up to 100 days a year. In spite of the challenges of overseas deployments, including the management of her responsibilities as the mother of young children, Anne was committed to her service in the Australian Army Reserve.

The second narrative is that of Chuong Nguyen,[25] a flight lieutenant and aviation medical officer in the RAAF. Chuong comes from a military family. His father served as a paratrooper in the Airborne Division of the RVNAF. His father's two half brothers also served in the RVNAF and were both killed in action, one in 1969 and the other in 1971. Chuong's mother's brother also served in the RVNAF and was killed in 1972. Chuong's parents knew each other before they left Vietnam as boat people. They reunited in Australia where they married. The family is Catholic. Chuong was born in 1990. He began a science degree at the University of Queensland in 2008, and 2010 was his first year of medicine. At the end of that year, he applied to become a medical officer in the RAAF. Once he completed his medical degree and his work as an intern and registrar in 2015, he went to Officer Training School (OTC), where he did eighteen weeks of training. He explains,

> Dad was in the airborne, which is a branch of the army. I wanted to join the army, but Mum was against it. We eventually compromised. That's why I picked the air force over the army.
>
> When I was growing up, my dad would occasionally talk about how he was in the military. We'd meet some of Dad's friends, and they were all Republic of Vietnam military. When I was younger, I wanted to follow what Dad did. Then I thought that I wanted to study, I wanted to go to university to do a profession, but was there a way for me to also follow what Dad was doing as well?

> The military did have their own university sponsorship program where they would pay a salary during service while you were studying. Then, when you finished, you owe those many years plus one in the service.
>
> Another reason why I wanted to do that was because growing up, my parents talked about coming across as refugees and not knowing anyone. Everyone they met was fairly open and welcoming to them. So I felt that a way to give back to Australia would be to serve and to provide other people with that opportunity as well.
>
> Dad supports me. He understood that collectively we had a debt to pay to Australia because they had taken us in when we had nowhere to go and this was a way to repay that, to provide others with the opportunities to come live a life free from war and extreme danger.

Chuong's narrative includes his account of his father's experience of post-traumatic stress disorder (PTSD). He recalls,

> Dad was treated for PTSD about seven or eight years ago. Up until then, he did speak about his experience during the war but not so much. When I was growing up, he was quite a private person. But when I started studying medicine, we were talking about flashbacks, dreams, and about being hypervigilant, and that's when Dad mentioned that yeah, he was having that.
>
> I can't remember where it was, but Dad was a radio operator, and he was shot and wounded. They were in a stream, he fell down in the water, and the unit medic ran over to help him. While the medic was helping him, the medic was shot and killed. It was that memory that played over and over for Dad. We call it survivor's guilt when you're there and someone else has been killed or maimed. He felt responsible. So I took him to the doctor's. He went to his GP [general practitioner] for counseling, and his GP had also volunteered during the war, so that helped him.

Chuong provides a striking portrayal of the source of his father's PTSD, including the haunting and recurrent image of the medic who was killed while helping his father. His narrative makes it clear that it was Chuong's medical studies that provided an avenue for the father to finally confide in his son.

The third narrative is that of Jacob Choi,[26] a captain in the Australian Army and a parachute rigger officer with the 9th Force Support Battalion.

When I interviewed him, he was at RAAF base Richmond, northwest of Sydney. Jacob was born in New Zealand in 1987. His background is mixed Vietnamese and Chinese. His mother was a refugee from Vietnam while his father was Hong Kong Chinese and served in the British Merchant Navy. His parents met in New Zealand. Jacob's mother knew Vietnamese and Cantonese, and his father Cantonese, Mandarin, and Hokkien. The common language at home was Cantonese. Jacob's family moved to Australia in 2001. He graduated from high school in 2004, became an Australian citizen in 2005, and studied at the American University in Washington, D.C., where he did two years in the U.S. Army Reserve Officer Training Corps (ROTC) program and completed a liberal arts degree. He taught at a high school for six months in the United States and six months in Australia in 2009 before joining the ADF in 2010. He trained for eighteen months at the Royal Military College Duntroon and asked for Long Tan company because his mother was Vietnamese. He clarifies,

> I joined the army for a few reasons, but one of them was definitely because my mum was a refugee from Vietnam.
>
> My mother's family left Saigon because her father was a minister of Baptist origin. Before the Vietcong got into Saigon, my family knew that his name was on a blacklist. They were tied to Americans in Saigon who were able to get them out to the airfield and fly them out. The irony is that the Hercules that got my mum out of Saigon is the same aircraft that I work with a lot during my job these days, especially as a paratrooper. So I have a lot of strong connections there that Mum keeps reminding me of. She has very vivid experiences of that transition as a refugee.
>
> I've always wanted to join the army. My mum has a really fond memory of me trying to join the New Zealand Air Force when I was fourteen. Obviously, they said no.
>
> My parents really didn't want me to join the army. Obviously, being a Vietnamese refugee, my mum had stark memories of firefights in Vietnam and taking shelter during explosions. She wasn't too happy with any interest I had in the military. But from 2001 onwards, especially with the war in Iraq and Afghanistan, I learned more about the army, especially through the news. The army suited me because it had the jobs that I wanted. When you're twenty-three years old, all you want to do is jump out of a plane and

have a parachute. So the army is the best place to do that. I don't regret it at all.

In terms of his identity, Jacob clarifies,

One thing I always tell people is that my professional belonging is the same as my national belonging. In terms of corporate identity, this is one of those rare instances where I was born in New Zealand, my mum is Vietnamese, my dad is Chinese, I went to study in America, I married a Singaporean, and the most Australian thing is that I serve in the army. My corporate identity is my personal identity as well.

Of his two heritage cultures, Jacob highlights the Vietnamese side and in particular his mother's refugee past, but he also points to the multiple cultures that formed him and continue to shape his life and military career as a Vietnamese Chinese New Zealander Australian.

Service in the Australian Defence Force

"A bicultural identity," suggest Abi Brooker and Jeanette Lawrence, "is a person's sense of self in relation to more than one culture, in an environment where multiple cultures co-exist. Immigrants and refugees . . . live their daily lives in interaction with their ethnic, heritage culture and in interaction with the mainstream Australian culture."[27] Anne Nguyen's and Chuong Nguyen's narratives reveal bicultural identities that are strongly embedded in both heritage and Australian cultures, while Jacob Choi's narrative reveals the flexibility and strength of his plural identity as an Asian Australian with multiple heritage and mainstream cultures. All three were able to negotiate the rich heritage of their Vietnamese family history as well as to embrace their Australian identity and their membership of the ADF. Their accounts acknowledge the South Vietnamese past—a collectivist framework of war, trauma, and mass migration—while positing individual trajectories that combine agency, adaptability and the ability to navigate multiple cultural contexts.

Although the narratives of Anne Nguyen, Chuong Nguyen, and Jacob Choi reveal distinct trajectories, three commonalities emerge. First, all three have learned from their family history. Their choice of career is predicated on their understanding of this history, partial and incomplete as it is. Both

Anne and Chuong come from military families in South Vietnam, and although numerous details are missing such as when and where family members served and in which units, this military past was instrumental in their decision to enlist in the Australian military. The trauma and PTSD experienced by many Vietnamese refugees are drivers for Anne's commitment to culture-specific counseling, as she underlines the dearth of counselors with the requisite linguistic and cultural skills. The need for counselors who have an understanding of refugees' histories and experiences including firsthand exposure to war, postwar state repression, and traumatic loss, is implicit in her narrative. In Chuong's case, trauma and PTSD form a point of connection between father and son, leading to the articulation of the source of the trauma for the father and to a means of dealing with PTSD. For Chuong, it also provided the impetus for his work as a medical doctor and air force officer. As for Jacob, his mother's experience as a refugee from Vietnam had a formative effect on him. He highlights the link between his military service and his family history from his mother's side, including his joining Long Tan company at the Royal Military College Duntroon.

Second, the narratives of all three articulate a clear understanding of what motivated their parents to act as they did by leaving Vietnam as refugees, citing political or religious persecution. In Anne's case, both grandparents had served in the RVNAF and the family would have been labeled *nguy* for that reason, but she also refers to the fact that her paternal family is Protestant. The postwar communist regime subjected "every type of religious activity to detailed government regulation."[28] The mix of "economic and persecutory reasons" that Anne refers to encompasses the difficult conditions that her family experienced under the postwar regime. As for Chuong, his father had served in one of the elite units of the RVNAF, and members of elite units were singled out for harsher detention measures in the reeducation camps.[29] Both of Chuong's parents lost close family members in the form of brothers killed in action during the war. The high personal cost of the war for his family and his father's recurrent memory of the unit medic who was killed while helping him illustrate the sequelae of war in the form of PTSD. Jacob, for his part, makes special note of the fact that his grandfather was a Baptist minister in South Vietnam and therefore blacklisted by the communists, and that is why the family had to evacuate Saigon in 1975. He draws a connecting line between the Hercules aircraft that his mother fled in as a refugee at the end of the Vietnam War with the Hercules aircraft that he works with as a paratrooper in

Australia in the twenty-first century. The three narratives provide a justification for their parents escaping from Vietnam and embarking on an uncertain journey in order to reconstruct lives in a different country and culture.

Third, all three assert their choice to serve in the ADF even in the face of opposition from parents or family members. Their decision to serve is filtered through the lens of gratitude and enables a means of forging their own career paths while paying tribute to their parents and acknowledging their history and heritage in the process. Although the issue of service and the desire to serve one's country are to be expected in the officer corps, what is distinctive about these three serving officers is that they refer specifically to their parents' refugee background and the fact that Australia had provided their families with a home. "Gratitude," writes Laura Searcy, "can be defined as the appreciation of what is valuable and meaningful to oneself."[30] In addition to mental health benefits such as positive affect and interpersonal connections, gratitude can also engender a greater sense of meaning, adaptability, and "protective resources against psychological distress."[31] This constitutes a constructive strategy for first- and second-generation refugees from conflict zones. Anne framed her reasoning in the context of service to the Vietnamese community as well as to Australia and contributing to humanitarian work—the army provided, she believed, a safe way for her to conduct this work. Chuong's words are even stronger in that he refers to the concept of debt—in other words, Australia had provided asylum and given his family a chance, and this was a debt that needed to be paid so that others would equally benefit. As for Jacob, his story highlights his multilayered cultural identity—the son of a Vietnamese refugee and a Chinese who had served in the British Merchant Navy, born in New Zealand, educated in New Zealand, Australia, and the United States, married to a Singaporean, and serving in the Australian Army. For all three, the notion of gratitude is tied to their parents' history of being refugees from Vietnam and granted asylum in Australia. "Indebtedness," notes Hidefumi Hitokoto, "is a moral emotion motivating people to reciprocate after receiving help."[32] Although gratitude and indebtedness can have negative connotations in the sense of "misplaced gratitude" by refugees toward host countries responsible for conditions in their home country,[33] in the Australian context, second-generation Vietnamese personnel frame these emotions in a constructive way. They provide a positive interpretation of their motivations for choosing a career in the military. Their responses reflect the "trustee" model of gratitude in which a debt of gratitude is likened to the acceptance of a deposit.[34] Deposits constitute a source of pride, and beneficiaries are not in a position of inferiority but are instead trustees of others' goodwill or concern.[35] They can therefore exercise their judgment and reciprocate.[36] As Jason D'Cruz argues, the "'trustee' model of gratitude fits well with a conception of the refugee as a responsible and answerable political actor, rather than exclusively as a victim who is passive."[37] For these Vietnamese Australian personnel, Australia's role as a country of asylum plays an important part as does their acknowledgment of their own family and community histories.

The narratives of all three can be grouped under the broad framework of belonging. As Faith Nibbs suggests, the term *belonging* "accords refugees . . . important agency while also giving weight to how a group simultaneously negotiates various memberships outside of the one-way connotation of integration."[38] Belonging in this context therefore refers to Vietnamese integrating into Australian society but Australia in turn being changed as a result of this. Jay Marlowe notes that

> politicians and the wider society are asking questions about the implications of welcoming refugees and what this might mean for the protection of national values, identity and security. Written between the lines of such concerns are implications of belonging—rarely defined but emotively experienced, particularly when these are perceived to be under threat.[39]

The narratives of first-generation Vietnamese bear the weight of the past and the collective mourning for a lost country. Belonging in the Australian context comes in the form of official acknowledgment of their service and their former homeland, entitlement to the service pension, full membership of the RSL, and participation in public commemorative marches such as Anzac Day. In turn, by embodying the experiences of the South Vietnamese and speaking their stories, RVNAF veterans have the capacity to highlight South Vietnamese perspectives and to shift and alter perceptions of the Vietnam War. As Official Historian Peter Edwards noted in 2006,

> What was strikingly different in the coverage of the 30th anniversary of the end of the war was the impact made by Australians of Vietnamese origin. Individuals, including former diplomats and officers of the former South Vietnamese regime, and their families told their stories, and in the process wove a new strand into the fabric of the Australian national narrative.[40]

For second-generation Vietnamese personnel in the ADF, belonging takes the form of being Australian while simultaneously claiming their Vietnamese history and heritage. Their narratives attest to their ease and proficiency in both heritage and mainstream cultures, revealing the flexibility and advantages of biculturality[41] (or in the case of Jacob Choi, of tetraculturality). While they acknowledge their family's past and a sense of collective loss and collective trauma, they do not let this past weigh them down. Their motivations to join the ADF appear to be based on aspects other than issues of racism, citizenship, and rights that often drive the enlistment of minorities in the military.[42] Hugh Smith noted in 1995 that "it is an article of faith . . . that armed forces reflect the nature of the society that raises and maintains them."[43] Examining the oral histories of Vietnamese personnel in the ADF sheds light not only on the motivations and perceptions of this minority but also on the legacy of war and of the refugee experience for second-generation humanitarian entrants from conflict zones. Issues of identity formation, belonging, and integration in refugee and immigrant communities are of central concern to Australia as a migrant nation. The interweaving of exchanges and stories between the first and second generations reveal Vietnamese Australian negotiations of their identity, their place, and the differing weight of the past in twenty-first-century Australia. The Vietnamese Australian experience highlights the importance of the host country acknowledging and incorporating the histories of refugee communities. The life histories and career trajectories of Vietnamese Australian personnel reveal their strong identification with both heritage and Australian cultures, an identification made possible by the positive conjuncture of official acknowledgment of the past paired with a sense of belonging in the present day.

Notes

1. Bao Vu, "Prestigious Medal for Australian Defence Force Academy Graduate Nam Nguyen," *Australia Network News*, January 28, 2014, http://www.abc.net.au/news/2014-01-25/an-viet-australian-defence-force-graduate-feature/5218584.

2. Vu, "Prestigious Medal."

3. Nam Nguyen, interview by the author, September 21, 2017, Campbell, Australian Capital Territory, Australia.

4. Egidius Patnistik, "Cadet of Vietnamese Descent the Best Graduate in Australia," *Kompas*, January 26, 2014. The wording "in his heart, his homeland is Australia" constitutes a direct quotation from Vu's article. http://internasional.kompas.com/read/2014/01/26/1751190/Taruna.Keturunan.Vietnam.Lulusan.Terbaik.di.Australia. My thanks to Peter Hamburger for signaling this article and for providing the English translation from the Indonesian.

5. These oral history interviews formed part of a pilot project conducted in 2017–2018 on Vietnamese serving in the Australian Defence Force.

6. Robert Perks and Alistair Thomson, "Introduction to the Third Edition," in *The Oral History Reader*, ed. Robert Perks and Alistair Thomson (London: Routledge, 2016), xiii.

7. Australian Bureau of Statistics, "Census Reveals a Fast Changing, Culturally Diverse Nation," June 27, 2017, https://www.abs.gov.au/ausstats/abs@.nsf/lookup/media%20release3.

8. Nancy Viviani, *The Indochinese in Australia 1975–1995: From Burnt Boats to Barbecues* (Melbourne: Oxford University Press, 1996), 1.

9. Mandy Thomas, "The Vietnamese in Australia," in *Asians in Australia: Patterns of Migration and Settlement*, ed. James E. Coughlan and Deborah J. McNamara (South Melbourne: Macmillan Education Australia, 1997), 275.

10. W. Courtland Robinson, *Terms of Refuge: The Indochinese Exodus and the International Response* (London: Zed Books, 1998), 127.

11. See United Nations High Commissioner for Refugees, *The State of the World's Refugees* (Oxford: Oxford University Press, 2000), 82; Jacqueline Desbarats, "Human Rights: Two Steps Forward, One Step Back?" in *Vietnam Today: Assessing the New Trends*, ed. Thai Quang Trung (New York: Crane Russak, 1990), 47–64; Linda Hitchcox, *Vietnamese Refugees in Southeast Asian Camps* (Basingstoke, UK: Macmillan in association with St. Antony's College, Oxford, 1990), 37–68; James M. Freeman and Nguyen Dinh Huu, *Voices from the Camps: Vietnamese Children Seeking Asylum* (Seattle: University of Washington Press, 2003), 7; Kieu-Linh Caroline Valverde, "From Dust to Gold: The Vietnamese Amerasian Experience," in *Racially Mixed People in America*, ed. P.P. Maria Root (Newbury Park, CA: Sage, 1992), 144–161; Steven DeBonis, *Children of the Enemy: Oral Histories of Vietnamese Amerasians and Their Mothers* (Jefferson, NC: McFarland, 1995); and Robert S. McKelvey, *The Dust of Life: America's Children Abandoned in Vietnam* (Seattle: University of Washington Press, 1999).

12. Robinson, *Terms of Refuge*, 50.

13. Returned Services League, Victorian Branch, "Minutes of Anzac Day Commemoration Council Meeting Held in the Board Room at Anzac House on Wednesday, 14 October 1981 at 5.30pm," 1–8. My thanks to the late Keith Rossi (1921–2016) for providing me with a copy of the minutes.

14. See Nathalie Huynh Chau Nguyen, *South Vietnamese Soldiers: Memories of the Vietnam War and After* (Santa Barbara, CA: Praeger, 2016), 163–181.

15. Nguyen, *South Vietnamese Soldiers*, 170.

16. Long Bui, *Returns of War: South Vietnam and the Price of Refugee Memory* (New York: New York University Press, 2018), 122–168.

17. Bui, *Returns of War*, 123.

18. Bui, *Returns of War*, 123.

19. See *U.S. Population Representation in the Military Services: Fiscal Year 2017 Summary Report* (Washington, DC: U.S. Office of the Under Secretary of Defense, Personnel and Readiness, 2018); and Karin De Angelis and David Segal, "Minorities in the Military," in *The Oxford Handbook of Military Psychology*, ed. Janice H.

Laurence and Michael D. Matthews (New York: Oxford University Press, 2012), 325–344.

20. See Susan J. Neuhaus and Sharon Mascall-Dare, *Not for Glory: A Century of Service by Medical Women to the Australian Army and Its Allies* (Brisbane: Boolarong Press, 2014), 244–252, 309; and Nguyen, *South Vietnamese Soldiers*, 22–24.

21. Statistics for July 1, 2002 to July 1, 2018 were provided to the author by Peter Twiss, Directorate of Workforce Information, Workforce Planning, Australian Department of Defence, on October 22, 2018. It should be noted that these statistics refer to personnel with "Vietnamese-sounding" names in the ADF.

22. Directorate of Workforce Information, Australian Department of Defence, 2018.

23. From this point on, I will use first names in order to avoid confusion as "Nguyen" is a common Vietnamese surname.

24. Anne Nguyen, interview by the author, October 13 and 20, 2017, Watson, Australian Capital Territory, Australia.

25. Chuong Nguyen, interview by the author, October 11, 2017, Amberley, Queensland, Australia.

26. Jacob Choi, interview by the author, September 15, 2017, Richmond, New South Wales, Australia.

27. Abi Brooker and Jeanette A. Lawrence, "Educational and Cultural Challenges of Bicultural Adult Immigrant and Refugee Students in Australia," *Australian Journal of Adult Learning* 52, no. 1 (2012): 69.

28. Nguyen Van Canh with Earle Cooper, *Vietnam under Communism 1975–1982* (Stanford, CA: Hoover Institution Press, 1983), 166.

29. See Nguyen, *South Vietnamese Soldiers*, 139–162.

30. Laura Searcy, "Gratitude," *Journal of Pediatric Health Care* 30 (2016): 517, http://dx.doi.org/10.1016/j.pedhc.2016.08.003.

31. Y. Joel Wong, Jesse Owen, Nicole T. Gabana, Joshua W. Brown, Sydney McInnis, Paul Toth, and Lynn Gilman, "Does Gratitude Writing Improve the Mental Health of Psychotherapy Clients? Evidence from a Randomized Controlled Trial," *Psychotherapy Research* 28, no. 2 (2018): 194, https://doi.org/10.1080/10503307.2016.1169332.

32. Hidefumi Hitokoto, "Indebtedness in Cultural Context: The Role of Culture in the Felt Obligation to Reciprocate," *Asian Journal of Social Psychology* 19 (2016): 16, https://doi.org/10.1111/ajsp.12122.

33. Jason D'Cruz, "Displacement and Gratitude: Accounting for the Political Obligation of Refugees," *Ethics and Global Politics* 1, no. 1 (2014): 14, https://doi.org/10.3402/egp.v7.22940. See also Yen Lê Espiritu, who refers to Vietnamese refugees in the United States as either "absent" or "good refugees" used to justify American imperialist aggression. Yen Lê Espiritu, "Thirty Years AfterWARd: The Endings That Are Not Over," *Amerasia Journal* 31, no. 2 (2005): xiii–xxiv, https://doi.org/10.17953/amer.31.2.v171j838l4455118.

34. Claudia Card, "Gratitude and Obligation," *American Philosophical Quarterly* 25, no. 2 (1988): 121.

35. Card, "Gratitude and Obligation," 121.

36. Card, "Gratitude and Obligation," 121.

37. D'Cruz, "Displacement and Gratitude," 14.

38. Faith Nibbs, *Belonging: The Social Dynamics of Fitting In as Experienced by Hmong Refugees in Germany and Texas* (Durham, NC: Carolina Academic Press, 2014), 223.

39. Jay Marlowe, *Belonging and Transnational Refugee Resettlement: Unsettling the Everyday and the Extraordinary* (London: Routledge, 2018), xi.

40. Peter Edwards, "The Fall of Saigon, 1975," RG Neale Lecture Series (Canberra: National Archives of Australia and the Department of Foreign Affairs and Trade, May 1, 2006), 13–14.

41. See Que-Lam Huynh, Angela-MinhTu D. Nguyen, and Verónica Benet-Martínez, "Bicultural Identity Integration," in *Handbook of Identity Theory and Research*, ed. Seth J. Schwartz, Koen Luyckx, and Vivian L. Vighones (New York: Springer, 2011), 833; and Seth J. Schwartz and Jennifer B. Unger, "Biculturalism and Context: What Is Biculturalism, and When Is It Adaptive?" *Human Development* 53 (2010): 26, https://doi.org/10.1159/000268137.

42. See, for example, James Burk, "Citizenship Status and Military Service: The Quest for Inclusion by Minorities and Conscientious Objectors," *Armed Forces and Society* 21, no. 4 (1995): 503–529; and Mohammed Ishaq and Asifa Hussain, "British Ethnic Minority Communities and the Armed Forces," *Personnel Review* 31, no. 6 (2002): 722–739, https://doi.org/10.1108/00483480210445999.

43. Hugh Smith, "The Dynamics of Social Change and the Australian Defence Forces," *Armed Forces and Society* 21, no. 4 (1995): 531.

18 Veterans' Reflections on Legacies of War in Việt Nam at Peace

MIA MARTIN HOBBS

Between 1981 and 2016, thousands of American and Australian Vietnam veterans returned to Việt Nam.[1] I interviewed over fifty veterans about their return to the region, examining why they returned and how they responded to the people and places of Việt Nam as the war receded further into history and memory. Veterans' returns evolved over the decades, from journeys of reconciliation, to healing missions, to commemorative pilgrimages. As they traveled through Việt Nam, returnees were faced with new stories and memories that contradicted their understanding of the war. Yet, the experience of returning to Việt Nam tended to verify and validate veterans' views on war legacies rather than challenge or change them. These oral histories demonstrate how survivors carry their war stories with them, drawing on new memories and experiences to make better sense of their past.

This chapter examines returnees' views on key war legacy issues in light of their returns to Việt Nam: perceptions of defeat (or victory) in Vietnam, the association of "their" war with war crimes, and the morality of the war. I did not pose direct questions to interviewees about loss, crimes, or morality, but most veterans raised these issues without prompting, which suggests that these are key legacies that continue to cause contention about the meaning of "their" war.

· · · · · ·

One of the lasting questions about Vietnam is why, how, and even whether the Western allies lost the war. Among returnees, one of the dominant reflections on the "reasons why we lost" was that communist victory was inevitable because the revolutionary willpower was such as to outlast any invading force. "It was never going to be a winnable show," Australian Army veteran Ric explained. "Even if America had the opportunity to attack North Vietnam [with ground troops], I don't think they'd have beaten the will of the people who just wanted a united country."[2]

This reasoning reproduced a prominent narrative at official Vietnamese sites of memory—namely, that the revolutionary victory stemmed from innate national characteristics of tenacity and fortitude.[3] Veterans absorbed this message in their interpretations of the loss of the war. Ric explained that "we went to their history museums, and we come away with the conclusion . . . if we were going to win, if the Americans were going to win that, if they were serious about winning it, they would have had to do things a whole lot different, and shot and killed every one of them, because they weren't giving up. They weren't going to give up at all. They'd just go down fighting, basically."[4] These state narratives were bolstered by interactions with local Vietnamese, most of whom had been taught at school about Việt Nam's history of resisting invasion. Official historians, such as Phan Huy Lê, Hà Văn Tấn, and Trần Quốc Vượng, produced for the regime what historian Patricia Pelley describes as "marxish" histories: informed by Marxist-Leninist theories but promoting a "history of broad social unity and . . . the 'tradition of resistance against foreign aggression.'"[5] All three historians were contributors and editors of the core history curriculum in Vietnamese schools, so it is reasonable to assume that veterans were given variations on this perspective from the Vietnamese they asked about the war. Expatriate veterans living in Việt Nam were particularly influenced by these ideas. David E., a former marine who lives in Đà Nẵng with his Vietnamese family, explained, "The French were here giving them shit for a hundred and fifty years, and then the Japanese were here really terrorizing them for a few years. And then the French come back in for a few more years. We're just here bombing the shit out of them for ten years. You know it was all part of their—they just take it in their stride, they just keep on chugging."[6]

Returnee understandings of revolutionary willpower was reinforced by soldier-to-soldier discussions. Every returnee described sitting down with revolutionary veterans and "meeting the enemy." Two groups of revolutionary veterans were responsible for meeting the majority of returnees in official capacity. One was D445, the National Liberation Front (NLF) battalion which fought Australians at the Battle of Long Tan. Many Australians reported meeting veterans of this battalion at veteran-expatriate bars in Vũng Tàu. The other was a group of senior military in Hà Nội, including General Giáp before his death in 2013. These senior officers met with the first group of American veterans to return in 1981 and with notable early returnees including Senator John McCain, Ambassador Pete Peterson, and General Hal Moore. Several early American returnees were members of the organization

Veterans for Peace (VFP), and by the mid-2000s, they had created their own Việt Nam–based chapter, which runs annual tours of Vietnam as a fundraiser for humanitarian projects. Each year, the tour group meets with senior military in Hà Nội. John K., a former marine who returned to Việt Nam on the 2016 VFP tour, recalled, "I talked to one of the guys in the army when I was there, and he said, 'You know, we were willing to fight as long as you guys wanted to fight. If you wanted the war to last five more years, ten more years, if you wanted it to last to 1999, we were perfectly willing to sacrifice all our kids. 'Cause when they came over the border, the DMZ [Demilitarized Zone], we never thought we'd see them again. So we would have done that. Regardless of what you folks did.' And I believe them. That's dedication."[7]

Returnees from across the political spectrum repeated this narrative of inevitable revolutionary victory. The majority of American returnees were strongly anti-war, in part because until 1995 the United States was hostile to Việt Nam. Returning to Việt Nam was a radical and defiant act, one undertaken primarily by radically anti-war veterans for whom the narrative of revolutionary willpower validated their political views. For more moderate and conservative Americans and for the majority of Australians, inevitable victory absolved veterans' governments of the responsibility of military failure. Making willpower the key to victory—over superior knowledge of terrain, intelligent strategy, military cohesion, and effective propaganda—erases American and Australian ignorance of Vietnamese history, culture, and local politics, the cruel fallacy of "destroy the town in order to save it" tactics, the low morale and friction among allied troops, and the powerful dissent of the international anti-war movement.[8]

The notion of the enemy's dedication and willpower influenced returnees' discussions of their Vietnamese allies. Many veterans suggested that the Western allies lost because the Republic of Việt Nam (RVN) was corrupt, its military was weak and cowardly, and its civilians were disloyal. "There was no unity in the South Vietnamese government. In the populace it was every man, woman and child for themselves," U.S. Army veteran Robert J. Reilly wrote.[9] "Basically, they didn't want to fight," Australian Army veteran Rod said. "I won't say they were cowards or anything like that, [but] they didn't really want to be in a fight."[10] This narrative of South Vietnamese weakness was closely entwined with the perception of revolutionary willpower. After he praised the "dedication" of a People's Army Việt Nam veteran, John K. added, "I don't think South Việt Nam had the will to fight. And without that, there's no way that we could send more arms, and more money, and we just would not have made it."[11]

Historian Carie Uyen Nguyen notes that although Republic of Việt Nam Armed Forces (RVNAF) soldiers were scapegoated in American popular culture as "incompetent cowards who often shirked their duties," her oral history research shows that veterans had much more complex perspectives: "Some Americans . . . believed the ARVN [Army of the Republic of Việt Nam] soldiers were good soldiers, fighting as hard as they could to defend their country; . . . others resented what they saw as an unequal burden."[12] It is likely that many veterans held both beliefs simultaneously. The emphasis on RVNAF weakness in return narratives suggests that engaging with contemporary Việt Nam undermined memories of an already-ambiguous RVN. If the political voice of social groups is silenced—as is the case for RVNAF veterans—their memory of the past is erased as a potential counter to the official representation. When veterans revisited the wartime space, symbolic meanings invested in two political entities were physically affirmed: Sài Gòn fell, but Hà Nội stands. Where revolutionary willpower and resilience were heavily emphasized, the story of RVN weakness and corruption was reinforced. The RVNAF were reduced to *ngụy*, "puppets," reiterating notions of dependency. Most veterans returned to Việt Nam with an agenda to meet and understand their enemy, and although some returnees also sought out former allies and RVNAF veterans, they generally had less success.[13] Many returnees found healing in the connections they forged with their former enemy. Perhaps for these connections to be sustained as veterans explored their shared experiences with revolutionary veterans, another figure—a new Other—was required to bear responsibility for the war.

American returnees' views of Vietnamese willpower often complemented their preexisting perception that Western intervention in Vietnam was wrongheaded. Entwined themes of Western hubris and Vietnamese resilience dominated veterans' discussions of strategy failure, as returning confirmed what many veterans had suspected when in the field. U.S. Army veteran Ralph described that on search-and-destroy missions, "we're going around, we're clearing land, and we just traveled through. You never stay and secure anything. So you realize, this can't last, because we're not holding land. . . . You could see that we weren't going to win anything, so we were just kind of there. Just hope you get through it, try to help your friend." Like many returnees, Ralph "used to think we could have won, but when you get back [to Việt Nam] and see the ineffectiveness of the bombing, I mean the Hồ Chí Minh trail, you can hardly think you'll control that by bombing."[14]

Australian returnees, in contrast, tended to combine findings from their returns with the revisionist perspective that political failure prevented the soldiers from winning by withdrawing them too soon. This perspective narrows the Australian Task Force (ATF) purpose in Vietnam: "Our charter was to cease the fighting in South Việt Nam, that's what we went over there for. When the Paris Peace Accords were signed in 1971 [sic], North signed a peace treaty with South. Our political masters then seen an avenue to get us out, 'cause it was unpopular. So we did what we had to do, we did achieve our goals."[15] Because the Australian presence in Vietnam was small and largely contained to the southerly province of Phước Tuy, it does not feature prominently in Vietnamese memorials and museums.[16] Australian Army veteran Les said that "there's a very strong resentment of what they call the American War, but they probably don't know we were in it. So we probably fly under the radar a bit."[17] This Australian absence from official Vietnamese memory of the war is taken as support for the idea that "we won *our* war." Historian Jeffery Grey notes that this idea is "tied to a persistent belief in American tactical incompetence and South Vietnamese cowardice," contrasted with the notion of superior tactical understanding by the Australians.[18]

Among more recent Australian returnees, some argued that the allies won the war because they limited communism's spread. "For them, it was a civil war," explained Robin. "For the Western world, it was a line in the sand against communism. And strategically, that worked."[19] These veterans did not draw from their return experiences to explain the argument, and they largely disregarded Vietnamese narratives. "Their interpretation is absolute nonsense," said Kevin, an Australian Army veteran; "Absolute nonsense. The [museum] tour guide was a mouthpiece for Hồ Chí Minh, virtually."[20] These vindicationists drew on counterfactual scenarios explored by prominent Australian historians. Peter Edwards, official historian at the Australian War Memorial, notes that "in the longer view one form of the domino theory gained a degree of credibility. This was the argument that that intervention . . . had served a useful purpose by delaying the fall of the RVN by ten years . . . [during which] numerous changes in Southeast Asia affected the regional impact of Hanoi's victory."[21] This line of argument was taken up by the Australian veteran community. Veterans Bruce Davies and Gary McKay argue that the war provided "improved strategic security" for Australia and that "the war provided a bulwark that allowed the peoples of the nearby Southeast Asia dominoes to prosper and to develop into mini economic powerhouses."[22] Veterans clung to this narrative that offered meaning to "their" war: "the Vietnam War did slow the communism war down, moving into other countries," army veteran Rodney said. "I know they went into Laos and Cambodia, but that was going to happen anyway, really. Might have stopped them going into Thailand, Malaya, you don't know."[23]

......

Returnees' discussions of why (or if) the war was lost were often linked to war conduct and to the issue of war crimes. Because my fieldwork concerned the return to Việt Nam, and out of ethical concern for research with subjects who may have trauma issues, none of my questions were about war crimes. However, many veterans visited Vietnamese museums that are notoriously explicit in their documentation of war crimes. The War Remnants Museum in Hồ Chí Minh City, for example, documents atrocities committed during the colonial period and in the Indochina wars, proposing that showing evidence of "the crime and consequences of war that the invasion force has caused to Vietnam" promotes "peace and solidarity between the peoples of the world."[24] Most veterans touched on the subject of war crimes when discussing war commemorations. Additionally, because of the lasting association between Vietnam and war crimes in public memory in Australia and the United States, they often brought up atrocities such as My Lai. How veterans made sense of their conduct in service, in light of the lingering association between Vietnam and war crimes, revealed an ongoing struggle to come to grips with profoundly unsettling information and to find culturally and morally comfortable ways of remembering violence.

Australian returnees agreed that Australian soldiers did not commit war crimes. "We didn't have a My Lai," Dave explained. "We shot the odd woman we saw in the bush under circumstances which were wartime circumstances."[25] Many Australian veterans were anxious to exonerate not only themselves but the entire ATF in Vietnam: "I don't know any Australian troop that ever raped a woman. And I don't know any Australian troop that ever killed a baby. You know? It went on, it most certainly happened, but no Australian troops were ever guilty of that. Certainly not the battalion that I served with."[26] In an extension of the "we won our war" narrative, many Australians made a point of comparing their honorable conduct to that of the Americans. Australian Army veteran John W. recalled his visit to the War Remnants Museum:

> I just looked at Graham and I said, "Thank fuck, thank fuck there is not a photo of an Australian in here." . . . I'm crying, like I am now. . . . I said, "Don't go in there. Do not go in there. That is not the

war I fought in. That's not the war I fought in." I had to walk away. That turned my stomach, that's just . . . the Vietnamese have every right, they have every right to be horrified as to what was done at My Lai, and Agent Orange, everything else like that. But I said to Graham, "Thank God there were no photographs of Australians in there." It was like we didn't exist.[27]

Thus, Australian returnees drew from Vietnamese exhibits featuring war crimes to support their preexisting notion that Australians committed no crimes. "The propaganda from the Việt Nam perspective was all directed pretty much toward the Americans anyway. And the museums are full of what they term 'American atrocity.' But it's propaganda in the main," said Graham S., an Australian Army soldier. "And as far as the Australian involvement was concerned, I think that we were honorable."[28]

I found three outliers to this consensus, two of whom were veteran-writers whose memoirs I drew from to support my research. Terry Burstall, the first Australian veteran to return in 1986, reflected on the "Australian War" after meeting with local Vietnamese who remembered the Australian presence: "War itself is an atrocity, but there was no need for the mindless brutality toward the civilian population."[29] Australian Army veteran Tony "Bomber" Bower-Miles agreed: "It didn't exactly win the hearts and minds of the people as you're driving this great steel rod down through grandma's chest."[30] Burstall and Bower-Miles both reported several instances of criminal conduct in their memoirs, including a common memory of "engineer's burials": "I blew up bodies. . . . It saved time digging a hole. They used to call it an engineer's burial. I was well aware of the psych ops angle of it because they'd always try and take their dead away with them. If you understand the Asian mind, you know they all want to go to the happy hunting ground in one piece and have a proper burial. So by blowing the body to shithouse, it will piss off the ones that are still alive."[31] Burstall also suggested that corpse mutilation and display was an established ATF method in Vietnam: a "policy of dumping VC [Vietcong] bodies in town market squares or dragging them behind Armoured Personnel Carriers (APCs), in sight of the village children, both methods supposedly meant to draw out further VC sympathisers."[32] One of my interviewees, Derrill, was an Australian Army veteran who had worked in psy ops during the war. Derrill also identified corpse desecration as a tactic after "an ambush at a place called Thừa Tích." Derrill explained that eleven NLF were killed by Australian forces at Thừa Tích. Some of the bodies were destroyed on the spot with an "engineer's burial" before a request came through from the Vietnamese district chief asking for the bodies to be returned to the village. The remaining bodies were strapped to APCs, rather than secured inside the vehicles, and transported to the village of Xuyên Mộc. As the Australians approached Xuyên Mộc, "these bodies supposedly fell off, according to [the Australians], and they dragged them into the village behind the APCs. And they all happened to be tied by the leg."[33]

Although these were the only veterans to identify crimes in Australian conduct, many others described or implied criminal actions, perhaps without knowing it themselves. Actions such as torture in interrogations, corpse mutilation for efficient burial or psychological warfare, bombing cities, strafing villages, individual and small-group civilian killings in free-fire zones, and the forced dislocation of civilians were described using military terminology: SOPs (standard operating procedure), task force policy, psyops. This suggests that veterans sometimes learned criminal actions as strategies or tactics and were unaware of the legal ambiguity or criminality of such actions. It also suggests that a military framework and language provided a level of psychic comfort for veterans when remembering such actions, implicitly justifying violence under an acceptable moral code and carving out space for the memory that Australian soldiers "did the job they were there to do, and they did it with honor."[34]

The differences between Derrill, Burstall, and Bower-Miles's descriptions of "engineer's burials"—as a regular practice versus an anomaly, with casual descriptions versus graphic detail—suggests that military frameworks clouded the ability of soldiers in combat to distinguish acceptable violence or proportional responses to threats from war crimes. Bower-Miles and Burstall served in the field and witnessed a great amount of violence and death. The strategic language used by Burstall and the rough army slang used by Bower-Miles suggests a practiced distance, indicating that the military framework provided a way of processing abject violence in a way that they could live with day to day. This framework appeared to limit veterans' considerations of the effects of their actions. In contrast, Derrill worked in psy ops: both distanced from the field and attuned to the psychic violence and moral violation of an engineer's burial. He described the "absolute horror" on the faces of villagers when they saw the APCs dragging bodies into Xuyên Mộc. Finally, both Bower-Miles and Burstall reported engineer's burials in books, which provided distance from their audience. Derrill spoke directly to me and thus may have felt social pressure to clarify his awareness of the illegal action. "It's actually a war crime," he said.

"It, to me, was a war crime. The bodies were blown up, that was the first thing, and the second thing is, dragging the bodies. I mean, they claimed it was accidental but bullshit."[35]

In contrast, the American anti-war returnees largely supported Vietnamese memories of atrocities in the war. They explained how the actions of troops in Vietnam turned the Vietnamese into an enemy and created what psychologist Robert J. Lifton describes as an "atrocity-producing situation"—a military culture that was "inevitably genocidal."[36] U.S. veteran and My Lai witness Ron said that "there were things that happened I think that were worse than My Lai over there, and the only thing is, I happened to be there that day, with the camera, and recorded some of the events [at My Lai]."[37] Many described a policy of shooting near civilians to "test" them. U.S. Army veteran Don explained that he refused to participate in destruction and killing on search-and-destroy missions and so was put on security, watching the villagers. He remembered asking, "'What happens if they run?' 'Well, that means they're a VC.' 'Well, then, what do you do?' They just look at you, like, you dumb shit. 'You shoot them.' They're pronounced guilty when they run."[38] Army veteran James described how this "test" turned into a game among soldiers outside of missions: "Guys taking out their rifles and shooting farmers from the truck, from the moving truck . . . that kind of thing was done all the time. You know, when we showed up, people were scared and they ran, and so the American soldiers and the officers assumed that they were running because they were guilty. Well, they were running to save their lives. And so they were killed for being frightened. And of course they were frightened because they knew they might be killed."[39] This game, itself derived from a "test," then turned into a "policy . . . to shoot near them. If they ran, jumped for cover, they were the enemy. . . . How many are gonna stand there? The instinct is going to be to jump."[40] For many veterans, therefore, My Lai came to signify something larger than the violence and death of one massacre: it was a single moment that embodied the Vietnam War.

Despite widespread discussion of the My Lai massacre among anti-war veterans, very few visited the Sơn Mỹ Memorial and Museum to the victims of the My Lai massacre. This may simply reflect lack of opportunity: Tịnh Khê is three hours by train or car from the nearest cities with any major tourism infrastructure. Others explained that they found it too painful to visit. Former marine Suel reacted forcefully when I asked if he had visited the site: "I won't go there. I absolutely refuse to go there. I don't want to deal with it. No, I've never been there, and I'll never go there."[41]

The few veterans I interviewed who had visited Sơn Mỹ were all sympathetic to Vietnamese war victims. However, they struggled with the ways the events of My Lai were memorialized. Ron, the U.S. Army photographer of the My Lai massacre, testified in 1976 that he had first sold his photographs of the My Lai massacre because he "wanted to get it off my chest, let the people know exactly what had happened."[42] He was glad that his images were on display in the War Remnants Museum because "American museums are trying to hide . . . what happened in Vietnam and that. And I think in Việt Nam they're trying to show more of a reality of what happened there." However, when I asked him about the exhibits at Sơn Mỹ, he said, "Some I can agree with; some I cannot agree with."[43] James, a proudly anti-war American veteran, remembered "some propaganda there" at Sơn Mỹ, with "one photograph in particular, of GIs, American GIs standing around smoking cigarettes and [the caption] said, 'GIs relaxing after the massacre.'"[44] This caption is not inaccurate: Seymour Hersh collected accounts from survivors and participants in the massacre who remembered GIs "taking a break, or loafing" while other soldiers continued the killing.[45] Yet, James felt so strongly about this caption that he "talked to the young woman guide there . . . I said, 'That's inappropriate, and you should revise that.' And I gave her some suggestions."[46]

Both men held the view that American violence against civilians was endemic during the war. However, when they were confronted with exhibits that remembered American violence in this way—as a casual, indifferent practice, rather than an aberrant, reactionary "snap" triggered by stress— they reacted defensively.[47] In the aftermath of war, both had questioned how and why their fellow soldiers could commit such acts of violence. The answers they found—military culture, ingrained racism and misogyny, psychological pressures of combat, and coping mechanisms for trauma—did not excuse but at least explained how people could learn to act with such brutality.[48] These factors of the American experience were rarely discussed in Vietnamese spaces for memory, and when they were, they were clinical and accusatory: flat dissections of enemy ideology and action. One caption reads, "America's secret documents about operation plan to kill civilians in Sơn Mỹ on March 16th, 1968." Another describes a 1969 bombing run through Quảng Ngãi: "The US bombing the area to rub out their crimes traces, one year later."[49] The focus of the Sơn Mỹ museum is the Vietnamese experience as victim of atrocity, not the American experience as perpetrator. As a result, these veterans found their feelings of solidarity tested by what they felt were exaggerated or one-sided representations.

Sơn Mỹ also tested Ron's personal war memory. He disapproved of "some of the objects they have there [at Sơn Mỹ], like you've probably seen the setup of the soldier and that, and all that? This one soldier holding the woman by the hair, that's a little ... kind of hard to comprehend. It could have happened there, I do not know, but the photographs tell the whole story there."[50] Ron was describing a nearly life-size clay statue of a GI forcing a woman onto the ground by her hair. His descriptions of inauthenticity at Sơn Mỹ were weighted by his sense of authority over My Lai memory: he was a witness to the massacre and so considered his memory, represented in his photographs, as the closest to "the whole story" or the historical truth. Yet in his 1976 testimony, he described conduct very similar to that depicted by the diorama: American soldiers were "more or less tormenting these people, especially that woman [indicating a photograph] at the front. They were grabbing her, and kicking her around."[51] Perhaps if the diorama presented this specific event in the way that he remembered it, he would not have disapproved. However, his critique avoids the basic difficulty of portraying atrocity: how to represent an event when cover-ups and ongoing warfare eradicated nearly all the evidence and only survivors' trauma remains.[52] His sense of authority over memory of My Lai also challenges how the Vietnamese tell their own story. Ron's images captured the event from one place and from the point of view of one U.S. Army photographer, but the massacre spanned four hamlets. Surviving the hundreds of murdered Vietnamese were the villagers who witnessed their deaths, and the diorama of the woman Ron describes is likely based on the memory of a survivor.[53]

Ron's response to the My Lai exhibit demonstrates a broader ambiguity toward the legacy of war crimes, an ambiguity shared by a handful of more recent American returnees. As diplomatic relations were normalized in the mid-1990s, so too was the idea of returning to Việt Nam. From the early 2000s, the political diversity of American returnees increased, and among these veterans there was a tension between their own memories and accepting the Vietnamese experience. "Calley was wrong, but My Lai, [there were] a lot of VC there," said U.S. Army veteran Mark, who first returned in 2009.[54] Some were uneasy about the singular focus on American crimes. U.S. Air Force veteran Jim felt that the United States had been "fairly up front" about My Lai and thought it was time for the SRV to acknowledge their crimes. "I mean, it took a while ... and yeah, we had a lot of soldiers that had a lot of stuff they really shouldn't've been doing. But that was a lot more out in the open than the Vietnamese government, which—now, there had been massacres too, on their side, of their own people, but you don't hear anything about that."⁵⁵ Veterans alluded to mass summary executions after the Battle for Huế in 1968 for evidence of revolutionary crimes. Yet, as Laderman notes, "There is no credible evidentiary basis for this version" of the "Hue Massacre."⁵⁶ The methodical execution of between 2,000 and 14,000 of civilians by revolutionary forces over three weeks was an apocryphal story that became embedded in Western popular memory of the war.⁵⁷ Returnees' focus on war crimes at Huế suggests that for some, the linking of war crimes and the U.S. military was an unfair distortion, and returning to Việt Nam may have exacerbated feelings of resentment because of the singular focus there on American atrocity. Air force veteran Mike M. said, "A lot of people wanted to lambast the United States for their dealings over there, but the communist regime was pretty brutal, too."⁵⁸

These ambiguous responses to American war crimes infuriated anti-war veterans. "I see so many people not being able to admit that it was wrong, it was criminal, and sinful, and they just can't admit it," Larry said. In response, he had embarked on a relentless pursuit of uncovering and exposing the "horror of it all." A former marine turned expatriate, Larry was preoccupied with the women's political prison, created by the French and handed over to the United States, on Côn Đảo Island. He often compared the brutal treatment of American prisoners of war to that at Côn Đảo, and he has created documentaries intended for American audiences about the prisons. "I want them to know," Larry said, "know more about what happened in this country."⁵⁹

. . . . . .

Discussions of war crimes were entwined with returnees' reflections on the broader meaning of the war. Anti-war veterans like Larry viewed Western involvement in the war as immoral. "Henry Kissinger is a war criminal, Nixon's a war criminal, a lot of them that were in the State Department," John A. said. "I would have danced on Lyndon Bain Johnson's grave, for escalating that war."⁶⁰ These anti-war returnees found solidarity through the Vietnamese state narrative of the war, which "underscore[s] a classic socialist construct of 'war between governments' and 'solidarity between people' . . . [which] recollects the US soldier as enemy *and* fellow victim of US imperial ambitions."⁶¹ In meetings with returning veterans, Vietnamese officials "inevitably point out that they have 'never had any animosity toward the American people.' American Governments, on the other hand, have 'lied and sought the destruction of our country.'"⁶² Veterans' views were hardened by returning to Việt Nam. "The longer I stay here, the more anti-war I get," Suel explained, "when I look at the devastation, what we did to these people for absolutely no reason. I mean there was not even a plausible reason for what we did. It just really hardened me, my thoughts. I am totally and completely anti-war now."[63]

In direct contrast, there were a handful of veterans who saw the war as moral, justified, and successful. Mostly Australian, these returnees linked Australia's national interest with the domino theory. Australian Army veteran David W. explained, "It was called the Yellow Peril, you know? . . . China was on the march, down into Indonesia. . . . I always wonder, if we hadn't—we might have won it."[64] The only American who agreed with this idea was Mark: "I don't think communism has expanded since Vietnam. . . . Communism doesn't work very well." He also thought "we did a lot of good here [during the war]. . . . This was a third world nation when we got here. Women didn't wear bras, most of them didn't wear tops when we got here in 1950-something. And then they taught them how to do that."[65] Mark's belief that the military presence educated the Vietnamese is classic orientalist paternalism, a perspective of Asia that was prevalent during the war. "We've taught them what freedom is like. We taught North Vietnam what freedom is like."[66]

Many veterans, from both nationalities, concluded that the war was simply "a horrible waste. Of time, effort, money, people. I think in the back of my mind I thought it was inevitable anyway."[67] This conclusion was very difficult for some, and facing the reality of wasted effort in peacetime Việt Nam was challenging. When U.S. Air Force veteran Heiko returned to Việt Nam, "I didn't really feel comfortable that the communists now owned this place, you know. I mean we busted our horns for so long, doing what we did. And now looking back at it, it wasn't really our war, but it just seemed a waste of people, and time, and bodies, and all of that kind of stuff, you know. That's what really came to mind, was all the people we lost. You know, it was sad."[68] Yet for others, returning provided some comfort. Francis explained that "when the war was officially ended, we thought if we left . . . we thought it was going to be a blood bath, and it was going to be terrible, and communism would take over, there'd be mass murder, all these terrible scenarios. It didn't really happen that way." Francis found that returning to Việt Nam "gave me the sense that all of our fears of what was going to happen [didn't], I mean on a small scale it did, but for the majority."[69]

· · · · · ·

Veterans' reflections about the legacies of the war demonstrate that rather than challenging their views, returning often reinforced their existing values and beliefs. This trend was apparent across political positions and all return periods for both Americans and Australians. Veterans' discussions of defeat (or victory) in Việt Nam, war crimes, and the morality of the war also demonstrate that these debates are far from settled. These war legacies are of ongoing importance to how veterans understand "their" war and their place in history.

Notes

1. This chapter is adapted from material in the author's book, *Return to Vietnam: An Oral History of American and Australian Veterans' Journeys* (Cambridge: Cambridge University Press, 2021). All rights reserved. I use "Việt Nam" to denote the country and "Vietnam" to indicate the war that veterans fought in and the place that they remember. About 1 percent (30,000) of U.S. soldiers and 5 percent (3,000) of Australian soldiers have returned to Việt Nam. These estimates are gathered from personal communication with veterans and tour guides.

2. Interview with Ric, telephone, August 5, 2016.

3. Christina Schwenkel, *American War in Contemporary Vietnam: Transnational Remembrance and Representation* (Bloomington: Indiana University Press, 2009), 91.

4. Interview with Ric.

5. Patricia Pelley, *Postcolonial Vietnam: New Histories of the National Past* (Durham, NC: Duke University Press, 2002), 61, 45.

6. Interview with David E., Đà Nẵng, April 8, 2016.

7. Interview with John K., Skype, August 2, 2016.

8. An unnamed major to journalist Peter Arnett in the aftermath of a battle in Bến Tre in which 456 civilians were killed. Peter Arnett, "Ruined Ben Tre, after 45 Days, Still Awaits Saigon's Aid: Regime Has Offered Nothing in Effort to Rebuild Town," *New York Times*, March 15, 1968, 3.

9. Robert J. Reilly, *Return of the Warriors: Vietnam War Veterans Face the Ghosts of Their Past on Their Personal Battlefields* (Victoria, Australia: Trafford Publishing, 2010), 111.

10. Interview with Rod, Vũng Tàu, August 19, 2016.

11. Interview with John K.

12. Carie Uyen Nguyen, "Whose War Was It Anyway?" *New York Times*, August 18, 2017.

13. RVNAF veterans are unrecognized by the Socialist Republic of Việt Nam and cannot freely organize as a community, making it nearly impossible for returning veterans to organize meetings with them.

14. Interview with Ralph, Skype, June 27, 2016.

15. Interview with Ray, Frankston, May 19, 2016.

16. The Australian Task Force was assigned the province of Phước Tuy, now Bà Rịa-Vũng Tàu, southwest of Sài Gòn. Just under 60,000 Australians served in Vietnam.

17. Interview with Les, Skype, July 1, 2016.

18. Jeffrey Grey, "In Every War but One? Myth, History and Vietnam," in *Zombie Myths of Australian Military History* (Sydney: NewSouth, 2010), 194, 195–196.
19. Interview with Robin, Carlton, July 25, 2016.
20. Interview with Kevin, Long Tân, August 18, 2016.
21. Peter Edwards, *Australia and the Vietnam War* (Sydney: NewSouth, 2014), 272.
22. Bruce Davies and Gary McKay, *Vietnam: The Complete Story of the Australian War* (Sydney: Allen & Unwin, 2012), 591.
23. Interview with Rodney, Vũng Tàu, August 17, 2016.
24. "General Introduction," War Remnants Museum, http://warremnantsmuseum.com/posts/introduction-general.
25. Interview with Dave, Carlton, June 27, 2016.
26. Interview with John W., Skype, May 23, 2016.
27. Interview with John W.
28. Interview with Graham S., telephone, June 23, 2017.
29. Terry Burstall, *A Soldier Returns* (Brisbane: University of Queensland Press, 1990), 187.
30. Tony "Bomber" Bower-Miles and Mark Whittacker, *Bomber: Vietnam to Hell and Back* (Sydney: Macmillan, 2009), 103.
31. Bower-Miles and Whittacker, *Bomber*, 104.
32. Terry Burstall, "Policy Contradictions of the Australian Task Force Vietnam, 1966," *Vietnam Generation* 3, no. 2 (1991): 44.
33. Interview with Derrill, Skype, June 27, 2016. This specific incident has been reported in the Australian media and discussed in another veteran's memoir. Matthew Benns, "Australian Federal Police May Investigate Claims Diggers Committed Atrocities during the Vietnam War," News.com.au, December 29, 2013; Don Tate, *The War Within* (Sydney: Murdoch Books, 2008), 263–264.
34. Interview with Peter, Melbourne, February 8, 2016.
35. Interview with Derrill.
36. Robert J. Lifton, *Home from the War: Vietnam Veterans—Neither Victims nor Executioners* (New York: Simon & Schuster, 1973), 41
37. Interview with Ron, Skype, April 5, 2016.
38. Interview with Don, Nha Trang, March 31, 2016.
39. Interview with James, Hà Nội, April 23, 2016.
40. Interview with Larry, March 18, 2016.
41. Interview with Suel, Đà Nẵng, April 14, 2016.
42. Testimony of Ronald Haeberle, April 23, 1970, in House Committee on Armed Services, *Investigation of the My Lai Incident,* 91st Congress, 2nd Session, 1976, 268.
43. Interview with Ron, Skype, April 5, 2016.
44. Interview with James. As of 2016, this caption reads, "The US soldiers with a 'cold look' after Sơn Mỹ massacre."
45. Seymour Hersh, *My Lai 4* (New York: Random House, 1970), 66.
46. Interview with James.
47. Exploring a similar response of American tourists to the War Remnants Museum, Scott Laderman argues that for American visitors, "the war was an Ameri-

can tragedy, and if the museum failed to acknowledge American suffering . . . then it was revealing its ideological bias." Scott Laderman, "From the Vietnam War to the 'War on Terror': Tourism and the Martial Fascination," in *Tourism and War*, ed. Richard Butler (London: Routledge, 2013), 33.

48. Both veterans recommended Nick Turse's *Kill Anything That Moves* to explain their attitude to atrocities in Vietnam.

49. Sơn Mỹ Memorial and Museum, April 4, 2016.

50. Interview with Ron.

51. Haeberle, testimony on *Investigation of the My Lai Incident*, 502.

52. Paul Williams, *Memorial Museums: The Global Rush to Commemorate Atrocities* (Oxford: Berg, 2007), 25. Charlie Company soldiers razed the hamlets after the massacre, and Quảng Ngãi Province was heavily bombed from 1969 until 1972 by RVNAF and American aircraft to cripple NLF resistance in the area.

53. The museum is directed by a survivor, Phạm Thành Công, and other survivors worked as guides at the memorial.

54. Interview with Mark, Đà Nẵng, April 14, 2016.

55. Interview with Jim, Hồ Chí Minh City, March 23, 2016.

56. Scott Laderman, *Tours of Vietnam: War, Travel Guides, and Memory* (Durham, NC: Duke University Press, 2009), 89.

57. The evidence suggests that NLF soldiers killed between 300 and 710 noncombatant police and RVN officials during the Tet offensive in Huế. U.S. Information Agency official Douglas Pike, who initially promoted the "bloodbath theory," acknowledged in 1988 that the numbers of those killed by the NLF were drastically inflated. Of the mass graves uncovered in Huế after the eight-week siege, many of the thousands of civilian fatalities were a result of American airpower, as well as an estimated 1,000 assassinated by RVN forces. Laderman, *Tours of Vietnam*, 89, 91–94, 116–117.

58. Interview with Mike M., Skype, May 20, 2016.

59. Interview with Larry, Đà Nẵng, April 18, 2016.

60. Interview with John A., Skype, August 12, 2016.

61. Schwenkel, *American War*, 26.

62. Bernard Weinraub, "American Veterans Treated Warmly in a Threadbare Hanoi," *New York Times*, December 22, 1981.

63. Interview with Suel.

64. Interview with David W., Vũng Tàu, August 17, 2016.

65. Interview with Mark.

66. Interview with Mark.

67. Interview with Ken, Carlton, May 25, 2016.

68. Interview with Heiko, Skype, May 10, 2016.

69. Interview with Francis, Skype, May 11, 2016.

19 Colonial Legacies of Dioxin Contamination in Vietnam and Australia

BOI HUYEN NGO

Ecologies of Uncertain Aftermaths— Colonial and War Aftermaths

Colonial legacies and histories within Vietnam and Australia have become entangled with dioxin contamination from the use of chemical herbicides. The herbicides used within both these countries are 2,4,5-T and 2,4-D; a mixture of both these herbicides in equal measure (50:50) has been militaristically categorized and known as Agent Orange ever since the Vietnam War. This chapter will explore the practices and procedures around the use of these herbicides and how colonial legacies have influenced the practices of spraying these herbicides in both Vietnam and Australia. Continuing the discussions earlier in this volume from Nathalie Nguyen and Mia Martin Hobbs on the device of storytelling to create larger architectures of knowledge around the Vietnam War and its aftermaths, this chapter will render visible the potential storytelling strategies that can structure our understandings of the past and the current urgencies of the present in decolonizing Western narratives around violence, health, and the environment in various contexts affected by war and colonization.

Two case studies will be explored in this chapter, one in the Vietnamese context and the other in the Australian context. This chapter will focus on the effects of the use of herbicides 2,4,5-T and 2,4-D which were used during the Vietnam War for Operation Ranch Hand between 1962 and 1971 and in the Kimberley region of Australia as an herbicide by the Western Australia Agriculture Protection Board between 1970 and 1985. In the Vietnamese context, the practice of executing Operation Ranch Hand in the Vietnam War will be analyzed through discourse analysis—examining the language around the operation plans and those who were part of it. In the Australian context, the decision making to systematically affirm the use of 2,4,5-T and 2,4-D within areas of marginalized communities of the Kimberley region throughout much of the 1970s and 1980s will be analyzed through content analysis of government documentation and media analysis. In addition, this chapter will explore the decisions and practices that continue to deny how the extensive use of these herbicides have affected the health and wellbeing of the Aboriginal Australian communities alongside veterans of the Vietnam War.

Dioxin contamination by 2,4,5-T and 2,4-D is a mode of violence that can be described as slow violence, where the cause and effect of the violence is not immediately visible, measurable, and tangible but rather, has a lag time between exposure and the enormity of the effects of exposure. An example is the 1976 Seveso disaster, where research has shown the long-term and large-scale effects of dioxin exposure to residential areas.[1] Dioxin contamination can seep slowly into the environment and the bodies through generations. Rob Nixon in his book *Slow Violence and the Environmentalism of the Poor* has addressed how there is a lack of acknowledgment or understanding of the enormity of war casualties beyond the immediate effects of violence, where fatalities are seen as swift killings rather than slow deaths.[2] Nixon wrote of slow violence, the mode of violence that is hidden and invisible, yet seeps into the everyday life of the people: "A violence that is neither spectacular not instantaneous, but rather incremental and accretive, its calamitous repercussions playing out across a range of temporal scales."[3] In relation to toxic legacies and contamination, he wrote, "How do we track the persistence of unofficial hostilities in the cellular domain, the untidy, attritional lethality that moves through the tissue, blood, and bones of combatants and non-combatants alike, moving through as well the living body of the land itself?"[4] Beyond the framework of cause and immediate effect, slow violence operates on a different and subjective framework in which the aftermaths of war and colonization are what he describes as open and uncertain. "Stories of the aftermath are protracted, convoluted, messy, open ended, and often discomforting to tell, particularly when—whether it's Noah's Ark or the 1991 Gulf War—the official narrative frame is unequivocally triumphalist."[5] In this research, we explore the nuanced continuation of colonial violence within Vietnam and Australia, a challenge that is noted by many scholars such as David Biggs, Rob Nixon, Edwin A. Martini, and Peter C. Van Wyck, among many others.

Edwin A. Martini has written in *Agent Orange: History, Science and the Politics of Uncertainty* of the integral violence within the unwillingness to understand the enormity of the possibilities around the effects of Agent Orange on landscapes, societies, and human bodies. "The failures of societies to address the total spread of dioxin through all these webs of production and transport constitutes a form of what Nixon calls slow violence."[6] David Biggs has noted the difficulty of writing about Agent Orange, with the challenge of "how to describe environmental phenomena with multiple and often divergent cascades of causal effects in different social, economic, and ecological settings."[7] He uses the concept of the drift in a very similar methodology of research to Peter C. Van Wyck's exploration of atomic legacies in his book *Highway of an Atom*, where he tracks the divergence of dioxin histories and how this can challenge established understandings of contamination. Biggs wrote, "By following drift, one can travel along disparate webs of social, political and physical factors playing into the initial commercial production or 'birth' of the herbicide, the political and ecological effects of its 'delivery' to mass markets and Vietnamese ecosystems, and the political and genetic stories associated with its degradation, half-life, 'death' and 'afterlife.'"[8]

Martini, Biggs, Nixon, and Van Wyck have made an overarching argument clear—that working with toxic legacies is part of an invisible violence that is drenched in uncertainty within the "open-ended, uncertain ecologies of the aftermath."[9] The challenge is to measure the immense and complex nature of responsibility in addressing uncertainty, and this need for responsibility is integral to address the violence of contamination that affects people to this day. This is akin to what Jacques Derrida described as the aporias of responsibility where "the concept of responsibility, like that of decision, would thus be found to lack coherence or consequence, even lacking identity with respect to itself, paralysed by what can be called an aporia."[10] Part of taking a social, political, and cultural responsibility for dioxin contamination in Vietnam and much of the Pacific is understanding that chemical contamination is not just an ecocidal tool of warfare. It is part of a legacy of colonization and capitalism, which needs to take into account how and where the chemicals are manufactured and how they are used or disposed after the war. Agent Orange has been manufactured in Australia.[11] We understand casualties now as not only direct victims of war but also the communities of people continually affected by the colonial legacies that place different values on life and health for different communities. Colonial legacies are part of the aftermath of chemical contamination.

Hence, when one explores the slow violence perpetrated by the spraying of Agent Orange, one explores the (ir)responsibilities of chemical warfare beyond a set space and time. Chemical warfare is slow violence seeping into temporality, into multiple environments, and into multiple bodies. It haunts, it insinuates, it multiplies, and then it appears. It becomes visible, materializing in sediments, in water, in blood, and in our mother's milk.

Chemical Agents 2,4,5-T and 2,4-D

The herbicides 2,4,5-T and 2,4-D were both used commercially and distributed for commercial sale prior to use in the Vietnam War. By 1958, 2,4-D and 2,4,5-T herbicides contributed to the majority of synthetic herbicides in the United States both in manufacturing and in consumption,[12] "a staple of the herbicide economy."[13] In creating the strategy for using herbicides as a military tool in the Vietnam War, army researchers at Fort Detrick created "Herbicide Mixture, Orange" which is a 50:50 mixture of these two commercial herbicides (2,4,5-T and 2,4-D). This was seen as a new tactical formula. It is the new and reformed militaristic purposes of 2,4,5-T and 2,4-D, rather than its chemical formula, that has created the label and what is known as Agent Orange. "These legal and bureaucratic procedures, more than chemistry, distinguished Agent Orange from near-identical commercial herbicides using a similar 50/50 mixture."[14] Hence, even though Agent Orange was technically used for exclusively military purposes, it consists of commercial herbicides of the time. Although Agent Orange is a military tool used in the Vietnam War, the same chemical agents of both 2,4,5-T and 2,4-D were used afterward for commercial, governmental, and agricultural purposes outside the context of the Vietnam War.

In the Vietnam War, from 1962 to 1971, the U.S. military used Agent Orange as a part of Operation Ranch Hand. The U.S. aim was to defoliate forest and rural areas in order to deprive the Vietcong guerrillas of food crops and cover. However, most of the crops destroyed were food sources for civilians, and as a result, widespread famine followed. As an ongoing consequence of Agent Orange spraying, sickness, diseases such as cancer, miscarriages, birth defects, disabilities, along with many other health issues are still being found throughout the generations in Vietnam, as well as among veterans of the Vietnam War and their offspring. In present-day Vietnam, the high levels of dioxin within the homeland soils and water as well as within the bodies of civilians is causing ongoing contamination: entering food chains, infiltrating water, soil, human tissue, and passing down generation after generation.

Diagnosis: Responsibility of the Story

The dioxin contamination or compound that is present in the herbicides 2,4,5-T and 2,4-D (hence, also Agent Orange) is 2,3,7,8-tetrachlorodibenzo-pdioxin (TCDD). This dioxin is formed within the manufacturing process. Both 2,4,5-T and 2,4-D can create TCDD within this process, but 2,4,5-T in particular has higher levels of TCDD compounds. Another factor to consider is that dioxin contamination is not stable and stagnant—conditions such as heat, for example through sun exposure, can heighten the TCDD compounds within the chemical agents.

An approach to ethical research is that when writing about chemical agents and its adverse effects on civilians and veterans, there is a recognition and understanding that chemicals do not work in predictable patterns, achieving predictable conclusions—especially given the particularity of different biological beings. Dioxin contamination affects different generations of families differently. It affects different environments, different fish, and different rivers differently. Many scientific studies have failed to fully resolve scientific questions on the correlation and links of dioxin to diseases due to the broad spectrum of symptoms and diseases as a consequence of dioxin exposure. There is the need for more inclusive ways of diagnosis to include clinical histories, stories, statistics of ongoing and recurring illness through the generations postexposure. A woman who was exposed to dioxin contamination through Agent Orange and has children with disabilities stated in an interview for social research on the impact of chemical warfare on women's reproductive health, "Vietnam is now a country of peace, extending hands to former enemies, but the victims of Agent Orange will never live in peace."[15] The struggle that many veterans and civilians face is that compensation and acknowledgment of the effects of dioxin contamination on their bodies and bodies of future generations is dependent on the Western biomedicine diagnosis framework and methodology.

Annemarie Jutel and Sarah Nettleton wrote about the current structures of Western biomedicine diagnosis in "Towards a Sociology of Diagnosis: Reflections and Opportunities."[16] Through the associated journal, there is a call from various scholars and medical experts to analyze the practices of diagnosis through the lens of historiography, culture, and sociology. They write that Western biomedicine diagnosis "validates what counts as disease; offers explanations and coheres patients' symptoms; legitimates illness, enabling patients to access the sick role; provides a means to access resources and facilitates their allocation; and forms the foundation of medical authority."[17] However, this framework can be limited in being able to diagnose dioxin contamination effects when disease and symptoms are inconsistent between individuals. In addition, the influence of politics has potentially affected the diagnosis of chemical contamination where recognition and responsibility of chemical contamination would ultimately lead to the need for compensation. Jutel and Nettleton referenced nuclear test veterans of the South Pacific Ocean where "the pursuit of biomedical explanation for their ailments is inseparable from the acknowledgment of liability . . . without a diagnosis, state recognition and ultimately compensation are impossible. Diagnosis, however, is politically charged, because it implies culpability."[18] Hence, both the lack of consistent symptoms among all victims within the biomedical diagnosis alongside the politically charged nature of diagnosis can limit and disregard the stories and experiences of dioxin contamination.

An example of the limits of the exclusively biomedical approach for diagnosis is the conclusions arrived at in the Australian Royal Commission report, *The Royal Commission on the Use and Effects of Chemical Agents in Australian Personnel in Vietnam* (1985), where many symptoms experienced by Australian veterans exposed to Agent Orange are attributed to stress and post-traumatic stress disorder (PTSD), "the same set of symptoms is often seen in survivors of nature and other disasters"[19] and in regard to lower mortality, "it is probably caused by an increase in risk taking behaviour, and in smoking, and in drinking connected with the Vietnam service."[20] The conclusion of the report is based on a particular study of science but with no account or acknowledgment of the veteran experience—no lengthy interviews, stories, or clinical histories are included in this report. The language of the conclusion has a patronizing tone: "So Agent Orange is Not Guilty and the chemical agents used to defoliate battle zones in Vietnam and to protect Australians from malaria are not to blame. No one lost. This is not a matter for regret but for rejoicing. . . . This is good news and it is the Commission's fervent hopes that it will be shouted from the rooftops."[21]

The Australian Royal Commission's conclusion forms part of a continuing pattern of denial of the effects of contamination from these chemical agents on marginalized people such as veterans, farmers, and Aboriginal Australians. The conclusion and the discourse in the Australian Royal Commission report demonstrates how the Western biomedical diagnosis method is utilized as a tool for the Australian government to avoid the responsibility of compensation. "In Agent Orange cases the uncertainty and the lack of convincing scientific proof have rewarded governments in Australia and chemical manufacturers of Agent Orange," writes Martini.[22] Responsibility in this Royal Commission Report was anchored in the need for traditional scientific evidence rather than having a fuller understanding of the intrinsic part of uncertainty and the infinite nature of dioxin contamination within stories and clinical histories. There is a need to encompass the understanding of individualized case-by-case scenarios of contamination of biological organisms, intergenerational effects, and landscapes. The structure of diagnosis utilized by most governments are part of a Western colonial structure that does not take into account storytelling and clinical histories as a part of diagnosis.

It should be understood that outside diagnosis for chemical contamination, the utilization of clinical histories, genetics counseling, and storytelling as part of diagnosis is already widespread in many medical practices such as in hospitals. An example is genetics counseling, which gathers family history to further understand diagnosis and disease, a practice adopted by many hospitals within Australia. Nancy H. M. Davenport, in her journal article "Medical Residents' Use of Narrative Templates in Storytelling and Diagnosis," wrote of how a community-orientated hospital in the United States, Bellwether Hospital, incorporated narrative storytelling as a part of diagnosis where "physicians through storytelling place any test or symptom in context; it is, in fact, how something gets cemented as a 'symptom' at all. Story trajectories then, are not by-products of the encounter; they are the work of the encounter."[23] Hence, storytelling and symptoms are analyzed together within this alternative diagnosis framework, and treatment follows once a physician makes sense of symptoms and sicknesses through a patient's story.[24] All of the below Vietnamese and Australian case studies are explored through the lens of understanding the lack of diagnosis incorporating clinical histories, genetics counseling, and storytelling for the victims of chemical contamination, and how this limitation further exacerbates inequalities that are part of the colonial legacies.

Cowboys and Indians: U.S. Colonial Discourses around Agent Orange

The various operations involving Agent Orange, including Operation Ranch Hand for the spraying of Agent Orange during the Vietnam War and

Operation Pacer HO for the disposal of Agent Orange after the war, utilize language and discourses to motivate veterans and workers around working with Agent Orange. One film on Operation Pacer HO uses disturbing language to outline some of the basic safety precautions when disposing Agent Orange involving the draining, rinsing, and crushing of Agent Orange barrels. The title of the film sequence is "Exposed with Pride," which was embraced by those involved in this operation.[25] Much of these discourses are adopted from colonial frameworks, showing a cultural and militaristic outlook concerning the environment, the Vietnamese people, and a lack of value for the health of themselves and civilians.

Regarding the name of Operation Ranch Hand, the definition of a ranch hand is a worker on a ranch in the United States where there is an implied association with farming and cultivating food. The irony is that the operation—the spraying of Agent Orange—was defarming, destroying, and colonizing through a military tactic of eradication—of forests, food sources, people.

At the website ranchhandvietnam.org containing veteran photographs and story archives about Operation Ranch Hand, veterans of this operation were proud to call each other cowboys. An example is the introductory statement on a page for the online gallery: "This Gallery is for all Cowboys to share their fondest memories and flying experiences with the rest of us."[26] The adoption of cowboys within the language among Ranch Handers also occurs in other sectors and parts of the U.S. military during the Vietnam War. In the context of analyzing the My Lai massacre, Michael Yellow Bird, in the article "Cowboys and Indians: Toys of Genocide, Icons of American Colonialism," wrote, "During the Vietnam War, the United States often thought of Vietnam in images of the American West and cast the Vietnamese in the role of Indians. It was common for American soldiers to refer to enemy territory (free-fire zones) as 'Indian Country' and for American soldiers to brutally massacre Vietnamese while fantasizing they were killing Indians."[27]

Similar to the colonial discourses that Yellow Bird was referring to in terms of the My Lai massacre, the title of Operation Ranch Hand presents the illusion of the Old West in that the soldiers refer to themselves as cowboys. Following on from this logic, then the Vietnamese are the Native Americans, and their environment is to be destroyed. The connection of the Old West to Operation Ranch Hand in the Vietnam War had obvious, deliberate, and even strategic connections to colonial sentiments in its textual referents to the colonization of Native Americans.

Smokey Bear

The so-called Ranch Handers of Operation Ranch Hand informally adopted a mascot—Smokey Bear, the U.S. mascot that successfully raised awareness about forest fires with its catchy slogan, "Only you can prevent the forest fires!" Smokey Bear debuted in 1947 and continues to be a recognized symbol in American culture. Smokey Bear is still used in wildfire prevention publicity. It is ironic that the Smokey Bear mascot, used by the U.S. Forest Service as an iconic figure to instruct the public on the risk of forest fires, was appropriated to signify the destruction of forests. The Forest Service motto was modified from "Only you can prevent the forest fire" to jokingly "Only you can prevent a forest." Modified posters of Smokey Bear were hung around the Ranch Hand buildings from 1965, mainly in Bien Hoa Air Base in Vietnam as well as training grounds in Virginia and Florida.[28]

However, the utilization of Smokey Bear may not be as ironic as it seems and may have colonial motivations. Jake Kosek's book *Understories: The Political Life of Forests in Northern New Mexico*, explores those motivations within the context of New Mexico and forest conservation programs, where Smokey Bear is perceived as colonizing by many of the communities in New Mexico such as the Indigenous and Chicano communities. A longtime forest worker Salomon Martinez stated that Smokey Bear "is a constant reminder that the woods are no longer ours. He watches over them like a prison guard. . . . He is not here to help people; he is here to kick us Chicanos out."[29] Around the area, posters of Smokey Bear have many bullet holes in them, showing the antagonism prompted by Smokey Bear in the community, where many expressed that Smokey Bear is the symbol of U.S. colonialism. The legacies and the mythologies of Smokey Bear are intertwined with the normative modes of race and nation. Kosek explored the colonizing aspect of Smokey Bear:

> Indeed, the imagined community of "the nation" is depicted implicitly within the Smokey Bear campaign with specific racial, gender and class segments of society presumed to stand in for the common interests of the larger nation. As a national symbol, Smokey thus nationalised prescribed behaviours by policing certain conduct within the forest. Even more powerful, however, Smokey came to embody the normative model citizen. He thus helped mold the proper relationship between American citizen and subject and reproduced boundaries of the national populace that excluded many

groups or individuals or at the very least, left open the question of whether and to what extent they were included.[30]

Alongside the colonizing aspect of Smokey Bear and how it is perceived as representing certain white notions of forest management is the U.S. Forest Service's own involvement in the Vietnam War. For years prior, the U.S. Forest Service advised the South Vietnamese in the development of their lumber industry.[31] However, in December 1965, the Joint Chiefs of Staff in the U.S. Department of Defense requested the Secretary of Defense grant approval to explore the possibility of forest fires as a military weapon for the Vietnam War, and this initiated research for the Defense Advanced Research Projects Agency.[32] They contracted the U.S. Forest Service to research and explore this potential weapon, hence the U.S. Forest Service was an active part of the research and military operation for the destruction of the environment. The adoption of Smokey Bear, a mascot for preventing forest fires for Operation Ranch Hand, is not ironic but is part of the continuation of colonial discourses and practices of the U.S. Forest Service within the context of the Vietnam War.

Adopting the Smokey Bear mascot and altering the posters only reinforced how Smokey Bear is used to normalize colonizing behavior and acts at this collective military level. Within the American context, Smokey Bear is still popular and used widely. Not only environmental destruction but environmental conservation is a form of control, including through the context of racism and histories of colonization. A way of understanding this is expressed through the words of the ecofeminist Rosemary Radford Ruether: "An ecological ethic must be an ethic of eco-justice that recognises the interconnection of social domination and the domination of nature."[33]

Dioxin Contamination in the Kimberley Region

Between 1970 and 1985, the Western Australia Agriculture Protection Board hired three hundred men to eradicate weeds from the Kimberley region using both 2,4-D and 2,4,5-T, the chemical agents and components of Agent Orange. Most of the workers handling these herbicides were Aboriginal Australians. These herbicides were used even after the various health concerns and health issues experienced by civilians and veterans in the aftermath of the Vietnam War suggested that the dioxin contamination of these herbicides (TCDD) had dangerous effects on the human body. Anthropologist Stephen Muecke wrote, "Someone decided to unload a cargo of unsellable Agent Orange on remote Indigenous Australia where its use didn't matter, where precariously employed young men need jobs."[34] Many interviews and accounts from the employees have shown that the employees were not aware of the dangers of these herbicides and their employers falsely assured them that the chemical was safe. Ron Delvin, a former worker of the Western Australia Agriculture Protection Board stated, "We were moving around the country spraying it all over the place, willy-nilly and being told it was safe, that you could drink it."[35] He mentioned that they were not given any protective gear or hazardous warnings.

It has been speculated in much reportage in the media that the herbicides given to the Aboriginal communities in the West Kimberley region were leftovers manufactured for the Vietnam War. A former worker, Carl Drysdale, expressed, "We actually asked if it came from Vietnam and we were laughed at and told it was harmless and just get on and do it and leave the research for the research people."[36]

The Western Australia Legislative Council wrote a report in 2004 titled *Report of the Standing Committee on Environment and Public Affairs in the relation to Chemical Use by the Agriculture Protection Board 1970–1985* in which they have stated that CIK (Chemical Industries Kwinana) chemicals manufactured the herbicides. The son of the late director of CIK, John Telford, said to the standing committee, "Absolutely no chemicals came in from Vietnam. If you knew the history of my father and his attitude towards Americans in Vietnam, you would know that would never happen."[37] However, with the owner deceased and the closure of CIK in 1985, there are no company records.[38] Hence, the question of whether the chemicals were imported from Vietnam is unconfirmed.

Most media reported the herbicide as Agent Orange, but the Western Australia Legislative Council refuses to accept that it was Agent Orange. The *Report of the Standing Committee on Environment and Public Affairs in the relation to Chemical Use by the Agriculture Protection Board 1970–1985* claim that since the chemicals 2,4-D and 2,4,5-T were used separately and not together, it is not Agent Orange: "Neither 2,4-D nor 2,4,5-T on their own constitutes Agent Orange. Agent Orange was never registered as a herbicide for use in Australia."[39] Although it is not what we would term Agent Orange and not the exact cocktail that the military researchers derived in Fort Detrick, what should be noted is the dioxin is still present whether 2,4,5-T is mixed with 2,4-D or on its own. As David Biggs expressed, Agent Orange is mainly a military term rather than a chemical one, used to differentiate it from herbicides in the commercial market. Although it is true that Agent Orange consists of a 50:50 mixture of 2,4-D and 2,4,5-T and not these chemicals separately, dioxin contamination (TCDD) is mainly derived from 2,4,5-T in its production process.

The *Report of the Standing Committee* also insists that CIK did follow the industry standards set out by the National Health and Medical Research Council in 1975 to regulate the level of TCDD dioxin of 2,4,5-T. However, the standing committee's notion that TCDD levels can be regulated is not accurate. I consulted with toxicologist Professor Andrew Dawson (Director, National Poisons Register and Clinical Toxicology, Royal Prince Alfred Hospital, Sydney), who mentioned that TCDD is formed during the manufacturing process, where a careful control of temperature can lower the TCDD, but also that TCDD is formed during storage where conditions of light and heat, for instance, can heighten TCDD levels. Therefore, the notion that the chemical end product always has a predictable and controlled concentration of TCDD is not correct.[40] An example of this is when the chemical is exposed to heat or, in the case of the next case study, fire.

Rogue Batch

In 1971, there was a factory fire in a chemical factory in Jurong, Singapore, in which the chemicals were fire damaged. Paper trails in the Tariff Board Inquiry files in the National Archives, Canberra, suggest that CIK did import fire-damaged chemicals to Brisbane, seeking reduced tariffs, with an invoice saying, "fire-damaged materials."[41] The director at the time, Robert Cecil Telford, wrote a letter to the tariff board dated December 21, 1972, requesting reduced tariffs. Telford provided proof of the damage to the imported chemicals, writing, "I am sending you a sample of the consignment. Normally it is yellow oily material. This stuff resembles molasses."[42] Furthermore, he wrote in a letter dated January 1, 1973, "We tried blending it in with pale amber product but due to its intense black colour even 3 to 4% was too much and our customers complained. . . . One of our greatest problems with this stuff is the presence of a sort of resinous partly soluble suspension that comes out of solution when customers add it with water. This blocks up jets and is quite impractical to use."[43] There are no confirmed documents within the report about what happened to this rogue batch of chemicals, but what is noteworthy in these letters is that they describe the color and consistency of this rogue batch—blackened, like molasses, and resinous in texture as opposed to yellow and oily.

This description of this rogue batch matched what was encountered by the workers of the Agriculture Protection Board. One of the workers, Carl Drysdale, described a strange batch in an ABC Radio interview: "Now this stuff that we got was dark brown, it was grainy, it blocked up the nozzles of the spray units, it was very thick and streaky. It definitely wasn't the regular run-of-the-mill 245-T. We certainly questioned where these drums came from because they were unmarked 44-gallon drums."[44] The striking similarity between the two descriptions of the chemicals by Robert Cecil Telford and worker Carl Drysdale and the lack of records as to what has happened to the imported rogue batch raises a question on whether the rogue batch was given to be sprayed in the Kimberley region.

Family members and the Indigenous community in the West Kimberley region are reeling from the intergenerational effects of dioxin contamination like in Vietnam. They experience higher portions of disabilities, early deaths, cancers, and miscarriages—like the people in Vietnam, like the veterans of the war. They are also fighting legally for compensation. Elders and members of the community, including Lucy Marshall, campaigner and Order of Australia recipient, are still seeking an acknowledgment and compensation for the contamination and the intergenerational haunting of dioxin contamination on the West Kimberley communities.[45]

Conclusion

Through looking at the trail of dioxin contamination, not only during the Vietnam War but also in its aftermaths, it is possible to discern a pattern akin to colonization. Chemical contamination becomes a tool in which the legacies of colonization continue in the so-called postcolonial world, whether it is in Vietnam or in Australia. It is a process in which certain bodies, environments, and lives are not as valued as others. As Nixon wrote, "Chemical and radiological violence, for example, is driven inward, somatised into cellular dramas of mutation that—particularly in the bodies of the poor—remain largely unobserved, undiagnosed and untreated."[46] It is a process of slow violence that seeps and haunts. There is a need to intersect the Vietnam War and its histories with colonizing practices that we see, particularly against Indigenous peoples. We need to understand that dioxin contamination can have different effects for different people and different environments. This is evident in research that alongside medical diagnosis, personal testimony, collective memory, oral histories, and clinical and family histories are needed for diagnosis. Scientific ambiguity is intrinsic and fundamental to the experience of contamination. As Biggs wrote, "Metabolic history and the metaphor of the drift present a path for more stories about environments, from toxic sites to human bodies, where there is neither a static victim or site nor a morally good or bad subject. Dioxin, like many environmental agents and phenomena, lacks intent."[47] Oral histories and personal testimonies can contribute to the processes of validation and acknowledgment for diagnosis, responsibility, and compensation toward those affected in the intergenerational communities. Decolonization is listening to stories.

Notes

The author would like to acknowledge, in gratitude, Professor Andrew Dawson (Director, Poisons Register and Clinical Toxicology, Royal Prince Alfred Hospital, Sydney) and Associate Professor Silas W. Smith (Clinical Associate Professor, Ronald O. Perelman Department of Emergency Medicine, NYU Grossman School of Medicine). Professor Dawson helped the author in clarifying the science around toxicology and has been generous and collaborative with sharing knowledge for many years. Associate Professor Smith has helped with clarifying toxicological reference material for this research.

1. Pier Alberto Bertazzi, Dario Consonni, Silvia Bachetti, Maurizia Rubagotti, Andrea Baccarelli, Carlo Zocchetti, and Angela Pesatori, "Health Effects of Dioxin Exposure: A 20-Year Mortality Study," *American Journal of Epidemiology* 153, no. 11 (2001): 1031–1044.

2. Rob Nixon, *Slow Violence and the Environmentalism of the Poor* (Cambridge, MA: Harvard University Press, 2011).

3. Nixon, *Slow Violence*, 2.

4. Nixon, *Slow Violence*, 217.

5. Nixon, *Slow Violence*, 200.

6. Edwin A. Martini, *Agent Orange: History, Science, and the Politics of Uncertainty* (Amherst: University of Massachusetts Press), 9.

7. David Biggs, "Following Dioxin's Drift: Agent Orange Stories and the Challenge of Metabolic History," *International Review of Environmental History* 4, no. 1 (2018): 7.

8. Biggs, "Following Dioxin's Drift," 11.

9. Nixon, *Slow Violence*, 200.

10. Jacques Derrida, *The Gift of Death* (Chicago: University of Chicago Press, 1995), 84.

11. Union Carbide Corporation (owned by DOW Chemicals since 2011) was one of the main manufacturers of Agent Orange and had a factory in Rhodes, NSW, manufacturing Agent Orange during the Vietnam War.

12. Biggs, "Following Dioxin's Drift," 15.

13. Biggs, "Following Dioxin's Drift," 16.

14. Biggs, "Following Dioxin's Drift," 18.

15. Anonymous interviewee cited in Le Thi Nham Tuyet and Annika Johansson, "Impact of Chemical Warfare with Agent Orange on Women's Reproductive Lives in Vietnam: A Pilot Study," *Reproductive Health Matters* 9 (2001): 163.

16. Annemarie Jutel and Sarah Nettleton, "Towards a Sociology of Diagnosis: Reflections and Opportunities," *Social Science and Medicine* 73, no. 6 (2011): 793–800.

17. Jutel and Nettleton, "Towards a Sociology of Diagnosis," 793.

18. Jutel and Nettleton, "Towards a Sociology of Diagnosis," 797.

19. Royal Commission on the Use and Effects of Chemical Agents on Australian Personnel in Vietnam and Phillip Evatt, *Final Report,* vol. 8 (Canberra: Australian Government Publishing Service, 1985), xv–26.

20. Royal Commission, *Final Report,* 8: xv–27.

21. Royal Commission, *Final Report,* 8: xv–38.

22. Martini, *Agent Orange,* 195.

23. Nancy H. M. Davenport, "Medical Residents' Use of Narrative Templates in Storytelling and Diagnosis," *Social Science and Medicine* 73, no. 6 (2011): 875.

24. Davenport, "Medicine Residents' Use," 880.

25. Martini, *Agent Orange,* 119.

26. "Photo Gallery," *About Operation Ranch Hand Vietnam South East Asia 1961–1971,* accessed November 5, 2020, http://www.ranchhandvietnam.org/gallery/.

27. Michael Yellow Bird, "Cowboys and Indians: Toys of Genocide, Icons of American Colonialism," *Wicazo Sa Review* 19 (2004): 43.

28. James G. Lewis, "On Smokey Bear in Vietnam," *Environmental History* 11 (2006): 598.

29. Jake Kosek, *Understories: The Political Life of Forests in Northern New Mexico* (Durham, NC: Duke University Press, 2006), 183.

30. Kosek, *Understories,* 213.

31. Martini, *Agent Orange,* 47.

32. Martini, *Agent Orange,* 46.

33. Rosemary Radford Ruether, "Toward an Ecological-Feminist Theology of Nature," in *Healing the Wounds,* ed. Judith Plant (Philadelphia: New Society Publishers, 1989), 149.

34. Stephen Muecke, "Day 12 /// Responding to Elizabeth Povinelli—Windjerrameru, The Stealing C*nts," E-flux Conversations, May 2015, https://conversations.e-flux.com/t/superconversations-day-12-stephen-mueke-responds-toelizabeth-povinelli-windjerrameru-the-stealing-c-nts/1733.

35. Ron Delvin cited in Gerry Georgatos, "Agent Orange Used as Herbicide throughout the Kimberley," *The Stringer: Independent News,* March 15, 2013, https://thestringer.com.au/agent-orange-used-as-a-herbicide-throughout-the-kimberley-1288#.X6KtE5MzbVo.

36. ABC: Background Briefing, *Chemical Consequences,* April 18, 2004, https://www.abc.net.au/radionational/programs/backgroundbriefing/chemical-conse quences/3408556.

37. Western Australia Legislative Council (Second Session of the Thirty-Sixth Parliament), *Report of the Standing Committee on Environment and Public Affairs in relation to Chemical Use by the Agriculture Protection Board 1970–1985,* Report 10,

October 2004, 21, https://www.parliament.wa.gov.au/Parliament/commit.nsf/(Report+Lookup+by+Com+ID)/CD08CE85AE2369D148257831003E960B/$file/ep.apb.041020.rpf.010.xx.a.pdf.

38. Western Australia Legislative Council, *Report of the Standing Committee*, 20, 23.
39. Western Australia Legislative Council, *Report of the Standing Committee*, 5.
40. Professor Andrew Dawson, Email correspondence with author, June 23, 2020.
41. Western Australia Legislative Council, *Report of the Standing Committee*, 33.
42. Western Australia Legislative Council, *Report of the Standing Committee*, 33.
43. Western Australia Legislative Council, *Report of the Standing Committee*, 34.
44. ABC: Background Briefing, *Chemical Consequences*.
45. Rebecca Trigger and Natalie Jones, "Queen's Birthday Honours: Lucy Marshall, Campaigner for Indigenous Agent Orange Victims in WA, Awarded Order of Australia," ABC News, June 8, 2015, http://www.abc.net.au/news/2015-06-08/queens-birthdayhonours-west-australians-recognised/6522804.
46. Nixon, *Slow Violence*, 6.
47. Biggs, "Following Dioxin's Drift," 30.

Acknowledgments

This volume began as a conference at Macquarie University in Sydney, Australia in August 2019. We would like to thank the university for sponsoring both the conference and Fred's visit to Australia as the 2019 Vice-Chancellor's Distinguished Visiting Fellow. We are grateful to Vice-Chancellor S. Bruce Dowton, Deputy Vice-Chancellor (Research) Sakkie Pretorius, and Executive Dean of the Faculty of Arts Martina Möllering for their support. Many thanks also to Barbara Keys for delivering the conference's keynote remarks and to everyone else who contributed to the conference and associated events: Helen Anderson, Michelle Arrow, Sean Brawley, Nicola Dew, Chris Dixon, Thom Dixon, Adele Garnier, Kyle Harvey, Kevin Jon Heller, Alison Holland, Julie Janson, Alexandra Kurmann, Michelle Lee, Jon Piccini, Erin Semon, Annabel Voysey, and Hoang Vu. The conference could not cover all of the war's varied regional dimensions and as a result this volume is not comprehensive in its coverage of the topic. Nevertheless, we hope this collection of essays will promote further study of the regional aspects of the conflict. At the University of North Carolina Press, Debbie Gershenowitz has been a wonderful editor, and we are grateful to everyone on the wider team who helped shepherd this book to publication. Thanks also to the two outside reviewers who provided valuable feedback on an early draft. Finally, allow us to express our immense gratitude to Jess, Lara, Gabrielle, and Rosemary, and to Danyel, Emma, and Joseph for their steadfast love and support.

Contributors

DAVID L. ANDERSON is professor of history emeritus at California State University, Monterey Bay, and senior lecturer of national security affairs at the U.S. Naval Postgraduate School. He is the author or editor of twelve books, including *Imperialism and Idealism: American Diplomats in China, 1861–1898* (1985), *The Columbia History of the Vietnam War* (2011), and *Vietnamization: Politics, Strategy, Legacy* (2020).

BRIAN CUDDY is lecturer in security studies at Macquarie University in Sydney, Australia. A historian of international politics and U.S. foreign relations, his research explores changing legal frameworks of national and international security in the twentieth century.

MATTIAS FIBIGER is assistant professor of business administration at Harvard Business School. A historian by training, he conducts research on international relations and political economy in Southeast Asia.

ZACH FREDMAN is assistant professor of history at Duke Kunshan University, where he teaches courses on U.S. foreign relations and modern China. His first book, *The Tormented Alliance: American Servicemen and the Occupation of China, 1941–1949* (2022), examines the U.S. military presence in China during World War II and the Chinese Civil War.

MARC JASON GILBERT is professor of history emeritus at Hawaiʻi Pacific University. He is author or editor of four books on the wars in Indochina, including *Why the North Won the Vietnam War* (2002), and author of related chapters in several books, such as *Vietnam and the West: New Approaches* (2010) and *Indochina in the Year of the Horse, 1966* (2016).

ALICE S. KIM received her PhD in Rhetoric from the University of California, Berkeley. Her dissertation, "Airport Modern" (2013), explores the genealogy of the postcolonial airport (Kimpo) through the lens of the contradictions of postwar South Korean industrialization and development. Her publications include "*Left* Out: 'People's Solidarity for Social Progress' and the Evolution of South Korean *Minjung* after Authoritarianism" in *South Korean Social Movements: From Democracy to Civil Society* (2011).

MARK ATWOOD LAWRENCE is professor of history at the University of Texas at Austin. He is author of *Assuming the Burden: Europe and the American Commitment to War in Vietnam* (2005), *The Vietnam War: A Concise International History* (2008), and *The End of Ambition: The United States and the Third World in the Vietnam Era* (2021).

JASON LIM is senior lecturer in Asian history at the University of Wollongong. He researches on Taiwan's relationship with Southeast Asia during the Cold War and on the history of the Chinese community in Southeast Asia.

JANA K. LIPMAN is a professor at Tulane University. She is the author of *In Camps: Vietnamese Refugees, Asylum Seekers, and Repatriates* (University of California Press, 2020) and the cotranslator of *Ship of Fate: The Memoir of a Vietnamese Repatriate* by Trần Đình Trụ (University of Hawai'i Press, 2017).

GREG LOCKHART is an Australian Vietnam War veteran and historian. Formerly of the Australian National University, his books include *Nation in Arms: The Origins of the People's Army of Vietnam* (1989) and *The Minefield: An Australian Tragedy in Vietnam* (2007). He is cotranslator with his wife Monique of *The Light of the Capital: Three Modern Vietnamese Classics* (1996), and his memoir *Weaving of Worlds: A Day on Île d'Yeu* is forthcoming.

FREDRIK LOGEVALL is the Laurence D. Belfer Professor of International Affairs at Harvard University. He is the author or editor of ten books, most recently *JFK: Coming of Age in the American Century, 1917–1956* (Random House, 2020). A native of Stockholm, Sweden, he is a former president of the Society for Historians of American Foreign Relations.

S. R. JOEY LONG is associate professor of history at the National University of Singapore. He is the author of *Safe for Decolonization: The Eisenhower Administration, Britain, and Singapore* (2011). His most recent book is a coedited volume (with Brian P. Farrell and David J. Ulbrich), *From Far East to Asia Pacific: Great Powers and Grand Strategy, 1900–1954* (2022).

CHRISTOPHER LOVINS is assistant professor of Korean history at the Ulsan National Institute of Science and Technology. He is the author of *King Chŏngjo, an Enlightened Despot in Early Modern Korea* (2019). He publishes on political legitimacy and early modern kingship, slavery, evolutionary approaches to the humanities, historical film, and science fiction.

MIA MARTIN HOBBS is a research fellow at Deakin University. An oral historian of war and conflict, she is the author of *Return to Vietnam: An Oral History of American and Australian Veterans' Journeys* (Cambridge University Press, 2021).

BOI HUYEN NGO's work explores Vietnamese migration and incorporates Aboriginal Australian and Vietnamese knowledge and storytelling in the attempt to decolonize knowledge and histories of Vietnam and Australia. She taught and guest lectured for five years at the University of Technology Sydney.

WEN-QING NGOEI is assistant professor of humanities at the Singapore Management University. His first book, *Arc of Containment: Britain, the United States, and Anticommunism in Southeast Asia* (Cornell University Press, 2019), traces how British decolonization and Southeast Asian anti-communism shaped U.S. empire in the wider region. His essays have appeared in *Diplomatic History*, *The Journal of American-East Asian Relations*, and *International Journal*.

NATHALIE HUYNH CHAU NGUYEN is professor of history at Monash University in Australia. An Oxford graduate and former ARC Future Fellow, she is the author of four books: *South Vietnamese Soldiers: Memories of the Vietnam War and After* (2016), *Memory Is Another Country: Women of the Vietnamese Diaspora* (2009), *Voyage of Hope: Vietnamese Australian Women's Narratives* (2005), and *Vietnamese Voices: Gender and Cultural Identity in the Vietnamese Francophone Novel* (2003).

NORIKO SHIRATORI is research fellow with the Research Center for Cooperative Civil Societies at Rikkyo University, Tokyo, lecturer in Asian studies at the School of Pacific and Asian Studies, University of Hawai'i at Mānoa, and research analyst in the state of Hawai'i executive branch. Her research explores transnational civic activism and social movements in the global 1960s and early 1970s.

LISA TRAN is professor of history at California State University, Fullerton. She is the author of *Concubines in Court: Marriage and Monogamy in Twentieth-Century China* (Rowman & Littlefield, 2015) and is currently working on a book manuscript on Asia in world history (under contract with Cambridge University Press).

A. GABRIELLE WESTCOTT is a doctoral candidate in history at the University of Connecticut, where she specializes in the history of U.S. foreign relations. Her dissertation, "Struggling for the Soul and Mind of a President," examines how the emotions and personalities of Lyndon B. Johnson and his advisers shaped U.S. policy toward Vietnam in 1968.

Index

$2,4$-D, 321, 322, 324, 325, 331. *See also* chemical agents; dioxin contamination; herbicides

$2,4,5$-T, 321, 322, 324, 325, 331, 332, 333. *See also* chemical agents; dioxin contamination; herbicides

$2,3,7,8$-tetrachlorodibenzo-pdioxin (TCDD), 325, 330, 332. *See also* dioxin contamination

Abe Shinzo, 107, 121
Aboriginal Australians, 10, 322, 326–327, 330
Abrams, Creighton, 132
Acheson, Dean, 69
activism, transpacific, 107, 111–120, 121. *See also* anti-war sentiment/activism; Beheiren; Iwakuni
Afghanistan, 137, 186
Africa, 7, 25. *See also individual countries*
African Americans, in military, 109, 111, 112, 113–114, 118
Afro-Asian nonaligned movement, 7
agency, of Vietnamese actors, 6
Agent Orange, 10, 311, 321, 323, 325, 330; in Australia, 14–15n40, 326, 330–332, 333; chemicals in, 332; colonial discourses around, 327; difficulty of writing about, 323; disposal of, 328; health issues and, 324; slow violence of, 324. *See also* chemical agents; dioxin contamination; TCDD; $2,4$-D; $2,4,5$-T
Agent Orange (Martini), 322–323
agitators, outside, 41. *See also* communism
agriculture, 144, 145, 147, 148–149, 153, 155

Agriculture Protection Board, 321, 330, 331, 333
Ahn Jung-hyo, 177
aid, U.S.: alignment and, 183; to ASEAN states, reduction in, 249; for contributing troops, 8, 197, 199; fisheries aid, 166; for French, 20; Indonesia and, 80, 81, 239–242, 246; legacies of, 239; military assistance programs, 205, 206, 209; to non-communist states, 237, 239; Philippines and, 189, 237, 239, 242, 246; South Korea and, 187–188, 197, 205–206, 208, 209; South Vietnam and, 147, 149, 150; Thailand and, 189; USOM, 151, 155
Aidit, D. N., 26
air war over North Vietnam, 95–96
Akaka, Daniel K., 102
Algeria, 185
Alliale, Camille, 25
allies, eternal, 193
allies, U.S., 6, 10; attempts to prolong U.S. involvement in war, 56; benefits to, 183; Clifford's distrust of, 63–64; commitment of, 56, 60–61; determination to resist communism, 60; legitimacy of U.S. involvement and, 65; vs. mercenaries, 204; perception of attitudes of, 62; race and, 204; representation of, 59; U.S. withdrawal from Vietnam and, 192. *See also* bases, U.S. military; Clifford, Clark; military coalition in Vietnam; status of forces agreements (SOFAs); troops, from Pacific region; *individual countries*
aloha, 88, 91, 99
ALP (Australian Labor Party), 32

American Tragedy (Kaiser), 69
American War, 1. *See also* Vietnam War
Anderson, David L., 7
Anderson, Patrick, 55
Ang Cheng Guan, 214–215
Anglo-Malaysian Defense Agreement, 249
ANPO Tōsō, 109
anti-colonialism, 3, 190. *See also* colonialism; decolonization; imperialism; nationalism; neocolonialism
anti-communism, 1, 7, 21, 163. *See also* Vietnam, South
anti-communist states, 1, 6–7, 26–27, 214, 231, 237. *See also* buying time thesis; Malaysia; Philippines; Singapore; Thailand
anti-war sentiment/activism, 54; American activists in Japan, 109–110; Cambodian incursion and, 98; GI resistance, 107, 108, 109, 111–120; in Hawai'i, 97, 98–99, 101; the Hobbit, 112, 114, 117–121; of returnees, 316; in Singapore, 218; transpacific, 107, 111–120, 121; in U.S., 218. *See also* Beheiren; Iwakuni
Anzac Day, 290
ANZAM (Australia, New Zealand, and Malaya), 45, 47
ANZUS (Australia, New Zealand, and United States) Pact, 24, 45, 47
áo dài, 167, 168
APACL (Asian People's Anti-Communist League), 7
Armstrong, Charles, 174
Army of the Republic of Vietnam (ARVN). *See* Republic of Vietnam Armed Forces (RVNAF); troops, from Pacific region
ASEAN (Association of Southeast Asian Nations), 49, 232, 233, 248–249, 250. *See also* Indonesia; Malaysia; Philippines; Singapore; Thailand
Asia, Southeast, 3, 27; American presence in, 227; Anglo-American relations in, 16; British withdrawal from, 218, 220, 249; challenges to regimes in, 214; communism's threat to, 233–234; conflict in, 248; doubts about endurance of U.S. power in, 248–249; export-oriented industrialization in, 243; indigenous communist movements in, 234–235; interconnectedness of, 21, 248 (*See also* domino theory); leadership changes in, 249; opponents of dictatorial rule in, 239; Soviet Union's agenda in, 236; stability of, 55; strategic importance of, 184; U.S. commitment to, 18. *See also* Association of Southeast Asian Nations (ASEAN); buying time thesis; domino theory; Pacific region; *individual countries*
Asian American Committee, 111
Asian People's Anti-Communist League (APACL), 7
Asia Pacific. *See* Asia, Southeast; Pacific region; *individual countries*
Association of Southeast Asian Nations (ASEAN), 49, 232, 233, 248–249, 250. *See also* Indonesia; Malaysia; Philippines; Singapore; Thailand
atrocities: portraying, 315. *See also* war crimes
Australia, 3; Aboriginal communities, 10, 322, 326–327, 330; absence from official Vietnamese memory of war, 309; Anzac Day, 290, 300; ANZAM, 45, 47; ANZUS, 24, 45, 47; assessment of Chinese forces, 4; British Empire and, 33–34, 35, 39, 41, 45, 48, 191; CPA in, 39, 40; decolonization and, 32, 34–37; determinants of Vietnam involvement, 48; domino theory and, 31, 32, 38–39, 41–43, 48, 49 (*See also* China, People's Republic of); entry into Vietnam War, 49; fear of communism in, 37, 39; geographic isolation of, 34; herbicides in, 321 (*See also* Agent Orange; dioxin contamination;

$_{2,4}$-D; $_{2,4,5}$-T); Immigration Restriction Act, 33; imperialism and, 31–32, 33; Indochina and, 47; interests of, 191; justification of participation in war, 31; Kimberley region, 321, 330–332, 333; *Konfrontasi* and, 24; Liberal/Country Party Coalition, 40; MACV and, 48; Malaya and, 46, 47; military intelligence and, 43, 48; motivations for participating in war, 187, 191, 193, 204–205; *Official History of Australia in Southeast Asian Conflicts 1948–1975*, 49; public opinion in, 191, 192 (*See also* anti-war sentiment/activism); R&R program in, 6, 13n28, 130, 133; race and, 4, 33, 35, 39, 133, 289; "red peril" rhetoric and, 32, 38–39; refugees in, 9, 273, 289, 297–298; Repatriation Acts Amendment Act (No. 2) 1979, 290; Returned and Services League of Australia, 290, 300; SEATO and, 46, 185 (*See also* SEATO); second-generation Vietnamese Australian military personnel, 288–301; security doctrine of, 193; Singaporean economy and, 217; strategic planning, 47; support for South Vietnam, 199; troops from, 7, 54, 56, 57–58, 182, 189–190, 201 (*See also* Australian Defence Force (ADF); military coalition in Vietnam; troops, from Pacific region); troops in Singapore, 216; as "true ally", 199, 204; U.S. and, 35, 45, 193; Vietnamese veterans in, 290–291, 295, 300; Vietnam policy, 41; war narratives in, 9; Western Australia Agriculture Protection Board, 321, 330, 331, 333; Western Australia Legislative Council, 14–15n40, 331, 332; white Australia policy, 33, 35, 39, 133, 289; withdrawal of troops from Vietnam, 192; in World War II, 33–34. *See also* Agent Orange; allies, U.S.; Australian Defence Force (ADF); Menzies, R. G.; Pacific region; troops, from Pacific region

Australia, New Zealand, and Malaya (ANZAM) alliance, 45, 47
Australia, New Zealand, and United States (ANZUS) Pact, 24, 45, 47
Australian-American Association, 133
Australian Charter, 33
Australian Defence Force Academy (ADFA), 288
Australian Defence Force (ADF): second-generation Vietnamese serving in, 288–301; veterans, 308–309, 310–312, 317, 326. *See also* troops, from Pacific region
Australian Labor Party (ALP), 32
Australian Secret Intelligence Service, 45
authoritarian regimes: economic growth and, 247; opponents of dictatorial rule in, 242–243; U.S. aid to, 242; Vietnam War's contribution to development of, 242. *See also* Philippines; Thailand
authority, distrust of, 108

Baker, Pamela, 275, 276
Bali Summit, 248
Bandung Conference, 7
Bangkok, 6. *See also* Thailand
Bangkok Declaration, 249
Bao Dai solution, 18, 21, 41, 42
bar girls, 136. *See also* rest and recreation (R&R) programs
Barthes, Roland, 168, 169, 171
bases, U.S. military, 2, 5–6; American goods available on, 163, 164; anti-war activism on, 121 (*See also* Iwakuni); fighter planes leaving for Vietnam from, 120; in Hawai'i, 92, 93 (*See also* Hawaiian land issue); local law and, 5 (*See also* status of forces agreements (SOFAs)); PCS and, 110; in Philippine territory, 3, 17, 18, 22; in South Korea, 163. *See also* Iwakuni; military, U.S.; status of forces agreements (SOFAs)

Index 345

Bashford, Alison, 2
Bayly, Christopher, 38
Beheiren (Betonamu ni Heiwa wo! Shimin Rengō [Citizens' Committee for Peace in Vietnam]), 107; American activists and, 109–111; American deserters and, 109; the Hobbit, 112, 114, 117–121; newsletters published by, 107, 111, 120; origins of, 108–111. *See also* Iwakuni
Beheiren Nyūsu, 107, 120. *See also* Beheiren
Bell, David, 150
Bell, James, 217
Bellwether Hospital, 327
belonging, 300–301
Berger, Samuel, 202
Berlin: division of, 37. *See also* Cold War; Germany
beteukong (Vietcong), naming of, 170–171
Bevins, Vincent, 77
bicultural identity, 297
Biden, Joe, 10
Biggs, David, 322, 323, 331, 334
Blackburn, Robert M., 198–199, 200, 203, 204
Black Panthers, 111
Black Power movement, 109, 111
Blang, Eugenie, 186
bluegill, 166, 167
Blue House raid, 204
Bonesteel, Charles, 207
Borneo, 23
Bower-Miles, Tony "Bomber", 311, 312
Brett, Judith, 34
Brezhnev, Leonid, 236
bridges in Japan, 113
Britain/British Empire: assessment of Chinese forces, 4; attempts to preserve empire, 17 (*See also* Malaysia; neocolonialism); Australia and, 33–34, 35, 39, 41, 45, 48; decline of empire, 25, 43, 45, 48, 187; French colonies and, 184; Hong Kong and, 273, 274, 279; Indonesia and, 73; influence in Southeast Asia, 16, 19 (*See also* Malaya; Singapore); Japan and, 48; Konfrontasi and, 24, 25; legacy of empire, 3, 16; New Zealand and, 190–191; refusal to join military coalition in Vietnam, 185, 186; restrictions on refugees, 273; SEATO and, 46, 185; Singapore and, 16, 17, 18, 21, 22, 23, 24, 25, 27, 216, 217, 220, 223, 245; U.S. and, 17, 19; withdrawal from Southeast Asia, 218, 220, 249; World War II and, 33. *See also* imperialism; MacDonald, Malcolm; neocolonialism
British Commonwealth Conference (1950), 41–42
Brook, Rob, 277, 278
Brooker, Abi, 297
Brown, Winthrop G., 202, 205, 206, 208, 209
Brown memorandum, 163
Brunei, 22
Bui, Long, 291
Bundy, William, 72, 129, 217–218
Burma, 24; China and, 19; decolonization and, 36; in domino theory, 42; independence movement in, 35; interconnected insecurity and, 19; MacDonald on, 20
Burns, John A., 91
Burstall, Terry, 311, 312
Burton, John, 35–36
Bush, George H. W., 102, 137
buying time thesis, 8, 14n38, 49, 226; analyzing, 232, 233; analyzing effects of Vietnam War and, 237–243; durability of, 231; Lee and, 226; limitations of, 250–251; mistaken assumptions in, 234; plausibility of, 231; proponents' claims, 232–233; refutation of, 232; Singapore and, 218. *See also* economic development/growth

Caldwell, Arthur, 49
Calley, William, 315
Cambodia, 27, 49, 235, 257; bombing campaigns in, 97; coup in, 82; ethnic Chinese refugees from, 266; Indonesia and, 82; legacies of war and, 9; SEATO and, 46, 185; U.S. incursion into, 82, 90, 97–98; in Vietnam War, 1
Camp Alpha, 130
Canada, 273
capitalism: dioxin contamination and, 323. *See also* economic development/growth
Carter, Jimmy, 202, 203
Casey, R. G., 37, 40
casualties, war: slow deaths, 322; Vietnamese, 98. *See also* dioxin contamination; war crimes
CATM/VN (Chinese Agriculture Technical Mission to Vietnam), 152, 153, 155
censorship, in South Korea, 174
Central Intelligence Agency (CIA), 71, 209; agents' participation in R&R programs, 130; on "barrier of US force" between China and Indonesia, 74; on communists in Southeast Asia, 236; on communist takeover of South Vietnam, 76; Indonesia and, 26, 74–75, 78, 79; intelligence estimate of Korea, 209; Singapore and, 216, 245; on threat of communism, 234
Centre for Strategic and International Studies (CSIS), 250
Chamberlain, Neville, 37
Chan, Sucheng, 259
Chang Lien-chun, 147
Chartered Industries, 221, 245
chemical agents, 10; rogue batch, 332–333. *See also* Agent Orange; dioxin contamination; TCDD; $2,4$-D; $2,4,5$-T
chemical violence, 333. *See also* Agent Orange; dioxin contamination; TCDD; $2,4$-D; $2,4,5$-T

Chen Cheng, 128
Chiang Kai-shek, 126, 129, 134, 136, 144. *See also* China, Republic of
Chifley, Ben, 35, 36, 40
China, 19; America's extraterritorial rights in, 126; anti-American riots in, 126; colonization of Vietnam, 142; communist seizure of mainland, 18 (*See also* China, People's Republic of); Jeep Girls, 136; rape by U.S. servicemen in, 127; Vietnam's relation with, 41, 257, 266
China, People's Republic of (PRC), 31, 32; ANZAM plans to defend Malaya from, 47; British Commonwealth's response to, 41; Chinese diaspora and, 257–259, 266; Cultural Revolution, 134, 219, 236; fears of expansion of, 19, 47, 77; inauguration of, 40; Indonesia and, 23–24, 25, 26, 74, 77, 79, 80, 81; in Korean War, 46; military aid to Vietnam, 237; Nixon's visit to, 192; rapprochement with U.S., 257; relation with Southeast Asian states, 17, 236; split with Soviet Union, 235, 237; support for national liberation movements, 236; support for North Korea, 184; support for North Vietnam, 186; Tiananmen Square protests/massacre, 271, 274, 280, 284; trade war with, 10; U.S. interests in Southeast Asia and, 43. *See also* Pacific region
China, Republic of (ROC; Taiwan), 126; agriculture in, 153; Chinese cultural renaissance movement, 134; Chinese Vietnamese and, 262, 276, 278; counteroffensive against mainland, 146; Diem's visit to, 149; economic development of, 146, 150, 156–157, 243; Fifth Four-Year Plan, 153; industry in, 153; JCRR, 147; KMT's move to, 143; Military Advisory Group, Vietnam, 7, 142; military prostitution in, 126, 127; MOFA,

China, Republic of (ROC; Taiwan) (cont.) 144–145, 146; R&R program in, 6, 127, 129–130, 134, 135, 136; regarded as pariah state, 142, 157; rights over American personnel in, 128; sex industry in, 137; SOFA, 129; South Vietnam and, 7, 142, 199 (*See also* ROC-RVN relations); Taipei Municipal Venereal Disease Control Institute, 133; Taiwan Garrison Command, 127; Tourism Council, 128, 129; tourism in, 243; U.S. and, 129, 150. *See also* Pacific region; rest and recreation (R&R) programs

China Productivity and Trade Centre, 150

Chinese Agriculture Technical Mission to Vietnam (CATM/VN), 152, 153, 155

Chinese Communist Party (CCP), 126, 260–261. *See also* China, People's Republic of; Mao Zedong

Chinese diaspora, 18, 19; communists in Asia and, 19–20; in Indonesia, 216; PRC and, 257–258; in Singapore, 216, 219–220, 248

Chinese residents in Vietnam, 144, 257, 258, 259–262; citizenship of, 262; communist government policies and, 258–259, 264, 265, 266, 267, 268n8; decision to leave, 257, 264–265; languages spoken by, 261–262; number of, 269n20; PRC and, 258, 260, 262; Taiwan and, 262; view of communism, 260–261. *See also* refugees from Vietnam, ethnic Chinese

Chin Peng, 235

Choi, Jacob, 295–297, 299, 301

Choi Dong-Ju, 201

Cholon, 9, 258, 259. *See also* Chinese residents in Vietnam

Choosing War (Logevall), 70

Chua, Daniel, 215

Churchill, Winston, 184

CIA (Central Intelligence Agency). *See* Central Intelligence Agency (CIA)

CIK (Chemical Industries Kwinana), 331, 332

civilians. *See* casualties, war; dioxin contamination; war crimes

"civilization", 33

civil rights movement, 108, 109

Clifford, Clark, 191; 8:30 Group, 61, 63, 64; allies and, 62, 63–64; assessment of Clifford-Taylor mission, 60; de-escalation/disengagement and, 55, 61; emotionality of, 66; on impossibility of U.S. victory, 60; reputation for pragmatism, 55; South Vietnamese and, 61, 62–64; turn against war, 54, 55–56, 58, 60, 61–66

Clifford Task Force, 61

Clifford-Taylor mission, 54, 55, 57, 58–59, 60, 62, 65, 191. *See also* Clifford, Clark; Taylor, Maxwell

clinical histories, 327

Cloke, Ken, 117

clothing, 162, 167, 168. *See also* "Vietnamese" skirt

coalition, military. *See* military coalition in Vietnam; troops, from Pacific region

"coalition of the unwilling", 182. *See also* military coalition in Vietnam; troops, from Pacific region

coffeehouse, GI, 112, 114, 117–121

Cold War, 16, 69, 163; beginning of, 37; in East and Southeast Asia, 142, 183–184; Hawai'i and, 87; Indonesia coup and, 77; nonaligned nations, 7, 23, 24, 80, 81, 82, 215, 220; Southeast Asia's noncommunist regimes and, 214; South Korea's importance in, 206; understanding regional developments and, 2. *See also* communism; Soviet Union

Coleman, Jonathan, 191

colonialism: aftermath of, 322 (*See also* dioxin contamination; violence, slow); dismantling legacies of, 10; in Hawai'i, 87; Korea and, 177; My Lai massacre

and, 328; Smokey Bear and, 329–330. *See also* decolonization; imperialism; neocolonialism
Commercial Import Program (CIP), 149
communism: Americanization of Vietnam conflict and, 17; containment of, 31, 49 (*See also* domino theory); gains in Indochina, 8; living under, 265; national sovereignty threatened by, 143; nonaligned nations, 7, 23, 24, 80, 81, 82, 215, 220; propaganda vs. economic reality, 264; reduction in risk of spread of, 76; Sino-Soviet split, 235, 237; threat to Southeast Asia, 233–234. *See also* anti-communism; Cold War; domino theory; Indonesian Communist Party (PKI); Malayan Communist Party (MCP); Vietminh
communist nationalists, 1. *See also* Vietnam, North
Communist Party of Australia (CPA), 39, 40
Communist Party of Indonesia (PKI), 22, 23, 25, 26, 71, 78, 79, 234; destruction of, 72, 74, 77, 78, 79, 83, 232, 239
Communist Party of Thailand (CPT), 234
communists, 298; Chinese residents in South Vietnam's views of, 260–261; opposition to Japanese occupation, 234. *See also* Vietnam
communist states, 20. *See also* China, People's Republic of; Soviet Union; Vietnam
Concerned Asian Scholars Committee, 111
conflict resolution, 117
Confrontation (*Konfrontasi*), 17, 23–26, 27, 71, 73, 78, 80, 216
conscientious objector (CO) status, 110
containment, arc of, 81
contamination, 334. *See also* dioxin contamination

cooperation, international, 8. *See also* troops, from Pacific region
corpse mutilation/display, 311–312
Cortright, David, 109, 111
cowboys, 328. *See also* Operation Ranch Hand
Cowley, Chris, 112
CPA (Communist Party of Australia), 39, 40
CPT (Communist Party of Thailand), 234
credibility, regional support for war and, 8
Cronkite, Walter, 96
CSIS (Centre for Strategic and International Studies), 250
Cuba, 201
cultural hierarchies, 7
cultural strategies, 5
Curtin, John, 33
Czechoslovakia, 37

Dassōhei Tsūshin, 107. *See also* Beheiren
Davenport, Nancy H. M., 327
Davies, Bruce, 309
Dawson, Andrew, 332
D'Cruz, Jason, 300
De Angelis, Karin, 291
death arising from inaction (Wangdo's principle), 173
deaths, slow, 322
debt, 299
decolonization, 2, 3, 32, 34–37, 234, 334. *See also* colonialism; imperialism; nationalism; neocolonialism; *individual countries*
defeat in Vietnam, 186. *See also* withdrawal from Vietnam, U.S.
Defense, U.S. Department of, 209
Defense Advanced Research Projects Agency, 330
de Gaulle, Charles, 185
de Lattre de Tassigny, Jean, 42
Delvin, Ron, 331
democracy, 208–209

Index 349

Democratic Republic of Vietnam (DRV; North Vietnam). *See* Vietnam, North
democratization, 247
Derrida, Jacques, 323
deserters, American, 108, 109, 119. *See also* anti-war sentiment/activism
detention, 271
development. *See* economic development/growth
diagnosis, 325–327, 333–334
dictatorial governments. *See* Korea, South
Dien Bien Phu, 45, 46, 143, 184
dioxin contamination: Aboriginal Australians and, 322, 330; colonization and, 321, 333; denial of effects of, 326–327; diagnosis and, 326–327, 333–334; effects of, 325; intergenerational effects of, 333; in Kimberley region, 330–332, 333; lack of consistent symptoms, 326; *Report of the Standing Committee*, 331, 332; responsibility for, 323, 327; scientific ambiguity of, 334; Seveso disaster, 322; as slow violence, 322; unpredictability of, 325. *See also* Agent Orange; chemical agents; TCDD; $2,4$-D; $2,4,5$-T
Dirlik, Arif, 3
division system, 178
domino theory, 1, 4, 9, 19, 31, 41, 48, 49, 59, 184, 190, 191, 232; Australia and, 31, 32, 38–39, 41–43, 48, 49; challenges to, 62; Clifford and, 58, 65; emergence of, 17, 20–21, 27; illegitimacy of, 55; Indonesia in, 69; Japan analogy, 43–44; Johnson administration's use of, 54, 59, 65; Koreans' belief in, 200; lack of evidence for, 32; problems with, 83; race and, 32; U.S. public opinion and, 59. *See also* communism
domino theory, reverse, 75, 78
Dongseo munhak (periodical), 165
Dorton, Bob, 113
Dower, Alan, 35

drift, concept of, 323
DRV (Democratic Republic of Vietnam; North Vietnam). *See* Vietnam, North
Drysdale, Carl, 331, 333
Dulles, John Foster, 184, 185
Duong Van Minh, 148

ecological ethic, 330
economic aid, U.S.. *See* aid, U.S.
economic despair, 265
economic development/growth, 6, 8; appeal of revolutionary movements and, 243; authoritarianism and, 247; buying time thesis, 8, 14n38; democratization and, 247; export-oriented industrialization, 155; as protection against communism, 143, 146; of ROC, 146, 150, 156–557, 243; in Singapore, 217, 223, 225; South Korea and, 208–209; in South Vietnam, 142, 144–145; in Thailand, 247–248; Vietnam War and, 233, 243. *See also* buying time thesis
Edwards, Peter, 300, 309
Egypt, 24–25
8:30 Group, 61, 63, 64
Eisenhower, Dwight D., 1, 20, 21, 59; Cold War coalitions in Southeast Asia, 183; on Dien Bien Phu, 46; domino theory and, 31; on Indonesia, 69
El Salvador, 235
Elsey, George, 62, 63
emigration. *See* refugees
emotion, 54, 55–56, 61–63, 66
empathy, 183
enemies, perpetual, 193
engineer's burials, 311–312
England. *See* Britain/British Empire
environmental consequences of Vietnam War, 173–174. *See also* Agent Orange; dioxin contamination
epidemiologists, 133
escalation in Vietnam, 27; claims about regional benefits of, 72; Hawai'i

delegation and, 94–97; Indonesia and, 71–75, 79–80; Japan and, 94; justification for, 71, 75; U.S.-British relations and, 73. *See also* Johnson, Lyndon B.; military coalition in Vietnam; troops, from Pacific region
Evatt, H. V., 35, 37
Ewing, Noam, 114
Executive Council (ExCo), 278
export markets, 243

Fadden, Arthur, 33, 40, 47
famine, 324
fangong dalu, 146
farmers, 326–27
"Fat Leonard" scandal, 125, 137
Fear, Sean, 6
feelings. *See* emotion
Fettling, David, 37
Fibiger, Mattias, 8, 9, 14n38
fish, "Vietnamese", 166–167, 169, 178
Fonda, Jane, 116
Fong, Hiram L., 90, 91–92, 95, 96, 97–99, 100
Food for Peace Program, 149
Ford, Gerald, 99
Foreign Affairs, Clifford's article in, 55, 59, 64, 65
foreign direct investment, in Southeast Asia, 245
foreign policy, U.S.: emotions in, 54; emphasis on Middle East, 10; Pacific region and, 10; as president's domain, 93, 98
forest fires, as military weapon, 330
forest management, 329–330
Forest Service, U.S., 329–330
Foster, John, 207
France: Algeria and, 185; Bao Dai solution, 18, 21, 41, 42; Chinese in Vietnam and, 144; colonialism, 183, 184; defeat in Vietnam, 42, 45, 46, 143, 184; mass culture, 168, 169; refusal to join military coalition in Vietnam, 185–186; SEATO and, 46, 185 (*See also* SEATO); U.S. aid to, 20, 21; war against Vietminh, 17, 18, 19–20; withdrawal from Indochina, 16. *See also* imperialism
Francis, Leonard Glenn "Fat Leonard", 125, 137
Fredman, Zach, 6
Free the Army (FTA) tour, 112, 116–117
Fujieda Mioko, 110

Gaddis, John Lewis, 183
Galbraith, Francis, 221
Gardner, Fred, 117, 118
Gardner, Lloyd C., 69
Gardner, Paul F., 81
garment industry, 170
gender, R&R and, 133
gender discrimination. *See* Mink, Patsy Takemoto
gender equality legislation, 102
genetics counseling, 327
Geneva Conference on Indochina, 143, 184, 186
Gent, Edward, 38
Germany, 37, 185, 186
Gilbert, Marc Jason, 5
Gilmore, Robert J., 35
Glenn Defense Marine Asia, 125
Godley, Michael, 258
Goh Keng Swee, 217, 223
Goldberg, Arthur, 95
Gough, Kathleen, 258
Graham, Peter, 276
gratitude, 299–300
Great Britain. *See* Britain/British Empire
Green, Marshall, 72–73, 75, 78, 79
Grey, Jeffery, 309
Griffin, Allen, 19–20
Gruening, Ernest, 95
Guam, 4
Guided Democracy, 234
Gulf of Tonkin Resolution, 91, 93

habeas corpus, 275–278, 279, 281. *See also* refugees from Vietnam, in Hong Kong
Hankyoreh, 165, 174, 177
Hankyoreh 21, 165, 174, 177
Han Xiaorong, 267
Harding, John, 44, 46–47, 48
Harper, Tim, 38
Harris, Kamala, 10
Harry, Ralf, 42
Hatfield, Mark, 100
Hawai'i, 4–5; *aloha*, 88, 91, 99; anti-war sentiment in, 97, 98–99, 101; Asian American population, 87–88, 90, 103; culture of mutual understanding in, 5; East-West Center in, 91; economy of, 87, 88; Indigenous land rights, 5 (*See also* Hawaiian land issue); Kaho'olawe, 102; native Hawaiian population, 87–88, 101, 102; native Hawaiian renaissance, 89; O'ahu Island, 5, 101; peace and, 89; Pearl Harbor attack, 33, 89; postcolonial conditions in, 87, 88, 90, 92; poverty in, 101; R&R program in, 13n28; reaction to withdrawal in, 99–100; response to Vietnam War, 88–103; statehood, 89, 92; support for, 93; tourism and, 93; training centers, 5; U.S. imperial relations in Pacific and, 5; U.S. military and, 92, 93, 99 (*See also* Hawaiian land issue); values of, 88, 91, 99, 103; Vietnam War's impact in, 87
Hawaiian land issue, 92–93, 97, 99, 101, 102
Hawaiian sovereignty movement, 89, 101
Hawai'i congressional delegation, 5, 88–92, 103; Cambodian incursion and, 97–98; commitments to peace, 93; end of Vietnam War and, 101–102; escalation and, 94–97; limited war and, 88, 93, 100; negotiated settlement and, 90, 96; Nixon's war policy and, 100; preference for soft power, 91; preserving Republic of Vietnam and, 93–94; relation with countries in Asia and, 91; on withdrawal, 95. *See also* Fong, Hiram L.; Inouye, Daniel K.; Matsunaga, Spark Masayuki; Mink, Patsy Takemoto
Haydock, John, 130
hearts and minds, winning, 5
Henke, Marina, 186, 188
herbicides, 321, 324, 325. *See also* Agent Orange; chemical agents; dioxin contamination; TCDD; $2,4$-D; $2,4,5$-T
Herring, George, 185, 186
Hersh, Seymour, 314
Highway of an Atom (Van Wyck), 323
Hiroshima, 115
historians, official, 306
Hitler, Adolf, 37, 75
Hitokoto, Hidefumi, 299
Hoa, 261. *See also* Chinese residents in Vietnam
Hoare, Richard, 282
Hobbit, the, 112, 114, 117–121
Ho Chi Minh, 18, 35, 41, 42, 69, 143, 309
Holt, Harold, 57, 190, 191
Holyoake, Keith, 190
home, symbol of, 34
Hong Kong, 271; Basic Law, 281; Britain and, 279; civil liberties in, 272, 277; control over future, 284; economic growth in, 243; ExCo, 278; habeas corpus and, 275, 278, 280, 281; handover to PRC, 273, 274, 275, 283, 284; individual asylum screenings in, 271; legal system, 279; LegCo, 278–283, 284; R&R programs in, 6; refugees in (*See* refugees from Vietnam, in Hong Kong); tourism in, 243
Hong Kong Human Rights Monitor, 280
Honolulu. *See* Hawai'i
Honolulu Conference, 62, 63, 64
Honolulu Star-Bulletin, 95
Hon Sui Sen, 225

hostess bars, 127, 128, 132. *See also* prostitution; rest and recreation (R&R) programs
Houston, Darrell, 131, 132, 133, 136
Hsu Shao-chang, 155
Huế, Battle for, 316
human rights, 202, 203
Humphrey, Hubert, 74, 189, 202
Hwang Suk-yong, 177

identity, bicultural, 297
Immerwahr, Daniel, 4, 5
imperialism, 3, 16, 17, 18; in Asia Pacific, 2; associative form of, 36; Australia and, 33; formal, reduction in, 3; maintaining, 18; Western, Japan's destruction of, 31. *See also* Britain/British Empire; colonialism; decolonization; France; neocolonialism
imperialism, U.S., 2, 4, 176; discourses around Agent Orange and, 327; extraterritorial, 5; informal, 3, 4, 27; overlap with British, 16; South Korea and, 177; territorial aspects of, 4. *See also* Hawai'i; Philippines; United States
imperium, 4
Improved Village Development Program, 153
indebtedness, 299
independence movements, 34. *See also* decolonization
India, 24; decolonization and, 36; independence of, 35, 37, 45; non-aligned status of, 185; SEATO and, 46; U.S. relationship with, 77. *See also* Asia, Southeast
Indian Communist Party, 37
Indian Peninsula, 3. *See also* Asia, Southeast
Indigenous peoples, 333. *See also* Aboriginal Australians
Indochina, 26, 41; Australia's strategic posture and, 47; China and, 19, 41; communist gains in, threat from, 8; in domino theory, 44; French defeat in, 16, 42, 45, 46, 143, 184; independence movement in, 35; interconnected insecurity and, 19; Japanese attack from, 47; MacDonald on, 20; perceived threats to, 43; U.S. commitment to, 27, 74; U.S. military withdrawal from, 70; U.S. support for French in, 20. *See also* Cambodia; France; Laos; Vietnam
Indonesia, 44, 205; American decision making in Vietnam and, 81; anti-Americanism in, 73; anti-communist stance of, 27; anxieties about, 248; army of, 73–74, 78, 79, 82, 234, 240, 242; Australia and, 36; Cambodia and, 82; China and, 23–24, 25, 26, 74, 77, 79, 80, 81; conditions in, 80–81; coup in, 49, 72, 73, 74–75, 77, 82, 216; CSIS, 250; in documentary record, 69, 70; in domino theory, 42; economy of, 223, 243, 246; ethnic Chinese in, 216; exports, 246; fear of communist takeover in, 48; foreign direct investment in, 245; Golkar, 242; implications of events in, 83; importance of, 4, 69; independence movement in, 35; international aid to, 239–242; *Kompas*, 288; *Konfrontasi*, 17, 23–26, 27, 71, 73, 78, 80, 216; Malaysia and, 216; massacre of "communists" in, 49; nationalism in, 71; nonaligned status of, 80, 81, 82, 185; orientation of, uncertainty about, 78, 80–81; PKI, 22, 23, 25, 26, 71, 78, 79, 234, 235, 239; PKI, destruction of, 72, 74, 77, 78, 79, 83, 232, 239; regional role of, 81–82; reorientation toward West, 240; Repelita, 239; resources of, 71; rise of New Order in, 239–242; risk of communism spreading and, 76; SEATO and, 46; Singapore and, 222, 226; Sjahrir, 35; Soedjatmoko, 232;

Indonesia (cont.)
  Soviet Union and, 79, 240; Sumitro, 240; *Supersemar*, 79; Thirtieth of September Movement, 26; Treaty of Amity and Cooperation and the Declaration of ASEAN Concord, 248; U.S. aid to, 237, 239, 240; U.S. and, 49, 78, 80, 81, 83; Vietnam connections, 82; Vietnam War and, 69–70, 71–82; West Irian and, 82. *See also* Asia, Southeast; Association of Southeast Asian Nations (ASEAN); Pacific region; Suharto; Sukarno
Indonesia-Malaysia Confrontation, 17, 23–26, 27
Indonesian Communist Party (PKI), 22, 23, 25, 26, 71, 78, 79; destruction of, 72, 74, 77, 78, 79, 83, 239
Indo-Pacific, 2. *See also* Asia, Southeast; Pacific region
industrialization/industry: export-oriented, 155; in ROC, 153; in South Korea, 170. *See also* economic development/growth
Inouye, Daniel K., 89–90, 94, 95, 96, 99; East-West Center and, 91; Hawai'i land issue and, 92, 101, 102; Nixon's war policy and, 100. *See also* Hawai'i congressional delegation
In Retrospect (McNamara), 77
Interagency Korean Task Force, 209
Inter-Governmental Group on Indonesia, 239
International Longshoreman and Warehousemen's Union (ILWU), 90
invasion, Vietnam's history of resisting, 306
Iran, 76, 77
Iraq War, 186, 200
Israel, 220
Ivory Coast, 25
Iwakuni, 6, 107, 113; Black GIs in, 109, 111, 113–114, 118; *Free the Army Tour* in, 112, 116–117; GI coffeehouse in, 112, 114, 117–121; GI resistance in, 107, 111–120; nuclear weapons in, 112, 115–117; town of, 107; transpacific activism in, 111–120, 121. *See also* anti-war sentiment/activism; bases, U.S. military; Beheiren; Japan
Iwakuni 13's Struggle, 113, 114
Iwase Jōko, 121

Jackson, Mississippi, 98
Jakarta. *See* Indonesia
Japan, 3; American activists in, 109–110; anti-war activism in (*See* Beheiren; Iwakuni); attack on Malaya, 44; bridges in, 113; British Empire and, 48; communist threat to, 31; conquest of Southeast Asia, 19, 20, 21; defeat in World War II, 108; destruction of Western imperialist order, 31; "downward thrust" of, 43, 47; economic growth in, 243; escalation in Vietnam and, 94; fighter planes leaving for Vietnam from, 120; Firearm and Sword Control Law, 120; Hiroshima, 115; jurisdiction over U.S. personnel in, 127, 128 (*See also* bases, U.S. military; Iwakuni); in Malay Peninsula, 18; military prostitution in, 137; occupation of Vietnam, 143; Okinawa, 4, 109–110; opposition to Vietnam War, 114; Pearl Harbor attack, 89; R&R programs in, 6, 243; refusal to join military coalition in Vietnam, 185; reparations to Saigon, 147; sex tourism and, 137; South Korea and, 203, 205; U.S. bases in, 109 (*See also* Iwakuni); U.S.'s relation with, 108, 120 (*See also* Beheiren; Iwakuni); in World War II, 17, 33, 43, 89; Yamaguchi prefecture, 107. *See also* Iwakuni; Okinawa; Pacific region
Japan analogy, 44, 47
Japanese Americans, 89. *See also* Hawai'i
Japanese Thrust, The (Wigmore), 43

Japan Socialist Party, 115
Japan-U.S. Security Treaty, 109, 114
JATEC Tsūshin, 107, 120. *See also* Beheiren
Jayawickrama, Nihal, 277
Jeep Girls, 136
Jema'ah Islamiyah, 242
Jeong Il-gwan, 206
Jessup, Philip, 19
Jiang Lianru, 134
Jo, Eun Seo, 200
Johnson, Lyndon B., 17, 184; Americanization of war in Vietnam, 233; anti-war returnees on, 316; approval ratings for, 218; on backing allies, 186; belief in possibility of victory, 66; Clifford-Taylor mission and, 54; Cold War coalitions in Southeast Asia., 183; de-escalation and, 61; domino theory and, 54, 59, 65; East-West Center and, 91; escalation in Vietnam and, 27, 75; explanation of decisions for U.S. combat role, 71; hardening of position, 62, 63, 83; Hawai'i land issue and, 92–93; Indonesia and, 74, 82; Inouye and, 89, 96; legitimacy of war and, 188; loyalty and, 97; more flags initiative, 182, 186, 192, 198–199, 204, 246; Park and, 202, 203; perception of attitudes in Pacific region, 8; public relations campaign, 75; *Pueblo* crisis and, 204; refusal to run for reelection, 97; on Suharto, 80; *The Vantage Point*, 75. *See also* escalation in Vietnam; United States
Jones, Howard Palfrey, 72
Jones, Matthew, 73
Jutel, Annemarie, 325–326

Kaho'olawe, 102
Kaiser, David, 69
Karnow, Stanley, 3
Katzenstein, Peter, 2, 4
Keith, Brian, 277

Kennan, George F., 76, 77, 78
Kennedy, Edward, 217
Kennedy, John F., 184, 201, 203, 208
Kent State University, 98
Kenya, 25
Kenyatta, Jomo, 25
Kim, Alice S., 7
Kim Ki Tae, 174
Kim Seong-eun, 205
Kim Young Ran, 175
Kintai, 113, 120
Kishi Nobusuke, 107
Kissinger, Henry, 59, 81, 82, 233, 316
KMT (Kuomintang), 143. *See also* China, Republic of
Kolko, Gabriel, 146, 147
Komer, Robert, 69, 202, 206
Konfrontasi (Confrontation), 17, 23–26, 27, 71, 73, 78, 80, 216
Korea, North, 204, 207
Korea, South (Republic of Korea; ROK): aid for, 187–188, 197, 205–206, 208, 209; anti-communist nationalism, 163; benefits of participation in Vietnam War, 163, 201, 209; censorship in, 174; China in, 43; committment to victory, 206; coup in, 197, 201; economy of, 164, 206, 243; effects of participation in Vietnam War, 208; experience of Vietnam War, 171, 172; fisheries aid, 166; human rights in, 203; incentives offered to, 188; industry in, 163, 170; Japan and, 205; MAP and, 209; military, 162, 163, 165, 177, 201–202, 205, 206, 209n1 (*See also* troops, from Pacific region; troops, South Korean); military prostitution in, 137; MINBYUN, 176; modernization in, 208–209; motivations for participating in Vietnam War, 187, 192, 193; National Guidance League, 175; participation in Vietnam War, 162, 165; political stability in, 209; portrayal of Vietnam War in popular culture, 198;

Korea, South (Republic of Korea; ROK) (cont.)
poverty in, 164, 200; public discourse on "Vietnam question" in, 174; R&R programs and, 130, 243; scholarship on participation in war, 198; sex tourism in, 137; South Vietnam and, 7, 199; stability in, 208; Syngman Rhee, 163, 175, 202; textile industry in, 162, 164, 170; troop commitments (*See* military coalition in Vietnam; troops, from Pacific region; troops, South Korean); Truth and Reconciliation Commission, 175; U.S. aid to, 208; U.S. goals for, 197, 208, 209; U.S. influence in, 163; U.S.'s relation with, 177, 187, 193, 202, 205, 209; "Vietnamese" imaginary in, 7, 164, 165, 170; "Vietnamese" modifier in, 166, 167, 169, 171–172, 176, 178; Vietnam War narratives in, 177. *See also* Park Chung Hee; troops, South Korean; "Vietnamese" skirt

Korean War, 20, 163, 176; atrocities by U.S. troops in, 165, 174, 175; China in, 46; distorted view of Koreans during, 176–177; No Gun Ri, 165, 174, 175

Kosek, Jake, 329

Kuala Lumpur, 6. *See also* Malaysia

Kuomintang (KMT), 143, 146, 262. *See also* China, Republic of

Kwak, Tae Yang, 203

Laderman, Scott, 316
Lai, Peter, 279
Lair, Meredith, 126
Laird, Melvin, 207, 208
Lam Van Tri, 152
Laos, 27, 49, 188, 235; bombing campaigns in, 97; China and, 23–24; legacies of war and, 9; SEATO and, 46, 185; secret war in, 130; in Vietnam War, 1
Lawrence, Jeanette, 297
Lawrence, Mark Atwood, 4

Lawyers for a Democratic Society (MINBYUN), 176
LBJ. *See* Johnson, Lyndon B.
Lee, Jin-kyung, 198
Lee, Min Yong, 201
Lee Cheuk-yan, 279–280
Lee Kuan Yew, 8, 21–22, 23, 24, 129, 136, 172, 215, 231; American investors and, 224; Bundy and, 217–218; on buying time, 226; Johnson and, 218, 219; support for Vietnam War, 219, 224; U.S. and, 214–219, 220, 226, 227
Lee Myung-bak, 175
Lee Yun-gi, 165–174, 176–178
legacies of Vietnam War, 9, 137, 233, 250, 305
legal services for GIs, 110, 116, 118, 119
LegCo (Legislative Council), 278–283, 284
Legislative Council (LegCo), 278–283, 284
Li, Gladys, 282
Lifton, Robert J., 313
Li Kwoh-ting, 145, 152–153, 156
Lim, Jason, 7
Lim Chong Yah, 215
Lim Kim San, 223
Lin, T. S., 134
Lipman, Jana K., 9
Lockhart, Greg, 3, 4
Lodge, Henry Cabot, 72, 79, 94
Logevall, Fredrik, 69–70, 186
Long, S. R. Joey, 8
Long Tan company, 298. *See also* second-generation Vietnamese Australian personnel
Lon Nol, 82
Lovins, Christopher, 7
loyalty, Johnson and, 97
Lu Ping, 273
Ly Hue My, 276

MAAG (U.S. Military Assistance Advisory Group), 126, 127
Macapagal, Diosdado, 249

MacDonald, Malcolm, 3, 19, 20, 37–38, 39–40, 41, 42, 43, 44, 45
MacDonald, Ramsay, 37
Machiavelli, Niccolò, 183
MACV (U.S. Military Assistance Command, Vietnam), 48, 182
Malaya, 4, 16, 23, 40, 71, 190, 248; alleged "communist insurrection" in, 37–38; Anglo-Malayan Defense Agreement, 22; ANZAM, 45, 47; Britain and, 18, 21, 37, 38, 47; communists in, 235; in domino theory, 42, 44; Far Eastern Strategic Reserve in, 45, 46; Gilmore on, 35; interconnected insecurity and, 19; resources of, 44, 46; SEATO and, 46; Tunku, 21, 22. *See also* MacDonald, Malcolm
Malayan Communist Party (MCP), 18, 19, 21, 38, 39, 44
Malay Peninsula: decolonization and, 36; resistance to Japanese occupation, 18
Malaysia, 17, 190, 231, 248; Alliance Party, 216; anti-communist stance of, 26; benefits from Vietnam War, 247; Britain and, 73, 249; communists and, 234, 235; economy of, 223, 243; establishment of, 23, 71; "Fat Leonard" scandal, 125, 137; foreign direct investment in, 245; insurgencies in, 232; *Konfrontasi* and, 17, 23–26, 27, 71, 73, 78, 80, 216; as neocolonial scheme, 23; prostitutes in, 134; R&R programs in, 6, 125, 243; racial tensions in, 248; refugees in, 272; Singapore and, 215, 216, 217, 220, 222, 226; Treaty of Amity and Cooperation and the Declaration of ASEAN Concord, 248; U.S. and, 23, 27, 49, 237, 239. *See also* Association of Southeast Asian Nations (ASEAN)
Malik, Adam, 74, 80, 250
Man, Simeon, 2, 3, 4, 5
Manila, 6. *See also* Philippines
Mao Zedong, 40, 41, 236. *See also* China, People's Republic of
MAP (Military Assistance Program), 206
Maphilindo, 248
Marcos, Ferdinand, 57, 129, 136, 189, 192, 214, 242, 246, 247, 249
marginalized people, 326–327. *See also* Aboriginal Australians
Marine Corps Air Station Iwakuni. *See* anti-war sentiment/activism; bases, U.S. military; Iwakuni
Marlowe, Jay, 300
Marshall, Lucy, 333
Marshall Islands, 4
Martinez, Salomon, 329
Martin Hobbs, Mia, 9, 321
Martini, Edwin A., 322–323, 327
masculinity, 137, 198. *See also* rest and recreation (R&R) programs
MASH (television series), 177
mass culture, French, 168, 169
Matsunaga, Spark Masayuki, 89–90, 91, 94, 95, 96; after war, 102; East-West Center and, 91; Hawai'i land issue and, 102; in military, 91–92; Nixon's war policy and, 100; USIP and, 102. *See also* Hawai'i congressional delegation
MCAS (U.S. Marine Corps Air Station). *See* bases, U.S. military; Iwakuni
McCain, John, 306
McCoy, Gerard, 278
McKay, Gary, 309
McMahon, Robert, 232
McMahon, William, 192
McNamara, Robert, 56, 72, 77, 96, 187, 206, 207, 233
MCP (Malayan Communist Party), 18, 19, 21, 38, 39, 44
"Medical Residents' Use of Narrative Templates in Storytelling and Diagnosis" (Davenport), 327
Melbourne Herald, 40
Melby, John F., 19, 20, 43, 44

Index   357

Menzies, R. G., 31, 32, 33–34, 36–37, 39, 40, 41, 45, 46, 47, 48–49, 191. *See also* Australia
mercenaries: definition of, 200; in Iraq War, 200; South Korean troops viewed as, 187–188, 197, 198–201, 204, 207; troops from Pacific region viewed as, 8, 182, 187, 199–200, 204, 243; vs. "true allies", 204; understanding of term, 200
Mercenaries and Lyndon Johnson's "More Flags" (Blackburn), 198–199
migration. *See* refugees
military, South Korean. *See* military coalition in Vietnam; troops, from Pacific region; troops, South Korean
military, South Vietnamese, 64, 148, 156, 182, 288, 290–291, 295, 300, 308
military, U.S.: African Americans in, 109, 111, 112, 113–114, 118; Asian representation in, 291; courts-martial, 112; deserters, 108, 119; "Fat Leonard" scandal, 125, 137; *First Team*, 133; GI coffeehouse, 112, 114, 117–121; Hawaiian lands held by, 89 (*See also* Hawaiian land issue); Hawai'i delegation and, 91–92; jurisdiction over personnel, 126–127, 128, 129 (*See also* bases, U.S. military; Iwakuni); legal discharge, 110–111; legal services for GIs, 110, 116, 118, 119; normalizing colonizing behavior, 330; Pacific Command, 5 (*See also* Hawai'i); prostitution organized by (*See* rest and recreation (R&R) programs); *Pueblo* crisis, 204; racism in, 111, 113–114; resistance in, 109, 110, 111–120 (*See also* anti-war sentiment/activism; Beheiren; Iwakuni); Singapore and, 217; SOFAs, 5–6, 127–128, 129; *Thunder*, 130; troop commitments, 182 (*See also* military coalition in Vietnam); underground GI newspapers, 112–113, 115, 117, 118, 120, 121; war crimes by, 165, 174, 175 (*See also* My Lai massacre); withdrawal from Indochina, 70. *See also* bases, U.S. military; rest and recreation (R&R) programs; veterans
Military Assistance Program (MAP), 206, 209
military coalition in Vietnam, 182; Australia in, 189–190; command of, 183, 187; incentives for participants, 192 (*See also* aid, U.S.); lasting effects on participants, 192; mercenary image of, 187; New Zealand in, 189, 190–191; participants' interests and, 183; participants' motivations, 187, 191, 192–193; Philippines in, 189; purpose of, 186; reexamination of Southeast Asian strategy, 191. *See also* allies, U.S.; more flags initiative; troops, from Pacific region; troops, South Korean; *individual countries*
Military Revolutionary Council (MRC), 148
Miller-Davenport, Sarah, 5
MINBYUN (Lawyers for a Democratic Society), 176
Ministry of Foreign Affairs (MOFA), 144–145, 146
Mink, Patsy Takemoto, 89–90, 95, 96, 98, 99, 100–101, 102. *See also* Hawai'i congressional delegation
Patsy T. Mink Equal Opportunity in Education Act (Title IX), 102
MOFA (Ministry of Foreign Affairs), 144–145, 146
Moon Jae-in, 175
Moore, Hal, 306
more flags initiative, 182, 185, 186, 192, 198–199, 204, 246. *See also* military coalition in Vietnam; troops, from Pacific region
Motono Yoshio, 108
MRC (Military Revolutionary Council), 148
Muecke, Stephen, 330–331

museums, Vietnamese: Sõn Mỹ Memorial and Museum, 313–315; War Remnants Museum, 310
Mussolini, Benito, 75
My Lai massacre, 188, 310, 311, 313–315, 328. *See also* war crimes
myth, Barthes's definition of, 169
mythical concept, 171

Narazaki Yanosuke, 115
narratives. *See* war narratives
Nasser, Gamal Abdel, 24–25
nationalism, 38, 190, 234; Indonesian, 71; in South Korea, 163. *See also* decolonization
National Lawyers Guild (NLG), 118
National Liberation Front (NLF), 1, 171
National Security Council (NSC), 3, 69, 208, 231
national security strategy, 183
NATO (North Atlantic Treaty Organization), 24, 128, 183, 186
Near North (Gilmore and Warner), 35
negotiated settlement, 88, 90, 96, 98. *See also* Paris Peace Accords; peace in Vietnam
Nehru, Jawaharlal, 24
nekolim, 23. *See also* neocolonialism
neocolonialism: in Asia Pacific, 2; British, 3–4, 17, 21–27 (*See also* Britain/British Empire; Malaysia); R&R programs and, 136; U.S. imperialism and, 4
Netherlands East Indies, 16, 18
Nettleton, Sarah, 325–326
neutralism, 60
New Guinea, 36
Ne Win, 24
New People's Army (NPA), 242–243
New York Times, 108
New Zealand, 7; ANZAM, 45, 47; ANZUS, 24, 45, 47; communist threat to, 31; cultural affinity with Britain, 190–191; *Konfrontasi* and, 24; motivations for participating in war, 187, 191, 193,
204–205; participation in R&R programs, 130; public opinion in, 191, 192 (*See also* anti-war sentiment/activism); SEATO and, 46, 185 (*See also* SEATO); security doctrine of, 193; Singaporean economy and, 217; support for South Vietnam, 199; troops in Singapore, 216; troops in Vietnam, 54, 56, 57, 58, 182, 189, 190–191, 192, 201 (*See also* military coalition in Vietnam; troops, from Pacific region); as "true ally", 199, 204; U.S. relations with, 193; withdrawal of troops from Vietnam, 192. *See also* Pacific region
Ng, Margaret, 281–282, 283
Ngo, Boi Huyen, 9–10
Ngo Dinh Diem, 4, 47, 144, 145, 146; economic development and, 146; overthrow of, 150; unpopularity of, 148; U.S. alliance with, 21; visit to Taipei, 149
Ngoei, Wen-Qing, 3, 4, 43–44, 49, 81, 215
Nguyen, Anne, 293–294, 297, 298, 299
Nguyen, Carie Uyen, 308
Nguyen, Chuong, 294, 297, 299
Nguyen, Nam, 288–289, 292
Nguyen, Nathalie Huynh Chau, 9, 321
Nguyen Cao Ky, 63, 95, 148
Nguyen Khanh, 148
Nguyen Khoa Nam, 288
Nguyen Ngoc Tho, 150
Nguyen Thi Binh, 101
Nguyen Thi Thanh, 176
Nguyen Van Thieu, 62, 63, 96, 99, 148, 153, 156, 186
Nibbs, Faith, 300
Nicaragua, 235
Nitze, Paul, 64
Nixon, Richard M., 4, 81, 97, 136, 184, 221, 316, 323; abuse of constitutional power, 100; Indonesia and, 70; plan for peace in Vietnam, 97; South Korean troops and, 207; support for policy of, 97–99; Vietnamization policy, 191; visit to China, 192

Nixon, Rob, 322, 333
Nixon Doctrine, 81, 192
NLF (National Liberation Front), 1, 171
NLG (National Lawyers Guild), 110
No Gun Ri, 165, 174, 175
nonaligned nations, 7, 23, 24; Indonesia, 80, 81, 82; Singapore, 215, 220
nonviolent direct action, 108
Noreui nalgae (Wings of melody; Lee), 165
Norodom Sihanouk, 82
North Atlantic Treaty Organization (NATO), 24, 128, 183, 186
Northern Marianas, 4
North Vietnam. *See* Vietnam, North
NPA (New People's Army), 242–243
NSC (National Security Council), 3, 69, 208, 231
nuclear weapons in Iwakuni, 112, 115–117

Obama, Barack, 10
Oceania, 2. *See also* Pacific region
oil, 246
Okinawa, 4, 109–110. *See also* Iwakuni; Japan
oligarchic power, enabled by Vietnam War, 248
Ono Nobuyuki, 114, 115
Operation Pacer HO, 328. *See also* Agent Orange; dioxin contamination
Operation Ranch Hand, 321, 324, 327, 329–330. *See also* Agent Orange; dioxin contamination
oral histories, 9, 289, 334. *See also* refugees from Vietnam, in Australia; second-generation Vietnamese Australian personnel
Organic Act, 92
orientalism, 136, 191, 317

pacification, 5
Pacific Counseling Services (PCS), 110, 111, 116, 118

Pacific region, 1, 2; effect of war and, 9; external intervention in, 2–3; geographic constructions of, 2; height of U.S. power in, 3; invention of, 3; motivations for supporting war, 8; threat to from communist gains in Indochina, 8. *See also* Asia, Southeast; *individual countries*
Pakistan, 46, 77, 185
Palethorpe, Nigel, 35
Palmerston, Lord, 193
Pan American Airways, 130
Pang Yang Huei, 146
PAP (People's Action Party). *See* People's Action Party (PAP); Singapore
pariah state, ROC regarded as, 142, 157
Paris Club, 239
Paris Peace Accords, 99, 155, 239, 309. *See also* peace in Vietnam
Park, Jinim, 177
Park, Tongsun, 203
Park Chung Hee, 163, 187, 188, 197, 199, 201–202, 203, 204, 205–206, 208. *See also* Korea, South
Park Geun-hye, 175
Park Young-han, 177
partners. *See* allies, U.S.; military coalition in Vietnam; troops, from Pacific region
paternalism, 89, 317. *See also* Mink, Patsy Takemoto
Pathet Lao, 188
patriarchy, 136. *See also* rest and recreation (R&R) programs
Pay Any Price (Gardner), 69
PCS (Pacific Counseling Services), 110, 111, 116, 118
peace, 89. *See also aloha*
peace in Vietnam: Beheiren and, 107 (*See also* Beheiren); Hawai'i congressional delegation and, 91, 93; initiatives, failed, 95; negotiated settlement, 88, 90, 96, 98; Nixon's plan for, 97; Paris Peace Accords, 99,

155, 239, 309; returnees' perception of outcome, 305–309. *See also* anti-war sentiment/activism
peacemaking institutions, 102
Pelley, Patricia, 306
Megan Ann Pelly Perpetual Memorial Award, 288
Penang: R&R programs in, 6. *See also* Malaysia
People's Action Party (PAP), 214, 216; American investors and, 224; authority of, 217; Chinese speaking base, 219; consolidation of rule, 226; economy and, 223; hold on power, 225–226; support for U.S. involvement in Vietnam, 218. *See also* Singapore
People's Republic of China (PRC). *See* China, People's Republic of (PRC)
Perk, Robert, 289
personal testimonies, 334
Peterman, Sidney, 110
Peterson, Pete, 306
Pham Ngoc Thach, 35
Pham Vang Ngoc, 152
Philippine Civic Action Group (PHILCAG), 189
Philippines, 231; anti-communism in, 21, 26; anxieties about Indonesia, 248; communists in, 234; economic benefits from Vietnam War, 246–247; foreign direct investment in, 245; insurgencies in, 232; nationalism in, 17; NPA, 242–243; participation in war, 56, 189, 192, 193; R&R programs in, 6, 129, 136, 243; refusal to recognize Malaysia, 248; SEATO and, 46, 185 (*See also* SEATO); support for South Vietnam, 199; Treaty of Amity and Cooperation and the Declaration of ASEAN Concord., 248; troops from, 7, 8, 57, 182, 191, 199–200, 246 (*See also* military coalition in Vietnam; troops, from Pacific region); U.S. aid to, 189, 237, 239, 242; U.S. and, 49, 193; U.S. bases in, 3, 17, 18, 22; withdrawal of troops from Vietnam, 191. *See also* Association of Southeast Asian Nations (ASEAN); imperialism, U.S.; Pacific region
Phung Hoan, 276
PKI (Indonesian Communist Party), 22, 23, 25, 26, 71, 78, 79, 234; destruction of, 72, 74, 77, 78, 79, 83, 232, 239
PKO (Protect Kahoʻolawe ʻOhana), 102
poker, "Vietnamese", 167, 169, 178
policymakers: emotionality of, 54; flawed certainties and, 83
politics of asymmetry, 143
politics of suffering, 198
Polynesian triangle, 2
Porter, William J., 206
postcolonialism, 34. *See also* decolonization
post-traumatic stress disorder (PTSD), 295, 298, 326
poverty, 243; in South Korea, 164, 200
power, soft, 90, 91–92, 183
pragmatism, Clifford's reputation for, 55
Prague, 37
PRC (People's Republic of China). *See* China, People's Republic of (PRC)
Presidential Task Force on Korea, 208
prostitution: "Fat Leonard" scandal, 125, 137; licensed, 131, 132, 133, 134; organized by military, 137; transnational, 136. *See also* rest and recreation (R&R) programs
Protect Kahoʻolawe ʻOhana (PKO), 102
protest: nonviolent direct action, 108. *See also* anti-war sentiment/activism
PTSD (post-traumatic stress disorder), 295, 298, 326
Pueblo crisis, 204

R&R (rest and recreation). *See* rest and recreation (R&R) programs
Rabel, Roberto, 190

race: allies and, 204; assessment of Chinese forces and, 4; Australia's involvement in Vietnam and, 31–32; "civilization" and, 33; domino theory and, 32; military control of Asia and, 36; R&R and, 133; security and, 47; support for war and, 199, 200; troops from Pacific region and, 204; white Australia policy, 33, 35, 39, 289. *See also* decolonization
racism, 89; in military, 111, 113–114; white Australia policy, 33, 35, 39, 133, 289. *See also* Mink, Patsy Takemoto
radiological violence, 333
rape, 126, 127
Rauch, Henrietta G., 98
Razak, Tun Abdul, 247
Reagan, Ronald, 231
red light districts, 137. *See also* prostitution; rest and recreation (R&R) programs
"red peril" rhetoric, 32, 38–39, 41
reeducation camps, 267
Refugee Concern Hong Kong, 275–278, 282
refugees, 2, 9; bicultural identity of, 297
refugees from Vietnam: Cold War narratives of, 257, 259; diversity among, 267; economic despair and, 265; ethnicity and, 266–267 (*See also* refugees from Vietnam, ethnic Chinese); motivations of, 267, 289, 298; number of, 257, 266; trauma and PTSD experienced by, 298. *See also* refugees from Vietnam, in Australia; refugees from Vietnam, in Hong Kong
refugees from Vietnam, ethnic Chinese: alleged ethnic persecution and, 266; concerns about economic discrimination, 259; decision to flee, 264–265; destinations of, 259–260; evacuation of, 264–265; habeas corpus and, 272; in Hong Kong refugee camps, 275–278 (*See also* refugees from Vietnam, in Hong Kong); relocation to PRC, 268nn4,8; with ROC travel papers, 276, 278; Sino-Vietnamese relations and, 257; views of Vietnam War, 262–264. *See also* Chinese residents in Vietnam
refugees from Vietnam, in Australia, 9, 289, 297–298. *See also* second-generation Vietnamese Australian personnel
refugees from Vietnam, in Hong Kong, 9; in closed camps, 273, 275; conditions in camps, 283; ethnic Chinese, 273, 275–278; habeas corpus petitions, 275–278; inequities between Chinese and Vietnamese migrants, 273; length of detention, 272, 273, 277–278; in open camps, 272, 278; questions provoked by, 284; refugee status of, 272; repatriation program, 274, 275; with ROC travel papers, 276, 278; screening process, 273–274; UNCHR and, 273; uprising in Whitehall Detention Centre, 280
refugee status, 271, 272. *See also* refugees from Vietnam, in Hong Kong
regional integration, 248, 249, 250. *See also* Association of Southeast Asian Nations (ASEAN)
Reilly, Robert J., 307
religious activity, 298
Repatriation Acts Amendment Act (No. 2) 1979, 290
Report of the Standing Committee on Environment and Public Affairs in the relation to Chemical Use by the Agriculture Protection Board 1970-198, 331, 332
Republic of China (ROC; Taiwan). *See* China, Republic of
Republic of Korea (ROK; South Korea). *See* Korea, South
Republic of Vietnam (RVN; South Vietnam). *See* Vietnam, South

Republic of Vietnam Armed Forces (RVNAF), 64, 148, 156, 182, 288, 308; veterans, 290–291, 295, 300. *See also* troops, from Pacific region; Vietnam, South
research, ethical, 325
resistance. *See* anti-war sentiment/activism; Beheiren; Iwakuni
responsibility, 323, 327
rest and recreation (R&R) programs, 2, 6, 13n28, 125–137, 243; in Australia, 133; competition in, 135; contracts with sex workers, 131; economy and, 129; effects of, 136–137; hostess bars, 127, 128, 132; hotels for Americans, 132; jurisdiction over U.S. personnel and, 127–128; opposition to focus on sex, 134; Orientalist fantasies and, 136; participation in, 136; reporting on, 131–132, 133; sex tourism and, 137; in Singapore, 218, 245; Taiwan and, 127, 129, 134, 136; in Thailand, 127, 246; threats to sovereignty, 135; VD and, 132–133, 134, 135. *See also* prostitution; sex; status of forces agreements (SOFAs)
Returned and Services League of Australia (RSL), 290, 300
returnees. *See* veterans, returnee
Reynolds, Robert, 126, 127
Rhee, Syngman, 63, 175, 202
ROC-RVN relations, 142; agriculture and, 147, 151–153, 155; assistance from ROC, 148–149; CATM/VN, 153, 155; desire for stability and, 148; economic goodwill mission, 145, 146; economic potential of South Vietnam and, 148; establishment of diplomatic relations, 144; evaluation of, 156; imbalance in, 143, 149–152; industrialization plans and, 145–146; MOFA report, 144–145, 146; postwar plans, 153, 155–56; Sino-Vietnamese Economic Cooperation Conferences, 149–155, 157; Sino-Vietnamese Trade

Promotion Group, 150; technical assistance, 151–153, 156
Rohingya genocide, 250
Roh Moo Hyun, 175
ROK (Republic of Korea; South Korea). *See* Korea, South
Romulo, Carlos, 249
Rostow, Walt W., 57, 66, 72, 233
Royal Commission on the Use and Effects of Chemical Agents in Australian Personnel in Vietnam, 326
RSL (Returned and Services League of Australia), 290, 300
Ruether, Rosemary Radford, 330
Rusk, Dean, 69, 71, 73, 79, 188, 189, 198, 206, 207, 218; belief in possibility of victory, 66; Park and, 202
Russia. *See* Soviet Union
RVN (Republic of Vietnam; South Vietnam). *See* Republic of Vietnam Armed Forces (RVNAF); Vietnam, South
RVNAF (Republic of Vietnam Armed Forces), 64, 148, 156, 182, 288, 290–291, 295, 300, 308. *See also* Vietnam, South

Sabah, 23, 24, 25
Saigon, 6, 7; ethnic Chinese in, 259 (*See also* Chinese residents in Vietnam); fall of, 156, 192, 257 (*See also* withdrawal from Vietnam, U.S.);
Saigon Daily News, 149
Sanger, Clyde, 42
Sarantakes, Nicholas Evans, 199
Sarawak, 23, 24, 25
Sato Eisaku, 107, 121
Scott, James, 234
Searcy, Laura, 299
SEATO (Southeast Asia Treaty Organization), 7, 22, 23, 24, 46, 47, 185, 188
second-generation Vietnamese Australian personnel, 288–301
Second Indochina War, 1. *See also* Vietnam War

Index 363

security, 8; interconnected, 19, 21 (*See also* domino theory); participation in coalition and, 193; race and, 47
Segal, David, 291
Seitz, Eric, 110, 111, 115–116, 118
self-interest, 183
Sembawang Shipyard, 225
Semper Fi (newspaper), 112–113, 115, 117, 118, 120, 121
Seveso disaster, 322
sex, 6; "Fat Leonard" scandal, 125; morale and, 127, 128; tourism and, 128, 129. *See also* rest and recreation (R&R) programs
sex industry, 137
sex tourism, 133, 137, 246. *See also* rest and recreation (R&R) programs
sex workers, 131, 133. *See also* rest and recreation (R&R) programs
Shen Chang-huan, 155
Shen Chong, 126, 127
Shiratori, Noriko, 6
Siam. *See* Thailand
signified, 171
signifier, 168, 169–170
Simpson, Bradley R., 77, 78
Singapore, 4, 16, 27, 215, 248; American investments in, 224–226, 227; anti-communist stance of, 26–27; anti-war activism in, 218; Britain and, 16, 17, 18, 21, 22, 23, 24, 25, 27, 216, 220, 249; buying time thesis and, 218; Chartered Industries, 221, 245; communications hub at, 44; communists in, 234; defense spending, 223; economic benefits from Vietnam War, 245; economic growth in, 8, 217, 223, 243; ethnic Chinese in, 216, 219–220, 248; exploitation of Cold War, 215; exports, 223, 245; foreign companies in, 223; foreign direct investment in, 245; Harris in, 10; Indonesia and, 23, 27, 216, 222, 226; interconnected insecurity and, 19; internal self-government, 21–22; Lee Kuan Yew, 8, 21–22, 23, 24; low labor costs, 227; MacDonald's analysis of, 20; Malaysia and, 71, 215, 216, 217, 220, 222, 226; military, 8, 220; nonaligned status of, 215, 220; R&R programs in, 6, 129, 136, 218, 243; scholarship on international history, 214–215; security of, 220; service industry in, 225; support for war, 8, 214, 218; tourism industry in, 245; Treaty of Amity and Cooperation and the Declaration of ASEAN Concord, 248; unemployment, 225; U.S. aid to, 237, 239; U.S. and, 27, 49, 214–219, 222, 227; Vietnam War's effect on, 215; water supply, 220; weapons from U.S., 220–222, 227; withdrawal of British forces from, 245. *See also* Association of Southeast Asian Nations (ASEAN); People's Action Party (PAP)
Sino-American Joint Commission on Rural Reconstruction (JCRR), 147
Sino-Vietnamese Economic Cooperation Conferences, 149–155
Sino-Vietnamese relations, 41, 257, 266
Sino-Vietnamese Trade Promotion Group, 150
skirt, "Vietnamese". *See* "Vietnamese" skirt
Slow Violence and the Environmentalism of the Poor (Nixon), 322
Smith, Hugh, 301
Smith, Walter, 208
Smokey Bear, 329–330
SNCC (Student Nonviolent Coordinating Committee), 111
SNIE (Special National Intelligence Estimate), 60
Soedjatmoko, 232
SOFAs (Status of Forces Agreements), 5–6, 127–128, 129
soldiers, Korean. *See* troops, South Korean
Solomon, Richard, 102

Sơn Mỹ Memorial and Museum, 313–315
South China Morning Post, 274, 277, 279, 281–282
Southeast Asia. *See* Asia, Southeast
Southeast Asia Treaty Organization (SEATO), 7, 22, 23, 24, 46, 47, 185, 188
South Sea, 2. *See also* Pacific region
South Vietnam. *See* Vietnam, South
Soviet Union, 18; agenda in Southeast Asia, 236; American deserters and, 109; expanding influence of, 37; financing of Cuba's involvement in civil war in Angola, 201; Indonesia and, 78, 79, 240, 242; in Malaya, 38; North Vietnam and, 184, 186, 207; split with China, 235, 237; Sukarno and, 23; Vietnam and, 237
Special National Intelligence Estimate (SNIE), 60
Spender, Percy, 41, 42, 43, 44
stability, 8, 55, 148
status of forces agreements (SOFAs), 5–6, 127–128, 129. *See also* bases, U.S. military; rest and recreation (R&R) programs
Stearman, William Lloyd, 231
stories, listening to, 334
storytelling, 10, 321, 327. *See also* war narratives
Stuart, Francis, 37
Student Nonviolent Coordinating Committee (SNCC), 111
Stur, Heather, 6, 10, 14n38
Suharto, 23, 26, 70, 82, 83, 222, 231–232, 239, 240, 242, 246, 249, 250; backing for Lon Nol, 82; coup in Indonesia, 72; international aid and, 239–242; nonalignment and, 80; *Supersemar*, 79; U.S. confidence in, 80; Vietnam War and, 74. *See also* Indonesia
Sukarno, 17, 21, 22–24, 35, 36, 48, 71, 77, 78, 79, 82, 216, 249; African views of, 25; China and, 25; failed plot against, 26; *Konfrontasi*, 71; marginalization of, 72, 74, 216; pro-Chinese orientation, 73; *Supersemar*, 79; U.S. relations with, 72. *See also* Indonesia
Sulzberger, C. L., 231
Sungkar, Abdullah, 242
Sun Yun-suan, 151, 152
Sweden, American deserters and, 109
Swynnerton, J. C. A., 16
Sydney: R&R program in, 6, 13n28. *See also* Australia
Sydney Daily Telegraph, 38–39
Symington, Stuart, 120
Symington Report, 120
syphilis, 133, 134

Taipei. *See* China, Republic of
Taipei Municipal Venereal Disease Control Institute, 133
Taiwan (Republic of China; ROC). *See* China, Republic of
Taiwan Garrison Command, 127
Taiwan Sugar Corporation, 145–146
Takahashi Taketomo, 108
Tan Te Lam, 276
Tarrow, Sidney, 111
Tatung Institute of Technology, 134
Taylor, Maxwell, 54, 59, 66, 191. *See also* Clifford-Taylor mission
TCDD ($_{2,3,7,8}$-tetrachlorodibenzo-p-dioxin), 325, 330, 332. *See also* dioxin contamination
Telford, John, 331
Telford, Robert Cecil, 332, 333
Tet offensive, 61, 96, 153, 191
textile industry, Korean, 162, 164, 170
Thailand, 76, 231; anti-communism in, 21, 26; China and, 19; CPT, 234; defense of Malaya and, 47; in domino theory, 42; economic benefits from Vietnam War, 245; economic growth in, 243, 247–248; foreign direct investment in, 245; Free Thai Movement, 234; Indonesia and, 248;

Thailand (cont.)
insurgencies in, 232; interconnected insecurity and, 19; interests of, 191; jurisdiction over U.S. personnel in, 128; MacDonald on, 20; participation in war, 56, 188–189, 191, 192, 193; R&R programs in, 6, 127, 246; refugees in, 272; SEATO and, 46, 185 (*See also* SEATO); sex industry in, 137; support for South Vietnam, 199; tourism in, 243, 246; Treaty of Amity and Cooperation and the Declaration of ASEAN Concord, 248; troop commitment and, 7, 8, 54, 57, 64, 182, 199–200, 246 (*See also* military coalition in Vietnam; troops, from Pacific region); U.S. and, 21, 49, 188–189, 193, 237, 239, 242. *See also* Association of Southeast Asian Nations (ASEAN)

U Thant, 95
Thatcher, Margaret, 273
Thomson, Alistair, 289
Tiananmen Square protests/massacre, 271, 274, 280, 284
Time magazine, 134
Title IX (Patsy T. Mink Equal Opportunity in Education Act), 102
Tito, Josef, 24
toilet, "Vietnamese", 167, 169, 178
Tokyo, 6. *See also* Japan
Tomita Hiroaki, 119
Toner, Simon, 6–7
tourism, 243; R&R programs and, 136; sex and, 128; in Singapore, 245; in Taiwan, 136; in Thailand, 246
"Towards a Sociology of Diagnosis" (Jutel and Nettleton), 325–326
toxic legacies, 323. *See also* Agent Orange; dioxin contamination
Tran, Lisa, 9
Tran Dang Vinh, 291
Tran Thien Khiem, 148
Tran Van Lam, 155
trauma, refugees and, 298

treaties. *See* status of forces agreements (SOFAs)
Treaty of Amity and Cooperation and the Declaration of ASEAN Concord, 248
"Trigonometric Functions" (Lee), 165–174, 176–178
troops, from Pacific region, 7–8, 54, 142, 182; aid and, 8, 197; desertions by, 64; funding for, 201; legitimacy of U.S. involvement and, 65; mercenary image of, 8, 182, 204, 243; more flags initiative, 182, 185, 186, 192, 198–199, 204, 246; motivations for sending, 204–205; from Philippines, 246; race and, 204; requested increase in, 57, 60–61 (*See also* Clifford-Taylor mission); from South Korea (*See* troops, South Korean); true allies vs. mercenaries, 199–200; war crimes committed by, 165. *See also* allies, U.S.; escalation in Vietnam; military coalition in Vietnam; veterans; *individual countries*
troops, South Korean, 7–8, 54, 56, 57, 162, 163, 165, 177, 182, 187, 197, 201–202, 205, 206, 209n1; benefits of sending, 201, 203, 204, 205; difference made by, 203; funding for, 206, 207; independent operation of, 201; Korean people's support for, 203–204; masculinity of, 198; mercenary characterization of, 187–188, 197, 198–201, 204, 207; modernization of military and, 205; motivations of, 200; North Korea and, 207; politics of suffering and, 198; U.S. concessions and, 199; veterans' positive attitude toward service, 198; volunteers, 209n1; wages of, 200; war crimes by, 165, 174, 175–176, 188; weapons for, 221; withdrawal from Vietnam, 192, 206–207. *See also* military coalition in Vietnam
Truman, Harry, 18, 20
Trump, Donald, 10

trust, 183
Truth and Reconciliation Commission, 175
Tsai Wei-ping, 128
Tsurumi Shunsuke, 114
Tsurumi Yoshiyuki, 108
Tunku Abdul Rahman, 21, 22
Tuy Hoa, 177

Understories (Kosek), 329
UNHCR (United Nations High Commissioner for Refugees), 271, 272, 273–274, 284
United Nations (UN), 23, 25, 95
United Nations High Commissioner for Refugees (UNHCR), 271, 272, 273–274, 284
United States: anti-war movement in, 54 (*See also* anti-war sentiment/activism); ANZUS, 24, 45, 47; Australia and, 35, 47; Britain's relation with, 17; building up of regional partners, 81; civil rights movement, 109; commitment to Southeast Asia, 18; cultural affinity with Britain, 191; domestic opinion on war, 4, 54, 219; economic aid to ROC ended, 150; fact-finding missions to Asia, 18–20; failed plot against Sukarno, 26; global power of, 3; imperialism of (*See* imperialism, U.S.); Japan's relation with, 108; legacies of war and, 9; legitimacy of involvement, 65; Malaysia and, 27; military (*See* bases, U.S. military; military, U.S.); Pearl Harbor attack, 33; perception of attitudes in Pacific region, 8, 59, 62; Philippines and, 17 (*See also* bases, U.S. military); public opinion in, 56, 59, 62, 75, 192 (*See also* anti-war sentiment/activism); reevaluation of Vietnam policy, 61; refugees and, 273; ROC and, 157; SEATO and, 46, 185 (*See also* SEATO); Singapore and, 27, 49, 214–219, 222, 227; Sino-American Joint Commission on Rural Reconstruction (JCRR), 147; South Korea's relation with, 205; South Vietnamese dislike of, 147; Vietnamese veterans in, 291; Vietnam's lack of threat to, 62; war narratives in, 9; weapons sold to Singapore, 220–222. *See also* aid, U.S.; allies, U.S.; bases, U.S. military; foreign policy, U.S.; imperialism, U.S.; Johnson, Lyndon B.; military, U.S.
United States Agency for International Development (USAID), 5, 81, 145, 150
United States Institute of Peace (USIP), 102
United States Operations Mission (USOM), 151, 155
USAID (United States Agency for International Development), 5, 81, 145, 150
U.S. Marine Corps Air Station (MCAS). *See* bases, U.S. military; Iwakuni
U.S. Military Assistance Advisory Group (MAAG), 126, 127
U.S. Military Assistance Command, Vietnam (MACV), 48, 182
USOM (United States Operations Mission), 151, 155
USSR. *See* Soviet Union

Valenti, Jack, 187
Van Campen, H. L., 120
van Schendel, Willem, 234
Van Wyck, Peter C., 322, 323
venereal disease (VD), 130, 132–133, 134, 135
veterans: Agent Orange and, 324, 325, 326–327, 328; return to Vietnam (*See* veterans, returnee);
veterans, anti-war, 307, 313–317
veterans, Australian: exposed to Agent Orange, 326; returnees, 308–309, 310–312, 317

veterans, Korean, 198. *See also* troops, South Korean

veterans, returnee, 9, 305; anti-war, 316–317; Australian, 308–309, 310–312; narrative of inevitable revolutionary victory, 305–307; narrative of South Vietnamese weakness, 307; perceptions of outcome, 305–309; understandings of revolutionary willpower, 306; view of war's morality, 305, 316–317; views of Vietnamese willpower, 308; views on war legacy issues, 305; war crimes and, 305, 310–316

veterans, Vietnamese, 290–291, 295, 300. *See also* Republic of Vietnam Armed Forces (RVNAF)

Veterans Entitlement Bill, 290

Veterans for Peace (VFP), 307

Vietcong, 170–171

Vietminh, 18, 19–20. *See also* Dien Bien Phu

Vietnam, 178; Bao Dai, 18, 21, 41, 42; China and, 24, 41; colonizers of, 143; communists in, 235 (*See also* Vietnam, North); dioxin contamination in, 321, 324, 333 (*See also* Agent Orange; dioxin contamination; $_{2,4}$-D; $_{2,4,5}$-T); division of, 143; in domino theory, 42; fish in, 166–167; French defeat in, 42, 45, 46, 143; Harris in, 10; independence of, 143; legacies of war and, 9; legitimacy of U.S. involvement in, 59; movement of people from, 9 (*See also* refugees from Vietnam); Palethorpe on, 35; refugees in Hong Kong and, 279–280; regional stability and, 58; resistance to invasion, history of, 306; Soviet Union and, 257; U.S. interests and, 48; U.S. security and, 62; U.S.'s relation with, 307

Vietnam, North (Democratic Republic of Vietnam; DRV), 1, 35, 235; air war over, 95–96; declaration of independence of, 35; fight against French, 184; Soviet Union's aid to, 207; support for, 184

Vietnam, South (Republic of Vietnam; RVN), 1, 88; agriculture in, 144, 145; anti-communist agenda, 148; APACL and, 7; Chinese in, 144, 156; coup in, 148, 150; diplomatic ambitions, 6–7; diplomatic relations with Asian countries, 142 (*See also* ROC-RVN relations); dislike of Americans, 147; economic development of, 142, 144–145, 146, 149; economic potential of, 145, 148; establishment of, 143; fall to communists, 156; goals and strategies of, vs. U.S.'s, 6; improved villages planned for, 152–153; industrialization plans, 145–146; instability in, 24; Japanese reparations to, 147; military, 64, 148, 156, 182, 288, 290–291, 295, 300, 308; MRC, 148; national culture, 6; preserving, 93–94; in regional and international contexts, 10; relation with anti-communist governments, 6–7; ROC's relation with (*See* ROC-RVN relations); SEATO and, 46, 185; troops in coalition, 182, 186 (*See also* military coalition in Vietnam; troops, from Pacific region); U.S. aid and, 147, 149, 150; U.S. influence in, 147. *See also* anti-communism; Saigon

"Vietnamese" fish, 166–167, 169, 178

"Vietnamese" imaginary in South Korea, 7, 164, 170. *See also* Korea, South

"Vietnamese" modifier, 166, 167, 169, 171–172, 176, 178

"Vietnamese" myth, 174

Vietnamese People's Army, 45

"Vietnamese" poker, 167, 169, 178

"Vietnamese" skirt (*wollam chima*), 162, 164, 167, 170, 172, 178; vs. *áo dài*, 168; demythologization of, 165, 168; name of, 164; in "Trigonometric Functions", 166

"Vietnamese" toilet, 167, 169, 178
Viet-Nam Information Notes, 59
Vietnamization policy, 191, 192. *See also* withdrawal from Vietnam, U.S.
"Vietnam's Moonlit Night" (song), 164
Vietnam War: allies' attempts to prolong U.S. involvement in, 56; Americanization of, 4, 17, 163, 170, 231, 233, 237; as American neocolonial expansionist war, 177; authority of Western narratives about, 9–10; committment to victory, 206; contexts of, 1, 2 (*See also* Asia, Southeast; Pacific region); costs of, 208; defeat in, 186; end of (*See* Paris Peace Accords; peace in Vietnam; withdrawal from Vietnam, U.S.); escalation of (*See* escalation in Vietnam); framed as regional conflict, 4, 54, 55, 56, 58–59, 66 (*See also* allies, U.S.); impossibility of U.S. victory, 55, 60, 61, 66, 74; justification for, 1, 8–9 (*See also* buying time thesis; domino theory); legacies of, 9, 137, 233, 250, 305; legitimacy of, 54, 188; names for, 1; official Vietnamese memory of, 309; participants in, 142 (*See also* military coalition in Vietnam; troops, from Pacific region); and political change elsewhere in Southeast Asia, 76; portrayal in popular culture, 198; regional attitudes toward, 8; regional drivers and effects of, 6; strength of Southeast Asia's non-communist states and, 237–243
violence, slow, 10, 322, 323, 324. *See also* Agent Orange; dioxin contamination
Võ Nguyên Giáp, 306
Vu, Bao, 288

Wain, Barry, 258
Waite, Gerald, 199, 200, 203, 204
Wall Street Journal, 280
Wanandi, Jusuf, 250

Wangdo's principle, 173
war, aftermath of, 322
war, limited, 93, 100
war crimes: documentation of, 310; engineer's burials, 311–312; My Lai massacre, 188, 310, 311, 313–315, 328; No Gun Ri, 165, 174, 175; returnees and, 305, 310–16; by South Korean troops, 165, 174, 175–176, 188; by U.S. troops, 175, 188. *See also* Agent Orange
war narratives, 9–10, 177
Warner, Denis, 35, 39–40, 43
Warnke, Paul, 62
War Powers Act, 100
War Remnants Museum, 310
Washington. *See* United States
Washino Masakazu, 119
Wei Daoming, 134
Westcott, A. Gabrielle, 4
Western Australia Agriculture Protection Board, 321, 330, 331, 333
Western Australia Legislative Council, 14–15n40, 331, 332
West Irian, 82
Westmoreland, William, 56, 61
Whitlam, Gough, 190
Widén, J. J., 191
Widjojo Nitisastro, 74
Wigmor, Lionel, 43
wildfire prevention, 329
Wilson, Harold, 71, 249
withdrawal from Vietnam, U.S., 81, 191, 192, 206–207; allies and, 192; Chinese residents in South Vietnam and, 263; drive for regional unity in Southeast Asia, 249–250; effects of, 95; evacuation of South Vietnam residents, 264–265; fall of Saigon, 156, 192, 257; Hawai'i and, 95, 99–100; justification of, 60. *See also* Paris Peace Accords
Wollam boom (Vietnam boom), 164
Womack, Brantly, 143

Index 369

women: Korean, 170. *See also* rest and recreation (R&R) programs
World Friendship Center, 112
World War II, 37; appeasement and, 75; Australia in, 33–34; Japanese Americans during, 89; Japanese reparations to Saigon, 147; Japan in, 33, 43, 47, 108; Jeep Girls in, 136; Pearl Harbor attack, 33, 89; rape by American servicemen during, 126
World Youth Conference, 37

Yeh Kung-chao, 144, 146
Yellow Bird, Michael, 328
"yellow peril" rhetoric, 41
Yen Chia-kan, 153, 155
Yoshioka Shinobu, 119
Yugoslavia, 24

Zhou Enlai, 23
Zomia, 234
Zone of Peace, Freedom, and Neutrality (ZOPFAN) Declaration, 249

www.ingramcontent.com/pod-product-compliance
Lightning Source LLC
Chambersburg PA
CBHW031751220426
43662CB00007B/366